"Students benefit from expert evaluation in finding [...] pastors want to keep up with new research done si [...] sors and librarians need to evaluate textbooks. All s [...] bibliography for guidance as to how to best use limited study time."

—**Steven Waterhouse**, Senior Pastor, Westcliff Bible Church, Amarillo, Texas

"As a pastor far removed from my seminary days, I am in need of a carefully selected list of books that will help me make informed choices when it comes to sermon preparation, Old and New Testament studies, Apologetics, Practical Theology and much more. Robert Yost has written an exceptionally well-compiled bibliography that has become a great addition to my library. He does an excellent job informing the reader of the relevance and quality of the sources he cites by offering succinct annotations about the book's usefulness."

—**Jeffrey Winter**, Senior Pastor, First Presbyterian Church, Haines City, Florida

"Every pastor who is serious about teaching the Scriptures must access the best tools for the trade, and the same is true for theological students. Dr. Yost has done pastors and students a service by providing a resource of resources. This annotated bibliography will quickly direct the pastor or student to the classics in the field as well as the most helpful resources for theological study."

—**Wesley C. McCarter**, Lead Minister, Rural Hall Christian Church, Winston-Salem, North Carolina

"Robert Yost has the spent the hours you can't in surveying a virtual library of biblical and theological texts. Pastors, students, and teachers looking to build a strong personal library along conservative and evangelical lines will find this work particularly helpful."

—**Trevor Smith**, Senior Pastor, Westminster Presbyterian Church, Charlotte, North Carolina

"Dr. Yost has done an admirable service in writing this much-needed resource. It provides a very good, broad basis for building one's own theological and practical library. It also serves as a ready tool for quickly finding books suggested on any given category included therein, either for one's own use or for answering others who ask for help on a given subject."

—**David K. Johnson**, University of Northwestern, St. Paul, Minnesota

"Pastors can now leave Cyril Barber's recommendations for the minister's library on the shelf. It served its generation. Robert Yost and his team have identified the tools for effective ministry that pastors will need in 2017 and beyond. Buy extra copies to share with seminary students building their libraries."

—**Frank Scurry**, President, Carolina Graduate School of Divinity

"With the rising cost of books, it is important for pastors/students to identify the best books as additions to a personal theological library. Theological research, as well as weekly preaching, must access the necessary resources, and often it is a challenge to sort through the multitude of books on a topic. Students and pastors will both benefit from this well-organized annotated bibliography to help guide them in sorting through the best books as well as the newer ones for use in ministry and research. An impressive text in its breadth, highly recommended as a reference tool to have on the shelf."

—**S. Donald Fortson III**, Reformed Theological Seminary, Charlotte, North Carolina

"A well-written, well-organized, and eminently practical tool for all serious students of the Word of God. It provides a much-needed guide to all of the essential works that should be present in the library of a minister of the gospel. As a former cross-cultural worker living for more than twenty years outside of his country of origin, I believe this work will prove to be an especially useful resource for anyone serving in a similar capacity today.

—**Steven A. Bailey**, Regional Director for Latin America, Encompass World Partners, Atlanta, Georgia

The Pastor's Library

The Pastor's Library

An Annotated Bibliography of Biblical and Theological Resources for Ministry

ROBERT A. YOST

Foreword by Eddie G. Grigg

WIPF & STOCK · Eugene, Oregon

THE PASTOR'S LIBRARY
An Annotated Bibliography of Biblical and Theological Resources for Ministry

Wipf & Stock
An Imprint of Wipf and Stock Publishers
199 W. 8th Ave., Suite 3
Eugene, OR 97401

www.wipfandstock.com

PAPERBACK ISBN: 978-1-5326-0098-2
HARDCOVER ISBN: 978-1-5326-0100-2
EBOOK ISBN: 978-1-5326-0099-9

Manufactured in the U.S.A.   SEPTEMBER 19, 2017

To my mother, Babara Yost Strawn,
who encouraged my love of books at an early age.

Contents

Foreword

MANY OF THE THOUGHT seeds we plant fall into minds and wills that are incapable of supporting the growth and development of that thought. Little did I know that such a thought seed I cast forth several years ago would develop into such a healthy resource for theological students and Christian ministers. In fact, it has evolved to be far more than I had ever envisioned.

Then Vice President of Academic Affairs, Dr. Robert A. Yost, and I were having one of our many meetings where we would sit down in my office and discuss administrative issues. As it would sometimes happen, the conversation drifted into the need for students to have guidance in spending their limited resources on good, solid library materials to carry them through their academic preparation into their ministerial or scholarly careers.

I confess that I was thinking of a ten- to twelve-page list that we could photocopy and hand out to our students, but I forgot to whom I was speaking. For you see, Dr. Yost has both the mind and the will capable of growth and development of an idea. In *The Pastor's Library: An Annotated Bibliography of Biblical and Theological Resources for Ministry*, Dr. Yost and several of his colleagues have pulled together annotated bibliographies of essential theological and biblical sources. This comprehensive resource is essential for theological students doing research on various ministry-related topics, as well as for pastors and Christian scholars involved in a teaching ministry.

As you peruse this work, do not be surprised if a thought seed is planted that God, through you, grows into a resource or tool to minister to others. I challenge you to let this work propagate thought seeds into your ministry and see what grows!

Eddie G. Grigg
President, Charlotte Christian College and Theological Seminary
Charlotte, NC

Preface

THIS BOOK IS AN annotated bibliography of biblical and theological resources.

My primary intended audience is pastors and theological students. My inspiration was the book *The Minister's Library*, by Cyril Barber, which was first published in 1974 and was a great help to multitudes of pastors and seminary students a generation ago. After several reprints and three supplements, the work has been out of print for over thirty years. My intention was not to cover the same ground that Barber did, but rather to produce a similar work in the same spirit.

The annotations in this work cover four broad areas of theological study: Old Testament, New Testament, Systematic Theology, and Practical Theology, with numerous subsections within each chapter. It is no surprise that the largest subsections under the Old and New Testament categories are commentaries. Many of the annotations are much more detailed than those of Barber or authors writing along the same lines in commentary reference guides. Some of the annotations have been written by experts in the field who are my friends and colleagues at Charlotte Christian College and Theological Seminary, as well as other fine institutions.

A final note: the annotations contained herein reflect evaluations that are highly subjective and are not meant to be the final word on the subject. They simply express one person's opinion.

Acknowledgments

To my wonderful wife, Tessie, who endured numerous lonely evenings and late dinners over the past year while I toiled away on this project. She is a real princess whom I love dearly!

To the library staff at Warner University who had to reshelve hundreds of books during my countless visits there for research.

To Dr. Eddie Grigg, the president of Charlotte Christian College and Theological Seminary, who gave me impetus to do this project.

To Jim Harmeling, who read sections and offered helpful suggestions as well as books I had missed.

To all of those on the faculty of Charlotte Christian College and Theological Seminary and other institutions who generously contributed their time and expertise on this project. As Dr. Stephen Stout suggested, I was like Tom Sawyer getting others to do the actual work of whitewashing the fence. I could not have completed the job without you wonderful and gracious folks.

To Dr. Stephen Stout who (again) guided, edited, and advised me on this project and who painted a section of the fence.

Abbreviations

BIBLE VERSIONS

ASV	American Standard Version
AV	Authorized Version
ESV	English Standard Version
KJV	King James Version
LXX	Septuagint
MT	Masoretic Text of the Hebrew Bible
NT	New Testament
NASB	New American Standard Bible
NIV	New International Version
OT	Old Testament
RSV	Revised Standard Version
TEV	Today's English Version

COMMENTARY SERIES

AB	Anchor Bible
ACCS	Ancient Christian Commentary on Scripture
AOTC	Apollos Old Testament Commentary
AYB	Anchor Yale Bible
BECNT	Baker Exegetical Commentary on the New Testament
BNTC	Black's New Testament Commentaries
BST	The Bible Speaks Today
BTCB	Brazos Theological Commentary on the Bible
CBC	Cambridge Bible Commentary on the NEB
CBSC	Cambridge Bible for Schools and Colleges
CC	The Communicator's Commentary
CCSS	Catholic Commentary on Sacred Scripture

EBC	The Expositor's Bible Commentary
ECC	Eerdman's Critical Commentary
EGT	The Expositor's Greek Testament
Hermeneia	Hermeneia: A Critical and Historical Commentary
IB	Interpreter's Bible
ICC	International Critical Commentary
Interp	Interpretation
NAC	New American Commentary
NICNT	New International Commentary on the New Testament
NICOT	New International Commentary on the Old Testament
NIGTC	New International Greek Testament Commentary
NIVAC	New International Version Application Commentary
OTL	Old Testament Library
OTS	Opening the Scriptures
Paideia	Paideia Commentaries on the New Testament
PNTC	Pillar New Testament Commentary
TNTC	Tyndale New Testament Commentaries
TOTC	Tyndale Old Testament Commentaries
WBC	Word Biblical Commentary
ZECOT	Zondervan Exegetical Commentary on the Old Testament

MISCELLANEOUS

ETS	Evangelical Theological Society
OP	Out of print
LCRL	Klock & Klock's Limited Classical Reprint Library
SBL	Society of Biblical Literature

LIST OF CONTRIBUTORS

David W. Baker: Professor of Old Testament, Ashland Theological Seminary, Doctor of Philosophy, University of London

Garry Baldwin: Pastor, Midwood Baptist Church, Charlotte, NC, Faculty, Charlotte Christian College and Theological Seminary, Doctor of Ministry, Carolina Graduate School of Divinity

Ryan Brandt: Instructor of Christian History and Theology, Grand Canyon University, Associate Editor, *Journal of Biblical and Theological Studies*, Doctor of Philosophy, Southern Baptist Theological Seminary

Bill Fleming: Head of Department of Pastoral Studies, Charlotte Christian College and Theological Seminary, Doctor of Ministry, Gordon-Conwell Theological Seminary

Eddie Grigg: President, Charlotte Christian College and Theological Seminary, Master of Divinity, Southeastern Baptist Theological Seminary, Doctor of Ministry, Emmanuel Baptist University

Lloyd L. Olsen Jr.: Faculty, Columbia College, Orlando, FL, Doctor of Ministry, Reformed Theological Seminary, Orlando, FL, Doctor of Philosophy, Christ Church, Oxford University

William Mounce: President, BiblicalTraining.org, Visiting Faculty, Carolina Graduate School of Divinity, Doctor of Philosophy, University of Aberdeen

Wade Singletary: Faculty, World Religions and Humanities, Polk State College, Winter Haven, FL, Master of Theological Studies and Master of Biblical Studies, Reformed Theological Seminary, Orlando, FL

Stephen O. Stout: Pastor, Shearer Presbyterian Church, Mooresville, NC, Faculty, Carolina Graduate Divinity School, Faculty, Charlotte Christian College and Theological Seminary, Doctor of Ministry, Covenant Theological Seminary, Doctor of Philosophy, Southeastern Baptist Theological Seminary

Ted Wright: Faculty, Charlotte Christian College and Theological Seminary, Master of Arts, Southern Evangelical Seminary

Chapter 1

Introduction

WHEN I WAS A student in seminary, I read somewhere that the length of a pastor's ministry in a particular church was often directly proportionate to the size of his theological library. The reasoning conveyed by this is that good pastors and preachers are often readers of good books. Conversely, poor pastors and preachers are all too often not serious readers. Readers of good books stretch their minds and thinking in ways that nonreaders do not. Please keep in mind that for every example of this rule of thumb, there is probably an exception. Early in my seminary studies as well as pastoral ministry, I was encouraged by certain friends to build the very best library that I could for ministry. I also saw several sad examples of small-minded pastors, who though they may have been godly men, were not readers and thus limited their ministries.

The purpose of this book is to assist students and pastors in making wise choices in building libraries for ministry. My personal theological orientation is evangelical and Reformed. Therefore, this book is intended primarily to assist those students and pastors who are in evangelical, Bible-believing colleges and seminaries rather than those in mainline denominations and institutions.

One will readily notice that this guide does not attempt to be complete in any sense of the word. My choices are highly selective, intending to be representative rather than comprehensive. I will say more about this in the next section. I have attempted to choose works that would be most helpful for a student or pastor who is trying to build a working pastor's library. Sometimes these works are from more of a liberal or critical perspective, particularly if they are seminal works in the history of the church. This book is also limited to works that were either originally written in the English language or were translated into it. There are many fine foreign-language works that did not make it into this guide. However, there are many excellent foreign-language authors whose works were translated into English and are included (e.g., G. C. Berkouwer, Karl Barth). I can say with complete assurance that the reader who uses this book with discretion can build a very fine and workable theological library for ministry. No doubt I have left out somebody's favorite book and I am certain to hear about it if I did. If that is the case, please let me know (robertyost@charlottechristiancollege.edu) and I will consider including it in my planned five-year supplement that I hope will be published in 2022.

While still a student in seminary back in the 1970s, I discovered Cyril Barber's *Minister's Library*, an exceedingly helpful work that became the shield at my right hand. At that time, while working two part-time jobs and attending seminary full time on an extremely limited income I began to purchase books to the end of building a working ministerial library. In the course of time, I also discovered David Scholar's *Basic Bibliographic Guide for New Testament Exegesis*, Frederick Danker's *Multipurpose Tools for Bible Study*, and Charles Spurgeon's *Commenting and Commentaries*. These were all quite enlightening and extremely helpful. They were a delight to read and they gave me direction in my quest.

WHY THIS BOOK?

In light of the fact that there are several very fine commentary guides available, such as Tremper Longman's *Old Testament Commentary Survey*, D. A. Carson's *New Testament Commentary Survey*, James Rosscup's *Commentaries for Biblical Expositors*, John Evans's *Guide to Biblical Commentaries and Reference Works*, and John Glynn's *Commentary & Reference Survey*, why is this book necessary? What led to the writing of this book? In 2012, two years prior to my retirement from the position of vice president of academic affairs at Charlotte Christian College and Theological Seminary,[1] the president of the institution, Eddie Grigg, was lamenting the absence of good, up-to-date bibliographic materials available for theological students who would like to build a theological library particularly from an urban ministries perspective. CCCTS is an urban school and many of its students are already working in pastoral ministry. Hence the need for reference books that would be helpful for pastors and other para-church workers. Which books are most valuable? Which are classics in the field? Which books or sets constitute the basic building blocks for a pastor's library? We were not talking about just commentaries, but books dealing with the nuts and bolts of pastoral ministry. What resources were available for a student or pastor wanting to begin acquiring such a library? Dr. Grigg and I discussed the issue from time to time, and upon my retirement on June 30, 2014, it was mutually agreed that a worthy project for a semi-retired research professor at CCCTS would be to compile an annotated bibliography that could be given to the students at the institution. Dr. Grigg had no idea of the scope of the project upon which I was embarking. He was thinking in terms of a few dozen typed sheets of paper that could be stapled together and given to students. I was thinking more in terms of *War and Peace*. We met somewhere in the middle. It was hoped that this project upon completion would be a resource to students at CCCTS as well as at the Carolina Graduate School of Divinity where I earned my doctor of ministry degree.[2]

Although there are numerous excellent resources available to students and pastors, that there is a need for such a project should be obvious to anyone familiar with the field of biblical and theological studies. Forty years ago when I was a seminary student, the only books of this nature readily available were the already mentioned books by Danker, Scholer, and Cyril J. Barber. These books are terribly dated now. Charles H. Spurgeon's

---

1. Hereafter CCCTS.
2. Sadly the institution closed its doors on June 30, 2016.

Commenting & Commentaries should also be mentioned, but it was originally published in 1876 and therefore lacks the products of over 140 years of scholarly research. My copy of Danker's book is the third edition, dated 1970, and my copy of Scholer's guide is the second edition, dated 1973. Barber's encyclopedic work is dated 1974. The major problem with all three books is that they are hopelessly out of date. Danker's book was revised and expanded in 1993. Scholer's book never was updated. Barber produced three supplements in 1976, 1978, and 1980, but today even the latest supplement is now over thirty-five years old. His original work was published by Baker, but now Moody Press holds the copyright. They are unwilling to update it, which is a real tragedy to pastors and students as it was the best and most comprehensive work of its kind from an evangelical perspective thirty or forty years ago. In addition to the problem of age in Danker's work, there is also the problem of theological bias. Danker cannot be called an evangelical by any stretch of the imagination, and his bias toward works that are more theologically liberal and highly critical in nature is evident. Danker's theological progression in the area of biblical inerrancy has been well documented in Harold Lindsell's seminal work, *The Battle for the Bible*. In like fashion, Scholer's helpful guide is also well out of date. His theological bent is more toward books that are conservative and hold to the authority of Scripture. However, the main problem with his book, beyond the issue of age, is that his comments are usually nonexistent. When Scholer does comment on a work, his comments are extremely pithy and of very little value to the beginning student or pastor.

Barber's excellent book was the industry standard, at least for pastors and students, when I was in seminary. It was indispensable for a generation of pastors and seminary students who were beginning to build a working theological library. Even though Barber published three supplements to his main work, those are now also out of date. Barber's book was excellent for its time, but it is missing the past thirty-five years of scholarship. One weakness of Barber's book and his supplements is that often his comments were not very detailed and sometimes his evaluations appeared to be inconsistent. Further the three supplements published by Baker demonstrated evidence of having been put together in haste. In 1966, unbeknownst to the writer, James Rosscup published *Commentaries for Biblical Expositors: An Annotated Bibliography of Selected Works*. It is possible that this volume escaped notice because it was not published by a major Christian publisher such as Baker or Zondervan. His work was revised and enlarged in 1983, 1993 and 2004, and it is now a bit out of date. It is also limited only to commentaries, and its theological bias is obvious. Its contents are heavily weighted toward works that are premillennial and dispensational. Also, many fine commentaries that are not evangelical, having a more liberal slant, are not included. It should be noted that some classics that are over one hundred years old are also not included.

Baker Academic in recent years has published two excellent works that have attempted to fill in some of the gaps: *Old Testament Commentary Survey*, by Tremper Longman III, and *New Testament Commentary Survey*, by D. A. Carson. Longman's work is now in its fifth edition (2013) and Carson's is in its seventh (2013). Both books have some strengths as well as some weaknesses.

Longman's book limits itself to commentaries with brief sections on one-volume commentaries and commentary sets and series, followed by an extensive section on individual commentaries. In each section, he provides the bibliographic information for the works along with about a paragraph of incisive and helpful evaluation. He completes each work or set with a rating from one to five. The book has a very straightforward and useful format that is very user friendly. The great limitation to Longman's work is that it is limited to commentaries and includes nothing else. Also, the great majority of works considered have been published within the past thirty years. One is hard pressed to find a work evaluated that is over fifty years old. Most older classics are not even mentioned. One bothersome feature of Longman's book is the failure of later editions to include books that were featured in earlier ones. Thus, if someone wants to read an evaluation of a certain commentary, if it is not included in the current edition, he must also purchase the earlier edition in which it appeared. This was likely a publisher decision, rather than author, generated to limit the size of the work, but the issue is real if one is searching for an evaluation that was included in an earlier edition.

Carson's book is somewhat more comprehensive than Longman's in that it includes New Testament introductions and New Testament theologies. Like Longman, Carson is brilliant in his area of study and his comments are always interesting and well worth reading. However, it is my opinion that Carson's work would have benefited from an approach more like Longman's in devoting a paragraph section to each work. Instead, Carson's treatment of each section is more of a rambling "stream of consciousness" approach in which some major works merit barely a sentence, if that. A more focused evaluation of each work considered would have been welcomed. Also, Carson does not include older commentaries in his evaluations, citing Spurgeon's nineteenth-century book to fill that gap. As I have already indicated, Spurgeon's work badly needs supplementing as it is now well over one hundred years old and some of his evaluations are no longer very helpful.

Two other books should be recognized: *A Guide to Biblical Commentaries and Reference Works*, by John F. Evans, and *Essential Bible Study Tools for Ministry*, by David R. Bauer. Both of these helpful encyclopedic works were discovered by me only in the past couple of years. How the excellent book by Evans escaped my notice is beyond me, but I wish I had discovered it twenty years ago. The Bauer book is more recent, but it is an impressive work of scholarship in its own right. The work by Evans, now in its tenth edition, is really an exceptional work. It is exhaustive and comprehensive in its scope. The author, a former Presbyterian pastor (PCA), is usually spot-on in his evaluations, which are from an evangelical and Reformed perspective. The main weakness is that it is heavily weighted toward commentaries. Pastors will find it most helpful in evaluating commentaries, but they will find little in the way of practical ministerial resources. The same can be said of Bauer's newer work, which is written from the perspective of a Wesleyan who teaches at Asbury Theological Seminary in Wilmore, Kentucky. Of the two, the work by Evans is the more conservative theologically and my preference, but I still appreciate many of the evaluations by Bauer and consider his contribution to this field to be substantial.

A final book should be noted, *Commentary & Reference Survey: A Comprehensive Guide to Biblical and Theological Resources*, by John Glynn. This helpful resource, now in its tenth edition, was first published in 1994 and last updated in 2007. As its title indicates, it is a comprehensive guide dealing not only with commentaries, surveys, theologies, ancient Near Eastern history, Jesus and the Gospels, Jewish background, popular and general references, biblical language resources, systematic theology, church history resources, but also including computer and Internet resources. Unfortunately, Glynn's book is simply a listing of resources. There are no comments or evaluations of each work save for a very few footnotes. Also, it contains little or nothing for the pastor who needs assistance in the area of practical theology. Although the book has several strengths such as each entry being delineated by codes marking whether it is Evangelical, Evangelical/ Critical, Conservative/Moderate, or Liberal/Critical, these are not enough to bridge the gap for students or pastors seeking a more detailed analysis of each book or a listing of resources in the area of practical theology. It is helpful, but hardly as comprehensive as its title would seem to suggest. More is needed.

This project hopefully combines the strengths of many of these works into one comprehensive work while, at the same time, negating some of their weaknesses. It provides needed updating of available materials for works such as those by Barber, Spurgeon, Danker, Scholer, and Rosscup. It also rounds out the material in those works by Longman, Carson, Evans, Bauer, and Glynn. Hopefully, it accentuates the strengths and negates the weaknesses of all of these works.

This volume hopefully fills a need for students, pastors, scholars, and laypersons in that it provides a comprehensive resource for those working in a particular field. Books have been selected in the particular areas of Old Testament, New Testament, Systematic Theology, and Practical Theology, which, in my opinion, would be most helpful to the theological student and/or pastor. For example, a student who is writing a research paper on the qualifications for elders and deacons in the local church setting could look under the section on the New Testament and find over a dozen commentaries on the Pastoral Epistles where the primary texts are found on this subject. Each commentary is evaluated and described. Exegetical commentaries based on the Greek text are designated, as are resources for the nonspecialist. My personal recommendations are also made, as well as salient quotations from certain experts in the field. Several of those experts currently serve on the faculty at CCCTS. The student could also look under the section titled "Practical Theology" and look under "Church Polity," where he would find numerous resources. In like manner, a pastor preaching through a book of the Bible would find suitable resources that would benefit him exegetically and homiletically. Laypersons seeking a book suitable for general Bible study would also find assistance. To that end I have included works by some writers that some of my friends and colleagues would look upon with horror at their inclusion (e.g., A. W. Pink, Warren Wiersbe). Early in my Christian life, I read Pink and he was a great benefit to me. He can still bless others. Likewise, Wiersbe's writing never fails to bless my soul.

Finally, this guide serves as a resource for students and pastors endeavoring to build a ministerial library. It has been my experience that pastors who have been in the ministry for any length of time usually acquire a working collection of reference books of use for Bible study, the construction of sermons, personal enrichment and spiritual growth, as well as to explain the "nuts and bolts" of ministerial tasks. Of course, this has changed drastically in recent decades with the proliferation of online sources and software programs. This guide assists them in making informed choices.

USE OF THIS GUIDE

A few preliminary comments are in order that this bibliography may be utilized judiciously. The purpose of this guide is not to list every book on a particular subject area or even every worthwhile book. Some writers have much more complete compilations than mine. For example, on the little book of Ruth alone, Evans lists sixty-two sources of which forty-four are annotated, whereas I mention thirteen. There are several books that are much more comprehensive than this guide particularly in the area of biblical commentaries and they are listed in the bibliography at the end of this book. Of particular interest would be the books by Barber, Carson, Evans, Bauer, and Longman to name just a few. Rather the purpose of this guide is to select books in the particular areas of Old Testament, New Testament, Systematic Theology, and Practical Theology which, in my opinion, would be most helpful to the student and/or pastor. Many of the works evaluated here are in the writer's personal library. In fact, this project began in my library and expanded out from there. It is almost impossible to keep up with the proliferation of new books being published every year. Some are listed in this guide, but not annotated due to availability. Works that are not are so designated as "Not evaluated for this edition."

All works selected for inclusion will include a bibliographic entry. Most will then be described, evaluated, and coded. A coding system has been devised in order to give readers some guidelines as to the most important works in a particular field. These codes appear in bold face to the left of the author's name in each bibliographic reference. They are as follows:

* Recommended. Should be obtained if available.

+ A recognized classic in the field. Most if not all in the reprint series such as the Klock & Klock Reprint Library are coded as such. They have passed the test of time and are recognized as classics by many.

? A work of liberal scholarship usually espousing some form of higher critical views. Use these books, but use them with some caution as they are not consistent with a conservative, evangelical position.

! A work that is technical and should be of most value to either the scholar or advanced student. Often at least intermediate language skills are required to use such a work with effectiveness. Some commentaries fall into this category.

It will be noticed that many annotations include quotations followed by the author's last name in parentheses. These will be from some of the books already mentioned by authors such as Spurgeon, Rosscup, Barber, Evans, Bauer, Longman, and Carson. They will receive attribution by having their names in parentheses after the quotation along with the page number where the quotation is found.[3] In many instances, these authors echo my evaluation of a particular work. In other cases, their evaluations are supplemental or they may even disagree with mine. The identification of these writers can be found in the bibliography at the back. In any event, all evaluations are subjective and simply

---

3. An exception to this rule would be if the quotation comes from one of Barber's three supplemental works.

reflect a particular writer's opinion. Because this guide's purpose is to serve the students and alumni at CCCTS, many of the annotations will be supplied by faculty members of Charlotte Christian College and Theological Seminary. The writer has also enlisted the assistance of scholars from other institutions of higher learning who are specialists in a particular field. Obviously, nobody is qualified to evaluate resources in every field covered in this guide. These annotations were often solicited by friends and colleagues when a book under consideration for inclusion was out of my specialty area or when I wanted to enhance the quality of this work. Their contributions appear in quotation marks and their names appear in bold face in parentheses after each quotation (e.g., **Fleming, Baldwin, Wright, Stout, Mounce** and the like). Their names as well as a brief biographical sketch with the credentials of each can be found on the page titled "List of Contributors." I would like to thank such persons for their contributions to this work. It could not have been completed without their generous assistance.

With respect to commentaries, every effort has been made to identify the eschatological perspective of the author at the end of the annotation with respect to books that deal with prophetic themes (e.g., Revelation, Matthew, Ezekiel, Isaiah, etc.). These are so designated as Premillennial, Amillennial, Postmillennial, and the like. Dispensational writers are also so designated if at all possible. If a work is written from a certain theological perspective, that is also so designated whenever possible (e.g., Reformed, Arminian).

CLASSICS AND OUT-OF-PRINT WORKS

C. S. Lewis suggested as a good rule of thumb that for every new book one reads, an older one should be read in between. That is probably very good advice. Some today read only the latest books and ignore the treasures of the past. That is, to my mind, shortsighted. Unfortunately, it may be the case that the classics are too often ignored because they are difficult to obtain.

Classics

A classic is a work that has stood the test of time. Its ideas have been judged against the great body of collective Christian thought over the centuries and is widely regarded as timeless and universal. It was Mark Twain who said that a classic is a book which people praise, but don't read. It is a sad reality that many today fail to mine the vast repository of the past. They read the current books, but not the timeless ones.

This guide, contrary to many similar ones, contains many classic works because I hold them in such high esteem. I was exposed to them very early in my seminary studies through the classic reprints published by such publishing houses as the James Family, James & Klock, Klock & Klock, Kregel, Eisenbrauns, and Banner of Truth. They did the church a great service by reprinting some of the great works that were all but forgotten. I purchased every one that I could get my hands on. Were it not for the efforts of these publishers and others like them, I might not have been exposed to the works of spiritual giants from the past such as John Eadie, Thomas Manton, Theodor Zahn, Charles Bridges, Joseph B. Mayor, Frederic Godet, William Jenkyn, Thomas Brooks, George Findlay, John Owen, Robert Johnstone, E. B. Pusey, and many others too numerous to list here. I stand in awe of their literary accomplishments and am in their debt.

Out-of-Print Books

Many of the books listed in this guide are now sadly out of print. Inclusion in this book was not predicated by their availability today. Many excellent books are no longer being published today. That is not to say that some publisher won't pick up the title and thankfully reprint it, but what it means is that you may need to do a little digging to find some books. Speaking as one who has haunted used bookstores over the past half century, I can say confidently that much of the joy in locating used books is the joy of discovery. Thankfully, in recent years it has become much easier to locate used books online. Some helpful online booksellers are:

abebooks.com

Alibris

Amazon

biblio.com

bookfinder.com

eBay

fetchbookinfo.com

Also, keep in mind that many older titles can be found in digital form online for free.

There are also numerous secondhand bookstores scattered across the United States. A listing of Christian bookstores can easily be found by Googling "Cramer's Corner." Dr. Cramer keeps a list of such bookstores current. Some other reliable used bookstores are:

Archives Bookshop

509 E. Walnut St.

Pasadena, CA 91101

(626) 797–4756

archivesbookshop.com

Kregel Used Books

525 Eastern Avenue Northeast

Grand Rapids, MI 49503

(616) 459–9444

www.kregel.com

Noah's Ark Book Attic

31 S. Trade St.

Tryon, NC 28782

(828) 859–5141

Zondervan

3900 Sparks Dr. SE

Grand Rapids, MI 49546

(800) 226–1122

www.harpercollinschristian.com/zondervan/

Baker

6030 East Fulton Road

Ada, MI 49301

(800) 877–2665

www.bakerbookstore.com/shop/usedbooks

Bright Light Books

161 East State Rd. 436

Fern Park, FL 32730

(407) 622–6657

SOFTWARE PROGRAMS

The past few decades have seen a revolution in the way that Bible study is done. The Internet gives students, pastors, and scholars access to reams of data that were unheard of when I was a student some forty years ago. Entire books and journal articles can now be found online. Likewise, exponential changes in computer technology and software programs have occurred at a dizzying pace. It has gotten to the point that some of us from a bygone age are having difficulty just keeping up with the technology. Personally, although I have a Logos subscription and have been trained in its use, I much prefer the feel of picking up an actual book. My way may be much slower, but it just feels better. Of course, were I thirty years younger, I likely would prefer using a Kindle to picking up a dusty tome. It is all a matter of preference.

Having said that, there are some excellent software programs available that many have found to be most helpful. The following Bible study programs are some of the most popular in use today. All of them operate across different platforms. Thus, they can be said to be cross-platform or multi-platform.

Probably the top three Bible study software programs are BibleWorks, Logos, and Accordance. All three have strong capabilities for the original languages and have a high percentage of overlap in those capabilities. BibleWorks is probably the most affordable program of the top three . Its focus is primarily on the original languages of the Bible and caters to students whether in college or seminary. For those studying the Bible in the original languages, this program is an excellent tool and the likely way to go for those on a limited budget. However, since its focus is on languages, the program lacks a supplemental library of resources such as commentaries and the like.

Logos is the software that I own and have used the most. It has excellent original language capabilities as well as a huge library of resources. Eight standard base packages are offered (Starter, Bronze, Silver, Gold, Platinum, Diamond, Portfolio, and Collector's Edition) ranging in price from a roughly $245, which is quite affordable, to over $10,000, which is not. Of course, the Platinum, Diamond, Portfolio, and Collector's Edition libraries offer a mind-boggling 1,214; 2,053; 3,046; and 5,132 number of resources, respectively. This software is a wonderful tool for those who can afford it. It even offers packages oriented to theological persuasion such as Anglican, Baptist, Lutheran, Methodist & Wesleyan, Orthodox, Pentecostal & Charismatic, Reformed, SDA, and Catholic. There is a help line that is available twenty-four hours a day.

Accordance was written to be used by the Mac, but now can be used by Windows users, too. It is quite impressive in its operation, extremely fast, and has many features. It tends to seek a middle ground between BibleWorks and Logos. My friend James Davis gave me a demonstration at ETS in 2015 on how to do Greek exegesis, and I was properly dazzled. The website has a store where one can purchase Academic Bundles ranging in price from about $400 to $1,000, numerous Add-On Bundles for varying prices, as well as add-ons for English, Greek, and Hebrew studies and international languages. Although this program does not cost as much as Logos, it is still not inexpensive. But it does offer the best of both worlds and can streamline your study. A word study that used to take me hours to do when I was in seminary can now be done in a fraction of that time. If finances are a consideration, this program offers more resources than BibleWorks and is much less expensive than Logos.

Other popular programs include Crosswire, e-Sword, OliveTree, The BibleAnalyzer, TheWord, WordSearchBible, YouVersion, and SourceView Bible. The software engines for most of these are free as are many of the modules.

A WORD ABOUT TRANSLITERATIONS

It is not exactly a secret that I am not a fan of transliterated Greek and Hebrew words. I realize that there is a place for transliterations for those readers who lack the requisite language skills to do advanced exegesis, but my opinion is that they are more of a hindrance to those who possess facility in either or both languages. I also admit that there are some very fine commentary series that commit this very sin. Series that come immediately to mind are the NICOT, NICNT, AOTC, PNTC, TOTC, and TNTC series. All of the aforementioned are excellent commentary series whose editors are some of the finest evangelical scholars working in their respective fields. Having said that, I admit that oftentimes I have struggled trying to figure out just which Hebrew or Greek word is being transliterated. When I was a student in seminary and during my time as a young pastor, I cut my teeth on commentary series such as the ICC, EGT, Meyer's Commentary on the New Testament, R. C. H. Lenski, and Alford's Greek Testament, as well as the old classic single-volume commentaries. Those writers simply assumed that a person doing exegetical work would be able to read biblical languages. A simple solution would be to use the actual Hebrew (and Aramaic) or Greek words and then to place a transliteration in parentheses. Problem solved! Such a solution would please both scholar and student, as well as the casual reader.

Chapter 2

Old Testament

OLD TESTAMENT INTRODUCTIONS

*Archer, Gleason L. *A Survey of Old Testament Introduction*. Rev. ed. Chicago: Moody, 2007.

> This book is the best up-to-date conservative approach to the problems of OT introduction. The first part of the book is especially valuable in that it covers the subject of General Introduction including the Hebrew Manuscripts and Early Versions, the Canon of the Old Testament, and the History of the Documentary Theory of the Pentateuch. Its separate treatment of Hebrew poetry is excellent. An earlier edition was my textbook while in seminary and remains a particular favorite. I have used it for many years as a textbook in the classes I teach on the subject. "Essential for evangelicals who wish to have an intelligent grasp of the OT" (Barber, 81).

Dick, Michael B. *Reading the Old Testament: An Inductive Introduction*. Peabody: Hendrickson, 2008.

> This book is an interactive introduction to the Hebrew Bible. It stresses "the role of the reader" according to the author. It presupposes no particular knowledge base or theological perspective on the part of the reader. According to the publisher, this work "provides readers with the critical methodologies and background information necessary to effectively explore the Old Testament."

?Eissfeldt, Otto. *The Old Testament: An Introduction*. Translated by Peter R. Ackroyd. New York: Harper & Row, 1965.

> This book is the standard treatment of the Old Testament from a liberal, form critical perspective. It includes sections on the Apocrypha and Pseudepigrapha.

*Gignilliat, Mark S. *Old Testament Criticism: From Benedict Spinoza to Brevard Childs*. Grand Rapids: Zondervan, 2012.

> This brief overview provides a concise survey of the representative figures of OT criticism and their theories and shows how they led to modern trends in OT interpretation. This book is engaging and informative and serves as a good introduction to the background and issues of modern OT interpretation.

*+Harrison, Roland Keith. *Introduction to the Old Testament*. Grand Rapids: Eerdmans, 1969.

> This book is the standard treatment of the Old Testament from a conservative perspective. It provides the most thorough discussion of the subject. Like Archer's work, it treats several topics of general introduction, such as the Development of Old Testament Study, Old Testament Archaeology, Ancient Near East Chronology, the Old Testament Text and Canon, and Old Testament History, Old Testament Religion, and Old Testament Theology. The book is especially valuable in the area of archaeology and criticism of the Graf-Wellhausen Hypothesis.

*Longman, Tremper, III, and Raymond B. Dillard. *An Introduction to the Old Testament*. 2nd ed. Grand Rapids: Zondervan, 2006.

> This book is a valuable moderately conservative approach to the problems of OT introduction. It lacks a separate section devoted to general introduction as Archer's work does, but rather approaches the topic on a book-by-book basis. This is a weakness of the book, though to be fair it does cover many such themes during the book discussions. The authors rethink some particular evangelical positions when the data does not support them and soberly weigh critical views against the biblical evidence. They may not always take my position, but I appreciate the fact that they do not blindly subscribe to accepted evangelical positions. The authors rarely pontificate, utilizing rather a careful irenic approach to the issues.

*Young, Edward J. *An Introduction to the Old Testament*. Rev. ed. Grand Rapids: Eerdmans, 1964.

> This book is an excellent introduction that focuses only on special introduction. While the book provides a useful introduction to the critical problems in OT study, it is dated and not abreast of current scholarly discussion. Still, this is a useful book to acquire, particularly if it can be obtained secondhand.

OLD TESTAMENT SURVEYS

Geisler, Norman L. *A Popular Survey of the Old Testament*. Grand Rapids: Baker, 1977.

> This book is a good basic survey of the Old Testament suitable for the undergraduate level as well as for laypersons. The book's main strength is its Christocentric approach to the Old Testament. Geisler, a distinguished conservative scholar and professor for many decades at some of the top evangelical institutions in the United States, sees Christ as the key to interpreting the OT. There are better works on the subject available, but this book is especially good for the beginning student.

*Hill, Andrew E., and John H. Walton. *A Survey of the Old Testament*. Grand Rapids: Zondervan, 1991.

> This book is an excellent general survey of the Old Testament from a conservative perspective. It is up to date on the latest trends in scholarship and takes a cautious approach on most issues. It may be too technical for undergraduate use. The publisher has just added in 2016 by the same authors a set of forty-seven supplemental lessons on five DVDs, titled *A Survey of the Old Testament Video Lectures: A Complete Course for the Beginner*.

*House, Paul R., and Eric Mitchell. *Old Testament Survey*. 2nd ed. Nashville: B&H Academic, 2007.

> A helpful survey of the OT, this treatment follows the canonical arrangement of the Hebrew Bible rather than the English arrangement. House is a noted OT professor at Beeson Divinity School and the former president of the Evangelical Theological Society, whereas Mitchell is a professor of OT at Southwestern Baptist Theological Seminary.

*LaSor, William Sanford, David Allan Hubbard, and Frederic Wm. Bush. *Old Testament Survey: The Message, Form, and Background of the Old Testament*. 2nd ed. Grand Rapids: Eerdmans, 1996.

> This edition is a thoroughly revised and updated treatment taking into account later research in the field of OT studies. After the deaths of LaSor and Hubbard, Bush recruited leading scholars in the field to assist in the completion of the revision: Robert E. Cooley on archaeology, as well as Leslie C. Allen, John E. Hartley, Robert L. Hubbard Jr., William B. Nelson Jr., Nancy Heidebrecht, and John E. McKenna. Although the title of this book reads "Survey," this book probably falls under the category of "Introduction." It is semi-technical and better suited for graduate and seminary students.

*Merrill, Eugene H. *A Historical Survey of the Old Testament*. Grand Rapids: Baker, 1966.

> This book is an excellent conservative treatment of the OT by a longtime OT professor at Dallas Theological Seminary. It is particularly helpful in how it treats the early chapters of Genesis. "A good brief evangelical survey to give a person quick perspective, especially helpful for introductory, beginning study" (Rosscup, 36).

*Schultz, Samuel J. *The Old Testament Speaks*. 2nd ed. New York: Harper & Row, 1970.

> Though this book is a survey, the book is particularly helpful in its treatment of certain problem passages, such as Joshua's long day and Jephthah's sacrifice. "This is an excellent general survey of Old Testament backgrounds and arguments of books" (Rosscup, 36).

Unger, Merrill F. *Introductory Guide to the Old Testament*. Grand Rapids: Zondervan, 1951.

> First published in 1951, this old standard is now dated and should be supplemented with more modern treatments. "An extensive treatment which ably sets forth the Mosaic authorship and unity of the Pentateuch, the date of the Exodus, Israel's conquest of Canaan, and the chronological problems of Joshua–Judges. Refutes the Deutero-Isaiah theory and rejects a late date for the book of Daniel" (Barber, 81).

OLD TESTAMENT THEOLOGY

*Goldingay, John. *Old Testament Theology: Israel's Gospel*. Downers Grove: IVP Academic, 2010.

*———. *Old Testament Theology: Israel's Faith*. Downers Grove: IVP Academic, 2006.

*———. *Old Testament Theology: Israel's Life*. Downers Grove: IVP Academic, 2009.

> Not published chronologically, this massive three-volume work, at over 2,700 pages, is a marvelous example of OT scholarship at its best. Volume 1 focuses on Israel's Gospel, the OT narratives from the creation to the first coming of Christ. Volume 2 focuses on Israel's Faith, an examination of the Prophets, the books of wisdom, and the Psalms. Volume 3 considers Israel's Life, her ethical, spiritual, and worshipping dimension. This exceptional theology is certainly Goldingay's *magnum opus*. It is not to be missed!

*House, Paul R. *Old Testament Theology*. Downers Grove: IVP Academic, 1998.

This book, by a well-respected OT scholar who presently serves as associate dean and professor of divinity at Beeson Divinity School, is a warm, balanced, and well-written overview of the field of OT theology following a canonical approach. Of particular value is the appendix titled "Old Testament Theology Since 1993" in which the author evaluates some of the major treatments published during the five-year span since the book's publication in 1998. Now that the book is approaching twenty years of age, an updated edition would be most welcome. Reformed.

*Kinlaw, Dennis F. *Lectures in Old Testament Theology*. Edited by John N. Ostwalt. Anderson, IN: Francis Asbury, 2010.

This excellent book is a compilation of lectures delivered in the classroom in 1993 by the former president of Asbury College. Kinlaw engagingly surveys the entire spectrum of OT theology in these thirty-one lectures. Wesleyan.

*Moberly, R. W. L. *Old Testament Theology: Reading the Hebrew Bible as Christian Scripture*. Grand Rapids: Baker Academic, 2013.

This engaging volume by a noted professor of theology and biblical interpretation at the University of Durham is a departure from conventional OT theologies. This book focuses on a few selective passages that the author considers to be representative of OT Scripture to uncover their characteristics and leading concerns, hence an OT theology. He also focuses on the hermeneutical issues involved in reading the Hebrew Bible as Christian Scripture. This book is readable and challenging.

*+Oehler, Gustav Friedrich. *Theology of the Old Testament*. Translated by George E. Day. Edinburgh: T. & T. Clark, 1873. Reprint, Minneapolis: Klock & Klock, 1978.

This work is a true classic in the field! It is an important book to which later OT theologians are indebted. Reformed.

*Payne, John Barton. *The Theology of the Older Testament*. Grand Rapids: Zondervan, 1962.

This theology was my textbook when I was in seminary. Very well written and eminently readable, this volume is an outstanding contribution to the field by a noted professor of OT at Covenant Theological Seminary. "An impressive work in the field of Biblical theology. Written from a thoroughly Reformed point of view" (Barber, 84). Reformed.

?Preuss, Horst Dietrich. *Old Testament Theology*. Vol. 1. OTL. Philadelphia: Westminster John Knox, 1995.

?————. *Old Testament Theology*. Vol. 2. OTL. Philadelphia: Westminster John Knox, 1996.

> In this monumental study, the author's aim is, in the tradition of OT scholars such as Walther Eichrod and Gerhard von Rad, to write a systematically oriented and structured theology of the OT. The systematic orientation is essential, according to Preuss, "because the Old Testament in the final analysis probably does not have a center" (1:20). The focus and methodology of this work is a detailed assessment of Israel's responses to God's acts of election and covenant with them as a people. His aim in this approach is to set forth what the Scriptures say about God and his relationship to his people in as comprehensive way as possible. A glaring weakness of this book is that Preuss undermines his arguments for unity by denying that the OT is actually God's revelation to man. All in all, this study is a major work representative of the best of liberal German scholarship of the latter twentieth century.

*Sailhamer, John. *Introduction to Old Testament Theology: A Canonical Approach*. Grand Rapids: Zondervan, 1999.

> This major study is an important evangelical proposal for utilizing a canonical, text-centered approach to the theology of the OT that is primarily hermeneutical and methodological. Sailhamer argues that OT theology needs to be text-based, canon-oriented, confessional, and diachronic. This book is a first-rate treatment that is both comprehensive and detailed in its methodology. Highly recommended!

*Waltke, Bruce K. *An Old Testament Theology: An Exegetical, Canonical, and Thematic Approach*. Grand Rapids: Zondervan, 2007.

> At 969 pages of text, this is a massive work of scholarship written by one of the leading OT scholars of this age. A Christian Book of the Year awarded by *Christianity Today* magazine! Not to be missed!

Zuck, Roy B., ed. *A Biblical Theology of the Old Testament*. Chicago: Moody, 1991.

> This theology was written by scholars from Dallas Theological Seminary and reflects the theological orientation of that institution. Consulting editors are Eugene Merrill and Darrell Bock. Merrill wrote the chapters on the Pentateuch, Chronicles, Ezra, Nehemiah, Esther, Ezekiel, and Daniel.

OLD TESTAMENT TEXT

*Elliger, K., and W. Rudolph, eds. *Biblia Hebraica Stuttgartensia*. Stuttgart: Deutsche Bibelstifung, 1966–1977.

> This Hebrew text represents a new and revised edition of Kittel's *Biblia Hebraica* (the first OT to be based on the Leningrad Codex, the oldest complete Hebrew Bible preserved), 3rd ed. Changes in this new work include a different typeface and a revision of the apparatus. The new critical apparatus no longer distinguishes between "major" and "minor" materials. The Greek citations are more often spelled out than interpreted. The apparatus continues to reflect the higher critical approach to the OT text with resultant subjective emendations. The Qumran material has been incorporated for Samuel and integrated into the apparatus for Isaiah (in BHK it was listed separately). The text is a nearly perfect copy of the MT as recorded in the Leningrad Codex.

Klein, Ralph W. *Textual Criticism of the Old Testament: The Septuagint after Qumran*. Philadelphia: Fortress, 1974.

> This guide is a useful little handbook for students of textual criticism. The author argues that the LXX provides access to the earliest discernible stages in the history of the OT text. The book includes a glossary of text critical terms with definitions.

*Vance, Donald A., George Athas, and Yael Avrahami, eds. *Biblia Hebraica Stuttgartensia: A Reader's Edition*. Peabody: Hendrickson, 2015.

> Finally, there is an edition of the OT that compares with *The UBS Greek New Testament: Reader's Edition*. This edition, according to the publishers, is for students with a basic understanding of biblical Hebrew. The publishers claim that students with only a year of Hebrew study and this edition are able to read the Hebrew Bible in its entirety.

HEBREW GRAMMARS

*Arnold, Bill T., and John H. Choi. *A Guide to Biblical Hebrew Syntax*. Cambridge: Cambridge University Press, 2003.

> Up to date, accessible, and user friendly. Highly recommended!

*+Gesenius, F. H. W. *Gesenius Hebrew Grammar*. Edited and enlarged by E. Kautzch. Revised by A. E. Cowley. 2nd ed. Oxford: Clarendon, 1910.

> Though dated now, this compilation has been the standard work for over a century. It remains perhaps the outstanding Hebrew grammar in English. A true classic!

*Pratico, Gary D., and Miles V. Van Pelt. *Basics of Biblical Hebrew*. 2nd ed. Grand Rapids: Zondervan, 2007.

*———. *Charts of Biblical Hebrew*. Grand Rapids: Zondervan, 2007.

> The authors have compiled a complete system that combines both inductive and deductive approaches for learning Classical Hebrew. The workbook contains almost three hundred pages of exercises along with a grammatical commentary on Gen 37:5–20. There are 130 of the most vital charts in the print version with a CD-ROM that has a complete collection of 450 charts. The grammar itself includes an interactive study-aid CD-ROM. If there is such a thing as an "Idiot's Guide to Learning Biblical Hebrew," this set is it! Recommended!

*Seow, C. L. *A Grammar for Biblical Hebrew*. Rev. ed. Nashville: Abingdon, 1995.

> An exceedingly helpful introductory grammar for biblical Hebrew, this book is not an introductory textbook. Its approach is to barrage the reader with numerous examples instead of one or two for illustration. Thus, it takes a bit longer to get to the actual Hebrew text. In addition, the order in which concepts are introduced can be mystifying at times, which relegates this work to the second tier of actual textbooks. But it is excellent for what it portends to be, an introductory grammar.

*Simon, Ethelyn, Linda Reshikoff, and Irene Motzkin. *A First Hebrew Primer: The Adult Beginner's Path to Biblical Hebrew*. 3rd ed. Oakland: EKS, 2005.

> This fine introductory grammar is excellent for the beginning student wanting to learn Hebrew. Its approach is systematic and comprehensive with thirty lessons, which include verb, grammar, and spelling charts, vocabulary lists, oral reviews, exercises, stories, biblical quotes, and an examination of the book of Ruth. Most of the words occurring over two hundred times in the Hebrew Bible are introduced.

*Waltke, Bruce K., and M. O'Conner. *An Introduction to Biblical Hebrew Syntax*. Winona Lake, IN: Eisenbrauns, 1990.

> This exceptional resource is an intermediate grammar of the Hebrew language. It is well written and the best work of its kind in the English language. Indispensable!

HEBREW LEXICONS

*Armstrong, Terry A., Douglas L. Busby, and Cyril F. Carr. *A Reader's Hebrew-English Lexicon of the Old Testament*. 4 vols. Grand Rapids: Zondervan, 1980.

> This handy tool is the counterpart to Kubo's *Reader's Greek-English Lexicon of the New Testament* and is intended to facilitate the rapid reading of the Hebrew OT by defining words that occur fifty times or fewer. Each entry is also keyed to BDB.

*+Brown, F., S. R. Driver, and C. A. Briggs. *A Hebrew and English Lexicon of the Old Testament*. Oxford: Clarendon 1907.

> This lexicon, based upon the lexicon of Gesenius, has been the standard work for over a century. It has not been superseded despite the fact that it does not include the results of discovered Semitic materials such as Ugaritic materials at Ras Shamra over the past century. Its arrangement by roots also makes it difficult to use for beginning students, but the publication of Einspahr's index has mostly alleviated this problem. It has higher critical tendencies, such as espousing the documentary hypothesis. It contains a separate Aramaic section. In spite of these weaknesses, it is indispensable in the study of Hebrew. "BDB exhibits greater understanding of the nuances of Hebrew than does Koehler-Baumgarner, and provides an indispensible tool in the Biblical preacher's workshop" (Barber, 79).

*Einspahr, Bruce. *Index to Brown, Driver & Briggs Hebrew Lexicon*. Chicago: Moody, 1976.

> This indispensable tool greatly simplifies the use of Brown, Driver, and Briggs's lexicon. It is especially necessary for beginning and intermediate students.

Gesenius, F. H. W. *Hebrew and Chaldee Lexicon to the Old Testament Scriptures*. Translated by S. P. Tregelles. Grand Rapids: Eerdmans, 1949.

> This helpful volume has been the standard abridged lexicon for students for many decades. It is less comprehensive than the works of Brown, Driver, and Briggs or Koehler-Baumgartner, but is still useful for students. It was first published in 1846 and is not abreast of current scholarship. Tregelles provided a conservative perspective by editing it, but this work is now hopelessly out of date. Aramaic is included with the Hebrew. "A brilliant, comprehensive classical and technical grammar indispensable for serious study" (Barber, 79).

Holiday, William L. *A Concise Hebrew and Aramaic Lexicon of the Old Testament*. Grand Rapids: Eerdmans, 1971.

> This book is an abridgement of Koehler-Baumgartner and can greatly facilitate the reading of Hebrew for the student. However, any serious work should be based on BDB or Koehler-Baumgartner. It contains a separate section on Aramaic.

*Koehler, L., and W. Baumgartner. *Lexicon in Veteris Testamenti Libros*. 2nd ed. Leiden: Brill, 1958. With supplement.

> The third edition is entirely in German whereas the second has some English translation. This lexicon has the advantages of being more current than BDB and of arranging words by alphabetic letter rather than by root, which would be of immense help to beginning and intermediate students. Its main disadvantage is that it does not provide the same philological insight as BDB.

*Owens, John Joseph. *Analytical Key to the Old Testament*. 4 vols. Grand Rapids: Baker, 1989.

> This comprehensive guide to the Old Testament greatly simplifies its study. It gives each word or phrase its grammatical identification, the page number in BDB where the word appears, and an English translation. I wish it had been available when I was in seminary. It would have saved me a lot of time and guesswork.

HEBREW CONCORDANCES

*Even-Shishan, Abraham. *A New Concordance of the Old Testament*. Jerusalem: Kiryat Sepher, 1984.

> This is complete and user friendly. Also available in an edition from Baker in Grand Rapids.

*Kohlenberger, John R., III. *The Hebrew-English Concordance to the Old Testament: With the New International Version*. Grand Rapids: Zondervan, 1998.

> This helpful concordance uses the Goodrick-Kohlenberger numbering system, which allows the user to cross-index to the other major lexicons. It is also keyed to the most popular translation in use today, the NIV.

*Mandelkern, Solomon. *Veteris Testamenti Concordantiae Hebraicae Atque Chaldaicae.* 2 vols. Graz, Austria: Akademische Druck-u. Verlagsanstalt, 1975.

> This two-volume set is the best concordance for serious Hebrew study. The text presented is in Hebrew. "The best concordance for a grammatical analysis of forms" (Barber, 80).

*+Wigram, George W. *The Englishman's Hebrew and Chaldee Concordance of the Old Testament.* 5th ed. London: Samuel Bagster, 1890. Reprint, Grand Rapids: Zondervan, 1970.

> Although this concordance is not exhaustive, the arrangement of the entries and the much cheaper price make this a more practical alternative for the general student than that of Mandelkern.

OLD TESTAMENT WORD STUDIES

*Botteweck, G. Johannes, Helmer Ringgren, and Heinz-Josef Fabry, eds. *Theological Dictionary of the Old Testament.* Translated by John T. Willis et al. Grand Rapids: Eerdmans, 2006.

> This highly anticipated dictionary, begun in 1970 with the publication of the first volume in German by Verlag W. Kohlhammer, was finally completed in 2006 with the publication in English of the fifteenth and final volume. This set is intended to be the OT counterpart to the Kittel-Friedrich *TDNT* and offers in-depth discussions of the key Hebrew and Aramaic words occurring in the OT. "The intention of the writers is to concentrate on 'meaning,' starting from the more general, everyday senses and building to an understanding of theologically significant concepts" (from the dust jacket). Approximately 1,150 key words are examined in this valuable work. This work is international and inter-confessional in scope. It reflects the form critical approach to the Old Testament. Used judiciously, this resource is invaluable for serious OT study.

*Clines, David J. A. *The Dictionary of Classical Hebrew.* 8 vols. Sheffield, UK: Sheffield Phoenix, 2011.

> Indispensable tool for the serious Hebrew student! Includes the biblical texts, as well as the Qumran materials, Ben Sira, and all known Hebrew manuscripts and inscriptions up to 200 CE.

*+Girdlestone, R. B. *Synonyms of the Old Testament*. Reprint, Grand Rapids: Eerdmans, 1948.

> Reprinted from the 1897 edition, this book is the standard treatment of the subject. It presents material in a topical manner and draws correlations to corresponding NT words by use of the LXX. Indispensable!

*Harris, R. L., G. L. Archer, and B. K. Waltke. *Theological Wordbook of the Old Testament*. 2 vols. Chicago: Moody, 1980.

> "This work has proved to be very helpful for concise comments on key OT words from a conservative and evangelical perspective. It is reasonably priced and quite friendly to a pastor who has only basic reading knowledge of Hebrew" (**Stout**).

SEPTUAGINT

Brock, S. P., C. T. Fritsch, and S. Jellicoe. *A Classified Bibliography of the Septuagint*. Leiden: Brill, 1973.

> This useful bibliography provides an extensive listing of works from 1900–1969 and a selective listing from earlier works.

*Chamberlain, Gary Alan. *The Greek of the Septuagint: A Supplemental Lexicon*. Peabody: Hendrickson, 2011.

> Essential for anyone working with the LXX.

!Fernandez Marcos, Natalio. *The Septuagint in Context: Introduction to the Greek Versions of the Bible*. Leiden: Brill, 2001.

> A broader and more technical work than that of Jobes and Silva.

*+Hatch, Edwin, and Henry Redpath. *A Concordance to the Septuagint and the Other Greek Versions of the Old Testament*. 2 vols. Oxford: Clarendon, 1875. Reprint, Graz, Austria: Akademische Druck-u. Verlagsanstalt, 1973.

> This two-volume set has been the standard work for over a century. "Indispensable for Greek word studies. Enables the student to trace the usage of NT words in the OT and Apocrypha" (Barber, 123).

*+Jellicoe, Sidney. *The Septuagint and Modern Study*. Oxford: Clarendon, 1968.

> This book was intended to update Swete's seminal work. It is now critical for work in the LXX.

*Lust, J., K. Eynikel, and K. Hauspie. *A Greek-English Lexicon of the Septuagint.* Rev. ed. Stuttgart: Deutsche Bibelgesellschaft, 2003.

> This book is a standard lexicon for this area of study.

*Jobes, K. H., and Moises Silva. *Invitation to the Septuagint.* Grand Rapids: Baker Academic, 2000.

> This book is the best general introduction available. A revised edition should be coming out soon. Unfortunately, the bibliography is rather sparse.

*Muraoka, T. *A Greek-English Lexicon of the Septuagint.* Louvain: Peeters, 2009.

> This book is a standard lexicon for this area of study.

*Rahlfs, Alfred, ed. *Septuaginta.* 2 vols. Stuttgart: Privilegierte Wurttembergische Bibelanstalt, 1935.

> This book is the standard edition of the LXX. "The finest modern critical work available" (Barber, 80).

*+Swete, Henry Barclay. *An Introduction to the Old Testament in Greek.* Revised by R. R. Ottley. New York: KTAV, 1968.

> Although dated in some respects and updated by Jellicoe's book, this work continues to be the most important handbook for the study of the Septuagint. "An indispensable, scholarly work long regarded as the standard critical introduction to the Septuagint" (Barber, 80).

Taylor, Bernard. *The Analytical Lexicon to the Septuagint: A Complete Parsing Guide.* Grand Rapids: Zondervan, 1994.

> For beginning students.

Thackeray, H. S. J. *A Grammar of the Old Testament in Greek according to the Septuagint.* Vol. 1, *Introduction, Orthography, and Accidence.* Cambridge: Cambridge University Press, 1909.

> Unfortunately this work was never completed. "An extremely helpful work on the grammar of the LXX. The proposed volume on syntax was never published. Excellent material on orthography, phonology, and morphology" (Barber, 80).

COMMENTARIES

The Entire Bible

?Albright, William Foxwell, and David Noel Freedman, eds. *The Anchor Bible*. New York: Doubleday, 1956–present.

> This series, begun in 1956, as a whole has decidedly liberal theological leanings. Some of the volumes are top notch and fairly conservative, but others are simply "out there." Each volume in the series must be evaluated individually. The goal of this series is to offer discussions that reflect a wide range of theological viewpoints. In 2007, Yale University Press purchased this series and is now in the process of publishing backlist titles as well as new ones. "An indispensable tool for scholars and certain ministers. . . . Usually emphasizes philology, historical background, and text, rather than theology. The volumes range in quality from excellent to horrible" (Longman, 7).

*+Calvin, John. *Calvin's Commentaries*. 22 vols. Reprint, Grand Rapids: Baker, 1974.

> This magnificent set is the result of the Calvin Translation Society in the nineteenth century. Calvin, of course wrote these wonderful commentaries in the sixteenth century well before the advent of higher critical views and modern linguistic studies. But this set is worth its weight in gold. Calvin was known as the "prince of expositors," and his work paved the way for later commentators. Preachers will draw a wealth of insight from Calvin's lucid comments. I cannot recommend his work highly enough. It can often be found secondhand. Please note that not all of the books of the Bible are covered here. Judges through Job in the OT and 2–3 John and Revelation in the NT are missing. "The more you read him, the more you'll appreciate his nuanced comments and rich theological insights" (Evans, 47). Reformed.

*Clendenen, E. Ray, ed. *The New American Commentary*. Nashville: B & H, 1991–2012.

> The commentaries in this series focus on two concerns. First, they allow the reader to understand the theological unity of each book and how they fit into Scripture as a whole. Second, they are nontechnical in nature so that their message is accessible to a wider reading audience. This series is based on the NIV and is written from a Baptist perspective. Authors are committed to a doctrine of inerrancy.

!*?Driver, S. R., A. Plummer, and C. A. Briggs, eds. *International Critical Commentary*. Edinburgh: T. & T. Clark, 1863–1924.

> This highly regarded scholarly commentary series had as its aim to utilize all available aids to biblical exegesis: linguistic, textual, archaeological, historical, literary, and theological. Originally edited by Driver, Plummer, and Briggs, it

has been in the hands of various editors over the years such as J. A. Emerton, C. E. B. Cranfield, and G. Stanton. The series is now in the process of reissuing its collection. For example, Cranfield's 1975 two-volume Romans commentary replaces the older Sanday and Headlam offering. The older volumes are still valuable for their exegetical insights. "They are best used by specialists and retain their value in spite of their age" (Longman, 11).

Freedman, David Noel, and Astrid B. Beck, eds. *The Eerdmans Critical Commentary*. Grand Rapids: Eerdmans, 1999–2012.

> The aim of this commentary series is to offer readers "clear insight into the biblical text, including its background, its interpretation, and its application" (from the preface). Contributors represent the best of modern scholarship and are inter-confessional. This series is aimed at serious readers as well as scholars. Unfortunately, Hebrew and Greek words are transliterated. As of 2015, eleven volumes have been published.

+Henry, Matthew. *Matthew Henry's Commentary on the Whole Bible*. 6 vols. Reprint, Old Tappan, NJ: Revell, 1708–10.

> Originally published in 1708–10, this helpful set continues to be reprinted. Henry tends to be wordy which makes for tedious reading at times, but his spiritual insights are superb. This commentary set has blessed numerous generations of preachers over the past two hundred–plus years. The essence of Henry's work can be purchased in a one-volume abridgement that usually stays in print. "Matthew Henry lived at a time when little emphasis was placed on the history and geography of the Holy Land. However, he was skilled in applying the truths of Scripture to the needs of those to whom he preached. . . . May still be consulted with real profit today" (Barber, 46). "Shrewd, practical comments" (Carson, 23). "You will find him to be glittering with metaphors, rich in analogies, overflowing with illustrations, superabundant in reflections. . . . Every minister ought to read Matthew Henry entirely and carefully through once at least" (Spurgeon, 3).

*+Jamieson, Robert, A. R. Fausset, and David Brown. *A Commentary, Critical, Experimental, and Practical on the Old and New Testaments*. 6 vols. Reprint, Grand Rapids: Eerdmans, 1945.

> Originally published in 1871, this helpful older set is based on the original languages, but is fairly accessible to the general user. For over a century, these volumes have been a mainstay for pastors. "This work grows on the user" (Barber, 46). "A really standard work. We consult it continually, and with growing interest" (Spurgeon, 40).

!*Kregel Exegetical Library*. Grand Rapids: Kregel Academic, 2011–present.

> This excellent new series is projected eventually to cover both testaments, but currently there are fewer than ten OT volumes. There is no general editor, but individual contributors are first rate: Eugene H. Merrill, Duane A. Garrett, Victor P. Hamilton, Robert B. Chisholm Jr., and the like. No transliterations are used! Highly recommended!

*Longman, Tremper, III, and Scot McKnight, eds. *The Story of God Commentary*. Grand Rapids: Zondervan, 2013–present.

> This series is aimed primarily at working clergy and devoted laypersons. Each commentary endeavors to accomplish three goals with each passage of Scripture: listen to the story, explain the story, and live the story. The general editors are highly respected in their fields. Longman is editor for the OT and McKnight for the NT. The volumes are generally well written and nontechnical.

?Mays, James Luther, ed. *Interpretation: A Bible Commentary for Teaching and Preaching*. Louisville: Westminster John Knox, 1982–2005.

> This commentary, as its subtitle suggests, is intended to be a nontechnical commentary resource for teachers and preachers. Although its theological stance is moderately critical, it tends to underplay many issues that divide scholars. The bibliographies tend to be extremely brief. There are forty-three volumes available. "This series bridges the gap between scholarly investigation and contemporary relevance. . . . Readable and interesting" (Longman, 12).

!Metzger, Bruce M., David A. Hubbard, and Glenn W. Barker, eds. *Word Biblical Commentary*. Grand Rapids: Zondervan, 1982–present.

> The contributors of this series are described in the preface as representing "a rich diversity of denominational allegiance. The broad stance of our contributors can rightly be called evangelical, and this term is to be understood in its positive, historic sense of a commitment to scripture as divine revelation, and to the truth and power of the Christian gospel." Some contributors might be regarded as more evangelical than others, but in a broad sense they are. The volumes in this series are scholarly and fairly technical. Initially published under the "Word" imprint, they were then issued under Thomas Nelson, which was then acquired by HarperCollins, which in turn assigned them to their Zondervan imprint. The OT editor is John D. W. Watts, and the NT, Ralph P. Martin. Older volumes in the series are now in the process of being replaced. One strength of this series is the voluminous bibliography that is included in each section.

Miller, Douglas B., and Loren L. Johns, eds. *Believers Church Bible Commentary*. Harrisonburg, VA: Herald, 1986–present.

> A cooperative project in process of several denominations in the Anabaptist tradition. Currently thirty volumes are available. "This series covering the entire Bible is directed toward pastors and Sunday school teachers. Writers represent church communities drawing upon evangelicalism, Anabaptism, and piety, such as the Brethren Church, Brethren in Christ, Church of the Brethren, Mennonite Brethren, and Mennonites. In addition to explanatory notes upon the text itself, a section looks at 'The Text in Biblical Context,' how themes are developed further in Scripture, and also at 'The Text in the Life of the Church,' showing the history of interpretation and application of the passage throughout church history and within various theological traditions" (**Baker**).

*Motyer, J. A., and J. R. W. Stott. *The Bible Speaks Today*. Downers Grove: IVP Academic, 1968–1983.

> This series is devotional in nature. According to Stott, the goal of each volume is to relate the message of the Bible accurately to contemporary life in an easy-to-read format. It succeeds in those goals admirably. At present fifty-five volumes are available. "The series is readable, accurate, and relevant" (Longman, 9).

*Muck, Terry, ed. *The NIV Application Commentary*. Grand Rapids: Zondervan, 1995–2014.

> Each commentary explores units of the text under three headings: original meaning, bridging contexts, and contemporary significance. This series has an impressive list of contributors and its volumes are particularly well written. Although its commentaries are not geared toward the scholar, these volumes are not lightweight. Teachers and preachers would benefit from this series.

*Oden, Thomas C., ed. *Ancient Christian Commentary on Scripture*. Downers Grove: InterVarsity, 2000–10.

> This twenty-nine-volume series is a compilation of the best early Christian exegesis from the second through eighth centuries on both the Old and New Testaments plus the Apocrypha. Highly recommended! "These volumes, produced by historical theologians and church historians, present excerpts from early interpretations of a text to give the flavor of interpretive tendencies of the past for readers who do not have the time to extensively research the voluminous primary material" (Longman, 8).

+Poole, Matthew. *A Commentary on the Holy Bible*. 3 vols. Reprint, Peabody: Hendrickson, 1985.

> First published in 1686, this classic work is again out of print. For over three hundred years, the set has been a mainstay of preachers in the English-speaking world. Poole died before completing his great work. From Isaiah 69 onward, his commentary was completed by others. "If I must have only one commentary, and have read Matthew Henry as I have, I do not know but what I should choose Poole. He is a very prudent and judicious commentator . . . not so pithy and witty by far as Matthew Henry, but he is perhaps more accurate, less a commentator, and more an expositor" (Spurgeon, 6). Reformed.

*Strauss, Mark L., and John H. Walton, eds. *Teach the Text*. Grand Rapids: Baker, 2013–present.

> This new set of commentaries on the entire Bible endeavors to bridge the gap between technical works and devotional ones. In each commentary, the discussion of each biblical text is limited to six pages and is divided into three main sections: "Understanding the Text," "Teaching the Text," and "Illustrating the Text." There are four subsections under "Understanding the Text": "The Text in Context," "Historical and Cultural Background," "Interpretative Insights," and "Theological Insights." As of this writing, nine volumes are available: 1 & 2 Samuel, Job, Ecclesiastes and Song of Songs, Matthew, Mark, Luke, Romans, 1 Corinthians, and Revelation. A total of twenty-two volumes are planned; as of 2015 nine have been published.

?Witherington, Ben, III, and Bill T. Arnold. *New Cambridge Bible Commentary*. Cambridge: Cambridge University Press, 2003–present.

> A mainstream critical series that "aims to elucidate the Hebrew and Christian scriptures for a wide range of intellectually curious individuals."

The Entire Old Testament

*?Ackroyd P. R., ed. *Old Testament Library*. Philadelphia: Westminster, 1962–2014.

> This helpful series must be used with care as its volumes were not written by evangelicals. As a whole, the commentaries are extremely helpful with respect to exegesis and historical backgrounds, but the series does not maintain a fidelity to Scripture. Many are translations of earlier German volumes. "This is a distinguished collection of commentaries written in the critical tradition" (Longman, 15).

*Baker, David W., and Gordon J. Wenham, ed. *Apollos Old Testament Commentary*. Grand Rapids: IVP Academic, 2002–present.

> This exciting new commentary series is firmly rooted in the latest evangelical scholarship written by international scholars who are both "exhibiting scholarly excellence along with practical insight for application" (editor's preface). Nine volumes are currently available: Leviticus, Deuteronomy, Joshua, Ruth, 1 & 2 Samuel, 1 & 2 Kings, Ecclesiastes & the Song of Songs, Daniel, and Haggai, Zechariah. The aim of the editors is to keep "one foot firmly in the universe of the original text, and the other in that of the target audience, which consists of preachers, teachers, and students of the Bible" (editors preface). Each volume seeks to offer a detailed exegesis of the Hebrew text as well as the historical and theological meanings. The nine volumes completed thus far are very well written, which indicates great promise for the completion of this series. However, one annoying feature is its use of transliteration instead of Hebrew words.

*Block, Daniel I. *Zondervan Exegetical Commentary on the Old Testament*. Grand Rapids: Zondervan, 2015–present.

> This promising new commentary series offers discourse analysis of the Hebrew Bible. Thus, it is very strong on exegesis, but much like its NT counterpart, ZECNT, it is very weak on introductory matters. Unfortunately, a weakness of this series is that it transliterates the Hebrew words. One can only wonder why a series that promotes itself as exegetical would eschew the use of the Hebrew and Aramaic words.

Cohen, A., ed. *Soncino Books of the Bible*. London: Soncino, 1946–61.

> This Jewish commentary, representing a traditional conservative Jewish viewpoint, contains the Hebrew text, a translation, and a commentary. It can be very helpful with regard to the text and interpretation.

*Harrison, R. K., and R. L. Hubbard, eds. *New International Commentary on the Old Testament*. Grand Rapids: Eerdmans, 1965–present.

> This series is a scholarly effort written in the evangelical tradition, but accessible to general audiences. Its history has been one of fits and starts. It began with E. J. Young's three-volume Isaiah commentary under his editorship, but never really got off the ground. That commentary was later removed from the series. It took off again under the editorship of R. K. Harrison who, upon his death, was replaced by R. Hubbard. The list of contributors includes some of the foremost scholars in the evangelical world. An extremely useful series that is consistently evangelical! Recommended.

!*+ Keil, F. C., and F. Delitzsch. *Biblical Commentary on the Old Testament.* 25 vols. Reissued in 10 vols. Grand Rapids: Eerdmans, 1975.

> Originally published in 1875 by two orthodox Lutheran OT scholars from Germany, this has been a standard for well over a century. It continues to be the best conservative exegetical commentary available on the OT. It belongs in the library of every pastor. The work of Delitzsch occasionally espouses higher critical views, but Keil is a bedrock conservative throughout. "An invaluable work which combines sound exegesis with solid exposition" (Barber, 82). "Their expositions, although dated, are solid and competent. They often give helpful theological commentary as well. . . . Makes a good backbone to a minister's library" (Longman, 12).

Walton, John H., ed. *Zondervan Illustrated Bible Backgrounds Commentary.* Grand Rapids: Zondervan, 2009.

> The aim of this series is to bring to life the cultural world of the OT through informative entries and full-color photographs and graphics. The pages are high quality glossy and the format is extremely pleasing to the eye. This series is primarily for laypersons and other nonspecialists.

*Wiseman, D. J., ed. *Tyndale Old Testament Commentaries.* Reprint, Downers Grove: IVP Academic, 2009–present.

> The entries in this commentary series are authored by respected British, American, South African, and Australian evangelical scholars. They are fairly brief and written for the nonspecialist. For the most part, they are very helpful and informative, emphasizing exegesis while not getting bogged down in minutiae. These commentaries are now in the process of being updated with David Firth as the main editor and Tremper Longman III as consulting editor. They promise to maintain the high standards of the original series.

The Pentateuch

*Alexander, T. Desmond, and David W. Baker, eds. *Dictionary of the Old Testament: Pentateuch.* Downers Grove: InterVarsity, 2003.

> At 954 pages including indexes, this dictionary contains a massive amount of material on the Pentateuch. Virtually every major topic and issue in these five books is explored in a meaningful and comprehensive manner given the constraints of the dictionary format. Further, it informs the reader and interacts with contemporary scholarship on the Pentateuch. Its list of contributors reads like a Who's Who of current evangelical scholarship. Highly recommended!

*+Green, William Henry. *The Higher Criticism of the Pentateuch*. New York: Scribner, 1895. Reprint, Grand Rapids: Baker, 1978.

> This book is a classic refutation of the Graf-Wellhausen documentary hypothesis by a professor of biblical and oriental literature at Princeton Theological Seminary.

*Hamilton, Victor P. *Handbook of the Pentateuch*. 2nd ed. Grand Rapids: Baker Academic, 2005.

> This helpful handbook offers balanced attention to the content of the five books of the Pentateuch. Although its content summaries are extremely useful, this volume goes well beyond that in summarizing current scholarly discussions on the Pentateuch and interacting with them from an evangelical perspective.

Holdcroft, L. Thomas. *The Pentateuch*. Oakland: Western, 1966.

> The book is helpful for beginning students, but its usefulness is limited by its brevity and heavily typological approach. This would be most helpful for laypersons beginning their study of the Pentateuch.

*Sailhamer, John H. *The Pentateuch as Narrative: A Biblical-Theological Commentary*. Grand Rapids: Zondervan, 1992.

> This book, written by a noted OT scholar who taught at Trinity Evangelical Divinity School, "focuses on the narrative and literary continuity of the Pentateuch as a whole," according to the back cover. It further states that "its central thesis is that the Pentateuch was written from the perspective of one who had lived under the Law of the Covenant established at Mount Sinai and had seen its failure to produce genuine trust in the Lord God of Israel." That pretty much sums up the content of the book. What it is not is a standard introduction such as written by Archer or Longman and Dillard. It is also not a book that interacts with the myriad critical theories surrounding the composition of those five books or a verse-by verse commentary. It is helpful for those seeking a better understanding of the place of this body of sacred literature in the lives of the Jewish readers of Moses' day and its demands upon them as a covenant community.

*Schnittjer, Gary Edward. *The Torah Story: An Apprenticeship on the Pentateuch*. Grand Rapids: Zondervan Academic, 2015.

> A beautiful book with high production values, this volume functions best as a textbook for undergraduate students. Each chapter concludes with a very helpful Interactive Workshop that includes a chapter summary, a list of key terms, challenge questions as well as ones for the more advanced students,

research project ideas, and a brief select bibliography. Well written and engaging. Very nicely done!

*Vogt, Peter T. *Interpreting the Pentateuch: An Exegetical Handbook*. Handbooks for Old Testament Exegesis. Edited by David M. Howard Jr. Grand Rapids: Kregel Academic & Professional, 2009.

> This extremely helpful volume is divided into three parts: an overview of the major themes of the Pentateuch, resources and strategies for interpreting and understanding these books, and how to understand and communicate the different genres encountered in them. The aim is to assist the reader in interpreting and communicating both law and narrative. With that goal in mind, the final section develops two examples: interpreting and communicating a legal text (Lev 19:28) and interpreting and communicating a narrative text (Gen 39). A must for OT students!

*Wolf, Herbert. *An Introduction to the Old Testament: Pentateuch*. Chicago: Moody, 1991.

> This commentary, written by an OT professor at Wheaton College, is a handy easy-to-use handbook for understanding the Pentateuch. It is well suited for the undergraduate student, but could also be used as a seminary text along with supplementary material. The book lacks in-depth treatment of many of the current critical issues one would expect in an introductory work, but for its purpose, it succeeds well in providing a useful tool for beginning study.

Genesis

*Alders, G. Ch. *Genesis*. Bible Student's Commentary. 2 vols. Translated by William Heynen. Grand Rapids: Zondervan, 1981.

> These two helpful volumes are part of a sixty-two volume set issued by Zondervan, *Korte Verklaring der Heilige*, which presents the best of evangelical Dutch commentaries from the 1930s and 1940s. This is an excellent commentary written from a Reformed perspective, which is useful to lay reader and scholar alike.

*Arnold, Bill T. *Genesis*. New Cambridge Bible Commentary. Edited by Ben Witherington III. New York: Cambridge University Press, 2009.

> This book, by an Asbury Theological Seminary professor, is a capable, broadly evangelical work in a critical series.

+Augustine. *On Genesis.* Works of Saint Augustine: A Translation for the 21st Century. Translated by Edmund Hill. Hyde Park, NY: New City Press, 2002.

A classic foundational work by the influential church father.

*?Brueggemann, Walter. *Genesis.* Interp. Edited by James Luther Mays. Atlanta: John Knox, 1982.

This commentary is a moderately critical treatment of the first book of the Bible. The author, professor of OT at Eden Theological Seminary, has based this provocative study on the RSV and is quite insightful at times. At other times, his comments tend to drift away from what the text is actually saying. "Often an exercise in speculation" (Rosscup, 42). "Always stimulating and insightful. His commentary concentrates on the final form of the text and focuses principally on the theology of the book" (Longman, 20).

*+Bush, George. *Notes on Genesis.* 2 vols. New York: Ivison, Phinney, 1860. Reprint, Minneapolis: James & Klock, 1976.

Though dated, this work remains a classic and contains much helpful material on the Hebrew text as well as being eminently useful for pastors.

*Cassuto, Umberto. *A Commentary on the Book of Genesis.* 2 vols. Jerusalem: Magnes, 1964.

This unfinished commentary was first published in Hebrew in 1949 after the author's untimely death. The first volume, *From Adam to Noah*, was completed by the author prior to his passing. The second volume, *From Noah to Abraham*, was completed by Israel Abrahams using Cassuto's notes. Thus, this commentary ends at 13:4 and the author's third volume, *Abraham to the Promised Land*, was never completed. Cassuto was a conservative Jewish scholar whose insights are often brilliant, occasionally pedestrian, but who always sheds light on the Hebrew text. He rejects the Documentary Hypothesis and takes many other conservative, traditional positions. "This is a solid commentary. . . . A brilliant philologist and literary scholar" (Longman, 20).

*Davis, John J. *Paradise to Prison: Studies in Genesis.* Grand Rapids: Baker, 1975.

This helpful volume is not a commentary as such, but still is very helpful for students wanting a better understanding of Genesis. "This is an excellent, well-documented and readable survey on some of the key passages and problems in Genesis" (Rosscup, 43).

!*+?Delitzsch, Franz. *A New Commentary on Genesis*. 2 vols. Translated by Sophia Taylor. Edinburgh: T. & T. Clark, 1888. Reprint, Minneapolis: Klock & Klock, 1978.

> A stand-alone technical commentary separate from the standard set by Keil and Delitzsch, these two volumes are a critical treatment which holds to the essential authorship by Moses, an incipient form of the Documentary Hypothesis, the "day age" theory, and the possibility of a final redaction after the exile. Of the two, Delitzsch was always the more liberal and those leanings are evident in this work. He appears to be on more solid ground in the second volume, which deals with chapters 12–50. Still very helpful for work on the Hebrew text.

!+?Driver, Samuel Rolles. *The Book of Genesis*. 12th ed. London: Methuen, 1926.

> First published in 1904, a classic critical commentary that adheres to the Documentary Hypothesis. "Perhaps the clearest, most valuable presentation of the issues from the old liberal perspective" (Evans, 73).

!+?Gunkel, Hermann. *Genesis*. Translated by Mark E. Biddle. Macon, GA: Mercer University Press, 1997.

> A hugely influential work for its form-critical approach to Genesis. First published in 1910. "Gunkel and Westermann are recognized as the best technical commentaries. Along with Hamilton and Wenham, these four would provide a working library on Genesis" (**Olsen**).

*Hamilton, Victor P. *The Book of Genesis 1–17*. NICOT. Edited by R. K. Harrison. Grand Rapids: Eerdmans, 1990.

*———. *The Book of Genesis 18–50*. NICOT. Edited by R. K. Harrison. Grand Rapids: Eerdmans, 1995.

> This two-volume study is a fine, well-balanced, conservative treatment of this foundational book. The author, a professor of religion at Asbury College in Wilmore, Kentucky, has written a fine commentary that stands as one of the very best available. Highly recommended! "Overall it is a standout commentary" (Rosscup, 44).

*Kidner, Derek. *Genesis: An Introduction and Commentary*. TOTC. Downers Grove: InterVarsity, 1967.

> This book is a valuable, but concise, conservative treatment of the book. An excellent commentary for laypersons, but pastors will want something more substantial. "Kidner has packed in a lot of understanding of word meanings, movements of thought in different parts of Genesis customs, God's purposes, and relationship to other parts of Scripture" (Rosscup, 45).

*Leupold, H. C. *Exposition of Genesis*. 2 vols. Grand Rapids: Baker, 1942.

> This book though dated remains one of the very best commentaries available on Genesis. It is very helpful for exegesis of the Hebrew text and thoroughly evangelical. "A most thorough, helpful exposition from the conservative standpoint" (Barber, 94). "This is one of the most valuable works to have on Genesis" (Rosscup, 46).

*Longman, Tremper, III. *Genesis*. Story of God Commentary. Edited by Tremper Longman III and Scot McKnight. Grand Rapids: Zondervan, 2016.

> At almost six hundred pages, this nontechnical commentary is long enough to cover the bases of this foundational book of Scripture. Longman is one the evangelical world's leading and most prolific OT scholars. As are all of his writings, this volume is well written and its conclusions are always thought-provoking and supported by the author's reasoning process. Evangelicals may not always agree with Longman's conclusions, particularly with respect to creation and the historicity of Adam and Eve, but they will certainly have their preconceived notions challenged. I do not always agree with Longman's conclusions, but I am always impressed by his depth of insight and honesty as he wrestles with the text.

*Matthews, Kenneth. *Genesis 1—11:26*. NAC. Edited by E. Ray Clendenen. Nashville: Broadman, 1996.

*———. *Genesis 11:27—50:26: An Exegetical and Theological Exposition of Holy Scripture*. NAC. Edited by E. Ray Clendenen. Nashville: Broadman, 2005.

> This two-volume work is an excellent treatment of Genesis. The author holds to the essential historicity of the events in the book including the creation account, but does not believe that the "days" of chapter 1 are necessarily literal twenty-four hour days. This is an excellent theological reading of the book which is enhanced by the author's substantial knowledge of the ancient Near East and its literature. "Offers a wealth of awareness about ancient culture and writings helpful to the background" (Rosscup, 47).

*+Murphy, J. G. *A Critical and Exegetical Commentary on the Book of Genesis*. Andover, MA: Draper, 1868. Reprint, Minneapolis: James Publications, n.d.

> This book is an excellent treatment of the Hebrew text, a true classic. Although over 150 years old, it has been superseded by more recent scholarship, but it still retains its devotional richness. It should be purchased if available. "A work of massive scholarship, abounding in rich and noble thought, and remarkably fresh and suggestive" (Spurgeon, 51).

*Ross, Allen P. *Creation and Blessing: A Guide to the Study and Exposition of the Book of Genesis*. Grand Rapids: Baker, 1988.

> This helpful volume is both scholarly and nontechnical making it accessible to the general reader. The commentary is long enough at 744 pages to have enough meat on its bones to more than adequately exposit the text in such a way that it is most helpful to students and pastors. The author deals with the text in sections, not verse by verse. "A major contribution, growing out of immense study in relevant literature of recent times dealing with ancient literature" (Rosscup, 47).

!?Skinner, John. *A Critical and Exegetical Commentary on Genesis*. ICC. Edited by S. R. Driver, A. Plummer, and C. A. Briggs. Edinburgh: T. & T. Clark, 1910.

> This book, along with most of the commentaries in this series, is highly critical and fairly representative of early twentieth-century critical scholarship on Genesis. The author holds to the Documentary Hypothesis and believes that the book is little more than a compendium of legends borrowed from the ancient Near East and adapted to suit the Hebrew reading audience. Although extremely dated, it is still helpful for exegesis and grammatical analysis, but of not much use to the pastor and impenetrable for the layperson.

?Speiser, E. A. Speiser. *Genesis*. AB. Edited by William F. Albright and David N. Freedman. Garden City: Doubleday, 1964.

> The author's liberal bias limits the usefulness of this book. It can still be very helpful with exegesis of the text and historical background. This book is limited in its usefulness for the pastor. There are much better books available. "Adopts and defends the documentary hypothesis, and interprets the entire book in light of liberal presuppositions. The translation of the text, word studies, comments on the customs and culture, and use of archaeology to illumine the events of the times, are particularly helpful" (Barber, 95).

?Von Rad, Gerhard. *Genesis*. OTL. Edited by G. Ernest Wright, John Bright, James Barr, and Peter Ackroyd. Rev. ed. Philadelphia: Westminster, 1972.

> This commentary, based on the RSV, is a revision of the author's work, which originally appeared in German in 1949. It was to be his last work completed prior to his death in 1971. Von Rad was an influential critical scholar whose work was a flag bearer for liberal OT studies. Evangelicals will find little help here. The author's exegesis is weak and he often takes positions that are untenable to evangelicals. For example, he accepts the Documentary Hypothesis as fact and regards much of the history presented in the narratives as either legendary or historically impossible. "An insightful, but critical commentary on Genesis. Von Rad is sensitive to theology and literature. . . . He argues for the Hexateuch and delineates sources" (Longman, 25).

*Waltke, Bruce K., and Cathi J. Fredricks. *Genesis: A Commentary*. Grand Rapids: Zondervan, 2001.

> A very fine commentary by perhaps the foremost evangelical OT scholar today. Waltke is a master interpreter who is expert in his understanding of the Hebrew text and grammatical nuances. An excellent addition to a pastor's library! "Exegetically insightful and theologically rich" (Longman, 25). "Pastors will value this most highly for its biblical theological reflection" (Evans, 70).

*Walton, John H. *Genesis*. Zondervan Illustrated Bible Backgrounds Commentary. Edited by John H. Walton. Grand Rapids: Zondervan, 2013.

> This beautiful little commentary provides the reader with much help in understanding the cultural milieu of the book of Genesis by explaining ancient Near East customs and traditions and how they relate. The photographs and graphics are first rate! Do not confuse this volume with the author's controversial *The Lost World of Genesis One*.

*Wenham, Gordon John. *Genesis 1–15*. WBC. Edited by Bruce M. Metzger, David A. Hubbard, and Glenn W. Barker. Nashville: Nelson, 1987.

*———. *Genesis 16–50*. Nashville: WBC. Edited by Bruce M. Metzger, David A. Hubbard, and Glenn W. Barker. Nashville: Nelson, 1994.

> Wenham, tutor in OT at Trinity College, Bristol, England, and professor emeritus of OT at the University of Gloucestershire, has produced a fine evangelical commentary that is extremely helpful on matters of the Hebrew text and exegesis. The author is a careful scholar who provides many useful insights. Although an evangelical, Wenham uses source criticism often referring to J and P sources. "High level of scholarship and his exegetical sensitivity" (Longman, 25). "One of the best evangelical biblical commentaries available on any book" (Evans, 70).

*?Westermann, Claus. *Genesis 1–11: A Commentary*. Translated by John J. Scullion. Minneapolis: Augsburg, 1984.

> These three volumes, by a highly regarded professor of OT and professor emeritus at the University of Heidelberg, were originally published in German in the Biblischer Kommentar series in 1974, 1981, and 1982. This commentary is a well-written and balanced treatment from a moderately critical perspective. Evangelicals can use it with profit, but its liberal bias limits its usefulness. "This commentary is a fully conceived approach that takes into account text, form, setting, interpretation, purpose, and thrust. It also provides excellent bibliographies for each section and synthesizes previous research" (Longman, 26). "This work is often disconcerting to the conservative in its

low view of the authority of the text, and often opposes conservative views. It has a large amount of material arbitrarily theorizing how the text came into the form we now have" (Rosscup, 50). "The most thorough exegetical treatment of Genesis" (Evans, 78). "Voluminous" (**Olsen**)!

Special Subjects in Genesis 1–11

Applegate, Kathryn, and J. B. Stump, eds. *How I Changed My Mind about Evolution: Evangelicals Reflect on Faith and Science.* Downers Grove: IVP Academic, 2016.

> A compilation of personal testimonies from evangelicals who believe that there is no conflict between the Bible's account of human origins and the science of evolution. Contributors include Scot McKnight, N. T. Wright, Richard Mouw, Tremper Longman III, Francis Collins, and John Ortberg. Some might question the "evangelical" credentials of some of the contributors. A provocative volume.

*Barrett, Matthew, and Ardel B. Caneday, eds. *Four Views on the Historical Adam.* Counterpoints: Bible & Theology. Edited by Stanley N. Gundry. Grand Rapids: Zondervan, 2013.

> Since the publication of Charles Darwin's *The Origin of Species* in 1859, the question of human origins has intrigued and perplexed *Homo sapiens*, including multitudes of Christians. This book clearly presents the four primary views on Adam held by evangelicals presented by some of the top scholars in the field. Denis O. Lamoureux writes on the "Evolutionary Creation View," John H. Walton on the "Archetypal Creation View," C. John Collins on the "Old-Earth Creation View," and William D. Barrick on the "Young Earth Creation View." The book concludes with two essays of pastoral reflection by Gregory A. Boyd and Philip G. Ryken. Boyd argues that a historical Adam is not essential to our Christian faith and Ryken counters that he is. Thought provoking!

*Carlson, Richard F., and Tremper Longman III. *Science, Creation, and the Bible: Reconciling Rival Theories of Origins.* Downers Grove: IVP Academic, 2010.

> Carlson is a physicist and Longman an OT scholar. Together they team to address how to reconcile scientific descriptions for the origin of the universe and man with the biblical data found primarily in Genesis chapters 1 and 2. They address the hermeneutical issues involved in attempting to interpret these two chapters. A good introduction to the current debate!

Camping, Harold. *Adam When? A Biblical Solution to the Time Table of the Earth.* Oakland: Family Stations, 1974.

> This volume presumes to create a timetable for the creation of the earth and events of Genesis 1–11. The author, who has had a controversial career to say the least, concludes that the date for creation was 11013 BC and Noah's flood was 4990 BC. This is an extremely interesting book, but it seems to me that the author's conclusions are a bit too pat and dogmatic.

!Collins, C. John. *Genesis 1–4: A Linguistic, Literary, and Theological Commentary.* Phillipsburg, NJ: Presbyterian & Reformed, 2006.

> "Fine, moderately technical work from a conservative, Reformed point of view" (**Olsen**).

Custance, Arthur C. *The Doorway Papers.* 10 vols. Grand Rapids: Zondervan, 1975–80.

> These ten volumes, by a Christian scientist and anthropologist, were originally published in more than sixty booklets. The titles of the ten volumes are as follows: *Noah's Three Sons*; *Genesis and Early Man*; *Man in Adam and in Christ*; *Evolution or Creation?*; *The Virgin Birth and the Incarnation*; *Time and Eternity and Other Biblical Studies*; *Hidden Things of God's Revelation*; *Science and Faith*; *The Flood: Local or Global? and Other Studies*; and *Indexes*. Extremely informative, interesting, and provocative!

Gish, Duane T. *Evolution: The Fossils Say NO!* 2nd ed. San Diego: Creation-Life, 1973.

> The author, who has a PhD in biochemistry from the University of California–Berkeley and was associate director of the Institute for Creation Research, argues in this volume that the fossil record does not support evolution as an explanation for human origins.

*Halton, Charles. *Genesis: History, Fiction, or Neither? Three Views on the Bible's Earliest Chapters.* Counterpoints: Bible & Theology. Grand Rapids: Zondervan, 2015.

> This book concentrates on Genesis 1–11 and attempts to apply three interpretative genres on three specific passages: the story of the Nephilim (6:1–4), Noah's ark (6:9—9:29), and the Tower of Babel (11:1–9). James K. Hoffmeier writes on "History and Theology," Gordon J. Wenham on "Proto-History," and Kenton L. Sparks on "Ancient Historiography."

Klingbell, Gerald, ed. *The Genesis Creation Account and Its Reverberations in the Old Testament.* Berrien Springs, MI: Andrews University Press, 2015.

> This book is a collection of essays by ten scholars, each writing on a different section, genre, or topic from the OT attempting to answer the following two

questions: How does the rest of Scripture relate to Genesis 1 and 2? Do the various authors of Scripture present creation theologies that align or diverge?

Lammerts, Walter E., ed. *Special Studies in Special Creation*. Grand Rapids: Baker, 1971.

> The thirty-one articles in this volume were selected from the *Creation Research Society Quarterly* (vols. 1–5) published from 1964–68. Contributors include such well-known writers in the field as John C. Whitcomb Jr., Henry M. Morris, Harold L. Armstrong, and Duane T. Gish. "A fascinating, scholarly volume which deals with the basic questions in the areas of special creation and presents arguments for its strong support" (Barber, 54).

*Lennox, John C. *Seven Days That Divide the World: The Beginning according to Genesis and Science*. Grand Rapids: Zondervan, 2011.

> This brief, extremely interesting, and easy-to-read book is by a professor of mathematics at the University of Oxford, who also wrote *God's Undertaker: Has Science Buried God?* Lennox attempts to define what the writer of Genesis meant in his account of the days of Genesis 1. Are they literal twenty-four-hour periods or a series of indeterminate time periods? The author explores different views on the subject and concludes that the earth is 4.5 billion years old.

*Moreland, J. P., and John Mark Reynolds, eds. *Three Views on Creation and Evolution*. Counterpoints: Bible & Theology. Edited by Stanley N. Gundry. Grand Rapids: Zondervan, 1999.

> This volume is one of the earlier Counterpoints volumes. It explores three views on the subject: "Young Earth Creationism" by Paul Nelson and John Mark Reynolds, "Progressive Creationism" ("Old Earth Creationism"), and "The Fully Gifted Creation" ("Theistic Evolution") by Howard J. Van Till. In addition, there are responses by scholars from the disciplines of biblical studies, theology, philosophy, and science (Walter L. Bradley, John Jefferson Davis, J. P. Moreland, and Vern S. Poythress).

Morris, Henry M. *The Genesis Record: A Scientific and Devotional Commentary on the Book of Beginnings*. Grand Rapids: Baker, 1976.

> This volume covers the entire book of Genesis, but its real value is in its treatment of chapters 1–11. "Valuable as corollary reading and of importance in any study of Genesis" (Barber).

———, ed. *Scientific Creationism*. San Diego: Creation-Life, 1974.

> This informative volume, prepared by the technical staff and consultants of the Institute for Creation Research, contains eight chapters that cover most of the discussion on the subject over fifty years ago. The chapters are: "Evolution or

Creation?," "Chaos or Cosmos?," "Uphill or Downhill?," "Accident or Plan?," "Uniformitarianism or Catastrophism?," "Old or Young?," "Apes or Men?," and "Creation according to Scripture." "Well written and well researched" (Barber).

*Walton, John H. *The Lost World of Adam and Eve*. Downers Grove: InterVarsity, 2015.

This seminal book is an examination of Genesis 2–3 particularly in light of the ancient Near East context. The author attempts to allow for a faithful reading of the text of Scripture along with full engagement with scientific findings to advance the human origins debate. This book is the logical continuation of the author's groundbreaking *The Lost World of Genesis One*. Winner of *Christianity Today's* 2016 Book Award in the category, Biblical Studies.

*————. *The Lost World of Genesis One: Ancient Cosmology and the Origins Debate*. Downers Grove: IVP Academic, 2009.

In this groundbreaking study, the author presents and defends eighteen propositions supporting a literary and theological understanding of Genesis 1. It is particularly helpful in that it emphasizes that ancient creation texts, including Genesis 1, are function oriented and that the Hebrew word for create concerns functions. Thus, he argues that days 1 to 3 in Genesis 1 establish functions and days 4 to 6 install functionaries. A seminal and mind expanding work!

Young, Davis A. *Creation and the Flood: An Alternative to Flood Geology and Theistic Evolution*. Grand Rapids: Baker, 1977.

This book, by a professor of geology at the University of North Carolina at Wilmington, attempts to mediate between flood geologists and theistic evolutionists. He presents a mediating position that is both biblical and scientific.

Exodus

*+Bush, George. *Notes on Exodus*. 2 vols. New York: Newman and Ivison, 1852. Reprint, Minneapolis: James & Klock, 1976.

This treatment is a conservative devotional exposition of the text that can be read with great value by the scholar as well as the pastor or student. "Bush's evangelical stance is wedded with thorough scholarly attention to detail in the Hebrew" (Rosscup, 52). "Of considerable value" (Spurgeon, 55). Apparently Spurgeon did not detect any plagiarism in this volume.

!*?Cassuto, Umberto. *A Commentary on the Book of Exodus*. Jerusalem: Magnes, 1967.

> This book is a complete treatment of the Hebrew text by a noted Jewish scholar. Although this is a critical commentary, the author's approach to many issues is conservative. His superb handling of the Hebrew text makes this book worth having. "He is sensitive to the literary artistry of Exodus and brilliant in his philological analysis" (Longman, 27).

!*?Childs, Brevard S. *The Book of Exodus*. OTL. Edited by Peter Ackroyd, James Barr, John Bright, and G. Ernest Wright. Philadelphia: Westminster, 1974.

> This outstanding scholarly commentary builds upon the principles outlined in the author's *Biblical Theology in Crisis*. Child's describes his purpose as "unabashedly theological" (from the preface). Each section of the commentary includes a new translation of the Hebrew text, textual criticism and philology, OT context, NT context, history of exegesis, and theological reflection within the context of the Christian canon. Childs often questions the historicity of events in the text's account. Use with caution. "This is one of the best commentaries on Exodus. . . . Although representing a critical perspective, this volume is valuable to evangelical ministers" (Longman, 27). "The work is more suitable for scholars or intense, advanced students who have discernment to weigh what is good and what is subjective theory pressed in. Though often liberal in its critical decisions, this work is frequently perceptive theologically to a discerning student who is . . . capable of gleaning the good and leaving the bad without being misled. In some ways its good points make it a serious example of an attempt at theological exegesis" (Rosscup, 53).

*Cole, R. Alan. *Exodus: An Introduction and Commentary*. TOTC. Downers Grove: InterVarsity, 1973.

> This book is a good, albeit brief, treatment of the book from an evangelical perspective. This is one of the better offerings in the Tyndale Old Testament Commentaries series.

*Davis, John J. *Moses and the Gods of Egypt*. Grand Rapids: Baker, 1971.

> This book is not a commentary as such, but more a study guide. Its strength is in synthesizing exegetical observations from the text and making them accessible to the student and pastor. "A valuable and informative series of studies fully abreast of the most recent archaeological and historical information. Makes available to Bible students a vast amount of material not normally accessible" (Barber, 96).

Dunnam, Maxie D. *Exodus*. CC. Edited by Lloyd J. Ogilvie. Waco, TX: Word, 1987.

> The popular Communicator's Commentary does not offer commentaries as such, but rather rich expositions valuable for the preacher and layperson. This volume by a noted Methodist pastor is no exception. The author applies the book of Exodus to today by emphasizing the dominant theme of the book, which he believes is lordship.

!?Durham, John I. *Exodus*. WBC. Edited by David A. Hubbard and Glenn W. Barker. Waco, TX: Word, 1987.

> Like most of the volumes in the popular WBC series, this volume furnishes much useful information particularly with the textual matters and exegesis. However, its adherence to higher critical scholarship casts much doubt on the author's conclusions in many areas. "The strength of this commentary is its focus on the theology of the text. Its weakness is its casual attitude toward the historicity of Exodus. Durham identifies the heart of the book's message as the presence of God with God's people" (Longman, 27).

*Enns, Peter E. *Exodus*. NIVAC. Edited by Terry Muck. Grand Rapids: Zondervan, 2000.

> An outstanding commentary that deals with the major themes of the book and their theological importance in a nontechnical, approachable way. Sometimes Enns can belabor the obvious, but there is much good to be said for this thoughtful study. "Incredibly insightful theological study" (Longman, 28).

*?Fretheim, Terence E. *Exodus*. Interp. Edited by James Luther Mays. Louisville: John Knox, 1991.

> This moderately critical commentary is interesting and particularly well written. At 316 pages of text, the author's treatment of the final form of the text is just enough, but not comprehensive or detailed. "This very readable volume is stimulating in discussing the theological message of the book" (Longman, 28).

!*Garrett, Duane A. *A Commentary on Exodus*. Kregel Exegetical Library. Grand Rapids: Kregel Academic, 2014.

> This fine commentary is a welcome addition to the KEL series. It begins with a thorough introduction of approximately 140 pages. Garrett devotes considerable space to the important matter of the date of the Exodus and related matters. The exegetical work is first rate. One helpful feature of this commentary is the author's "Theological Summary of Key Points" at the end of each section of text. This would be very helpful for the preacher or teacher.

*Gispen, W. H. *Exodus*. Bible Student's Commentary. Translated by Ed van der Maas. Grand Rapids: Zondervan, 1982.

> This book is another offering from the *Korte Verklaring der Heilige*. It is, as are all of the books in the series, very helpful to both pastor and student, as well as to the scholar. Of particular interest are Gispen's special sections on the plagues and the character of Moses.

*Hamilton, Victor P. *Exodus: An Exegetical Commentary*. Grand Rapids: Baker Academic, 2011.

> This volume is an excellent treatment of the book of Exodus by a noted OT scholar and longtime professor at Asbury University. It is from an evangelical perspective and is helpful to scholar and pastor alike. However, its use of transliterations rather than the Hebrew text could be an annoyance for scholars and limit its usefulness. "This excellent commentary by an able interpreter focuses on exegesis and thus provides its own translations with notes as well as a good treatment of the text's meaning without much further theological or canonical reflection" (Longman, 28–29).

Meyer, F. B. *Devotional Commentary on Exodus*. London: Purnell, n.d. Reprint, Grand Rapids: Kregel, 1978.

> As the title suggests, this is not an exegetical commentary and thus not of much help to the serious scholar or student. However, Meyer was a master preacher and his book is full of sermonic material and helpful applications.

*+Murphy, James G. *A Critical and Exegetical Commentary on the Book of Exodus*. Boston: Halliday, 1868. Reprint, Minneapolis: James Publications, 1976.

> This book is an old classic by a noted evangelical scholar. Although it is dated and not up to date on the latest linguistic and archaeological data, it can still be used with profit by pastors and students. At times the reading is a bit ponderous and plodding due to the archaic writing style, but like reading the Puritans, it is often worth the effort. "The result of laborious study by a scholar of ripe learning" (Spurgeon, 56).

Pink, Arthur W. *Gleanings in Exodus*. Reprint, Chicago: Moody, 1981.

> Rich expositions written on a nontechnical level. Ideal for laypersons.

*Stuart, Douglas K. *Exodus: An Exegetical and Theological Exposition of Holy Scripture*. NAC. Edited by E. Ray Clendenen. Nashville: Broadman, 2006

> An excellent contribution to the NAC series. Stuart is a highly respected OT scholar who writes clearly and well and is a staunch evangelical. This is a must for any pastor who is preaching through Exodus!

Vonk, Cornelis. *Exodus*. OTS. Translated by Theodore Plantinga and Nelson D. Kloosterman. Amsterdam: Buijten & Schipperheijn, 1991. Reprint, Grand Rapids: Christian's Library, 2013.

> This volume was originally published in Dutch as *De Voorzeide Leer*. Deel I. *De Heilige Schrift Exodus*. This study, written by a popular Dutch Reformed preacher during the middle third of the twentieth century, is not a technical commentary for the scholar, but rather a series of devotional studies covering the main themes and motifs in the book of Exodus with primary emphasis on the concept of Covenant.

Decalogue

*Clowney, Edmund P. *How Jesus Transforms the Ten Commandments*. Edited by Rebecca Clowney Jones. Phillipsburg, NJ: Presbyterian & Reformed, 2007.

> This thoughtful volume was completed just prior to the author's death in 2005. This edition is annotated. Reformed.

Davidman, Joy. *Smoke on the Mountain*. Philadelphia: Westminster, 1971.

> An engaging and readable study of the Ten Commandments by the wife of C. S. Lewis.

Douma, J. *The Ten Commandments: Manual for Christian Life*. Translated by Nelson D. Kloosterman. Phillipsburg, NJ: Presbyterian & Reformed, 1996.

> Dutch Reformed.

Greenman, Jeffrey P., and Timothy Larsen, eds. *The Decalogue through the Centuries: From the Hebrew Scriptures to Benedict XVI*. Louisville: Westminster John Knox, 2012.

> This collection of essays surveys the ways in which major Christian thinkers such as Aquinas, Barth, Calvin, Luther, and Wesley understood and applied the Ten Commandments throughout Christian history.

?Hauerwas, Stanley M., and William H. Willimon. *The Truth about God: The Ten Commandments in Christian Life*. Nashville: Abingdon, 1999.

> Two popular writers, a professor at Duke Divinity School and a popular Methodist preacher, expound not only what the Ten Commandments say about God, but what they say about those who attempt to follow them. Wesleyan.

*?Miller, Patrick D. *The Ten Commandments*. Interp. Louisville: Westminster John Knox, 2009.

> Although not an evangelical treatment, this book is well worth consulting for pastors.

*Mohler, R. Albert, Jr. *Words From the Fire: Hearing the Voice of God in the 10 Commandments*. Chicago: Moody, 2009.

> A rich and penetrating exposition by the president and Joseph Emerson Professor of Christian Theology at the Southern Baptist Theological Seminary.

*Packer, J. I. *Keeping the Ten Commandments*. Wheaton: Crossway, 2008.

> Packer is certainly one of the most influential Christian thinkers of the past fifty years and any book that he has written is well worth reading. This book is a collection of brief, penetrating chapters that include discussion questions and ideas for further study at the end of each chapter. Any pastor preaching a series on the Ten Commandments should consult this book. Reformed.

*Ryken, Philip Graham. *Written in Stone: The Ten Commandments and Today's Moral Crisis*. Phillipsburg, NJ: Presbyterian & Reformed, 2010.

> A collection of incisive sermons preached by the former pastor of Philadelphia's Tenth Presbyterian Church who is now president of Wheaton College. Highly recommended! Reformed.

*+Watson, Thomas. *The Ten Commandments*. Reprint, Edinburgh: Banner of Truth, 1965.

> This Puritan classic, first published in 1692 as part of *A Body of Practical Divinity*, is a warm and rich exposition of the Decalogue. When I preached a series on the Ten Commandments thirty years ago, I found Watson's writing to be a gold mine of practical application.

Leviticus

*+Bonar, Andrew. *A Commentary on Leviticus*. Reprint, Edinburgh: Banner of Truth, 1966.

> This book is a devotional commentary first published in 1846. This is arguably the best conservative older treatment of the book. It is a true classic in the field. "One of the great works on this portion of God's Word" (Barber, 97). "Very precious" (Spurgeon, 60). "A lovely devotional and theological exposition by one of the godliest ministers Scotland ever knew" (Evans, 89).

*+Bush, George. *Notes, Critical and Practical on the Book of Leviticus*. New York: Newman and Ivison, 1852. Reprint, Minneapolis: James Family, 1979.

> This book is an extremely helpful volume that uses the Hebrew text. It is rightfully considered a classic by many. "A book which pastors will find exceedingly useful" (Barber, 97)!

Gane, Roy. *Leviticus, Numbers*. NIVAC. Edited by Terry Muck. Grand Rapids: Zondervan, 2004.

> Extremely and practical and helpful volume for wading through the maze of religious rituals particularly in Leviticus.

*Harrison, R. K. *Leviticus: An Introduction and Commentary*. TOTC. Edited by D. J. Wiseman. Downers Grove: InterVarsity, 1980.

> This brief treatment is a very helpful generally conservative work by a noted OT scholar.

*+Kellogg, S. H. *The Book of Leviticus*. New York: Armstrong, 1899. Reprint, Minneapolis: Klock & Klock, 1978.

> This book is a true classic that was justifiably reprinted by Klock & Klock in their LCRL in 1978. "This lucid broader work is one of the best theologically on Leviticus" (Rosscup, 63). "An exemplary study" (Barber, 97).

*Kiuchi, Nobuyoshi. *Leviticus*. AOTC. Edited by David W. Baker and Gordon J. Wenham. Downers Grove: InterVarsity, 2007.

> This very fine commentary is another excellent offering in the promising Apollos Old Testament Commentary series. At just over five hundred pages, this volume does justice to the text of Leviticus with flair and passion. Kiuchi brings the themes of this book, often assumed to be dull and stodgy, to life. This is an outstanding treatment by a top-notch scholar. "Kiuchi is an expert on Levitical ritual law as well as a sensitive exegete and theologian. . . . Highly recommended" (Longman, 32).

Noordtzij, A. *Leviticus*. Bible Student's Commentary. Translated by Raymond Togtman. Grand Rapids: Zondervan, 1982.

> This book is another commentary in the fine *Korte Verklaring der Heilige* series and has much to commend itself. However, it must be read with discernment as it is not as conservative as some of the other offerings in the series. For example, he suggests that some parts of Leviticus are of later origin than Moses.

?Noth, Martin. *Leviticus*. OTL. Edited by Peter Ackroyd, James Barr, John Bright, and G. Ernest Wright. Philadelphia: Westminster, 1977.

> This surprisingly skimpy volume is at once helpful at times and at other times infuriating. There is some useful information for evangelicals, but the author's extremely liberal theological stance along with the brevity of his comments make for a commentary that is highly uneven at best. "Depends on a theory of literary compositions according to scholarly guesswork and subjective reasoning. . . . Readers need to be alert to discern where Noth is delivering speculation from his sources agenda and not the text itself. He is often clear, but sometimes unclear and incomplete" (Rosscup, 64).

Vasholz, Robert I. *Leviticus: A Mentor Commentary*. Dublin: Mentor, 2007.

> Not reviewed for this edition.

*Wenham, Gordon J. *The Book of Leviticus*. NICOT. Edited by R. K. Harrison. Grand Rapids: Eerdmans, 1979.

> This book is an excellent conservative scholarly treatment of the book in the usually reliable NICOT series. "Wenham has provided a fascinating and extremely helpful discussion of what most Christians regard as a drab book. He does an excellent job of explaining the holiness laws and their function in ancient Israel. It is a well-written commentary" (Longman, 34).

Numbers

*Ashley, Timothy R. *The Book of Numbers*. NICOT. Edited by R. K. Harrison and Robert L. Hubbard Jr. Grand Rapids: Eerdmans, 1993.

> This ambitious undertaking makes a serious contribution to the body of literature on this often neglected book. The author, a Baptist minister in La Crosse, Wisconsin, and former professor of biblical studies at Acadia Divinity College in Wolfville, Nova Scotia, has produced a well-written and accessible commentary that interacts with scholarly views. His arguments disputing the census and numbers accounts in the book are interesting, but not convincing.

He questions the reliability of some of the contents of the book. Despite these cautions, this volume is one of the better commentaries available on Numbers. "He not only deals with the technical problems of the book but also demonstrates the relevance of the book for theology" (Longman, 34).

!*?Budd, Philip J. *Numbers*. WBC. Edited by David A. Hubbard and Glenn W. Barker. Waco, TX: Word, 1984.

There is much to commend this weighty volume in the highly regarded WBC by a noted British OT scholar. There is much help for the scholar and serious student seeking assistance in exegesis of the text. However, the author accepts higher critical views of literary sources and regards the incidents in the book to reflect Jewish traditions rather than authentic history. This is one of the volumes in the series that is questionably evangelical. "It employs a source-critical methodology in a way that will offend some evangelicals. It is weak in biblical theology" (Longman, 35).

*+Bush, George. *Note on Numbers*. Chicago: Ivison & Phinney, 1858. Reprint, Minneapolis: James & Klock, 1976.

This study is a very helpful, but dated, commentary by a noted scholar based on the Hebrew text. I cut my teeth on the Bush series while a student in seminary and I loved them! "Succinct, helpful comments" (Barber, 97).

*Cole, Dennis R. *Numbers: An Exegetical and Theological Exposition of Holy Scripture*. NAC. Edited by E. Ray Clendenen. Nashville: Broadman, 2001.

This excellent conservative commentary includes a substantial discussion of the book's literary structure. As its title indicates, it is also a very strong theological exposition of the book. Cole holds to essential Mosaic authorship of the book, but falters in concluding that the large numbers in the census accounts are hyperbole. There is robust interaction with previous scholarship on the book.

Gane, Roy. See section on Leviticus.

!?Gray, George Buchanan. *A Critical and Exegetical Commentary on Numbers*. ICC. Edited by S. R. Driver, A. Plummer, and C. A. Briggs. Edinburgh: T. & T. Clark, 1903.

A thorough technical commentary that, over a century old, is now outdated. For many years, this was the best scholarly treatment of the book. It is still widely consulted by students and scholars, but it needs to be supplemented with more recent works.

*?Levine, Baruch A. *Numbers 1–20*. AB. Edited by William Foxwell Albright and David Noel Freedman. New York: Doubleday, 1993.

*?———. *Numbers 21–36*. AB. Edited by William Foxwell Albright and David Noel Freedman. New York: Doubleday, 2000.

> These two volumes are a major resource in the study of this book. Levine, the Skirball Professor of Bible and Ancient Near Eastern Studies at New York University, has contributed a learned and well-written treatment to the literature surrounding this book. At just about one thousand pages, he leaves few stones unturned. However, he assumes the Documentary Hypothesis as factual, which colors many of his findings. "About Levine's erudition there is no doubt, and all serious students of Numbers must have this book. . . . Those more concerned about the final form of the book will find the introductory material especially tedious" (Longman, 35–36).

*Noordtzij, A. *Numbers*. Bible Student's Commentary. Translated by Ed van der Maas. Grand Rapids: Zondervan, 1983.

> This volume is another commentary in the *Korte Verklaring der Heilige* series and brings a depth of learning to many issues in Numbers. He in most cases defends traditional conservative scholarly views with a few notable exceptions. "A very able treatment of the text, word study, background, and relation to other Scripture" (Rosscup, 68).

*?Olson, Dennis T. *Numbers*. Interp. Edited by James Luther Mays. Louisville: Westminster John Knox, 2012.

> One of the better volumes in the series by a noted interpreter of the book of Numbers. Olson is strong in tracing the theological themes of the book, but his writing reflects the tired old liberal claptrap with regard to the manner and date of composition. Use with care. "No one has had a larger influence in recent years on our understanding of the theological theme of the book" (Longman, 36).

Philip, James. *Numbers*. CC. Waco, TX: Word, 1987.

> This book is another offering in the excellent CC by a leading evangelical pastor in Scotland. It is not a particularly valuable volume for help in exegesis, but abounds in practical application for the preacher and layperson.

Stubbs, David L. *Numbers*. BCTB. Edited by R. R. Reno. Grand Rapids: Brazos, 2009.

> According to the dictates of the series, the author provides a theological reading of the book. He takes a Christological approach.

*Wenham, Gordon. *Numbers: An Introduction and Commentary*. TOTC. Downers Grove: InterVarsity, 1981.

> As are all of the commentaries in the TOTC series, this volume is a brief treatment of the text, but is replete with helpful details and application. This is a very helpful volume for the pastor or teacher by a noted OT scholar.

Deuteronomy

*Block, Daniel I. *Deuteronomy*. NIVAC. Edited by Terry Muck. Grand Rapids: Zondervan, 2012.

> At just over eight hundred pages, this commentary is a weighty volume both in length and in depth. True to the primary aim of the series, this volume endeavors to apply the text and to assist the reader in the process of moving from original meaning to contemporary significance. Block, a well-respected OT scholar, accomplishes this admirably. The three headings under which each unit is examined are original meaning, bridging contexts, and contemporary significance. Anyone studying Deuteronomy would benefit much from reading this commentary, but preachers would especially find assistance. This is a worthwhile library acquisition for preachers and teachers.

!?Christensen, Duane L. *Deuteronomy 1:1—21:9*. WBC. Edited by Bruce M. Metzger, David A. Hubbard, and Glenn W. Barker. Nashville: Nelson, 2001.

!?———. *Deuteronomy 21:10—34:12*. WBC. Edited by Bruce M. Metzger, David A. Hubbard, and Glenn W. Barker. Nashville: Nelson, 2002.

> This massive commentary breaks new ground in Deuteronomic studies and is geared primarily to the specialist. At about nine hundred pages, it is thorough and quite detailed. Of particular value to scholars are the extensive bibliographies of scholarly works. This study will not be of much use to evangelical pastors or students (unless very advanced), but OT scholars need to be aware of Christensen's ideas. "Sometimes ponderous comments on verses" (Rosscup). "This commentary is not for the timid. It is technical and also presents new theories about the nature of Deuteronomy" (Longman, 38).

*Craigie, Peter C. *The Book of Deuteronomy*. NICOT. Grand Rapids: Eerdmans, 1976.

> This study is an outstanding scholarly, mid-level treatment of the text by a noted conservative OT scholar. Like all commentaries in the NICOT series, this book is aimed at the serious student of Scripture, but is not overly technical. It contains a very helpful introduction to the book along with a select bibliography and three appendices geared more to the serious scholar.

*+Cumming, John. *Book of Deuteronomy: Sabbath Morning Readings on the Old Testament*. London: John Farquhar Shaw, 1856. Reprint, Minneapolis: Klock & Klock, 1982.

> This book by a noted nineteenth-century Scottish preacher is not a commentary, but rather a series of expositions or devotions on the book of Deuteronomy. There is good reason that the publishers included this gem in its LCRL. It abounds with devotional warmth and application. There is not much help for the scholar here, but for the preacher and layperson there is much to commend it.

!?Driver, Samuel R. *A Critical and Exegetical Commentary on Deuteronomy*. ICC. Edited by S. R. Driver, A. Plummer, and C. A. Briggs. 3rd ed. Edinburgh: T. & T. Clark, 1965.

> This work, originally published in 1895, is an example of a commentary pervaded by higher critical views, which severely limits its usefulness for conservative students and scholars. It is helpful for exegesis, but its usefulness is limited to that. Danker, himself no evangelical, writes that this work "has long been the standard" (262) and is considered the classic older commentary among liberal scholars. Use with caution.

*?Lundbom, Jack R. *Deuteronomy: A Commentary*. Grand Rapids: Eerdmans, 2013

> Not reviewed for this edition.

*McConville, J. G. *Deuteronomy*. AOTC. Edited by David W. Baker and Gordon J. Wenham. Downers Grove: InterVarsity, 2002.

> This fine volume is one of the earlier volumes in the AOTC series. It purports to take "a fresh approach" to the book. The author attempts with some success to cast Deuteronomy as a narrative with all the components of a story such as plot, scene, character, and dramatic tension. McConville, professor of OT theology at the University of Gloucestershire in Cheltenham, England, is sensitive to the modern history of interpretation and takes a canonical approach in that he attempts to answer the question of how the completed text has meaning for its readers. Well written, interesting, and provocative! "Conservatives and critics alike will find obstacles to accepting it" (Longman, 39).

*Merrill, Eugene H. *Deuteronomy*. NAC. Edited by E. Ray Clendenen. Nashville: Broadman, 1994.

> A major commentary by a senior OT scholar that really shines in exculpating the structure and unity of the book. As always, Merrill's writing in engaging and informative. The author, a longtime faculty member at Dallas Theological Seminary, is a staunch conservative and this volume reflects those evangelical values consistently.

*?Miller, Patrick D. *Deuteronomy*. Interp. Edited by James Luther Mays. Louisville: John Knox, 1990.

> One of the better commentaries in this series.

!?Nelson, Richard D. *Deuteronomy*. OTL. Edited by James L. Mays. Louisville: Westminster John Knox, 2002.

> This volume replaces the dated von Rad commentary in the series. This book has limited value for the evangelical pastor, but is a must for scholars working in Deuteronomy.

*Ridderbos, J. *Deuteronomy*. Bible Student's Commentary. Translated by Ed M. van der Maas. Grand Rapids: Regency Reference Library, 1984.

> This book is another commentary in the *Korte Verklaring der Heilige* series by one of the most highly regarded OT Dutch Reformed scholars of the mid-twentieth century. This helpful offering by a conservative refutes higher critical views for the most part and is valuable in dealing with the text. "Ridderbos is theologically sensitive and exegetically insightful" (Longman, 40).

*Thompson, J. A. *Deuteronomy*. TOTC. Edited by D. J. Wiseman. Downers Grove: InterVarsity, 1974.

> This book is an exceptional commentary that should be on the shelf of every student who studies or preaches on this book. Unfortunately, the author makes some concessions to critical scholarship, but these do not negate the value of this fine book. Perhaps the finest nontechnical, popular treatment available. "A well-documented treatise, rich in Near Eastern culture, which ably expounds Moses' final message to God's people" (Barber). "Stimulating and full of helpful information" (Longman, 40).

*Woods, Edward J. *Deuteronomy*. TOTC. Edited by D. J. Wiseman. Downers Grove: InterVarsity, 2011.

> This volume replaces the 1974 one by J. A. Thompson. Woods holds to the conservative fifteenth-century BC date for the composition of the book. A worthy replacement that is up to date on current scholarly issues.

*Wright, Christopher. *Deuteronomy*. New International Biblical Commentary. Edited by F. F. Bruce. Peabody: Hendrickson, 1996.

> An outstanding treatment of the book based on the NIV.

The Historical Books

*Arnold, Bill T., and H. G. M. Williamson, eds. *Dictionary of the Old Testament: Historical Books*. Downers Grove: IVP Academic, 2005.

> An indispensable reference tool for anyone working in the Historical Books!

*Chisholm, Robert B., Jr. *Interpreting the Historical Books: An Exegetical Handbook*. Handbooks for Old Testament Exegesis. Edited by David M. Howard Jr. Grand Rapids: Kregel Academic & Professional, 2006.

> This handbook is the inaugural volume in the HOTE series. This helpful volume explores the components of narrative-setting, characterization, and plot. It then examines the major theological themes of each of the twelve books.

*Hamilton, Victor P. *Handbook on the Historical Books*. Grand Rapids: Baker, 2001.

> This volume is more of a survey of the Historical Books than an actual handbook. It abounds with charts and helpful discussions of problems, such as the offer of Jepthtah's daughter, along with helpful bibliographies after each section.

Holdcroft, L. Thomas. *The Historical Books*. Oakland: Western, 1952.

> This book is useful only as a brief survey suitable for the layperson. It is quite dated and is very heavy in using typology.

*Howard, David M., Jr. *An Introduction to the Old Testament: Historical Books*. Chicago: Moody, 1993.

> This book is an excellent introduction to this section of the OT by a noted OT scholar. Very helpful and concise!

Joshua

*+Blaikie, William Garden. *The Book of Joshua*. London: Hodder & Stoughton, 1908. Reprint, Minneapolis: Klock & Klock, 1978.

> This book is another very helpful volume from Klock & Klock's wonderful LCRL series. It is not a commentary as such, but is comprised of brief chapters detailing the major themes, persons, and events of the book of Joshua. It is extremely well done, exceedingly helpful especially to the preacher, and a delight to read. "One of the finest books ever written on this section of God's Word. Treats Israel's history under Joshua admirably. Filled with practical lessons for everyday living. Warmly recommended" (Barber, 99)!

!*?Butler, Trent C. *Joshua*. WBC. Edited by David A. Hubbard and Glenn W. Barker. Waco, TX: Word, 1985.

> This book is another questionably evangelical offering in the WBC series. While there is much to commend this volume with regard to exegesis, the author is not an evangelical in this writer's judgment. "This is a well-researched and thought-out commentary, full of philological, textual, and exegetical information and insight" (Longman, 42). Of particular value to the serious scholar are the extensive bibliographies at the beginning of each section.

*Davis, John J. *Conquest and Crisis: Studies in Joshua, Judges and Ruth*. Grand Rapids: Baker, 1969.

> This study is not a commentary as such, but rather an excellent treatment of the central themes of Joshua, Judges, and Ruth. The author, a noted OT scholar and longtime professor at Grace Theological Seminary, grapples with the difficult problems in the books from a conservative perspective and valiantly defends the evangelical positions.

*Goslinga, C. J. *Joshua, Judges, Ruth*. Bible Student's Commentary. Translated by Ray Togtman. Grand Rapids: Regency Reference Library, 1986.

> This commentary, originally published in 1927, is one of the strongest offerings in the Dutch Reformed *Korte Verklaring der Heilige* series. Although it is dated and does not reflect recent scholarship, it is still an excellent commentary that offers help to the scholar and student in many areas. Goslinga adheres to traditional conservative views on many of the issues in the three books, but he dates the writing of Ruth during the reign of Solomon. "This is a substantial conservative commentary. . . . Verses in the book are handled with deep reverence" (Rosscup, 77).

*Hess, Richard S. *Joshua*. TOTC. Edited by D. J. Wiseman. Downers Grove: InterVarsity, 1996.

> An exceptional achievement particularly in spite the space limitations of the series. This is a thoroughly evangelical treatment that is a must-buy for pastors and students. "An adept interpreter of the literary and theological aspects of the book" (Longman, 44).

*Howard, David M. *Joshua: An Exegetical and Theological Exposition of Holy Scripture*. NAC. Edited by E. Ray Clendenen. Nashville: Holman Reference, 1998.

> A thoroughly conservative treatment of the book by a noted OT scholar and professor of OT at Bethel Seminary in St. Paul, Minnesota. This volume is one of the strongest offerings in a weak field. The author is a previous president of ETS.

*Hubbard, Robert L. *Joshua*. NIVAC. Edited by Terry Muck. Grand Rapids: Zondervan, 2009.

>   Not reviewed for this edition.

Huffman, John A., Jr. *Joshua*. CC. Waco, TX: Word, 1986.

>   This offering in the popular CC was written by a popular Presbyterian pastor who draws parallels between the time of Joshua and the present day. This is not a commentary for the serious scholar or student, yet it abounds in devotional material for the preacher or layperson. It is a rich exposition.

Pink, Arthur W. *Gleanings in Joshua*. Chicago: Moody, 1964.

>   This book is a very rewarding devotional study, but like all of Pink's writings tends to overemphasize typology. Pink died before the completion of this book and most of the material in chapters 20–23 were written by James Gunn of Midland, Ontario. "Deeply devotional, manifests a comprehensive grasp of Scripture, contains clear outlines, and abounds in edifying material" (Barber, 99). This volume would be particularly useful for preachers and laypersons.

*Pitkanen, Pekka M. A. *Joshua*. AOTC. Edited by David W. Baker and Gordon J. Wenham. Downers Grove: InterVarsity, 2010.

>   This is a very good commentary, after the style of the series, on a very controversial book. The hundred-page introduction is very helpful in attempting to deal with some of the issues in the book. The author's commentary is also good for the most part, but weak in some areas. For example, the author's discussion on the genocide issue in chapter 6 is weak and almost patronizing. He also bends over backwards to be fair to critical scholars and does not engage them as robustly as many would like.

*Woudstra, Marten H. *The Book of Joshua*. NICOT. Grand Rapids: Eerdmans, 1981.

>   As with all of the entries in the NICOT series, this book is very helpful especially in the area of exegesis. One of the best modern evangelical commentaries available on Joshua. "There are some good literary observations, but much more could be done in this area" (Longman, 46).

Judges

*Block, Daniel I. *Judges, Ruth: An Exegetical and Theological Exposition of Holy Scripture.* Edited by E. Ray Clendenen. Nashville: Holman Reference, 1999.

> In a weak field, pride of place clearly goes to this excellent commentary on the Judges portion. This massive volume is a fine evangelical treatment that deserves a place on every preacher's shelf. Block is one of the finest OT interpreters today. "Fills a huge hole as it provides a careful treatment of introductory matters, adequate and balanced exegesis, and good theological interpretation" (Evans, 112).

!+Burney, Charles Fox. *Notes on the Hebrew Texts of Judges and Kings.* 2 vols. Reprint, New York: Ktav, 1966.

> Recommended by Danker (262) for its treatment of the Hebrew text, this commentary was originally published in 1903 and 1930. The reprint edition has an extensive introduction by W. F. Albright. It has been hugely influential and is still cited in the scholarly literature. Interestingly, it is available in a Kindle edition. "Abounds in textual, philological, historical, geographical, and archaeological material" (Barber, 99).

*+Bush, George. *Notes on Judges.* New York: Newman & Ivison, 1852. Reprint, Minneapolis: James & Klock, 1976.

> This book is the final volume of the classic reprint series of commentaries on OT books by George Bush. It is a careful and detailed commentary based on the Hebrew text and is a gold mine for scholars and preachers alike. "Of considerable value" (Spurgeon, 64).

!*Butler, Trent. *Judges.* WBC. Edited by David A. Hubbard and Glenn W. Barker. Rev. ed. Grand Rapids: Zondervan, 2014.

> This volume is a revision of the 2009 commentary. I have not seen a copy of the revised edition. However, the 2009 offering was a surprisingly conservative treatment of the book, particularly in light of the author's Joshua volume in this series a quarter century previously. This commentary is an exhaustive effort, which covers most of the bases especially in the exegetical and linguistic areas. As per usual in this series, the bibliographies are extensive and helpful.

!*Chisholm, Robert B., Jr. *A Commentary on Judges and Ruth.* Kregel Exegetical Library. Grand Rapids: Kregel Academic, 2013.

> This volume is a serious, exegetical commentary for the serious student, scholar, and pastor. The author is department chair and professor of OT studies at Dallas Theological Seminary. The commentary is most helpful on several

levels. The 105-page introduction is a gold mine of material. In the exposition, each narrative section has a translation, an outline, an explanation of the literary structure, and exposition. Of particular value to the preacher and teacher is the section titled "Message and Application" at the end of each section. This part includes thematic emphases, theological principles, and homiletical trajectories. Each homiletical trajectory includes a preaching idea. Even if a preacher's Hebrew is not sharp, he can benefit from these applications. Any preacher doing a series from this book should purchase this commentary.

Cundall, Arthur E., and Leon Morris. *Judges and Ruth*. TOTC. Edited by D. J. Wiseman. Downers Grove: InterVarsity, 1968.

> Cundall wrote the Judges portion and Morris the Ruth. The commentary by Morris is far superior to that by Cundall. Unfortunately, the two are bound together and cannot be purchased separately. For an excellent nontechnical treatment of Judges, purchase Webb or Wood. "*Judges* follows many of the higher critical theories. The exposition, however, is clear and helpful" (Barber, 99).

*Davis, John J. See section on Joshua.

*+Fausset, A. R. *A Critical and Expository Commentary on the Book of Judges*. London: Nisbet, 1885. Reprint, Minneapolis: James & Klock, 1977.

> This book an excellent scholarly study by a noted evangelical Anglican of the nineteenth century. It is a monumental work that should be purchased when available. It is truly one of the classic works on this portion of God's Word. "Remains one of the finest comprehensive and scholarly treatments for the expositor" (Barber, 99). Anglican.

*Goslinga, C. J. See section on Joshua.

!?+Moore, George Foot. *A Critical and Exegetical Commentary on Judges*. ICC. Edited by S. R. Driver, A. Plummer, and C. A. Briggs. Edinburgh: T. & T. Clark, 1895.

> For many decades this was the standard critical commentary, but because of its age it has been superseded by other more recent works. It can still be helpful for its linguistic insights, but is of extremely limited value for the average pastor.

*Webb, Barry G. *The Book of Judges*. NICOT. Edited by R. K. Harrison and Robert L. Hubbard. Grand Rapids: Eerdmans, 2012.

> This fine commentary is a comprehensive, conservative treatment of the text. The author, senior research fellow emeritus in OT at Moore Theological College in Sydney, Australia, has contributed a fine mid-level work that is helpful particularly in dealing with some of the problem passages in the book of Judges. For example, Webb does not backpedal the tough cases and concludes

that Jephthah's daughter was indeed offered as a burnt offering. He concludes that the bitterest blow to her was not her impending death, but the fact that she had to die young and childless.

*+Wiseman, Luke H. *Practical Truths from Judges*. London: Hodder & Stoughton, 1874. Reprint, Grand Rapids: Kregel, 1985.

This helpful volume is not so much a commentary as it is a book of essays covering major events, persons, and themes from the period of the Judges. Entire sections are devoted to Barak, Gideon, Jephthah, and Samson. There is not much help here for the exegete as textual matters are rarely addressed, but it is full of homiletical gems and application for the preacher. Of Wiseman's writing, Spurgeon writes, "He does it in a powerful style. . . . A man of fullness, and judiciousness; in fact, a wise man" (Spurgeon, 65).

*Wood, Leon. *Distressing Days of the Judges*. Grand Rapids: Zondervan, 1975.

Written by a solid evangelical scholar, this study remains one of the best books available on Judges and Ruth. This treatment is a detailed exegetical study of the period from Othniel to Samuel and yet is easy to read and extremely helpful to scholar and layperson alike. "It is one of the most valuable books on the period of the judges and on character sketches of the main judges" (Rosscup, 82).

Younger, K. Lawson. *Judges, Ruth*. NIVAC. Edited by Terry Muck. Grand Rapids: Zondervan, 2002.

Not reviewed for this edition.

Ruth

Atkinson, David. *The Wings of Refuge: The Message of Ruth*. BST. Downers Grove: InterVarsity, 1983.

This book is an excellent offering in the popular the BST series. Atkinson ably sets forth the major themes of the book in an engaging and readable way. The author, chaplain of Corpus Christi College, Oxford, demonstrates an awareness of critical views, but there is little interaction with them. This is a book for the preacher or layperson, but the serious scholar or student will receive little help here in exegesis of the text.

Barber, Cyril J. *Ruth: An Expositional Commentary*. Chicago: Moody, 1983.

As the title states, this study is an expositional rather than an exegetical commentary. The author includes an introduction which demonstrates an awareness of current scholarly research and which refutes liberal critical views. It also deals with such questions as date, authorship, and the books place in the canon of the OT. It is especially helpful for preachers and laypeople.

*Block, Daniel I. See section on Judges.

!*———. *Ruth*. ZECOT. Edited by Daniel I. Block. Grand Rapids: Zondervan, 2015.

> Daniel Block is one of the most respected evangelical OT scholars in the field. He is the Gunther H. Knoedler Professor of OT at Wheaton College and a prolific writer and editor. This exceptional commentary provides discourse analysis and interpretation of the Hebrew text and is exceedingly helpful on exegesis. This is the best technical commentary from an evangelical perspective.

!*Chisholm, Robert B., Jr. See section on Judges.

*+Cox, Samuel. *The Book of Ruth*. London: Religious Tract Society, n.d. Reprint, Minneapolis: Klock & Klock, 1982.

> This volume, an offering in Klock & Klock's LCRL, is the most famous work of the nineteenth-century British preacher Samuel Cox. The language is a bit archaic and stilted, but this book should be consulted by anyone attempting to preach on the book of Ruth. It is devotional in approach and of little value to the serious scholar. "Exhibits a remarkable understanding of human nature, and provides its readers with a work of real merit" (Barber, 100).

*Cundall, Arthur E., and Leon Morris. See section on Judges.

*Davis, John J. See section on Joshua.

*+Fuller, Thomas. *The Book of Ruth*. London: Tegg, 1868. Reprint, Minneapolis: Klock & Klock, 1982.

> This offering in Klock & Klock's LCRL was very rare and difficult to obtain prior to this reprinting. The book is comprised of a series of addresses given by the seventeenth-century Anglican rector Thomas Fuller at St. Benet's Church in Cambridge from 1630–31. "Quaint and pithy, and lit up with flashes of his irrepressible wit" (Spurgeon, 66).

*Goslinga, C. J. See section on Joshua.

*Hawk, L. Daniel. *Ruth*. AOTC. Edited by David W. Baker and Gordon J. Wenham. Downers Grove: InterVarsity, 2015.

> This volume is a fine commentary on an often-neglected book that interacts engagingly with current scholarship. This is perhaps the finest contemporary stand-alone commentary on this book available. Between Hubbard and Hawk, the little book of Ruth is well served.

*Hubbard, Robert L., Jr. *The Book of Ruth*. NICOT. Edited by R. K. Harrison and Robert L. Hubbard Jr. Grand Rapids: Eerdmans, 1988.

> This excellent commentary is the best mid-level treatment available on this little historical book. It contains an extensive introduction that deals extensively with such issues as canonicity, literary criticism, the genealogy of 4:18–22, authorship and date, legal backgrounds, and themes. The author does careful exegesis and deals with the text in such a way that the book comes alive. Hubbard really does justice to the book. "The commentary as a whole demonstrates careful scholarship, a lively writing style, and balanced judgment. . . . One of the very best of the series" (Longman, 50).

Younger, K. Lawson. See section on Judges.

Samuel

?Ackroyd, Peter R. *The First Book of Samuel*. CBC. Edited by P. R. Ackrody, A. R. C. Leaney, and J. W. Packer. Cambridge: Cambridge University Press, 1971.

> This slender volume is moderately critical and intended for the nonspecialist. "A clear writing style and often is of help on the reading of a given text, historical setting, customs and explanation of the passage" (Rosscup, 85).

*Andrews, Stephen J., and Robert D. Bergen. *I & II Samuel*. Holman Old Testament Commentary. Edited by Max Anders. Nashville: Holman Reference, 2009.

> The goal of this series, according to the back cover, is, "When you've got the time, this series offers a detailed interpretation based on the popular NIV text. When time is short, this series delivers an essential understanding of the OT with unsurpassed clarity and convenience." This volume, written by two different OT scholars, for the most part delivers on that promise. Its exposition is deep enough for the serious student to derive benefit and the format is user friendly enough for laypersons to use it with ease. This book is more than a reworking of Bergen's work on these books in the NAC series. This volume offers a new and fresh approach to the text.

Arnold, Bill T. *1 & 2 Samuel*. NIVAC. Edited by Terry Muck. Grand Rapids: Zondervan, 2003.

> Not reviewed for this edition.

*Baldwin, Joyce G. *1 and 2 Samuel*. TOTC. Edited by D. J. Wiseman. Downers Grove: IVP Academic, 1988.

> An excellent nontechnical commentary for pastors and laypersons. Baldwin's work is always characterized by careful scholarship. "A concise, competent, clear evangelical work" (Rosscup, 86).

*Bergen, Robert D. *1, 2 Samuel*. NAC. Edited by E. Ray Clendenen. Nashville: B & H, 1996.

> This study is an important conservative work by a professor of OT at Hannibal-LaGrange College in Hannibal, Missouri. This is one of the best and most complete commentaries available on these two books. "His excellent work reflects wide knowledge of biblical literature in the text and in footnotes" (Rosscup, 86). "Competent and readable . . . sensitive to historical, literary, and theological issues" (Longman, 52).

*+Blaikie, W. G. *The First Book of Samuel*. London: Armstrong, 1887. Reprint, Minneapolis: Klock & Klock, 1978.

> This study is an exceptional exposition full of devotional insights and richness. It is not a technical commentary, but that does not negate its usefulness to preachers. "One of the finest devotional commentaries ever produced" (Barber, 100).

*+Blaikie, W. G. *The Second Book of Samuel*. London: Armstrong, 1893. Reprint, Minneapolis: Klock & Klock, 1978.

> See comments on the author's work of 1 Samuel. "A work that deserves a place in every Bible student's library. Perceptive and enlightening" (Barber, 101).

*?Brueggemann, Walter. *First and Second Samuel*. Interp. Edited by James Luther Mays. Louisville: John Knox, 1990.

> This moderately critical commentary is particularly well written and a great resource to the preacher or teacher working through these two books. At only 357 pages of text, Brueggemann is sometimes terse in his comments and he often ignores or downplays interesting sections. "A fascinating study of Samuel. His writing style is not just engaging but also exciting" (Longman, 53). "About the best exposition one could hope for from the critical side" (Evans, 123).

*Chisholm, Robert B., Jr. *1 & 2 Samuel*. Teach the Text Commentary Series. Edited by Mark L. Strauss and John H. Walton. Grand Rapids: Baker, 2013.

> This interesting commentary, in the TTTCS, is well written, accessible, and nontechnical. Chisholm, professor of OT and department chair at Dallas Theological Seminary, writes for pastors and well-informed laymen who do not have either the time or the expertise to wade through detailed, exegetical commentaries and want to grasp quickly the most important data on the text. Chisholm communicates that well. Particularly interesting and helpful are his insights in each section under the section "Teaching the Text." Many of his applications could be used as sermon outlines. His thoughts under "Illustrating the Text" are varied and imaginative such as his mention of writers including Bunyan, C. S. Lewis, and George MacDonald and film directors such as Speilberg and DeMille. A lot of thought went into the suggested applications in this volume.

*Davis, John J. *The Birth of a Kingdom: Studies in I–II Samuel and I Kings 1–11*. Grand Rapids: Baker, 1970.

> This fine survey treatment covers the period of Samuel and the united monarchy up through 1 Kings 11. It is a very helpful volume, written by a professor of OT at Grace Theological Seminary, and it possesses the virtues of being scholarly, conservative theologically, and well written. "Illuminates the historical record of the Books of Samuel and Kings, draws information from the comparative literature of the ancient Near East on social and political conditions prevailing at the time, and highlights the Biblical text with material from archaeological investigations. A valuable book" (Barber, 100).

*Deane, William John. *Samuel and Saul: Their Lives and Times*. London: Nisbet, n.d. Reprint, Minneapolis: Klock & Klock, 1983.

> This classical reprint issued by Klock & Klock is not a textual commentary, but rather a biography of Samuel and Saul along with a commentary on the events of their lives. Anyone consulting it would be spiritually nourished.

*Firth, David G. *1 & 2 Samuel*. AOTC. Edited by David W. Baker and Gordon J. Wenham. Downers Grove: InterVarsity, 2009.

> This worthwhile commentary is the best mid-level, nontechnical commentary available on these two books. The book is well written, interesting, and covers the main issues adequately. "Firth is sensitive to literary concerns, serious about the book's historical issues, and insightful on its theological teaching" (Longman, 53).

!?Hertzberg, Hans Wilhelm. *I & II Samuel*. OTL. Rev. ed. Translated by J. S. Bowden. Edited by G. Ernest Wright, John Bright, James Barr, and Peter Ackroyd. Philadelphia: Westminster, 1960.

> An older critical work by a revered German professor of OT at the University of Kiel, this volume is strong in exegesis, but at over fifty years of age showing its antiquity. Should be supplemented with more contemporary works that are evangelical in approach.

*+Kirk, Thomas. *Saul: The First King of Israel*. Edinburgh: Elliot, 1896. Reprint, Minneapolis: Klock & Klock, 1983.

> Like the work by Deane, this is a biographical study rather than a commentary as such. This monograph, along with that of Deane, was reprinted together in one volume by Klock & Klock, and is well worth consulting. Both works are not technical scholarly works, but are of great value to the preacher and anyone teaching the book of 1 Samuel.

*Tsumura, David Toshio. *The First Book of Samuel*. NICOT. Edited by R. K. Harrison and Robert L. Hubbard. Grand Rapids: Eerdmans, 2007.

> This commentary is an excellent evangelical treatment of the text that does a good job of dealing with the exegetical details without getting too technical. The author explains the myriad textual transmission problems by arguing for the Masoretic textual tradition and explaining that such alleged textual corruptions are in reality functions of the Hebrew language in place during the time of writing. "Strengths are in the area of history and grammatical study (using discourse analysis for the above-the-sentence level)" (Longman, 55).

Kings

*Beal, Lissa M. *1 & 2 Kings*. AOTC. Edited by David W. Baker and Gordon J. Wenham. Downers Grove: InterVarsity, 2014.

> This excellent commentary is a fine evangelical treatment of these two historical books that is fairly detailed and comprehensive without being overly technical. The author, professor of OT at Providence Theological Seminary in Otterburne, Manitoba, takes conservative, evangelical positions on most issues, but also demonstrates awareness of other scholarly views without weighing down the general reader with unwanted details. This commentary is very valuable for teachers and preachers working in these two historical books.

*?Cogin, Mordechai. *I Kings*. AYB. Edited by William Foxwell Albright and David Noel Freedman. New Haven: Yale University, 2001.

> This excellent treatment completes the projected two volume work begun by Cogin and Hayim Tadmoor fifteen years previously. The promised introduction to the entire compendium of Kings is included here. This volume, by the professor of biblical history at the Hebrew University of Jerusalem, is especially well written and informative particularly with regard to the historical background of the book. "Like the previous contribution, this one emphasizes history and ancient Near Eastern background but is also sensitive to literary qualities. Especially interesting is his discussion of sources of Kings in the introduction" (Longman, 56).

*?Cogan, Mordechai, and Hayim Tadmor. *II Kings*. AYB. Edited by William Foxwell Albright and David Noel Freedman. New Haven: Yale University, 1988.

> This study by two Mesopotamian studies professors is a helpful and well-written treatment that concentrates on the Mesopotamian historical background of this book. As the two books of Kings in the Hebrew Bible are in reality one book, this book was originally slated as a two-volume study with the 2 Kings volume being written first (for whatever reason). The introduction in this volume is almost nonexistent, having been planned for inclusion in the first volume.

*Davis, John J. See section on Samuel.

*+Farrar, F. W. *The First Book of Kings*. London: Hodder & Stoughton, 1903. Reprint, Minneapolis: Klock & Klock, 1981.

> This excellent offering in Klock & Klock's LCRL is not a verse-by-verse commentary, but rather a series of essays covering the persons and events of the books. Farrar demonstrates a decided preference for the LXX over the MT. "Valuable expository studies by a great preacher, a profound scholar, and a man of unparalleled literary activity, who exercised considerable influence as a theologian and lecturer" (Barber, 101).

*?Gray, John. *I & II Kings: A Commentary*. OTL. Edited by Peter Ackroyd, James Barr, John Bright, and G. Ernest Wright. 2nd ed. Philadelphia: Westminster, 1970.

> This book is a massive critical commentary not as detailed in its philological detail as Montgomery's work, but still including "a vast amount of archaeological and exegetical material" (Barber, 101). "This has been the classic commentary on Kings for the past forty years. Gray presents especially detailed work on chronology and sources from a critical perspective. There is not much theological commentary" (Longman, 57).

*House, Paul. *1, 2 Kings*. NAC. Nashville: B & H, 1995.

> This book, by noted conservative OT scholar and Beeson Divinity School professor, is an outstanding addition to the lauded NAC. It is user friendly and scholarly, but not limited in usefulness to scholars. The author, a former president of the Evangelical Theological Society, is solid in his evangelical convictions and has produced one of the very best conservative treatments of these books. One often wishes that his exposition of the text were more detailed, but that is a minor quibble over such an excellent commentary. "The introduction to the commentary gives excellent and clear exposition of the issues surrounding the interpretation of the book" (Longman, 58). Reformed.

?Jones, G. H. *1 and 2 Kings*. New Century Bible Commentary. Edited by Ronald E. Clements and Matthew Black. 2 vols. Grand Rapids: Eerdmans, 1984.

> A strongly critical work that is based on the RSV, these two volumes contain little to commend theological conservatives. From the author's rejection of Thiele's reasonable theories of co-regencies to his tendency to see sections of text as outright fiction, this is a good commentary to bypass. This writer is baffled by Longman's assessment. "One of the best in the series" (Longman, 58).

Konkel, August H. *1 and 2 Kings*. NIVAC. Edited by Terry Muck. Grand Rapids: Zondervan, 2006.

> Not reviewed for this edition.

!*+?Montgomery, James A., and Henry Snyder Gehman. *A Critical and Exegetical Commentary on the Book of Kings*. ICC. Edited by S. R. Driver, A. Plummer, and C. A. Briggs. Edinburgh: T. & T. Clark, 1951.

> Although this volume is a critical commentary from the very liberal ICC series, it is often lauded as the best volume in the set. It is the classic treatment of the Hebrew text and as such is valuable to conservative and critical scholars alike. "The archaeological material throwing light on the era of the monarchy and the divided kingdom, plus the philological study, make the book very helpful" (Rosscup, 90). "One of the foremost critical studies on the Hebrew text" (Barber, 101).

*+Rawlinson, George. *The Lives and Times of the Kings of Israel and Judah*. London: James Nisbet, 1889. Reprint, Lynchburg, VA: James Family Christian Publishers, 1979.

> Helpful biographical studies of the Hebrew kings beginning at the time of the divided kingdom. "Still valuable for its correlation of sacred and profane history" (Barber, 101).

*Thiele, Edwin Richard. *The Mysterious Numbers of the Hebrew Kings*. Reprint, Grand Rapids: Kregel Academic & Professional, 1994.

> Originally published in 1951 and later revised in 1965 and 1983, this very helpful volume does a very credible job of grappling with the chronological issues surrounding the Hebrew kings from a conservative perspective. Not all of the problems are solved, but this book provides a solid framework for serious study. "For the serious student, it is an indispensable work" (Rosscup, 91).

*Whitcomb, John C. *Solomon to the Exile: Studies in Kings and Chronicles*. Grand Rapids: Baker, 1971.

> This study is an excellent, easy-to-read brief survey of Kings and Chronicles from a conservative perspective. The author was a noted OT professor at Grace Theological Seminary for many years. This book is not a commentary as such, but follows a survey approach. It is especially useful for undergraduate students and laypersons. It covers the period of history from 1 Kings 12 through 2 Kings.

Chronicles

*+Bennett, W. H. *An Exposition of the Books of Chronicles*. London: Armstrong, 1908. Reprint, Minneapolis: Klock & Klock, 1983.

> This addition to Klock & Klock's LCRL is not so much a verse-by-verse commentary as it is a thematic approach dealing with such varied issues as Heredity, Statistics, Family Traditions, the Jewish Community in the Time of the Chronicler, Teaching by Anachronism, the Priests, the Prophets, and Satan. The book also deals with the major kings and their reigns. In the foreword to the book, Cyril Barber in deploring the paucity of serious older works on the subject, calls this book "the only substantive work worthy of serious consideration."

*Braun, Roddy. *1 Chronicles*. WBC. Edited by David A. Hubbard and Glenn W. Barker. Waco, TX: Word, 1986.

> There is much to commend this moderately conservative treatment of this book by a noted Lutheran OT scholar. The author takes a rather loose approach in interpreting some historical matters, but all in all this is a fairly helpful volume particularly in the areas of exegesis of the text, historical background and customs, and geography. As with most volumes in the WBC, use with care. As this book is now over thirty years old, more recent treatments are to be preferred. "A very helpful discussion of all aspects of the book. Good bibliographies, sensitive exegesis, and helpful comments on Old Testament theology" (Longman, 60).

!?Curtis, Edward Lewis, and Albert Alonzo Madsen. *A Critical and Exegetical Commentary on the Books of Chronicles*. ICC. Edited by Samuel Rolles Driver, Alfred Plummer, and Charles Augustus Briggs. Edinburgh: T. & T. Clark, 1910.

> A very liberal work that discounts the historicity of these two books. Valuable only for technical issues related to the text. Quite dated.

*Dillard, Raymond B. *2 Chronicles*. WBC. Edited by Bruce M. Metzger, David A. Hubbard, and Glenn W. Barker. Waco, TX: Word, 1987.

> This excellent commentary is very well done containing many helpful and interesting details on the text along with excellent bibliographies. The late author, who taught OT language and literature at Westminster Theological Seminary, has contributed a fine study to the literature on a book that has often been overlooked. Dillard sometimes cuts his conclusions a bit too thin for a work that purports to be evangelical. "This commentary makes 2 Chronicles come alive. It is superb in its analysis of the theological message, given 2 Chronicle's composition in the postexilic period. It is one of the few Old Testament commentaries that explores connections with the New Testament" (Longman, 61).

Hill, Andrew E. *1 & 2 Chronicles*. NIVAC. Edited by Terry Muck. Grand Rapids: Zondervan, 2003.

> Not reviewed for this edition.

!*?Japhet, Sara. *1 and 2 Chronicles: A Commentary*. OTL. Edited by James L. Mays. Louisville: Westminster John Knox, 1993.

> A marvelous, moderately critical commentary in a very liberal series, this volume covers most of the bases and is a must purchase for all serious students of these books. Of limited value to the average pastor, but a treasure for the scholar. The author, a Jewish scholar, is the Yehezkel Kaufmann Professor of Bible at the Hebrew University of Jerusalem.

!?Klein, Ralph W. *1 Chronicles*. Hermeneia. Edited by Thomas Kruger. Philadelphia: Fortress, 2006.

!?———. *2 Chronicles*. Hermeneia. Edited by Thomas Kruger. Philadelphia: Fortress, 2012.

> An excellent technical two-volume commentary that is a must for serious students and scholars. Its price may be prohibitive for many pastors. "Magnificent" (Evans, 139)!

*?Knoppers, Gary N. *I Chronicles*. AYB. Edited by William Foxwell Albright and David Noel Freedman. 2 vols. New Haven: Yale University, 2004.

> This study, by the head of the Department of Classics and Ancient Mediterranean Studies at Pennsylvania State University, is a very well-written and detailed commentary. It is extremely helpful with textual matters. "Written with great detail and erudition, Knoppers navigates well many of the critical issues of the book. . . . He presents the view that Chronicles is well understood as 'rewritten Bible,' but does not provide much theological reflection, in keeping with the purpose of the series" (Longman, 62).

!*Merrill, Eugene H. *A Commentary on 1 & 2 Chronicles*. Kregel Exegetical Library. Grand Rapids: Kregel Academic , 2015.

> This excellent commentary is a fine effort by a noted OT scholar. The author, professor emeritus of OT studies at Dallas Theological Seminary, is a sure-footed guide to OT history and he brings a conservative evangelical perspective to the Hebrew text. On the negative side, however, are the numerous editorial and proofreading errors in this volume. Perhaps the absence of a general editor has exacerbated this problem.

?Myers, Jacob M. *I Chronicles*. AB. Garden City, NJ: Doubleday, 1965.

> Like most volumes in the AB series, the author's liberal bias in this work limits the use of this commentary. As the dust cover of the book reads, "I Chronicles is to be neither accepted as a faithful narrative of the Davidic period nor dismissed as a fanciful, imaginative recreation of that history. It must be taken as an important clue to the biblical process." Myers, formerly a professor of OT at the Lutheran Theological Seminary in Gettysburg, Pennsylvania, published this commentary in 1965 and it has been superseded by other works. The author is inconsistent in his treatment of the history covered in Chronicles. In some cases he defends the accuracy of the text, whereas in others he questions it. "Myers concentrates on issues of history and text and is of very little help in the area of theology. Recent commentaries are much better" (Longman, 62).

?————. *II Chronicles*. AB. Garden City, NJ: Doubleday, 1965.

> See comments under the author's commentary on 1 Chronicles. "Attempts to validate the text, focuses upon the theology of 2 Chronicles, and is particularly helpful for the way the writer blends archaeological data with the narrative" (Barber, 101).

*Selman, Martin J. *1 Chronicles*. TOTC. Edited by D. J. Wiseman. Downers Grove: InterVarsity, 1994.

*———. *2 Chronicles*. TOTC. Edited by D. J. Wiseman. Downers Grove: InterVarsity, 1994.

> At just under six hundred pages, these two volumes are concise, evangelical, and readable. Although not a technical commentary, it is quite informative and aimed at pastors and informed laypersons. The extensive introduction is very helpful. Highly recommended!

*Thompson, J. A. *1, 2 Chronicles: An Exegetical and Theological Exposition of Holy Scripture*. NAC. Edited by Ray Clendenen. Nashville: Holman Reference, 1994.

> A serviceable conservative treatment aimed at pastors and students.

*Whitcomb, John C. See section on Kings.

Ezra and Nehemiah

*+Adeney, Walter F. *Ezra and Nehemiah*. New York: Hodder & Stroughton, n.d. Reprint, Minneapolis: Klock & Klock, 1980.

> This book by a noted British Congregationalist minister and professor of NT exegesis and church history at London University in the late nineteenth and early twentieth centuries is a welcome addition to Klock & Klock's LCRL. The author allows the text to speak for itself in this able treatment. It is full of insight and golden nuggets. "A work which can be read with profit by both pastor and layperson" (Barber, 102).

!?Batten, Loring Woart. *A Critical and Exegetical Commentary on the Books of Ezra and Nehemiah*. ICC. Edited by S. R. Driver, A. Plummer, and C. A. Briggs. Edinburgh: T. & T. Clark, 1913.

> For decades this was the standard technical commentary for linguistic and exegetical analysis. Although it still retains much of its value, it has been superseded by more recent works.

*Breneman, Mervin. *Ezra, Nehemiah, Esther: An Exegetical and Theological Exposition of Holy Scripture*. NAC. Edited by Ray Clendenen. Nashville: Holman Reference, 1993.

> A concise, conservative treatment of these three books. Well written and engaging.

*Fensham, F. Charles. *The Books of Ezra and Nehemiah*. NICOT. Grand Rapids: Eerdmans, 1982.

> This commentary is a fine evangelical treatment of these two books. The author's presentation of introductory matters is particularly helpful. For example, his discussion of the chronological sequence of Ezra and Nehemiah is conservative and traditional in its approach. He prefers the view that Ezra arrived in Jerusalem in 458 BC prior to Nehemiah's arrival in 445 BC. This study is not as detailed as that of Williamson. "An evangelical effort knowledgeably rich in exegesis with a firm grasp of Hebrew, matters of introduction, and solid explanation of many of the verses. He shows a more meaningful grip on the relationship of the material in Ezra and Nehemiah than Williamson and is better overall" (Rosscup, 97–98).

*Kidner, Derek. *Ezra and Nehemiah: An Introduction and Commentary*. TOTC. Edited by D. J. Wiseman. Leicester: InterVarsity, 1979.

> An exceptional brief treatment of these two books, Kidner is a master of simplifying complex material and making it understandable. Here he is concise and eminently readable as always.

!*?Williamson. H. G. M. *Ezra, Nehemiah*. WBC. Edited by David A. Hubbard and Glenn W. Barker. Waco, TX: Word, 1985.

> This exceptional commentary, by a lecturer in Hebrew and Aramaic at Cambridge University, is a detailed evangelical treatment of these two historical books. Although this is a very scholarly study, it is not impenetrable to the average reader as some of the books in the WBC series often are and can be quite helpful to the layperson as well as the scholar and pastor. This is probably the best technical commentary available on these two books. "This is a comprehensive, scholarly commentary written by a highly competent evangelical scholar" (Longman, 66). "Highly respected in the general scholarly community" (Rosscup, 101).

Esther

*Baldwin, Joyce G. *Esther: An Introduction and Commentary*. TOTC. Edited by D. J. Wiseman. Downers Grove: InterVarsity, 1984.

> Baldwin, formerly dean of women at Trinity College, Bristol, has contributed several fine volumes in this series. This is a very fine commentary that is very helpful for scholar and student alike. However, that being said, she appears to doubt the historicity of some events in the book while holding to its having a "historical nucleus" (24). "Baldwin combines a keen literary and theological

sense with a firm and intelligent opinion concerning the book's historicity. The commentary is well written and based upon thorough research" (Longman, 66).

*Breneman, Mervin. See section on Ezra-Nehemiah.

Jobes, Karen. *Esther*. NIVAC. Edited by Terry Muck. Grand Rapids: Zondervan, 1999.

> Not reviewed for this edition. However, the author is a highly respected NT and LXX scholar and Bible translator whose works are of a uniformly excellent quality. "Without a doubt this is the best commentary to buy on Esther" (Longman, 67).

*?Moore, Carey A. *Esther*. AB. Edited by William Foxwell Albright and David Noel Freedman. Garden City, NJ: Doubleday, 1971.

> This commentary, at a rather sparse 118 pages including four appendices, is nonetheless a fairly capable treatment of the text. The introduction, at thirty-two pages (not included in the 118 pages of actual commentary), is quite lengthy and helpful particularly in dealing some of the issues surrounding the book such as canonicity and historicity. The book also includes a lengthy bibliography that was quite extensive and helpful at the time of writing in 1971, but is now quite dated and needs revision to reflect forty-four-plus years of scholarship.

Poetical Books

!?Alter, Robert. *The Wisdom Books: Job, Proverbs, and Ecclesiastes*. New York: Norton, 2010.

> Alter's translation is magisterial; his commentary less so. Read this book for the beauty of his translation, but read Estes or someone more evangelical for reliable commentary. The author sees Job as a character from a fable and sections of Proverbs as written in either the Persian or Hellenistic periods.

*Bullock, C. Hassell. *An Introduction to the Old Testament: Poetic Books*. Chicago: Moody, 1988.

> This helpful volume is an excellent introduction to the Historical Books that is not too technical. Highly recommended!

!Crenshaw, James L. *Old Testament Wisdom: An Introduction*. 3rd ed. Louisville: Westminster John Knox, 2010.

> For several decades, this book has been the standard critical introduction to the Hebrew books of wisdom. Many of Crenshaw's conclusions will be unpalatable to evangelicals. Supplement this work with that of Estes or Bullock.

*Estes, Daniel J. *Handbook on the Wisdom Books and Psalms*. Grand Rapids: Baker Academic, 2005.

> This handbook is an exceptionally helpful volume from a conservative, evangelical perspective. There are enlightening articles on special topics in the Proverbs such as on cheerfulness, contentment, humility, and parenting. Highly recommended!

*Futato, Mark D. *Interpreting the Psalms: An Exegetical Handbook*. Handbooks for Old Testament Exegesis. Edited by David M. Howard Jr. Grand Rapids: Kregel Academic & Professional, 2007.

> This handbook is the second entry in the excellent HOTE series. Futato upholds the high standards set Chisholm set with the first volume. This book's treatment of Hebrew poetry is particularly helpful.

*Longman, Tremper, III, ed. *Dictionary of the Old Testament: Wisdom Poetry & Writings*. Downers Grove: IVP Academic, 2008.

> An indispensable tool for anyone working in the area of Hebrew wisdom literature and poetry.

?Von Rad, Gerhard. *Wisdom in Israel*. Nashville: Abingdon, 1972.

> This seminal work, when it came out in German in 1970, was groundbreaking. Von Rad, professor of OT at the University of Heidelberg for many years, saw Hebrew wisdom literature as Israel's willingness to ground her faith in encounter with the world as the creation of God. "Attempts to correlate the place of knowledge in the religious experience of God's people" (Barber).

Yoder, Calvin Sanford. *Poetry of the Old Testament*. Scottdale, PA: Herald, 1948.

> This book is a very basic introduction to the poetry of the Old Testament. It is a very helpful book in many ways, but is not up to date with current scholarship and sorely in need of revision. Its lack of an appendix limits its usefulness.

Job

*Alden, Robert L. *Job*. NAC. Edited by E. Ray Clendenen. Nashville: B & H, 1993.

> This volume is a detailed exegetical treatment of the book of Job, much more detailed than the author's work on Proverbs. Like his work on Proverbs, this book is insightful and a delight to read. It is an extremely helpful volume. He leans toward the historicity of Job the man. "He fails, however, to recognize the central issue of the book, which is the nature and origin of wisdom" (Longman, 68–69).

*Andersen, Francis I. *Job: An Introduction and Commentary*. TOTC. Downers Grove: InterVarsity, 1976.

> This study is possibly the best conservative scholarly work available on Job. It is an exemplary and thorough work of scholarship. "An excellent treatment which maintains a high standard of evangelical scholarship" (Barber). "Andersen has provided one of the best modern and informed expositions of the text of Job" (Rosscup, 102).

Burrell, David B. *Deconstructing Theodicy: Why Job Has Nothing to Say to the Puzzle of Suffering*. Grand Rapids: Brazos, 2008.

> This interesting and provocative book is not a commentary. Rather, it is a theological and philosophical reflection on the major movements of the book. Burrell, a professor of philosophy and theology at the University of Notre Dame, concludes that the book of Job is an affirmation that God hears and heeds the cries of anguish of his people. It includes a chapter by A. H. Johns, an Islamic scholar ("A Comparative Glance at Ayyub in the Qur'an"). This is a rather slim volume at 142 pages, but it does contribute to the discussion on the subject of suffering in the life of the believer. Roman Catholic.

!*Clines, David J. A. *Job 1–20*. WBC. Edited by David A. Hubbard and Glenn W. Barker. Nashville: Nelson, 1989.

!*———. *Job 21–37*. WBC. Edited by David A. Hubbard and Glenn W. Barker. Nashville: Nelson, 2006.

!*———. *Job 38–42*. WBC. Edited by David A. Hubbard and Glenn W. Barker. Nashville: Nelson, 2011.

> At over 1,500 pages, this moderately conservative commentary is a massive treatment of the book of Job. It is extremely detailed and strong particularly in the areas of exegesis and presentation of various views of the book. Clines apparently leaves no stone unturned in this remarkable study. Some of his conclusions may be untenable or confusing to evangelicals, but overall this

is an exceptional effort by the professor emeritus of biblical studies at the University of Sheffield. "Clines has written a stimulating and insightful commentary on the book of Job. It is stimulating in the sense that it will get the reader thinking about the book and its issues. It is provocatively written. It is strong in literary and theological analysis. It is long because he extensively discusses linguistic, philological, and textual issues. The bibliographies are incredibly good" (Longman, 69).

*+Gibson, Edgar C. S. *The Book of Job*. London: Methuen, 1899. Reprint, Minneapolis: Klock & Klock, 1978.

This volume is a very fine older commentary by a lecturer at the University of Cambridge. Gibson begins his book with a very fine introduction followed by his exposition of the text. Of particular value to the reader are his comments prior to each section of text explaining the writer's theme for that section. As are all of the volumes in Klock & Klock's LCRL, this volume is well worth purchasing if it can be found. "A valuable exposition. Deserves a place in the library of every pastor" (Barber, 103).

!*?Habel, Norman C. *The Book of Job*. OTL. Edited by James L. Mays, Carol A. Newsom, and David L. Petersen. Louisville: Westminster John Knox, 1985.

A scholarly, critical treatment that has enjoyed a stellar reputation by scholars. It is worth purchasing. "Concentrates particularly on literary features and theology" (Longman, 70).

*Hartley, John E. *The Book of Job*. NICOT. Edited by R. K. Harrison. Grand Rapids: Eerdmans, 1988.

A weighty and detailed evangelical treatment of the book. Highly recommended!

*Longman, Tremper, III. *Job*. Baker Commentary on the Old Testament Wisdom and Psalms. Edited by Tremper Longman III. Grand Rapids: Baker, 2012.

Longman has set a high standard by his work in this series. A substantial commentary that hits the right balance for pastors and students. The author attempts "to give a theological explanation that sees the book's main theme as connected to the question of the source of true wisdom" (Longman, 71).

*Pope, Marvin H. *Job*. AB. Edited by William Foxwell Albright and David Noel Freedman. Garden City, NJ: Doubleday, 1977.

This volume is a capable treatment of the text. It was originally published in 1965 and needs to be supplemented by more modern studies. "This one's strength is its philological analysis. Pope . . . is a very sound practitioner of comparative Semitics. This is a solid commentary" (Longman, 71).

Ross, Hugh. *Hidden Treasures in the Book of Job: How the Oldest Book in the Bible Answers Today's Scientific Questions*. Grand Rapids: Baker, 2011.

> Unlike most other volumes on Job that do not qualify as commentaries, this one does not explore the book through the prism of theodicy, but rather through science. This book is totally unique, provocative, well written, and engaging all at the same time. The author is a Christian astronomer who is founder and president of Reasons to Believe. He covers issues such as lessons from animals, dinosaurs, the origin of soulish and spiritual qualities, and creation and Genesis controversies.

Walton, John H. *Job*. NIVAC. Edited by Terry Muck. Grand Rapids: Zondervan, 2012.

> Not reviewed for this edition.

Psalms

*+Alexander, Joseph Addison. *The Psalms: Translated and Explained*. Edinburgh, 1873. Reprint, Grand Rapids: Baker, 1977.

> Though about 150 years old, this commentary by a respected nineteenth-century OT professor at Princeton remains one of the very best available on the Psalms. The exegetical work is exceptional. It is essentially a reworking of the German Hengstenberg's famous commentary on the Psalms. According to the preface of the original 1850 publication, "The original design was to make that work, by abridgment and other unessential changes, more acceptable and useful to the English reader than it could be in the form of an exact translation" (1). "Contains genuine scholarship and evangelical warmth which are singularly missing from many commentaries today" (Barber). "Occupies a first place among expositions. It is a clear and judicious explanation of the text and cannot be dispensed with" (Spurgeon, 81).

*Craigie, Peter. *Psalms 1–50*. WBC. Edited by David A. Hubbard and Glenn W. Barker. Waco, TX: Word, 1983.

*Tate, Marvin E. *Psalms 51–100*. WBC. Edited by David A. Hubbard and Glenn W. Barker. Dallas: Word, 1990.

Allen, Leslie C. *Psalms 101–150*. WBC. Edited by David A. Hubbard and Glenn W. Barker. Waco, TX: Word, 1983.

> This three-volume treatment of the Psalms was written by three different authors in non-chronological order: Craigie 1–50 in 1983, Tate 51–100 in 1990, and Allen 101–150 in 1983. Allen's contribution is the weakest of the three; Tate's the strongest. Craigie is a renowned Ugaritic scholar whose helpful

comments are more measured and cautious than the questionable specula-
tions of Dahood. As his commentary is the first in the series, his volume
contains the introduction. This set should be supplemented by a commentary
that is strong on theology, such as the one by Van Gemeren.

*+Cox, Samuel. *The Pilgrim Psalms: An Exposition of the Psalms of Degrees*. New York:
Randolph, 1874. Reprint, Minneapolis: Klock & Klock, 1983.

A masterful exposition of Psalms 120–134 by a masterful nineteenth-century
expositor from the UK.

!?Dahood, Mitchell. *Psalms*. AB. Edited by William Foxwell Albright and David Noel
Freedman. 3 vols. Garden City: Doubleday, 1965.

This three-volume set is a very fine commentary in many respects, particularly in shedding light on word meanings, but disappointing in others. Dahood
has obviously gone overboard in stressing the parallels between Northwest
Semitic texts to bring out the meaning of the Hebrew text. Some of his parallels are dubious at best. "A highly critical work in which the author, relying
heavily upon contemporary linguistic materials and stressing the relationship
of hymnic literature to the Ugaritic texts found at Ras Shamra, tries to capture
and present the meaning of the original Hebrew. Helpful for the expositor"
(Barber, 105). "There is no methodological control, and even Ugaritic scholars cannot evaluate his arguments. Nonspecialists will be at a total loss. In
short, this commentary is very eccentric" (Longman, 73).

*DeClaisse-Walford, Nancy, Rolf A. Jacobson, and Beth Laneel Tanner. *The Book of
Psalms*. NICOT. Edited by Robert L. Hubbard. Grand Rapids: Eerdmans, 2014.

This commentary is a massive, at just over one thousand pages, volume that
packs a lot of punch on such a long biblical book. This book reads sometimes
like a tag team effort with the psalms divided among the three authors and
the name of the author of each section displayed at the end of each section. Of
particular value are the sections written by Jacobson, each of which includes
a reflection on the psalm. These reflections contain much useful application
for pastors and teachers.

*+Dickson, David. *A Commentary on the Psalms*. 2 vols. Glasgow, 1834. Reprint,
Minneapolis: Klock & Klock, 1980.

A rich and warm exposition by a noted seventeenth-century Scottish cov-
enanter. This is the best Puritan commentary on the Psalms and a true classic.
For those wise folks who love the Puritans, this one is a must-buy! Originally
published in one volume in 1655 in London, this two-volume work is a reprint of the 1834 Glasgow edition. "Heavily laden with richness" (Rosscup,

109). "A rich volume dripping fatness. Invaluable to the preacher. Having read and re-read it, we can speak of its holy savour and suggestiveness. We commend it with much fervor" (Spurgeon, 84).

*Goldingay, John. *Psalms*. Baker Commentary on the Old Testament Wisdom and Psalms. 3 vols. Edited by Tremper Longman III. Grand Rapids: Baker, 2006–8.

The amazingly prolific Goldingay has produced a real treasure-house of exegesis and theological reflection. It is a substantial treatment that deserves a place on every preacher's shelf. "The best Psalms commentary for the meaning of the book in its original setting" (Longman, 74).

!?+Gunkel, Hermann. *The Psalms: A Form Critical Introduction*. Philadelphia: Fortress, 1962.

This study is a classic treatment in form criticism and biblical interpretation. Evangelical pastors seeking homiletical assistance will find little here of value. "A foundational work which attempts to locate the Psalms in their different sociological settings (*Sitz im Leben*) and their corresponding literary form (*Gattung*). Radical in its approach, but helpful for its analysis of literary forms" (Barber, 104).

*Kidner, Derek. *Psalms: An Introduction and Commentary*. TOTC. Edited by D. J. Wiseman. 2 vols. Leicester: InterVarsity, 1973.

As are all volumes in the generally helpful TOTC series, these two volumes are very brief but of uniform high quality. Kidner, a noted OT scholar and warden of Tyndale House, Cambridge, has produced an excellent and helpful treatment of the English text, much like his commentary on the Proverbs in the same series. "Highly recommended for its theological insight and practical bent. . . . The introductory material, particularly the discussion of the meaning of the difficult words in the psalm titles, is very helpful. This commentary is well worth the price" (Longman, 75).

*Leupold, H. C. *Exposition of the Psalms*. Grand Rapids: Baker, 1969.

Like all of the commentaries by this noted OT scholar and longtime professor at the Evangelical Lutheran Theological Seminary, this study is an excellent, in-depth treatment. It is helpful to scholar and student alike and rewards careful reading. "It is one of the better works on Psalms in regard to providing competent, pertinent material of a serious nature to the pastor, teacher, or layman" (Rosscup, 110). "A rewarding expository treatment" (Barber, 105). Amillennial.

*+Maclaren, Alexander. *The Psalms*. 3 vols. New York: Hodder & Stroughton, n.d. Reprint, Minneapolis: Klock & Klock, 1981.

> This classic exposition is by one of England's nineteenth-century pulpit masters and a true gem. "A masterful treatment" (Barber, 105).

*?Mays, James Luther. *Psalms*. Interp. Edited by James Luther Mays. Louisville: John Knox, 1994.

> Mays somehow manages to cover all 150 psalms in 451 pages of text. By focusing on the message of the individual psalms themselves and bypassing critical issues and discussions, the author crams a lot of nontechnical information and useful application into a compact commentary that is occasionally too brief to be of much assistance. "An exciting new commentary that focuses on the literary expression and theological message of the Psalms. It approaches the Psalms as rich statements of faith in God. He has a good feel for the Psalms as individual compositions as well as for the structure of the book as a whole" (Longman, 76).

*Scroggie, W. Graham. *The Psalms*. Old Tappan, NJ: Revell, 1965.

> This helpful volume is a wonderful collection of brief studies on each of the 150 psalms written for the general reader in mind. This volume is highly recommended for the pastor. "This is an excellent *synthesis* on each of the 150 psalms, with homiletical outlines, choice quotes and concise glimpses of the thought" (Rosscup, 113).

*+Spurgeon, C. H. *The Treasury of David*. Reprint, Peabody: Hendrickson, 1988.

> This classic set seems never to go out of print. Spurgeon was a giant of the pulpit in nineteenth-century London and is still read and often quoted today. He read widely, particularly the Puritans, and his preaching and writings show the results of that. He can still be read with profit and enrichment today. When you read Spurgeon, you are feeding your soul. "Richly rewarding, deeply devotional and pleasingly relevant" (Barber, 106).

Proverbs

Aitken, Kenneth T. *Proverbs*. Daily Study Bible. Edited by John C. L. Gibson. Louisville: Westminster John Knox, 1986.

> The topical format utilized in this book renders it difficult to use for students seeking immediate assistance on a particular verse. "The introduction to this volume is one of the more critical of the series, although the bulk of the

commentary provides helpful information. Interestingly, Aitken orders the material in Proverbs 10 and afterward in a topical rather than textual format" (Longman, 78).

Alden, Robert L. *Proverbs: A Commentary on an Ancient Book of Timeless Advice*. Grand Rapids: Baker, 1983.

> This study is a brief treatment of the book in which the author comments on each verse in capsule form. This book is very helpful to the beginning student or pastor, but of limited value to the exegete seeking detailed assistance on the text.

*?Clifford, Richard J. *Proverbs*. OTL. Edited by James L. Mays, Carol A. Newson, and David L. Petersen. Louisville: Westminster John Knox, 1999.

> This study is a very good commentary, but not an evangelical treatment. "This commentary puts . . . emphasis on text criticism, philology, and ancient Near Eastern background" (Longman, 78).

Cohen, A. *Proverbs*. Soncino Books of the Bible. Edited by A. Cohen. London: Soncino, 1946.

> This brief commentary by a noted Jewish scholar is particularly helpful for those seeking to know the traditional Jewish interpretation of a particular verse.

?Davis, Ellen F. *Proverbs, Ecclesiastes, and the Song of Songs*. Westminster Bible Companion. Louisville: Westminster John Knox, 2000.

> Aimed primarily at laypersons, this volume takes a moderately critical approach.

!*Fox, Michael V. *Proverbs 1–9*. AYB. Edited by William Foxwell Albright and David Noel Freedman. New Haven: Yale University, 2000.

> This study is exceptionally well done and quite helpful. "This is an excellent commentary both because the series allows more space than other commentaries and because Fox is a master interpreter" (Longman, 78).

!*————. *Proverbs 10–31*. AYB. Edited by John J. Collins. New Haven: Yale University, 2009.

> This book is an excellent commentary by a master interpreter. A comprehensive and full treatment. "Brilliant" (Evans, 175).

*Garrett, Duane A. *Proverbs, Ecclesiastes, Song of Songs.* NAC. Edited by E. Ray Clendenen. Nashville: Broadman, 1993.

> A very helpful, conservative treatment of these three books. Garrett's exposition of the Proverbs will be of particular value to pastors. I found Garrett's treatment of the Proverbs to be particularly valuable.

*Kidner, Derek. *The Proverbs: An Introduction and Commentary.* TOTC. Downers Grove: InterVarsity, 1964.

> This study is a very helpful albeit brief work that focuses on key themes in Proverbs. The textual treatment is brief, but the author does compare it with apocryphal wisdom books and parallels in ancient Near Eastern literature. "He often helps on proverbs that seem to clash, and has insights on how to view the ones that generalize and do not work in some cases" (Rosscup, 117).

*Longman, Tremper, III. *Proverbs.* Baker Commentary on the Old Testament Wisdom and Psalms. Edited by Tremper Longman III. Grand Rapids: Baker Academic, 2007.

> This study is an exceptional commentary exceeded only by Waltke's work. It is exceedingly helpful both for the scholar and the student. My only complaint is that the work utilizes transliterations rather than the actual Hebrew text. This is the curse of the modern age. The book contains a very helpful appendix containing twenty-eight brief essays on topics ranging from Anger to Women/Wife. Every preacher who preaches on the Proverbs should consult this commentary.

!?McKane, William. *Proverbs: A New Approach.* OTL. Edited by Peter Ackroyd, James Barr, John Bright, and G. Ernest Wright. Philadelphia: Westminster, 1970.

> This study is of uneven quality, but helpful at times. There are better more up-to-date works available. "This commentary is a significant contribution to the study of Proverbs, even if the critical conclusions are difficult to appreciate. . . . Invaluable for the study of the language. . . . A must for scholarly inquiry into Proverbs, but of doubtful value to the layperson or pastor" (Longman, 80). "Very learned and critical" (Evans, 177).

!*Murphy, Roland E. *Proverbs.* WBC. Edited by David A. Hubbard and Glenn W. Barker. Nashville: Nelson, 1998.

> Although this offering in the WBC by an emeritus professor of biblical studies at Duke University is not an evangelical commentary, it is still extremely helpful in exegesis of the text. Murphy denies Solomon's authorship of any of the proverbs. "Murphy is a preeminent interpreter of Wisdom Literature" (Longman, 80).

Perowne, T. T. *The Proverbs*. CBSC. Edited by A. F. Kirkpatrick. Cambridge: Cambridge University Press, 1899.

> This old commentary is a very brief treatment of the book and has been superseded by more modern works. It is worth purchasing if it can be picked up secondhand.

Plaut, W. Gunther. *Book of Proverbs: A Commentary*. Jewish Commentary for Bible Readers. Edited by Chaim I. Essrog. New York: Union of American Hebrew Congregations, 1961.

> This commentary is primarily for Jewish lay readers by a rabbi who field-tested his material in an extensive adult Jewish education program at the Mount Zion Hebrew Congregation of Saint Paul, Minnesota. For those desiring to know how Jews, both ancient and modern (up to the time of writing), interpreted the Proverbs, this is a very helpful volume. Christian pastors will find much material that is of use to them.

?Scott, R. B. Y. *Proverbs, Ecclesiastes*. AB. Edited by William Foxwell Albright and David Noel Freedman. New York: Doubleday, 1965.

> This commentary is by far the weakest volume in the Anchor series. At only 187 pages for Proverbs and sixty-five pages for Ecclesiastes, it is a brief treatment in the extreme. The notes are sparse and not particularly illuminating. A huge disappointment! How did this volume get past the editors? "This is not one of the better commentaries in the Anchor series. It represents a classically critical approach to Proverbs. It is not particularly strong in any area of research. . . . Ecclesiastes is treated very briefly, almost like an afterthought" (Longman, 81).

!? Toy, Crawford H. *A Critical and Exegetical Commentary on the Book of Proverbs*. ICC. Edited by Samuel Rolles Driver, Alfred Plummer, and Charles Augustus Briggs. Edinburgh: T. & T. Clark, 1899.

> This book is a very technical treatment of the Hebrew text. The author was a radical critic who dates the composition of the book no earlier than 300 BC. It was the standard critical work a hundred years ago, but has been superseded by more modern works. It is still helpful for those wrestling with the Hebrew text.

*Treier, Daniel J. *Proverbs & Ecclesiastes*. BCTB. Edited by R. R. Reno. Grand Rapids: Brazos, 2011.

> This is a helpful theological commentary by a noted evangelical scholar who teaches at Wheaton College. "A stimulating supplement to a more traditional exegetical and biblical-theological commentary" (Longman, 81).

*Waltke, Bruce K. *The Book of Proverbs*. NICOT. Edited by R. K. Harrison and Robert L. Hubbard. 2 vols. Grand Rapids: Eerdmans, 2004.

> This is "hands down" the very best commentary, new or old, on the Proverbs. Waltke, a highly respected OT scholar who has taught at Dallas Theological Seminary and Reformed Theological Seminary, has produced a massive work of scholarship that is mid-level, but helpful both to the academy and the church. It is simply magisterial and without peer. Highly recommended!

Whybray, R. N. *The Book of Proverbs*. CBC. Edited by P. R. Ackroyd, A. R. C. Leaney, and J. W. Packer. Cambridge: Cambridge University Press, 1972.

> This book is a very brief treatment of the Proverbs based on the New English Bible. The introduction, at just over fourteen pages, is too sparse. "A good competent study of the book from a critical perspective" (Longman, 82).

Ecclesiastes

!*Bartholomew, Craig G. *Ecclesiastes*. Baker Commentary on the Old Testament Wisdom and Psalms. Edited by Tremper Longman III. Grand Rapids: Baker Academic, 2009.

> This study is the finest commentary available on the book today. Bartholomew provides almost ninety pages of introduction to the book including discussions devoted to Canonicity, the History of Interpretation, and Authorship. He argues against Solomonic authorship of the book on both internal and external grounds. "Excellent commentary, especially strong in history of interpretation and biblical theology" (Longman, 82).

+Bridges, Charles. *A Commentary on Ecclesiastes*. Reprint, Edinburgh: Banner of Truth, 1961.

> This classic, first published in 1860, is essentially a series of sermons on each verse of the book. Although any book written by Bridges is well worth reading, this is one of his weaker efforts. Spurgeon writes that "he gives us nothing very new" (106). "Deeply devotional, but manifesting a weakness in the exposition of the successive stages of the Biblical writer's thought" (Barber, 107).

!*?Crenshaw, James L. *Ecclesiastes*. OTL. Edited by James L. Mays. Louisville: Westminster John Knox, 1987.

> Crenshaw has produced a capable treatment of this book, but many of his conclusions will not be satisfying to evangelicals. For example, he dates the writing of the book after the exile and he concludes that the writer is a bitter skeptic. Frankly, I don't understand Longman's endorsement of this book. "Highly recommended" (Longman, 83).

?Davis, Ellen F. See section on Proverbs.

*Fredericks, Daniel C., and Daniel J. Estes. *Ecclesiastes & The Song of Songs*. AOTC. Edited by David W. Baker and Gordon J. Wenham. Downers Grove: InterVarsity, 2010.

> Fredericks wrote the Ecclesiastes portion of this commentary and Estes the Song of Songs. Regarding Fredericks's contribution, it is markedly inferior to that of Estes. Most interpreters of Ecclesiastes understand *hebel* to be "meaningless." Fredericks, however, argues extensively that it is to be understood in the book as "temporary," which influences his entire understanding of the book. This "hobby horse" of the author makes his contribution the weakest book treatment of the otherwise fine AOTC series. Estes, on the other hand, has written a very fine commentary on Song of Songs. His introduction includes a fine discussion of interpretational approaches. The author believes that the book is best understood as an anthology of love poems. One would hope that in future editions of this commentary, they would be separated into the two books that they actually are and bound separately.

*Garrett, Duane A. See section on Proverbs.

Ginsburg, Christian D. See section on Song of Songs.

*+Hengstenberg, Ernest W. *A Commentary on Ecclesiastes*. Edinburgh: T. & T. Clark, 1869. Reprint, Minneapolis: James & Klock, 1977.

> This study is an outstanding nineteenth-century commentary by a conservative German scholar. It is a worthy addition to the scholarly library of reprints by James & Klock. He argues against Solomonic authorship of the book. "A conservative exposition based a thorough study of the original text" (Barber, 107). "This is one of the finest, most scholarly old works on Ecclesiastes" (Rosscup, 121).

*Leupold, H. C. *Exposition of Ecclesiastes*. Grand Rapids: Baker, 1952.

> Published in 1952, this excellent treatment of Ecclesiastes remains one of the very best evangelical works available on the subject. As are all of Leupold's commentaries, this book is a thorough and scholarly exegesis of the text from a solidly conservative Lutheran point of view. "An exceptional treatment based upon a careful exegesis of the text and revealing the emptiness of formalism and the discontent with life which follows attempts to solve its problems outside implicit faith and trust in God's providence" (Barber, 107).

*+McDonald, James M. *The Book of Ecclesiastes Explained*. New York: Dodd, 1856. Reprint, Minneapolis: Klock & Klock, 1982.

> This book is a worthy addition to Klock & Klock's LCRL. MacDonald, a noted nineteenth-century Princeton professor, devotes more than one hundred pages to his introduction before delving into a careful exegesis of the text. "The content of each expository study gives evidence of his careful exegesis" (Barber). "Thoroughly exegetical, with excellent 'scopes of argument' following each division: to be purchased if it can be met with" (Spurgeon, 109).

!?Murphy, Roland E. *Ecclesiastes*. WBC. Edited by David A. Hubbard and Glenn W. Barker. Nashville: Nelson, 1992.

> This moderately conservative treatment of Ecclesiastes is by one of the premiere experts on Hebrew wisdom literature. Murphy, George Washington Ivey Emeritus Professor of Biblical Studies at Duke University, denies Solomonic authorship and alleges that there are contradictions in the book. However, the discerning student may benefit if read with care. "There are better commentaries to get at the original meaning and theological significance of Ecclesiastes" (Longman, 86).

Scott, R. B. Y. See section on Proverbs.

Shaw, Benjamin. *Ecclesiastes* (title subject to change). Carlisle, PA: Banner of Truth.

> Forthcoming in 2017.

*Treier, Daniel J. See section on Proverbs.

*+Wardlaw, Ralph. *Exposition of Ecclesiastes*. Philadelphia: Rentoul, 1868. Reprint, Minneapolis: Klock & Klock, 1982.

> A rare and hard-to-obtain classic. Purchase if found. "Is always good" (Spurgeon, 110). "Well worth reading" (Barber).

Song of Songs

*Carr, G. Lloyd. *The Song of Solomon: An Introduction ad Commentary*. TOTC. Edited by D. J. Wiseman. Downers Grove: InterVarsity, 1984.

> This commentary is one of the better offerings in the TOTC series. Carr takes a literal approach to interpreting the book. The author, a professor at Gordon College in Boston, is solidly evangelical and careful in his scholarly approach. "This is a good popular exposition of the Song. Much scholarly research stands behind it" (Longman, 88).

?Davis, Ellen F. See section on Proverbs.

Duguid, Iain M. *The Song of Songs*. TOTC. Edited by David G. Firth. Downers Grove: InterVarsity, 2015.

> Not reviewed for this edition. However, this is a series update and is intended to replace Carr's work, which is one of the better offerings in the older series. The series update includes discoveries from the ancient Near East since the publication of Carr's work in 1984, more emphasis on linguistics, and a revised exegetical format.

*+Durham, James. *An Exposition of the Song of Solomon*. Reprint, Carlisle, PA: Banner of Truth, 1982.

> Durham, who lived from 1622–1658, was one of the foremost Scottish Reformed theologians of the Puritan age. This volume, first published in 1840, is one of his masterpieces. It is warm, rich, and thoughtful. "Durham is always good, and he is at his best upon the Canticles" (Spurgeon, 112).

!?Exum, J. Cheryl. *Song of Songs*. OTL. Edited by James L. Mays. Louisville: Westminster John Knox, 2005.

> This volume will be of limited value and interest to evangelical pastors. "A brilliant reading by a leading literary critic" (Evans, 189).

*Fredericks, Daniel C., and Daniel J. Estes. See section on Ecclesiastes.

*Garrett, Duane A. See section on Proverbs.

*Garrett, Duane, and Paul House. *Song of Songs / Lamentations*. WBC. Edited by Bruce M. Metzger. Nashville: Nelson, 2004.

> A refreshingly evangelical treatment by two top-notch conservative OT scholars in an uneven series. Garrett was responsible for the Song of Songs, a more technical commentary than his NAC volume. House wrote the Lamentations portion. These two Bible books in one volume is an unusual pairing, but the commentaries are solid, particularly the one done by House.

*Ginsburg, Christian D. *The Song of Songs and Coheleth*. Library of Biblical Studies. Edited by Harry M. Orlinsky. Prolegomenon by Sheldon H. Blank. New York: Ktav, 1970.

> This study is a famous older work by a noted Jewish scholar first published in 1857. It includes a prolegomenon by Sheldon H. Blank, which attempts to update certain discussions. "It is one of the better older works with help on exegesis, customs, views" (Rosscup, 121). "In spite of the fact that the writer never completed this work, and never had access to the materials from Ras

Shamra, he has left for posterity a scholarly work which retains much of its original value and interest" (Barber, 107).

Glickman, S. Craig. *A Song for Lovers*. Downers Grove: InterVarsity, 1976.

This book was an outgrowth of Glickman's 1974 ThM thesis at Dallas Theological Seminary, titled "The Unity of the Song of Solomon." This is a generally helpful volume that takes a consistently literal interpretation of the book and applies it to love and marriage today.

*Hess, Richard S. *Song of Songs*. Baker Commentary on the Old Testament: Wisdom and Psalms. Grand Rapids: Baker Academic, 2005.

This book is the final volume in the Wisdom and Psalms subsection of the Baker Commentary on the Old Testament. Although a strong case could be made for excluding Song of Songs from the category of Wisdom Literature, this volume is included nonetheless. These volumes are very helpful particularly to the scholar. However, the transliteration of Hebrew words instead of the actual Hebrew text is a distraction at least to this reader. "Hess provides a detailed analysis of this book of Old Testament love poetry. He provides excellent philological analysis and shows keen poetic sensibility. He is an expert in ancient Near Eastern background and also provides very helpful theological comments on the book" (Longman, 91).

*Longman, Tremper, III. *Song of Songs*. NICOT. Grand Rapids: Eerdmans, 2001.

This commentary is an important recent treatment of this book. The author, Robert H. Gundry Professor of Biblical Studies at Westmont College, in Santa Barbara, California, is one of the most highly regarded evangelical OT scholars writing today, if not the most prolific. This volume provides a lengthy introduction that deals effectively with the important interpretive issues such as genre and ancient Near Eastern background. Longman deals with the authorship issue at length, but does not come down decisively on Solomonic authorship. He sees the book as best understood as an anthology of twenty-three love poems.

*Pope, Marvin H. *Song of Songs*. AB. Edited by William Foxwell Albright and David Noel Freedman. Garden City, NJ: Doubleday, 1973.

At 701 pages of text, this study is a massive treatment of the book as well as the major issues surrounding it. The introduction itself is well over two hundred pages and full of useful information. At over forty years of age, this volume is now a bit dated, but still needs to be consulted by any serious student of the book. "This commentary contains a wealth of linguistic, literary, and historical information. The history of interpretation, comparative sections, and 55 page bibliography are worth the price of the book" (Longman, 93).

Prophetic Books

General Works on the Prophets

*Boda, Mark J., and Gordon McConville, eds. *Dictionary of the Old Testament: Prophets.* Downers Grove: IVP Academic, 2012.

> Indispensable for anyone working in the OT prophets. A wonderful scholarly tool!

*Bullock, C. Hassell. *An Introduction to the Old Testament: Prophetic Books.* Rev. ed. Chicago: Moody, 2007.

> First published in 1986, this book remains an excellent introductory guide to the prophetic books. The 2007 revision was basically cosmetic. Bullock's treatment is not detailed enough to delve into all of the complex scholarly issues in any depth, but he does provide a useful overview of the major issues. His approach to the text is chronological, not canonical, as he moves from the Neo-Assyrian Period to the Neo-Babylonian Period and finally to the Persian Period. Highly recommended for the undergraduate level!

Chalmers, Aaron. *Interpreting the Prophets: Reading, Understanding and Preaching from the Words of the Prophets.* Downers Grove: IVP Academic, 2015.

> Not reviewed for this edition.

*Freeman, Hobart E. *An Introduction to the Old Testament Prophets.* Chicago: Moody, 1968.

> Though somewhat dated, this book remains one of the best general introductions to the OT prophets available. "An excellent study of prophetism which discusses each prophetic book with regard to its nature, date, author, historical background and problems. Particularly helpful on the problem of the efficacy of OT sacrifices" (Barber, 108–9). Premillennial.

*Hays, J. Daniel. *The Message of the Prophets: A Survey of the Prophetic and Apocalyptic Books of the Old Testament.* Grand Rapids: Zondervan, 2010.

> This book is an excellent choice for an undergraduate survey class on the prophets. It is beautifully laid out and well written. The layout is extremely attractive and visually appealing. Each chapter has a selective bibliography for further reading, discussion questions, and writing assignments, which reinforce the content of the material.

+Heschel, Abraham J. *The Prophets*. Peabody, MA: Prince, 1962.

> This provocative book is a look at the prophets of Israel from a Jewish rabbinic perspective. It is well written and quite readable.

*Van Gemeren, Willem A. *Interpreting the Prophetic Word: An Introduction to the Prophetic Literature of the Old Testament*. Grand Rapids: Zondervan, 1990.

> A solid introduction to the prophetic literature aimed more at pastors and students. One wishes that Zondervan had paid as much attention to the layout of the book as it did to the volume by Hays.

*Wood, Leon J. *The Prophets of Israel*. Grand Rapids: Baker, 1979.

> The author, a noted professor of OT at Grand Rapids Baptist Seminary until 1976, has provided an excellent introduction to the study of the prophets of Israel. He pays particular attention to the continuity between both writing and non-writing prophets. According to the book's dust jacket, "A continuity exists between Israel's earlier non-writing prophets and its later prophets. Both must be studied to acquire a thorough understanding of Israelite prophecy." "A careful and reverent treatment of the place, importance, and teaching of the OT prophets. Should be in every preacher's library" (Barber). Premillennial.

Isaiah

*+Alexander, Joseph Addison. *Commentary on the Prophecies of Isaiah*. Reprint, Grand Rapids: Zondervan, 1962.

> This study is an exemplary verse-by-verse treatment based on the Hebrew text first published in 1846 by a noted nineteenth-century Princeton professor of OT. The exegetical work is extensive and there are seventy-eight pages devoted to introductory matters. "Makes the writer's genuine scholarship and evangelical warmth available to a new generation of expositors. A classic!" (Barber, 109) "We cannot too strongly recommend it" (Spurgeon, 120). Amillennial.

!*?Childs, Brevard S. *Isaiah*. OTL. Edited by James L. Mays, Carol A. Newsom, and David L. Petersen. Louisville: Westminster John Knox, 2001.

> This commentary takes a critical approach to Isaiah's prophecy. Childs believes that the final form of the book is the result of layers of redaction and numerous authors and denies supernatural inspiration. This book, like the author's Exodus commentary, should be used, but with great caution. "Well worth getting is Child's canon-conscious take on the book. Though not quite

as well done in depth and detail as his much earlier Exodus commentary, it is helpful to see how he manages what he considers to be the compositional history of the book with the final form's theological message" (Longman, 94). "The work reflects incredible interaction with scholarly theory, and is for a smaller group of scholars of this pursuit. But it cannot rate well overall for usefulness in many sections to others, even the maturely diligent, to whom more forthright works are available" (Rosscup, 129).

*+Kelly, William. *An Exposition of the Book of Isaiah.* 4th ed. London: Morrish, 1871; Minneapolis: Klock & Klock, 1979.

This is a classic work by a noted Plymouth Brethren writer. It is primarily an exposition of the English text, but the author does utilize the Hebrew. Premillennial. Dispensational.

*Leupold, H. C. *Exposition of Isaiah.* 2 vols. Grand Rapids: Baker, 1968.

This commentary is an excellent and detailed exposition of the English text, but it is based on an intimate acquaintance with the Hebrew text. The author defends the unity of the book and takes conservative, evangelical positions in all matters. "A satisfying exposition" (Barber, 110). "A fine commentary" (Rosscup, 131). Amillennial.

*Motyer, J. Alec. *Isaiah: An Introduction and Commentary.* TOTC. Edited by D. J. Wiseman. Reprint, Downers Grove: InterVarsity, 2009.

This volume, first published in 1994, is an excellent, nontechnical treatment of Isaiah, which will be of inestimable value to pastors and students. Do not confuse this book with the author's 1993 stand-alone work on the same subject. Both are excellent.

*———. *The Prophecy of Isaiah: An Introduction & Commentary.* Downers Grove: InterVarsity, 1993.

Longer and more detailed than the author's 1994 TOTC volume, this is an outstanding treatment of the book from a conservative viewpoint. First rate! "It is thoroughly researched and thought-out. It represents the best of a conservative evangelical approach to the book at the end of the twentieth century" (Longman, 96).

*Oswalt, John N. *The Book of Isaiah, Chapters 1–39*. NICOT. Edited by R. K. Harrison and Robert L. Hubbard Jr. Grand Rapids: Eerdmans, 1986.

*———. *The Book of Isaiah, Chapters 40–66*. NICOT. Edited by R. K. Harrison and Robert L. Hubbard Jr. Grand Rapids: Eerdmans, 1998.

> This excellent commentary is the best mid-level, nontechnical work available on this book of prophecy. These two volumes replace E. J. Young's three-volume work in the New International Commentary on the Old Testament series. The author, formerly professor of OT and Semitic languages at Trinity Evangelical Divinity School in Deerfield, Illinois, and currently visiting distinguished professor of OT at Asbury Theological Seminary, is solidly evangelical and takes conservative positions throughout these two volumes. For example, Oswalt argues that a single author wrote the entire book, which certainly goes against the prevailing scholarly opinion. Interestingly, the second volume came out twelve years after the first. "A decidedly and dependably conservative approach" (Evans, 197). Amillennial.

*———. *Isaiah*. NIVAC. Edited by Terry Muck. Grand Rapids: Zondervan, 2003.

> This volume is a more accessible and less technical treatment than his massive two-volume NICOT commentary. This book is outstanding and will be of great value to pastors. Highly recommended!

Ridderbos, J. *Isaiah*. Bible Student's Commentary. Translated by John Vriend. Kampen, The Netherlands: Kok, 1950–51. Reprint, Grand Rapids: Zondervan, 1985.

> Originally published in Dutch under the title *Korte Verklaring der HeiligeSchrift*, this conservative commentary is intended for nonspecialists who do not know Hebrew. The Zondervan reprint uses the NIV. This commentary is quite helpful in many ways, but its brevity limits the depth of its treatment of this complex book of prophecy. The author argues for the unity of the prophecy with some minor glosses by Isaiah's disciples. Somewhat weak on the theology of the book. "Ridderbos is a top flight scholar" (Longman, 97). Reformed. Amillennial.

?Watts, John D. W. *Isaiah*. WBC. 2 vols. Edited by David A. Hubbard and Glenn W. Barker. Waco, TX: Word, 1985.

> Watts, formerly a professor at Southern Baptist Theological Seminary in Louisville and Fuller Theological Seminary, has produced a moderately liberal commentary on the canonical form of the book in the uneven WBC. The author holds to a fifth-century date for the book after a long redaction history. Whatever belonged to the historical Isaiah was hopelessly diluted. "Watts proposes a twelvefold structure to the book (in two parts [chaps. 1–39; 40–66]) that follows a kind of chronological flow. . . . This is an interesting and provocative commentary" (Longman, 98).

Webb, Barry G. *The Message of Isaiah*. BST. Edited by J. A. Motyer. Downers Grove: InterVarsity, 1997.

> Not reviewed for this edition.

*Young, Edward J. *The Book of Isaiah: Chapters 19–39*. NICOT. Edited by R. K. Harrison. Grand Rapids: Eerdmans, 1956.

*———. *The Book of Isaiah: Chapters 1–18*. NICOT. Edited by R. K. Harrison. Grand Rapids: Eerdmans, 1969.

*———. *The Book of Isaiah: Chapters 40–66*. NICOT. Edited by R. K. Harrison. Grand Rapids: Eerdmans, 1972.

> These three volumes, by the revered professor of OT at Westminster Theological Seminary until his death in 1970, were projected to be the first installment in the NICOT series. Unfortunately, the project sputtered soon after publication with only a few volumes being written. The series has since been revived and is now going strong with John Oswalt's two volumes replacing Young's work. This work is excellent for its exegetical insights and should be purchased if found in a secondhand store. "Young was a meticulous and detailed scholar, which is evident in his work here. He is a better philologist than literary scholar or biblical theologian, but the commentary is well worth the money" (Longman, 99). Amillennial.

Jeremiah

!*?Allen, Leslie C. *Jeremiah*. OTL. Edited by William P. Brown, Carol A. Newsom, and David L. Petersen. Louisville: Westminster John Knox, 2009.

> This addition to the OTL replaces the volume by Carroll, which was one of the weaker offerings in the series. This commentary, while more conservative than most in the series, is not evangelical, but will be of great help in dealing with textual issues.

*Bright, John. *Jeremiah: A New Translation with Introduction and Commentary*. AB. Edited by William Foxwell Albright and David Noel Freedman. Garden City: Doubleday, 1965.

> Although the AB series is usually fairly liberal across the board, this surprisingly conservative commentary stands out as a real jewel. John Bright was a noted OT scholar and professor at Union Theological Seminary in Richmond and a student of W. F. Albright at Johns Hopkins University. This is not an evangelical commentary, but it still is a valuable tool for those studying the book of Jeremiah. It contains a new translation of the text, and extensive

introduction, and critical notes. "This is one of the better commentaries on Jeremiah, although it is written from a moderately critical angle. Bright has good theological and literary sense. One disconcerting feature of this commentary is its arrangement. Bright has chosen to depart from Jeremiah's more topical arrangement and has commented on the text in a reconstructed chronological order" (Longman, 100).

!Craigie, Peter C., Page H. Kelley, and Joel F. Drinkard Jr. *Jeremiah 1–25*. WBC. Edited by J. D. W. Watts. Nashville: Nelson, 1991.

Harrison, R. K. *Jeremiah and Lamentations*. TOTC. Edited by J. D. Wiseman. Downers Grove: InterVarsity, 1973.

At one time revered for its solid scholarship and conservative point of view, it is now dated and of limited value. Superseded by Lalleman's volume in the series.

*Huey, F. B., Jr. *Jeremiah, Lamentations*. NAC. Edited by E. Ray Clendenen. Nashville: Holman Reference, 1993.

At 512 pages, this is a rather substantial treatment of these two books considering the series. It is now a bit dated, but of primary use to pastors.

!Keown, Gerald L., Pamela J. Scalise, and Thomas G. Smothers. *Jeremiah 26–25*. WBC. Edited by J. D. W. Watts. Nashville: Nelson, 1995.

Begun by Craigie whose untimely death derailed the project, it was completed by five scholars. Therefore, this is a commentary written by committee with predictable results. Useful though on technical matters.

*Laetsch, Theo. *Jeremiah Bible Commentary*. St. Louis: Concordia, 1952.

This commentary, by a noted conservative Lutheran OT scholar and professor at Concordia Seminary, also covers Lamentations. Though dated now, it remains one of the best conservative expositions of the book. Amillennial.

*Lalleman, Hetty. *Jeremiah and Lamentations*. TOTC. Downers Grove: InterVarsity, 2013.

This volume is a replacement for Harrison's 1973 commentary. Lalleman, tutor in OT studies at Spurgeon's College in London, wrote her PhD thesis titled "Jeremiah in Prophetic Tradition." Her treatment of the text is exceptional.

!*?Lundbom, Jack R. *Jeremiah 1–20*. AB. Edited by William Foxwell Albright and David Noel Freedman. New York: Doubleday, 1999.

!*?———. *Jeremiah 21–36*. AB. Edited by William Foxwell Albright and David Noel Freedman. New York: Doubleday, 2004.

!*?———. *Jeremiah 37–52*. AB. Edited by William Foxwell Albright and David Noel Freedman. New York: Doubleday, 2004.

> At just around two thousand pages, this commentary is a massive study of the book that is particularly strong in its treatment of the Hebrew text. It is learned, well written, and a compendium of information on this prophetic book. This replaces the Bright volume in the series. This set is quite expensive; if you pay list price, it will run more than $250, quite out of reach of the budget of most pastors. "This is a brilliant commentary on the book in its original meaning, though Lundbom is not interested in Jeremiah's theology. A must-buy for those ministers and scholars who are really interested in looking at the book" (Longman, 104).

!?McKane, William P. *A Critical and Exegetical Commentary on Jeremiah*. ICC. Edited by J. A. Emerton, C. E. B. Cranfield, and G. N. Stanton. 2 vols. Edinburgh: T. & T. Clark, 2000.

> At $290 this set is way out of the price range of most. Likewise, it is beyond the intellectual capacity of most. "Meticulous textual and philological work and very critical" (Evans, 210). "A must for all scholars, it is just as well ignored by most laypersons and ministers" (Longman, 104).

*Thompson, J. A. *The Book of Jeremiah*. NICOT. Edited by R. K. Harrison. Grand Rapids: Eerdmans, 1980.

> This commentary is a standard evangelical treatment of the book by a noted OT scholar and professor at the University of Melbourne in Australia. It includes an exhaustive introduction of over one hundred pages, along with a very helpful detailed outline of the book, and an extensive bibliography. "This is the most detailed evangelical commentary of recent vintage" (Rosscup, 142). "Well worth getting" (Longman, 104). Amillennial.

Lamentations

!?Berlin, Adele. *Lamentations.* OTL. Edited by James L. Mays. Louisville: Westminster John Knox, 2002.

> An excellent technical commentary by the Robert H. Smith Professor Emerita of Biblical Studies at the University of Maryland, my alma mater. A must for scholars and serious students, but of limited use to evangelical pastors.

*?Dobbs-Allsopp, F. W. *Lamentations.* Interp. Edited by James L. Mays. Louisville: Westminster John Knox, 2002.

> A worthwhile critical commentary that surprisingly is very helpful to preachers in spite of some questionable conclusions about the judgment of God. "A very sensitive theological and existential interpretation of the book" (Longman, 105).

*Garrett, Duane, and Paul House. See section on Song of Songs.

Harrison, R. K. See section on Jeremiah.

Hillers, Delbert R. *Lamentations.* AYB. 2nd ed. Edited by William Foxwell Albright and David Noel Freedman. New Haven: Yale University Press, 1992.

> This volume is the second edition of a study that was first published in 1972 by the W. W. Spence Professor of Semitic Languages at Johns Hopkins University. This treatment is a helpful commentary that is particularly strong in pointing out the book's Near Eastern literary background. There are also helpful discussions on the "Liturgical Use of Lamentations" and "Poetic Meter and Related Rhythmic Features."

*Huey, F. B., Jr. See section on Jeremiah.

*Laetsch, Theo. See section on Jeremiah.

*Lalleman, Hetty. See section on Jeremiah.

*Wright, Christopher J. H. *The Message of Lamentations.* BST. Edited by J. A. Motyer. Downers Grove: IVP Academic, 2015.

> A brief, but eminently useful, exposition of the book. Of particular value for pastors.

Ezekiel

!*?Allen, Leslie C. *Ezekiel 20–48*. WBC. Edited by Bruce M. Metzger, David A. Hubbard, and Glenn W. Barker. Grand Rapids: Zondervan, 2015.

> Completes what Brownlee started. Allen's work is much stronger than that of Brownlee and less eccentric. A vast improvement!

*Block, Daniel. *The Book of Ezekiel*. NICOT. Edited by Robert L. Hubbard Jr. 2 vols. Grand Rapids: Eerdmans, 1997–98.

> At over 1,700 pages, this is a substantial and satisfying treatment of the text that all pastors and students should own. Highly recommended! "This is an outstanding work" (Evans, 216).

!?Brownlee, William H. *Ezekiel 1–19*. WBC. Edited by David A. Hubbard and Glenn W. Barker. Waco, TX: Word, 1986.

> This unfinished commentary reflects what Brownlee was able to complete prior to his death. It is a capable work in many respects and the author had a fairly high view of Scripture. However, he saw the final form of the book as reflecting considerable redaction activity over the centuries. "The introduction overall reveals a scholar given to radical critical theory. . . . A disappointment" (Rosscup, 146). "Basically a museum piece already" (Evans, 219).

*Duguid, Iain M. *Ezekiel*. NIVAC. Edited by Terry Muck. Grand Rapids: Zondervan, 1999.

> A solid nontechnical treatment particularly useful for pastors.

!*?Eichrodt, Walther. *Ezekiel*. OTL. Edited by Peter Ackroyd, James Barr, John Bright, and G. Ernest Wright. Philadelphia: Westminster, 1970.

> A technical, critical work that is mainly of value for its discussions of OT theology. Eichrodt contributed two volumes in the same series on the subject.

*+Fairbairn, Patrick. *An Exposition of Ezekiel*. Edinburgh: T. & T. Clark, 1851. Reprint, Minneapolis: Klock & Klock, 1979.

> This classic commentary is a breath of fresh air to the reader. It is a bedrock conservative treatment of the English text with extensive references to the Hebrew. It is accessible to general readers and helpful to pastors and scholars. Amillennial.

Feinberg, Charles Lee. *The Prophecy of Ezekiel: The Glory of the Lord*. Chicago: Moody, 1969.

> This study is a helpful treatment for pastors and students based upon the English text. The material in this commentary first appeared in serial form in the missionary magazine the *Chosen People*. "The best work on the subject" (Barber, 112)! Premillennial. Dispensational.

*Taylor, John B. *Ezekiel: An Introduction and Commentary*. TOTC. Edited by D. J. Wiseman. Downers Grove: InterVarsity, 1969.

> This handy little volume, in keeping with the series goals, is particularly helpful for the pastor and beginning student. "Must be read with discernment" (Barber). Anglican.

*Wright, Christopher J. H. *The Message of Ezekiel: A New Heart and a New Spirit*. BST. Edited by J. A. Motyer. Downers Grove: IVP Academic, 2001.

> An excellent nontechnical exposition that is particularly valuable for pastors.

!*?Zimmerli, Walther. *Ezekiel 1: A Commentary on the Book of the Prophet Ezekiel, Chapters 1–24*. Hermeneia. Philadelphia: Fortress, 1979.

!*?————. *A Commentary on the Book of the Prophet Ezekiel, Chapters 25–48*. Hermeneia. Philadelphia: Fortress, 1982.

> Originally published in German in 1969, this massive critical work is a must for serious students of the book. At $164 for the set, it is beyond the price range of most pastors, but it is most valuable for its detailed analysis of the text. "Represents the best of critical thought on the book" (Longman, 111). "This magisterial work reflects a lifetime of assiduous textual, form-critical, and tradition-history research" (Evans, 223).

Daniel

*Baldwin, Joyce G. *Daniel: An Introduction and Commentary*. TOTC. Edited by D. J. Wiseman. Downers Grove: InterVarsity, 1978.

> As are all of the books in this series, this is a fairly brief, but capable, verse-by-verse treatment of the text. The introduction is substantial, over sixty pages, and particularly well done. There is substantial interaction with liberal viewpoints throughout the book. "This commentary contains a wealth of information and careful exegetical insight. Baldwin is a balanced and sane exegete, which is important to note in a commentary on a book that attracts some wild ideas. Baldwin is solidly conservative but not rigid" (Longman, 111).

Boutflower, Charles. *In and Around the Book of Daniel*. London: Society for Promoting Christian Knowledge, 1923. Reprint, Grand Rapids: Kregel, 1977.

> This book is not a verse-by-verse commentary, but rather an examination of prophecy in the book of Daniel. It includes chapters on four of the most important prophecies in the book as well as explanations of Daniel's prophetic dreams. The author defends the orthodox view of the book and contains much excellent historical material. This volume is a real favorite of Barber.

*Culver, Robert Duncan. *Daniel and the Latter Days*. Rev. ed. Chicago: Moody, 1977.

> This commentary by a premillennial scholar is especially valuable for its comparison of the premillennial, amillennial, and postmillennial views in the book of Daniel. "Scholarly and well-documented" (Barber). Premillennial.

*?Goldingay, John E. *Daniel*. WBC. Edited by David A. Hubbard and Glenn W. Barker. Dallas: Word, 1989.

> This commentary is a most learned and comprehensive treatment of Daniel's prophecy. The author's splendid research and extensive introduction and bibliographies, particularly of the secondary literature, are to be commended. Unfortunately, many of his conclusions will be untenable to evangelicals. For example, Goldingay essentially denies predictive prophecy in that he dates the writing of the book to the second century, thus postdating the writing after fulfillment. He also believes that the historical content of chapters 1–6 are simply stories with a mythological base. "Gives insight into historical, literary, and theological issues concerning the book. . . . It would be a major mistake to ignore this important commentary while studying Daniel" (Longman, 112). "Painfully loose on matters of date and historicity" (Evans, 224).

Lang, G. H. *The Histories and Prophecies of Daniel*. Grand Rapids: Kregel, 1940.

> This helpful commentary, by a leading British Plymouth Brethren clergyman, is based upon the Revised Version. It is very innovative and shows the result of independent thinking. "Combines extensive research with a comprehensive view of the prophetic Scriptures" (Barber, 113). Premillennial. Postribulational.

*Leupold, H. C. *Exposition of Daniel*. Columbus, OH: Wartburg, 1949. Reprint, Grand Rapids: Baker, 1969.

> This study is another fine scholarly commentary from a noted evangelical Lutheran OT professor. Very helpful for pastors and teachers and has stood the test of time. "Of particular value for its exegetical treatment of the text" (Barber, 113). "Quite detailed and helpful" (Rosscup, 156). Amillennial.

*Longman, Tremper, III. *Daniel*. NIVAC. Edited by Terry Muck. Grand Rapids: Zondervan, 1999.

> A capable treatment by a seasoned OT scholar. "The theme of the whole book is that in spite of present difficult circumstances, God is in control and will defeat the forces of evil and oppression" (Longman, 113). "A great expositional and theological help" (Evans, 224).

*?Lucas, Ernest C. *Daniel*. AOTC. Edited by David W. Baker and Gordon J. Wenham. Downers Grove: InterVarsity, 2002

> This commentary receives high marks for its clear exposition of the text of Daniel. However, it receives low marks for viewing the book as an intermingling of story and fact. Evangelicals will not be convinced by the author's arguments for a second-century date of composition.

Miller, Stephen R. *Daniel*. NAC. Edited by E. Ray Clendenen. Nashville: Broadman & Holman Reference, 1994.

> A capable, conservative treatment of the text. Premillennial. Dispensational.

!+Montgomery, James Alan. *A Critical and Exegetical Commentary on the Book of Daniel*. ICC. Edited by S. R. Driver, A. Plummer, and C. A. Briggs. Edinburgh: T. & T. Clark, 1927.

> After almost ninety years since its publication, this book is still an important commentary for its exegesis of the text. Very technical! Not for pastors with weak Hebrew skills. At one time, "Montgomery's technical commentary was *the* starting point in scholarly discussion. It still is *a* key starting point" (Evans, 227).

*+Pusey, E. B. *Daniel the Prophet*. Oxford: Parker, 1869. Reprint, Minneapolis: Klock & Klock, 1978.

> Pusey, the Regius Professor of Hebrew at Oxford from 1828–1880, has made a solid contribution to the study of this book. This commentary, another volume in Klock & Klock's fine LCRL, is actually a compilation of nine lectures delivered in the Divinity School of the University of Oxford and is a detailed scholarly treatment of the book. "His greatest contribution is in historical backgrounds" (Rosscup, 158). "To Dr. Pusey's work on Daniel all subsequent writers must be deeply indebted" (Spurgeon). Amillennial.

Walvoord, John F. *Daniel: The Key to Prophetic Revelation*. Chicago: Moody, 1971.

> This commentary published in 1971 by the president of Dallas Theological Seminary remains one of the finest works available from a dispensational

premillennial perspective. Dispensationalism has been in a state of evolution in recent decades and this volume does not reflect those discussions. "Emphasizes the genuineness of the prophet and his writings, and provides a clear interpretation of the book. Thorough, well outlined, and well documented" (Barber, 113). Premillennial. Dispensational.

*+Wilson, Robert Dick. *Studies in the Book of Daniel.* 2 vols. Reprint, Grand Rapids: Baker, 1979.

This set is a paperback reprinting of a classic work first published in 1917. Wilson, a staunchly conservative OT scholar at Princeton Theological Seminary, has provided an indispensable guide to the book of Daniel. He does not shy away from the many difficult interpretive problems in the book, and he ably defends its historical accuracy and integrity. "This is one of the outstanding conservative defenses of historical matters in Daniel" (Rosscup, 160). "A most valuable work" (Barber)! Amillennial.

*Wood, Leon. *A Commentary on Daniel.* Grand Rapids: Zondervan, 1973.

This study is a fine verse-by-verse commentary by a noted professor of OT at Grand Rapids Baptist Bible Seminary. This book can be used by the more advanced student and pastor as well as by the layperson. "A fascinating and enlightening commentary which expounds the historical setting of the book, unfolds its prophetic message, and provides readers with a fresh, accurate translation of the text" (Barber, 113). Premillennial. Dispensational.

*Young, Edward J. *The Prophecy of Daniel: A Commentary.* Grand Rapids: Eerdmans, 1949.

This excellent commentary by a longtime professor of OT at Westminster Theological Seminary is considered a classic by many. It is an outstanding and thorough treatment of the text that is of great value to the exegete. Young defends Daniel's authorship as well as the historical accuracy of the book. Although it is almost seventy years old, this still is a "must have" volume for pastors and students who are studying the book of Daniel. It is one of the finest conservative works available. "A painstaking exegetical exposition" (Barber, 113). Amillennial.

Minor Prophets

*Feinberg, Charles L. *The Minor Prophets.* Chicago: Moody, 1976.

This compilation by a former professor of OT at Dallas Theological Seminary and Talbot Seminary, was originally published in five volumes from 1948 to

1952. It is rather dated now and not up to date on current research trends, but is still valuable for giving an overview of each book. "These studies are valuable for their historical and cultural contribution" (Barber). Premillennial. Dispensational.

*Hailey, Homer. *A Commentary on the Minor Prophets*. Grand Rapids: Baker, 1972.

This very accessible study is ideal for pastors and laypersons. Amillennial.

*Laetsch, Theo. *Bible Commentary the Minor Prophets*. St. Louis: Concordia, 1956.

This study is an excellent conservative treatment of the Minor Prophets by a Lutheran scholar. It is scholarly, yet devotional, with helpful verse-by-verse exegesis of the text as well as historical data and useful exposition. "Laetsch deals with the text verse-by-verse, grapples with difficult phrases and explains them, uses the Hebrew extensively, and presents illuminating word studies. The lucid presentation helps make it a very interesting commentary to read" (Rosscup, 165). Amillennial.

*McComiskey, Thomas Edward, ed. *The Minor Prophets: An Exegetical and Expositional Commentary*. 3 vols. Grand Rapids: Baker Academic, 1992–98.

This out-of-print series endeavors to give the Minor Prophets a strong evangelical treatment. With such notable scholars as Joyce Baldwin, J. A. Motyer, F. F. Bruce, Tremper Longman III, Douglas Stuart, and Bruce Waltke contributing, it certainly succeeds in that attempt. This set is top to bottom exceptionally well done and a necessary acquisition for anyone preaching through or studying the Minor Prophets. Purchase it if you can find it. It sorely needs to be reprinted. "This is the best anthology of commentaries on the Minor Prophets available" (Longman, 13).

?Smith, George Adam. *The Book of the Twelve Prophets*. Rev. ed. 2 vols. New York: Harper, 1928.

This collection is a scholarly, critical treatment that is often cited in literature on the Minor Prophets. Evangelicals will disagree with some of the author's conclusions such as his belief that Jonah was non-historical. However, this commentary is well written and can often be helpful. It is worth acquiring if it can be picked up secondhand.

*Tatford, Frederick A. *The Minor Prophets*. 3 vols. Sussex: Prophetic Witness, 1974. Reprint, Minneapolis: Klock & Klock, 1982.

This valuable reprint in Klock & Klock's LCRL is a three-volume compilation of twelve volumes that were originally published from 1971–1974 by the Prophetic Witness Publishing House. Each of the twelve books included is a concise, but helpful, exposition of the main message of the prophet's message. The book titles are especially imaginative and evocative such as *Prophet of a Broken Home* for Hosea and *Prophet of Social Injustice* for Amos.

*+Von Orelli, C. *The Twelve Minor Prophets*. Translated by J. S. Banks. Edinburgh: T. & T. Clark, 1897. Reprint, Minneapolis: Klock & Klock, 1977.

This study is an excellent, however not extensive, treatment of the writings of the Minor Prophets. It is a welcome addition to Klock & Klock's LCRL by a noted nineteenth-century German scholar. Though a contemporary of Ewold, Graf, and Welhausen during the ascendance of German higher criticism, Von Orelli managed to remain moderately conservative and defend the integrity of the Old Testament. "Ably expounds the teaching of these prophetic writings and provides valuable historical and linguistic data" (Barber).

Hosea

!*Andersen, Francis I., and David Noel Freedman. *Hosea*. AB. Edited by William Foxwell Albright and David Noel Freedman. Garden City: Doubleday, 1980.

This detailed and informative commentary is one of the better offering in the YABC series. At over six hundred pages, it is massive and sometimes tries to accomplish too much. The introduction and bibliography are excellent. Its discussions are sometimes too detailed for the casual student or pastor to follow. Despite these limitations, anyone preaching or teaching the book must consult this important work. Andersen and Freedman are first-rate Hebrew scholars. "This book is marred a little by a syllable-counting approach to meter" (Longman, 115). "The authors have no theological system on eschatology" (Rosscup, 167).

*Dearman, J. Andrew. *The Book of Hosea*. NICOT. Edited by R. K. Harrison and Robert L. Hubbard. Grand Rapids: Eerdmans, 2010.

This excellent commentary is perhaps the best mid-level treatment of this book available. It is particularly well done. "Hosea is a complex book, but Dearman is up to the task. As a Hebraist, he provides an excellent translation of the difficult Hebrew. His literary and historical skills help him unravel difficult exegetical issues. He is also sensitive to Hosea's theological contribution" (Longman, 115).

*Garrett, Duane A. *Hosea, Joel*. NAC. Edited by E. Ray Clendenen. Nashville: Holman Reference, 1997.

> A stellar nontechnical treatment of these two books. Garrett is an engaging and careful writer. Excellent for pastors!

!?Harper, William Rainey. *A Critical and Exegetical Commentary on Amos and Hosea*. ICC. Edited by Samuel Rolles Driver, Alfred Plummer, and Charles Augustus Briggs. Edinburgh: T. & T. Clark, 1905.

> This commentary is fairly typical of commentaries in the ICC series in that it is excellent on exegesis of the text and theologically liberal. It is now over a century old and should be supplemented with more recent works. It has been superseded in the series. "Valuable for its textual analysis and discussion of the traditional views of these prophecies, but it is of limited value to the preacher who is interested in getting to the heart of a passage" (Barber, 115).

*Hubbard, David Allan. *Hosea*. TOTC. Edited by D. J. Wiseman. Downers Grove: IVP Academic, 2009.

> A well-researched and well-written commentary that is surprisingly scholarly for the series. "Sound scholarship and extensive research" (Longman, 116).

!*?Mays, James Luther. *Hosea: A Commentary*. OTL. Edited by G. Ernest Wright, John Bright, James Barr, and Peter Ackroyd. Philadelphia: Westminster, 1969.

> Although the OTL series is decidedly liberal, this moderately critical work is one of the better offerings. Surprisingly accessible for the pastor. "Mays has detailed exegesis and comments of a theological nature for pastors and students" (Rosscup, 169). "Mays concentrates on the theological meaning of the text to the subordination of philology, text, and other exegetical concerns" (Longman, 116).

!*?Mcintosh, A. A. *A Critical and Exegetical Commentary on Hosea*. ICC. Edited by J. A. Emerton, C. E. B. Cranfield, and G. N. Stanton. London: T. & T. Clark, 1997.

> A substantial upgrade over Harper. Moderately critical. Somewhat weak on theological reflection.

*+Morgan, G. Campbell. *Hosea: The Heart and Holiness of God*. Westwood, NJ: Revell, 1934. Reprint, Grand Rapids: Baker, 1974.

> A collection of brilliant sermons by a true master of the pulpit. Morgan was the pastor of Westminster Chapel in London prior to D. Martyn Lloyd-Jones. Even today, nearly a century after he preached, Morgan's sermons are models of the art of exposition. Pastors will love this volume.

*Smith, Gary V. *Hosea, Amos, Micah*. NIVAC. Edited by Terry Muck. Grand Rapids: Zondervan, 2001.

> An outstanding treatment of these three books that will especially be appreciated by pastors. Although this is not a technical commentary, Smith does not skimp on the exegesis. Anyone preaching through these books will want to purchase this work.

*Stuart, Douglas. *Hosea-Jonah*. WBC. Edited by Bruce M. Metzger, David A. Hubbard and Glenn W. Barker. Waco, TX: Word, 1987.

> This excellent commentary on the first five of the Minor Prophets is a welcome conservative treatment, which is not always the case in the uneven WBC series. The author, a professor of OT at Gordon-Conwell Theological Seminary in Massachusetts, is a noted evangelical scholar and coauthor with Gordon Fee of the excellent book *How to Read the Bible for All Its Worth*. Stuart is a careful scholar and this commentary is particularly well researched and written. His study is particularly strong in the areas of exegesis and historical background. Of special value is his general introduction, which demonstrates the prophetic dependency on pentateuchal blessings and curses. This book is certainly one of the stronger offerings in the series. "This is one of the best recent commentaries on the Minor Prophets. It is a must-buy for everyone preaching on these books. It is intelligently conservative and emphasizes theology without ignoring the other aspects of the text" (Longman, 117).

Joel

?Allen, Leslie C. *The Books of Joel, Obadiah, Jonah and Micah*. NICOT. Edited by R. K. Harrison. Grand Rapids: Eerdmans, 1976.

> This volume is a detailed commentary that will reward careful study by both scholar and student. The author, formerly of London Bible College and more recently at Fuller Theological Seminary, takes some untenable positions especially for evangelicals, such as the dating of Joel and Obadiah and the historicity of Jonah. "Extensive research into the historic setting coupled with interesting information on the etymology of certain words makes this book worthy of serious consideration" (Barber).

*Baker, David W. *Joel, Obadiah, Malachi*. NIVAC. Edited by Terry Muck. Grand Rapids: Zondervan, 2006.

> A very solid and satisfying exposition and application of these three brief books that will particularly benefit pastors.

!?Barton, John. *Joel and Obadiah*. OTL. Edited by James L. Mays. Louisville: Westminster John Knox, 2001.

> A capable critical commentary that demonstrates a keen awareness of the literature on this book.

!?Crenshaw, James L. *Joel*. AYB. Edited by William Foxwell Albright and David Noel Freedman. New Haven: Yale University Press, 1995.

> This volume is not up to the quality of some of the other AYB or AB offerings on the individual Minor Prophets, such as those of Adele Berlin, Paul Raabe, Jack Sasson, or Andrew Hill. It is a difficult and ponderous read. One almost misses seeing the forest for the trees. There are better treatments on Joel available such as the volumes by Baker, Barton, Dillard, Garrett, and Hubbard. "Readers grope in darkness" (Rosscup, 172). "The most valuable liberal work" (Evans, 241).

*Garrett, Duane A. See section on Hosea.

*Hubbard, David A. *Joel and Amos: An Introduction and Commentary*. TOTC. Edited by D. J. Wiseman. Downers Grove: InterVarsity, 1989.

> An excellent nontechnical treatment of these two books. Particularly useful for pastors and laypersons.

*Stuart, Douglas. See section on Hosea.

!?Ward, William Hays, John Merlin Powis Smith, and Julius August Bewer. See section on Micah.

Amos

*!Andersen, Francis, I., and David Noel Freedman. *Amos*. AB. Edited by David Noel Freedman and William Foxwell Albright. Garden City: Doubleday, 1989.

> At over one thousand pages, this is a massive and comprehensive commentary on a very short book of prophecy. Obviously, this is not for the casual student or unprepared pastor. One can lose sight of the forest for the trees. However, for the advanced student, pastor with good Hebrew skills, or scholar, this volume is a must. "This is among the best, most complete commentaries on Amos" (Evans, 242).

*+Cripps, Richard S. *A Commentary on the Book of Amos*. London: SPCK, 1929. Reprint, Minneapolis: Klock & Klock, 1981.

> Klock & Klock has done a service to students and scholars alike by adding this title to their LCRL. Cripps, a longtime lecturer at St. John's College, Cambridge, produced a volume that is very helpful in the exegesis of the text, but is influenced by higher critical views.

!?Harper, William Rainey. See section on Hosea.

*Hubbard, David A. See section on Joel.

*Mays, James Luther. *Amos: A Commentary*. OTL. Edited by G. Ernest Wright, John Bright, James Barr, and Peter Ackroyd. Philadelphia: Westminster, 1969.

> This study is a capable treatment from a moderately critical perspective. It is one of the better offerings in the OTL. Evangelicals will likely take issue with the author's conclusion that the author of 9:11–15 was someone "in Judah during the exilic period" (166). "Building upon the historical setting, expounds the content and form of the book" (Barber, 115). "A well-respected liberal work with much good information on many parts of the book" (Rosscup, 175).

*Motyer, J. A. *The Day of the Lion: The Message of Amos*. BST. Edited by J. A. Motyer and John R. W. Stott. Downers Grove: InterVarsity, 1974.

> This study is a well-written and helpful commentary, written on a popular level but with a substantial research base. Motyer is a top OT scholar. "A helpful examination of the Book of Amos which relates the message of this OT prophet to the needs of the present day" (Barber). "Succeeds in making the message articulate, often bringing out stimulating and refreshing lessons and applying them to people today" (Rosscup, 176).

!*?Paul, Shalom M. *Amos: A Commentary on the Book of Amos*. Hermeneia. Edited by Frank Moore Cross, et al. Philadelphia: Fortress, 1991.

> A first-rate technical treatment of the text that ranks up there with Andersen and Freedman. This volume is not a replacement for Wolff, but rather a supplement. Surprisingly conservative, this is very readable and more accessible than the AB volume. "He writes clearly, and his work is extremely well researched" (Longman, 123). "An impressive work" (Evans, 244).

*Smith, Gary V. See section on Hosea.

*Stuart, Douglas. See section on Hosea.

Obadiah

Allen, Leslie C. See section on Joel.

*Alexander, T. Desmond, David W. Baker, and Bruce Waltke. *Jonah, Obadiah, and Micah*. TOTC. Edited by D. J. Wiseman. Downers Grove: InterVarsity, 1988.

> Baker, a top-notch OT scholar and professor at Ashland Theological Seminary, wrote the Obadiah portion of this commentary, Alexander the Jonah section, and Waltke on Micah. At just over two hundred pages, this little volume seems to cover all of the bases. The pastor not delving into technical areas of the text will find this book to be a tremendous help and a trustworthy guide.

*Baker, David W. See section on Joel.

!?Barton, John. See section on Joel.

*Block, Daniel I. *Obadiah*. ZECOT. Edited by Daniel I. Block. Grand Rapids: Zondervan, 2013.

> This slim volume, at 116 pages, does an adequate job of expositing the text of the OT's shortest book. The introduction is fairly sketchy and Block, along with many scholars both evangelical and liberal, dates the prophecies of Obadiah in the exilic period, which is problematic in the view of the writer. This is probably the best work available. Unfortunately, there are few evangelical options on this brief book of prophecy.

Gaebelein, Frank E. *Four Minor Prophets: Obadiah, Jonah, Habakkuk, and Haggai*. Chicago: Moody, 1970.

> This little book is a devotional commentary of particular value for laymen. The author attempts to distill the message of the prophets Obadiah, Jonah, Habakkuk, and Haggai for today's world.

*+Marbury, Edward. *Obadiah and Habakkuk*. London: Nisbet, 1865. Reprint, Minneapolis: Klock & Klock, 1979.

> Originally published in separate volumes in London in 1649–50, this Puritan classic is a warm, nontechnical exposition of these two books. Warning: There are numerous Latin quotations included. "His spirituality of mind prevents his learning becoming dull" (Spurgeon, 135).

!*?Raabe, Paul R. *Obadiah*. AYB. Edited by William Foxwell Albright and David Noel Freedman. New Haven: Yale University Press, 1996.

> An outstanding scholarly commentary by a professor of OT at Concordia Seminary in St. Louis. This work is substantial and detailed and leaves few stones unturned. One of the very best works available on this short book.

*Stuart, Douglas. See section on Hosea.

!?Ward, William Hays, John Merlin Powis Smith, and Julius August Bewer. See section on Micah.

!?Watts, John D. W. *Obadiah: A Critical Exegetical Commentary*. Grand Rapids: Eerdmans, 1969.

> At one time this was *the* commentary to consult for serious study of this book. Now there are better options. "Packs a remarkable amount of relevant and helpful information in a very small compass" (Bauer, 198).

Jonah

Aalders, G. Charles. *The Problem of the Book of Jonah*. London: Tyndale, 1948.

> A brief, conservative apologetic for the historicity of the book.

*Alexander, T. Desmond, David W. Baker, and Bruce Waltke. See section on Obadiah.

Allen, Leslie C. See section on Joel.

*Bruckner, James K. *Jonah, Nahum, Habakkuk, Zephaniah*. NIVAC. Edited by Terry Muck. Grand Rapids: Zondervan, 2004.

> An excellent nontechnical treatment of these four short books. Pastors will particularly love this volume.

*+Fairbairn, Patrick. *Jonah: His Life, Character, and Mission*. Reprint, Grand Rapids: Baker, 1980.

> First published in 1849, this book has rightly achieved classic status. It is not a technical commentary on the Hebrew text, but is rich in insight and application. "Regarded as one of the ablest expository treatments available" (Barber, 116). "This work is well done, and is by far the ablest English treatise on this prophet" (Spurgeon, 136).

Gaebelein, Frank E. See section on Obadiah.

!*?Limburg, James. *Jonah*. OTL. Edited by James L. Mays. Louisville: Westminster John Knox, 1988.

> An excellent technical commentary in the critical tradition. Of limited use to the average evangelical pastor. "A fine summary statement of a moderate critical analysis of the literary and theological dimensions" (Longman, 128).

*+Martin, Hugh. *The Prophet Jonah: His Character and Mission to Nineveh*. Reprint, London: Banner of Truth, 1958.

> This edition is a reprint of the 1877 edition. A warm, devotional exposition. Spurgeon perhaps engaged in hyperbole in his comments particularly in light of his endorsement of Fairbairn. "A first-class exposition of Jonah! No one who has it will need any other" (Spurgeon, 137).

!?Mitchell, Hinckley G., John Merlin Powis Smith, and Julius A. Bewer. See section on Haggai.

*?Sasson, Jack M. *Jonah*. AB. Edited by William Foxwell Albright and David Noel Freedman. New York: Doubleday, 1990.

> This excellent treatment of the little book of Jonah has much to commend itself. There is an interesting section on interpretations in which the author explores different views of the book. His essay, "Jonah as History or Fiction," is a sane discussion of the subject. Unfortunately, the author does not commit himself to either position. He skillfully skirts the issue, but to his credit does not totally rule out a historical foundation for the book. "This provocative commentary . . . is well worth adding to a reference library" (Longman, 128).

*Stuart, Douglas. See section on Hosea.

Micah

Allen, Leslie C. See section on Joel.

*Alexander, T. Desmond, David W. Baker, and Bruce Waltke. See section on Obadiah.

!*Andersen, Francis I., and David Noel Freedman. *Micah*. AB. Louisville: Westminster John Knox, 2000.

> At 664 pages, this volume is a massive work. It has a price tag to match its prodigious girth and may be beyond the range of most pastors. However, this commentary is worth the price. It is a must-buy for the serious student and Bible scholar. Weak on theology. "The most comprehensive commentary available" (Evans, 252).

*Barker, Kenneth L., and Waylon Bailey. *Micah, Nahum, Habakkuk, Zephaniah*. NAC. Edited by E. Ray Clendenen. Nashville: Holman Reference, 1998.

> Barker wrote the Micah and Habakkuk portions of this commentary; Bailey contributed Nahum and Zephaniah. This is a solid, well-written commentary by two fine OT scholars. The Bailey sections tend to be a bit stronger with more up-to-date research than the Barker ones. However, this is an excellent commentary for the pastor or Bible teacher to acquire. Premillennial on Micah and Habakkuk.

*Smith, Gary V. See section on Hosea.

!?Smith, Ralph L. *Micah-Malachi*. WBC. Edited by David A. Hubbard and Glenn W. Barker. Waco, TX: Word, 1984.

> This commentary is a rather ambitious undertaking considering the space limitations. While it is a helpful treatment of these seven Minor Prophets in many respects, the author, formerly a professor of OT at Southwestern Baptist Theological Seminary, is unable to do justice to the task at hand in a mere 342 pages of text and he makes some concessions to higher criticism. His treatment of Nahum is particularly skimpy. However, his exposition is good and this is a solid effort for the most part. "He has good bibliographies, discusses views, gives a wealth of information on text, exegesis, background, etc. and often is clear" (Rosscup, 183).

*Waltke, Bruce. *A Commentary on Micah*. Grand Rapids: Eerdmans, 2007.

> A superb, most useful commentary on the book for student and scholar alike. If you are preaching on Micah, this is a must-buy! "Overall, the most helpful commentary on Micah for Christian proclamation and instruction" (Bauer, 202).

!? Ward, William Hayes, John Merlin Powis Smith, and Julius A. Bewer. *A Critical and Exegetical Commentary on Micah, Zephaniah, Nahum, Habakkuk, Obadiah, and Joel*. ICC. Edited by Samuel Rolles Driver, Alfred Plummer, and Charles Augustus Briggs. Edinburgh: T. & T. Clark, 1911.

> It is my opinion that the ICC editors attempted to do too much by compiling these six books together with three different authors. They were unable to do justice to the project. However, this volume is a starting point for technical work in these books. It is virtually impossible to find secondhand, but it has been reprinted in an exact reproduction by BiblioBazaar in 2010.

Nahum

*Baker, David W. *Nahum, Habakkuk, Zephaniah*. TOTC. Edited by David Firth. Downers Grove: IVP Academic, 2009.

> One of the new second-generation commentaries in this series, this very brief treatment (120 pages) of these three prophetic books is well written and enlightening. It is unfortunate that the constraints of the series did not allow for more elucidation. This commentary is most helpful for laypersons and pastors with little Bible training. "An engaging writing style and an emphasis on theology and historical background" (Longman, 133). Wesleyan.

*Barker, Kenneth L., and Waylon Bailey. See section on Micah

> "Bailey has contributed a strongly written, well-thought-out, and well-researched analysis of Nahum that is sensitive to the important theological themes" (Longman, 133).

*Bruckner, James K. See section on Jonah.

!?Christensen, Duane. *Nahum*. AYB. Edited by David Noel Freedman. New Haven: Yale University Press, 2009.

> A remarkably complete and exhaustive moderately critical commentary that covers all the bases and then some. One problem for users is sifting through all of the extraneous material. A must for serious students; of limited value for most pastors. "Not for the faint-hearted" (Evans, 256)!

*+Maier, Walter A. *The Book of Nahum: A Commentary*. St. Louis: Concordia, 1959. Reprint, Minneapolis: James Family, 1977.

> This very fine commentary, by the voice on the "Lutheran Hour" for many years, is perhaps the best available treatment of this often-neglected little book of prophecy. This was one of the first reprints by James Family and it is a real treasure. Dated now, but still retains much of its usefulness. "A lengthy, critical commentary in which every word of each verse is evaluated and expounded in the light of the theme of the book. A valuable study" (Barber, 116). "This is a very fine detailed work by a conservative and is highly desirable for the serious student" (Rosscup, 184–85).

!*?Roberts, J. J. M. *Nahum, Habakkuk, and Zephaniah*. OTL. Edited by James L. Mays. Louisville: Westminster John Knox, 1991.

> A technical, critical commentary that is full of detail and helpful for pastors who are willing to mine its riches. "Probably the leading critical interpretation of these three books" (Evans, 257).

*Robertson, O. Palmer. *The Books of Nahum, Habakkuk, and Zephaniah*. NICOT. Edited by R. K. Harrison and Robert L. Hubbard Jr. Grand Rapids: Eerdmans, 1990.

> This volume is not one of the stronger offerings in the NICOT series. Nevertheless, it is a very fine commentary by a bedrock conservative OT scholar who formerly taught at Westminster Theological Seminary and Covenant Theological Seminary. Unfortunately, Nahum has not gotten much attention by commentary writers over the years, which enhances the value of this volume. In my judgment, however, the three prophetic books do not get the full treatment in this work, which is right around 350 pages. The bibliographies are especially brief. "Robertson excels in theological analysis and pastoral application. The commentary is weak in philological and other technical details" (Longman, 134–45). Reformed. Premillennial.

*Smith, Gary V. See section on Jonah.

!?Smith, Ralph L. See section on Micah.

!?Ward, William Hays, John Merlin Powis Smith, and Julius August Bewer. See section on Micah.

Habakkuk

*Baker, David W. See section on Nahum.

*Barker, Kenneth L., and Waylon Bailey. See section on Micah.

*Bruckner, James K. See section on Jonah.

Gaebelein, Frank E. See section on Obadiah.

Henderson, E. Harold. *The Triumph of Trust*. Little Rock, AK: Baptist Publishing, 1980.

> This book is a slim volume for general readers that deals primarily with the three questions posed and answered by the prophet Habakkuk. It concludes with a chapter titled, "The Continuing Significance of Habakkuk." The outlines would make this work especially valuable for preachers.

*+Marbury, Edward. See section on Obadiah.

!*?Roberts, J. J. M. See section on Nahum.

*Robertson, O. Palmer. See section on Nahum.

Smith, Ralph L. See section on Micah.

!?Ward, William Hays, John Merlin Powis Smith, and Julius August Bewer. See section on Micah.

Zephaniah

*Baker, David W. See section on Nahum.

*Barker, Kenneth L., and Waylon Bailey. See section on Micah.

*?Berlin, Adele. *Zephaniah*. AB. Edited by William Foxwell Albright and David Noel Freedman. New York: Doubleday, 1994.

> This excellent commentary, written by a professor of Hebrew Bible and Near Eastern literature at the University of Maryland, is perhaps the finest treatment of this little book of prophecy available. The author's introduction is most helpful in sorting out the issues surrounding this book, but she prefers to take a mediating position on the authorship question acknowledging a historical personage named Zephaniah, but not going so far as to ascribe the book's composition to him. "Berlin is known as an exceptional practitioner of the literary method, and she does not disappoint us in this commentary, which shows great sensitivity to such issues as intertextuality. She also helpfully discusses text, semantics, historical issues, and theological message" (Longman, 138).

*Bruckner, James K. See section on Jonah.

!*?Roberts, J. J. M. See section on Nahum.

*Robertson, O. Palmer. See section on Nahum.

Smith, Ralph L. See section on Micah.

!?Ward, William Hays, John Merlin Powis Smith, and Julius August Bewer. See section on Micah.

Haggai

*Baldwin, Joyce G. *Haggai, Zechariah, Malachi*. TOTC. Edited by D. J. Wiseman. Downers Grove: InterVarsity, 1972.

> As are all of the books in this series, this study is a fairly brief, but capable, verse-by-verse treatment of the text by a frequent contributor, Joyce G. Baldwin of Trinity College, Bristol. "A very insightful, conservative commentary" (Longman, 140).

*Boda, Mark J. *Haggai, Zechariah*. NIVAC. Edited by Terry Muck. Grand Rapids: Zondervan, 2004.

> This volume is one of the more substantial volumes in the series. Although it is excellent on application, it deals with some of the more technical issues

as well as theological ones. "Both exegetically and theologically, this work is deeply satisfying" (Evans, 262).

Gaebelein, Frank E. See section on Obadiah.

*Meyers, Carol L., and Eric M. Meyers. *Haggai, Zechariah 1–8*. AB. Edited by William Foxwell Albright and David Noel Freedman. Garden City: Doubleday, 1987.

*———. *Zechariah 9–14*. AB. Edited by William Foxwell Albright and David Noel Freedman. Garden City: Doubleday, 1993.

> These two volumes constitute an excellent treatment of the prophecies of Haggai and Zechariah. At almost a thousand pages combined, this commentary is a massive and wonderfully comprehensive study of both books that is rich in historical and archaeological detail. The first volume including Haggai's prophecy vies with Taylor's excellent NAC treatment for pride of place among studies on this tiny book. "This is a wonderfully written and researched commentary that I have found extremely provocative and largely persuasive" (Longman, 144).

!?Mitchell, Hinckley G., John Merlin Powis Smith, and Julius A. Bewer. *A Critical and Exegetical Commentary on Haggai, Zechariah, Malachi, and Jonah*. ICC. Edited by Samuel Rolles Driver, Alfred Plummer, and Charles Augustus Briggs. Edinburgh: T. & T. Clark, 1912.

> The unusual grouping of the prophecies covered in this commentary is explained in the preface. The book of Jonah is placed at the end of the series "not only because it was composed at a much later date than the traditional order suggests, but also because it is of a different character from the other prophets." Not one of the stronger offerings in the old ICC series.

Petterson, Anthony R. *Haggai, Zechariah, & Malachi*. AOTC. Edited by David W. Baker and Gordon J. Wenham. Downers Grove: IVP Academic, 2015.

> This brief commentary attempts to treat three prophetic books in just over four hundred pages of text. Less than one hundred pages each are devoted to Haggai and Malachi, with Zechariah getting the longest treatment at just over two hundred pages. Thus, this volume is not exhaustive by any means and some things get short shrift. The project is simply too ambitious considering the page restraints. Having said that, Petterson is an evangelical who takes the authority of the text seriously. He holds to one author of Zechariah, for example. This is a well-written and interesting commentary primarily aimed at the nonspecialist.

Smith, Ralph L. See section on Micah.

!*Taylor, Richard A., and E. Ray Clendenen. *Haggai, Malachi*. NAC. Edited by E. Ray Clendenen, Kenneth A. Matthews, and David S. Dockery. Nashville: Broadman & Holman, 2004.

> This commentary, particularly the Haggai portion written by Taylor, is particularly well done. Taylor, a noted OT and Syriac scholar at Dallas Theological Seminary, has produced what is perhaps the finest conservative scholarly commentary available on the book of Haggai. He was my professor and ThM thesis reader when I was a student at Capital Bible Seminary. His meticulous research and professionalism has always impressed me. The Clendenen volume is definitely on the lighter side. "A very serious, well-researched exposition of the book. The prose and the footnotes may get a bit heavy for laypeople, but ministers and scholars will appreciate the reflection and interaction with other scholars" (Longman, 142).

*Verhoef, Pieter A. *The Books of Haggai and Malachi*. NICOT. Edited by R. K. Harrison. Grand Rapids: Eerdmans, 1987.

> This study is a fine conservative commentary by the emeritus professor of OT, University of Stellenbosch, South Africa. Its treatment is extensive and scholarly and offers much good introductory material. "He does a careful job of exegeting the Hebrew text. He also explores the theological message . . . and traces their themes into the New Testament. This commentary is more academic in style than many others in the NICOT series; thus, it is recommended as a scholarly guide to both of these prophetic books" (Longman, 142).

Zechariah

Baldwin, Joyce G. See section on Haggai.

*Boda, Mark J. *The Book of Zechariah*. NICOT. Edited by R. K. Harrison and Robert L. Hubbard. Grand Rapids: Eerdmans, 2016.

> At 782 pages of text, this commentary is a massive work of impeccable scholarship. The introduction is fifty-three pages which includes a nine-page very helpful and up-to-date bibliography. Thus, the commentary on the text is well over seven hundred pages of painstaking and exhaustive scholarship. The voluminous footnotes ensure that this volume will serve students and pastors as well as scholars. This work will surely set the standard for this book of prophecy for decades to come.

————. See section on Haggai.

Feinburg, Charles L. *God Remembers: A Study of Zechariah*. Portland: Multnomah, 1965.

> This study is one of the better premillennial commentaries available on the book. The author was for many years a professor of OT at Dallas Theological Seminary and Talbot Seminary. "A valuable study that expounds in depth and detail" (Barber, 117). Premillennial. Dispensational.

*Leupold, H. C. *Exposition of Zechariah*. Grand Rapids: Baker, 1956.

> This study is the final volume of this author's series of OT commentaries and the quality is just as high as its predecessors. It is a richly rewarding study by a noted OT professor at the Evangelical Lutheran Theological Seminary. Though somewhat dated, this is still one of the best scholarly commentaries available on this book. "Provides a serious, technical study of the prophetic predictions of Zechariah from an amillennial viewpoint. Very helpful" (Barber, 117). Amillennial.

*Meyers, Carol L., and Eric M. Meyers. See section on Haggai.

!?Mitchell, Hinckley G., John Merlin Powis Smith, and Julius A. Bewer. See section on Haggai.

*+Moore, Thomas V. *A Commentary on Zechariah*. New York: Carter, 1856. Reprint, Edinburgh: Banner of Truth, 1958.

> This study is a Reformed devotional commentary by a nineteenth-century US Presbyterian. It is not a technical commentary, but rather an exposition whose stated purpose in the publisher's foreword "combines such scholarship and devotion in a form which the ordinary believer is well able to follow" (p. 5). "A capital book. Most useful to ministers" (Spurgeon, 139). Amillennial.

Petterson, Anthony R. See section on Haggai.

Smith, Ralph L. See section on Micah.

*Unger, Merrill F. *Zechariah: Prophet of Messiah's Glory*. Grand Rapids: Zondervan, 1963.

> This commentary is a detailed work by a revered professor of OT at Dallas Theological Seminary. Each section of the text has an outline and at the top of the page is the author's translation of the text with the commentary at the bottom. A weakness is that the introductory matters are very brief, comprising only six pages. "A valuable exposition based upon the original text" (Barber, 117). Premillennial. Dispensational.

*+Wright, Charles Henry Hamilton. *Zechariah and His Prophecies*. London: Hodder and Stroughton, 1879.

> This volume, a welcome addition to Klock & Klock's LCRL, is not a commentary as such, but rather is comprised mainly of eight lectures delivered at the University of Oxford in 1878 by a noted OT scholar and professor at Trinity College, Dublin. It includes a new translation with notes on the Hebrew text along with a critical and grammatical commentary of seventy-three pages at the end of the book.

Malachi

*Baker, David W. See section on Joel.

Baldwin, Joyce G. See section on Haggai.

*Kaiser, Walter C., Jr. *Malachi: God's Unchanging Love*. Grand Rapids: Baker, 1984.

> This study is a fine commentary, by the former dean and vice president at Trinity Evangelical Divinity School and president at Gordon-Conwell Theological Seminary, that demonstrates how to practice exegesis of the text. The author illustrates the principles described in his excellent *Toward an Exegetical Theology*. "A practical commentary that combines scholarly tidbits with pastoral concern" (Longman, 145). Premillennial.

!?Mitchell, Hinckley G., John Merlin Powis Smith, and Julius A. Bewer. See section on Haggai.

Petterson, Anthony R. See section on Haggai.

Smith, Ralph L. See section on Micah.

*Taylor, Richard A., and E. Ray Clendenen. See section on Haggai.

Verhoef, Pieter A. See section on Haggai.

The Apocrypha and Pseudepigrapha

!*Charles, R. H. *The Apocrypha and Pseudepigrapha of the Old Testament*. 2 vols. Oxford: Clarendon 1913.

> This set has been the standard critical work for decades since its publication in 1913.

*Charlesworth, James H. *The Old Testament Pseudepigrapha*. 2 vols. Garden City: Doubleday, 1983.

> According to the editor's preface, this book "is designed for the scholar and the interested non-specialist." The organization of the books is according to literary types rather than chronological or an alphabetical listing.

*Coogan, Michael, ed. *The New Oxford Annotated Apocrypha: New Revised Standard Version*. 4th ed. Oxford: Oxford University Press, 2010.

> This book is the standard edition of the Apocrypha in English. It includes a brief introduction to the Apocryphal/Deuterocanonical Books as well as an introduction to each book which includes: Name and Canonical Status; Authorship, Text, and Date of Composition; Contents and Structure; and Interpretation and Guide to Reading.

*deSilva, David A. *Introducing the Apocrypha: Message, Context, and Significance*. Grand Rapids: Baker Academic, 2002.

> This excellent introduction to the Apocrypha includes a detailed introduction to the collection as a whole, as well as fine treatments of each book. The author helps fill in the holes in most Christians' understanding of the intertestamental period. It is scholarly, while at the same time eminently readable and accessible.

*Metzger, Bruce M. *An Introduction to the Apocrypha*. New York: Oxford University, 1957.

> Until the publication of deSilva's work, this introduction has been the standard introductory work to this grouping of ancient noncanonical books. "A comprehensive examination of the books of the Apocrypha together with an evaluation of their history and significance" (Barber, 186).

Chapter 3

New Testament

NEW TESTAMENT BACKGROUND

*Arnold, Clinton E., ed. *Zondervan Illustrated Bible Backgrounds Commentary*. 4 vols. Grand Rapids: Zondervan, 2002

> "This work gives excellent background information and pictures of events, sites, and customs mentioned in the NT, organized passage by passage in NT order, making it quite useful for a busy pastor, especially for finding pertinent sermon illustrations" (**Stout**).

*Burge, Gary M., Lynn H. Cohick, and Gene L. Green. *The New Testament in Antiquity*. Grand Rapids: Zondervan, 2009.

> This unique work shows how Jewish, Hellenistic, and Roman cultures meshed in first-century Palestine and provided the cultural milieu in which the NT authors wrote their books and letters. This volume is well written and informative. Indispensable!

*+Fairweather, William. *The Background of the Epistles*. Edinburgh: T. & T. Clark, 1935. Reprint, Minneapolis: Klock & Klock, 1977.

> In this classic work, Fairweather endeavors to provide a "bird's-eye view of the world of thought and action lying behind the Epistles" (preface, viii). Although Pauline studies have taken leaps and bounds since its writing, it is still an invaluable work that repays careful study. "An indispensable work" (Barber).

*+————. *The Background of the Gospels.* 3rd ed. Edinburgh: T. & T. Clark, 1920. Reprint, Minneapolis: Klock & Klock, 1977.

> This classic study carefully blends history and theology and is most helpful for a proper understanding of the life and ministry of Jesus. "A very important older work which traces the historical and doctrinal themes of the intertestamental period and the preparation of the Graeco-Roman world for the coming of Christ" (Barber, 132).

*Jeremias, Joachim. *Jerusalem in the Time of Jesus: An Investigation into Economic and Social Conditions during the New Testament Period.* Translated by F. H. and C. H. Cave. Philadelphia: Fortress, 1969.

> This book is an indispensible work on the subject. "A valuable investigation into the economic and social conditions which prevailed during NT times" (Barber, 134).

Machen, J. Gresham. *The New Testament: An Introduction to Its Literature and History.* Carlisle, PA: Banner of Truth, 1976.

> Published almost forty years after Machen's death, this helpful book includes chapters on the historical background of Christianity, the early history of Christianity, Christianity established among the Gentiles, and the principles and practice of the gospel.

Tenney, Merrill C. *New Testament Times.* Grand Rapids: Eerdmans, 1965.

> At over fifty years of age, this work still retains much of its value and should be purchased if found in a secondhand store. Includes a valuable discussion of the sources behind NT history as well as investigations into the political scene, the cultural tensions, and the Jewish heritage influencing the world of the NT. "A valuable reconstruction of the cultural milieu into which Christ was born and in which the apostolic church developed" (Barber, 134).

NEW TESTAMENT INTRODUCTIONS

Barker, Glenn W., William L. Lane, and J. Ramsey Michaels. *The New Testament Speaks.* New York: Harper & Row, 1969.

> This book is an excellent introduction to the message of the NT. At almost fifty years of age, it is a bit dated and should be supplemented with more recent works. However, it is surprisingly conservative and evangelical in its assessments. For example, the authors uphold the traditional view of Pauline authorship of the Pastoral Epistles.

?Boring, M. Eugene. *An Introduction to the New Testament: History, Literature, Theology*. Louisville: Westminster John Knox, 2012.

> This volume is a learned work aimed at beginning college or seminary students. Some of the conclusions arrived at by the author will be untenable to most evangelicals. For example, he holds that there is no doubt that Paul's second letter to the Corinthians is the result of editorial work after leaving his hand. Further, he holds that the Pastoral Epistles reflect a church situation much later than the first century and therefore could not have been written by Paul.

*Carson, D. A., and Douglas J. Moo. *An Introduction to the New Testament*. 2nd ed. Grand Rapids: Zondervan, 2005.

> This exceptional work is the standard introduction from an evangelical perspective. Its scholarship is impeccable and the authors' positions are defensible and cautious. Highly recommended!

*Guthrie, Donald. *New Testament Introduction*. 3rd ed. Downers Grove: InterVarsity, 1970.

> This one-volume edition by the noted lecturer in NT language and literature at the London Bible College was originally published in three volumes. It is moderately conservative, extremely well written, and quite helpful in dissecting the major issues in NT study. This has been the standard work for decades. A fourth revised edition came out in 1989.

Harrison, Everett F. *Introduction to the New Testament*. Grand Rapids: Eerdmans, 1971.

> This book is not as detailed or as technical as Guthrie's highly regarded introduction. It is showing its age. "Vies with Guthrie's for Number 1 position in modern conservative introductions" (Barber, 127).

*Köstenberger, Andreas J., L. Scott Kellum, and Charles L. Quarles. *The Cradle, the Cross, and the Crown: An Introduction to the New Testament*. Nashville: B & H Academic, 2009.

> "An easy to use and very informative NT introduction, *CCC* is written from a conservative evangelical viewpoint by Baptist professors (they defend Pauline authorship of the Pauline epistles and Petrine authorship for 2 Peter) and is excellent for classroom use, as each chapter includes study questions, discussion points, and suggested bibliographies. One would be hard-pressed to find a better NT Introduction than this one" (**Stout**).

*+Zahn, Theodor. *Introduction to the New Testament.* Translated by John Moore Trout et al. 3 vols. Grand Rapids: Kregel, 1953. Reprint, Minneapolis: Klock & Klock, 1977.

> Although now dated, this remains a classic conservative treatment. It was first published in English having been translated from the original German in 1909. Klock & Klock did a service to the scholarly community by including this work in their LCRL. Purchase it if available. "Magisterial" (Carson, 34).

NEW TESTAMENT SURVEYS

Achtemeier, Paul, Joel Green, and Marianne Meye Thompson. *Introducing the New Testament.* Grand Rapids: Eerdmans, 2001.

> This volume is a good intermediate text for beginning students and laypersons. It is not technical and is easily accessible.

Bailey, Mark, and Tom Constable. *Nelson's New Testament Survey.* Nashville: Nelson, 2003.

> Not reviewed for this edition.

*Elwell, Walter A., and Robert W. Yarbrough. *Encountering the New Testament: A Historical and Theological Survey.* 3rd ed. Grand Rapids: Baker Academic, 2013.

> This overview is an excellent book for use in the classroom from a conservative, evangelical perspective. There is a companion website for the book with resources for both student and professor.

*+Gundry, Robert H. *A Survey of the New Testament.* 5th ed. Grand Rapids: Zondervan, 2012.

> First published in 1970, this now classic work is in its fifth edition and has been a standard for both undergraduate and graduate students for over four decades. It is arranged into five sections. Part 1 is titled "Political, Cultural, and Religious Antecedents" while part 2 is "Literary and Historical Materials." The final three sections deal with the text itself, with part 3 titled "The Four Canonical Gospels and Acts," part 4, "The Letters," and part 5, "The Apocalypse." Each chapter contains an overview, study goals, important terminology, review questions, discussion questions, and helpful bibliographies. This book is exceptionally well done in its design, scholarly without being too technical, and well written. A set of eighteen supplemental video lectures on two DVDs are now available from the publisher.

Tenney, Merrill C. *New Testament Survey*. Grand Rapids: Eerdmans, 1961.

> This book was a standard work on the subject a half century ago, but it has been superseded by more recent works. It is still worth consulting and can be useful for undergraduate students, pastors, and nonspecialists.

NEW TESTAMENT THEOLOGY

*+Bernard, Thomas Dehany. *The Progress of Doctrine in the New Testament*. New York: American Tract Society, 1896. Reprint, Minneapolis: Klock & Klock, 1978.

> This classic work is the compilation of the Bampton Lectures delivered at the University of Oxford in 1864. The result is a panoramic view of the scope of NT theology from the Gospels to the Apocalypse, marked by evangelical fidelity and solid scholarship.

*Bock, Darrell L. *A Theology of Luke and Acts*. Biblical Theology of the New Testament. Edited by Andreas J. Köstenberger. Grand Rapids: Zondervan, 2012.

> This masterpiece explores the theology of the Gospel of Luke and the book of Acts. The author demonstrates convincingly that Luke's purpose in writing was to "show that the coming of Jesus, Christ, and Son of God launched the long-promised new movement of God" (from chapter 1). "Indispensable" (Carson, 64).

*Davids, Peter H. *A Theology of James, Peter, and Jude*. Biblical Theology of the New Testament. Edited by Andreas J. Köstenberger. Grand Rapids: Zondervan, 2014.

> The general epistles have often suffered from neglect. The author has written major commentaries on the epistles James, 1–2 Peter, and Jude and is eminently qualified to write a theology of this portion of the general epistles. He traces common themes and issues found in these epistles such as Greco-Roman background, theology, Christology, view of the source of sin, eschatology, implied authorship and pseudonymity, and ecclesiological stance. A strength of this volume is its survey of recent scholarship and where it is going.

*Guthrie, Donald. *New Testament Theology*. Leicester: InterVarsity, 1981.

> Weighing in at 982 pages of text not to mention a thirty-six-page bibliography, this is a massive, encyclopedic work that takes a thematic approach to each topic. While it is an impressive work of scholarship by the noted vice-principal and lecturer in New Testament at London Bible College, it is not without its problems. It is possible for the reader to become weighted down by all the details. "A mammoth work. . . . Perhaps there is not as much synthesis for

each theme as one might expect: the price paid for this otherwise attractive format is that readers might finish their study without too much of an idea of, say Paul's distinctive contribution to NT theology as a whole, but with only an idea of his contribution to certain themes" (Carson, 35).

*Ladd, George Eldon. *A Theology of the New Testament*. Grand Rapids: Eerdmans, 1974.

This magisterial work has for decades been a standard introduction to the subject to multitudes of college and seminary students. It is clear, comprehensive, and readable. There is a 1993 revised edition by Donald Hagner, one of Ladd's students at Fuller Theological Seminary, that updates and enhances Ladd's classic work.

*+Lloyd-Jones, D. Martyn. *The Cross*. Westchester, IL: Crossway, 1986.

This engaging masterpiece of NT theology is a published collection of sermons preached at Westminster Chapel, London, in the fall of 1963. As always, Lloyd-Jones is worth reading and not to be missed.

*+Milligan, George. *The Theology of the Epistle to the Hebrews*. Edinburgh: T. & T. Clark, 1899. Reprint, Minneapolis: James Family, 1978.

This study is a major work of scholarship by the famous coauthor of *The Vocabulary of the Greek Testament* with James Hope Moulton. It predicts today's current interest in NT theology. "This is one of the most significant works to be reprinted in recent years. It treats concisely matters of authorship and date, etc., and then systematizes the theology of the Epistle in light of God's covenants with Israel" (Barber).

*Morris, Leon. *New Testament Theology*. Grand Rapids: Academie, 1986.

This treatment is a fairly brief and nontechnical approach to New Testament theology. It is readable and accessible for the nonspecialist.

*Schreiner, Thomas R. *New Testament Theology: Magnifying God in Christ*. Grand Rapids: Baker Academic, 2008.

This excellent volume by the James Buchanan Harrison Professor of New Testament Interpretation at Southern Baptist Theological Seminary in Louisville focuses on two overarching themes: (1) the unity of redemptive history and the kingdom of God, and (2) the glory of God through the work of Christ and the empowering presence of the Holy Spirit. At 866 pages of text, it is a massive undertaking, but not to be missed. Schreiner is an important voice in NT studies today.

*Stott, John R. W. *The Cross of Christ*. Downers Grove: InterVarsity, 1986.

> This book is a readable and engaging modern restatement of the NT theology of the cross by a master preacher and scholar.

*Thielman, Frank. *Theology of the New Testament: A Canonical and Synthetic Approach*. Grand Rapids: Zondervan, 2005.

> This massive volume, at 725 pages of text along with thirty-five pages of works cited, by a Presbyterian scholar and professor of NT at Beeson Divinity School, Birmingham, Alabama, is at once readable and engaging. "Habitually avoids entering into the cut and thrust of debate within the discipline of biblical theology, with the result that his book is a better introduction to the actual theological content of the NT documents than to the discipline of biblical theology or to the interface of theology and history—but if one must choose to tilt in one direction or another, this is a better choice than its opposite. Thielman manages to be broadly comprehensive and genuinely edifying—a fine achievement" (Carson, 36–37). Reformed.

Zuck, Roy B., ed. *A Biblical Theology of the New Testament*. Chicago: Moody, 1994.

> Written for the nonspecialist by the faculty of Dallas Theological Seminary and reflecting the theological perspectives of that institution. Premillennial. Dispensational.

NEW TESTAMENT HISTORY

Barrett, C. K., ed. *The New Testament Background: Writings from Ancient Greece and Roman Empire That Illuminate Christian Origins*. Rev. ed. San Francisco: HarperSanFrancisco, 1995.

> A collection of primary sources (the Roman Empire, the papyri, inscriptions, philosophers and poets, the Gnostics, mystery religions, Jewish history, Rabbinic literature and Rabbinic Judaism, Qumran, Philo, Josephus, the LXX and Targums, apocalyptic literature, and mysticism) that gives the reader necessary background to the world of the NT.

*Bruce, F. F. *New Testament History*. Garden City: Anchor, 1972.

> This study has been the standard work on the subject since its publication in England in 1969. Although it has been superseded by later works, it still should be consulted. It is a delight to read. "A well-documented, brilliantly written, generally conservative history which covers the entire NT era and will remain a standard for years" (Barber, 137).

*+Deissmann, Adolf. *Light from the Ancient East: The New Testament Illustrated by Recently Discovered Texts of the Graeco-Roman World.* Translated by Lionel R. M. Strachan. London: Hodder & Stoughton, 1909. Reprint, Peabody: Hendrickson, 1995.

> A classic study of nonliterary Greek and Latin texts that shed important light on the text, language, history, and literature of the NT. Invaluable for our understanding of biblical Greek.

*+————. *Bible Studies: Contributions Chiefly from Papyri and Inscriptions to the History of the Language, the Literature, and the Religion of Hellenistic Judaism and Primitive Christianity.* Translated and revised by Alexander Grieve. Edinburgh: T. & T. Clark, 1923. Reprint, Winona Lake, IN: Alpha, 1979.

> This classic study was first published in 1901. See remarks on the author's *Light from the Ancient East.*

!*Evans, Craig A. *Ancient Texts for New Testament Studies: A Guide to the Background Literature.* Grand Rapids: Baker Academic, 2005.

> An invaluable overview of the background literature for the study of the NT. This helpful guide is a roadmap to the multiplicity of texts of which the NT specialist must be familiar. Indispensible for both serious students and scholars!

*Evans, Craig A., and Stanley E. Porter, eds. *Dictionary of New Testament Background.* Downers Grove: InterVarsity, 2000.

> Indispensable guide to the Jewish and Greco-Roman backgrounds of the NT.

*Ferguson, Everett. *Backgrounds of Early Christianity.* 3rd ed. Grand Rapids: Eerdmans, 2003.

> The standard and best introduction to the world of the NT and the early church. A top-notch introduction for college and seminary students, one of its most valuable features is the inclusion of excellent bibliographies at the beginning of each chapter and end of each subsection. Engaging, readable, and accessible for all levels of interest.

*Green, Joel B., and Lee Martin McDonald, eds. *The World of the New Testament: Cultural, Social, and Historical Contexts.* Grand Rapids: Baker Academic, 2013.

> Contains a cornucopia of information on the various contexts from which the NT emerged from a blue-ribbon team of specialists. Essential for understanding the world of the NT and the early church.

Hedrick, Charles W., and Robert Hodgson Jr., eds. *Nag Hammadi, Gnosticism, and Early Christianity*. Peabody: Hendrickson, 1986.

> This collection of thirteen essays, published in memoriam of George W. Mac-Rae, who died in 1985, focuses on the relationship of Gnosticism and the early church. The contributors are all internationally recognized scholars in the disciplines of Gnosticism, NT studies, or early church history.

*Rudolp, Kurt. *Gnosis: The Nature and History of Gnosticism*. San Francisco: Harper & Row, 1984.

> A scholarly and readable treatment of a difficult subject. One of the best resources available.

!*+Schürer, Emil. *The History of the Jewish People in the Age of Jesus Christ*. 2 vols. English version revised and edited by Geza Vermes and Ferus Millar. Edinburgh: T. & T. Clark, 1973.

> The revision of this magisterial study, first published in 1885, updated a true classic. Covers the period from 175 BC to AD 135. Not to be missed! "Still regarded as one of the most authoritative treatments of first-century Judaism.

Witherington, Ben, III. *New Testament History: A Narrative Account*. Grand Rapids: Baker, 2001.

> Not reviewed for this edition.

!*Yamauchi, Edwin M. *Pre-Christian Gnosticism: A Survey of the Proposed Evidences*. 2nd ed. Grand Rapids: Baker, 1983.

> This important study explores the relationship of Gnosticism to the development of Christianity and the NT. Yamauchi, a noted evangelical scholar and professor at Miami University, analyzes the evidence used by scholars to support their theory that Gnosticism preceded the emergence of NT Christianity and furnished the building blocks of the new religious movement. He also exposes the methodological fallacies used to support their views. "A technical treatise revealing the extremely fluid state of Gnostic study" (Barber).

NEW TESTAMENT USE OF THE OLD TESTAMENT

!*Archer, Gleason L., and Gregory Chirichigno. *Old Testament Quotations in the New Testament*. Chicago: Moody, 1983.

> This impressive work of scholarship was conceived for the 33rd annual meeting of the Evangelical Theological Society, which met in Toronto in late 1981.

The conference theme for that year was "Relationships between the Testaments." The format is set up like a synopsis with four columns on each two pages of text. The four columns list the Masoretic Text, the LXX, the NT, and Commentary. "What is presented in this book is both a commentary and a tool to help students and scholars alike examine the lexical and syntactical relationships of the Old Testament quotations used in the New Testament" (from the preface). Highly technical!

*Beale, G. K., and D. A. Carson, eds. *Commentary on the New Testament Use of the Old Testament*. Grand Rapids: Baker Academic, 2007.

This massive work of scholarship endeavors to analyze OT citation in the NT as well as probable allusions. Editors G. K. Beale and D. A. Carson have assembled a top-notch team of NT scholars to accomplish this very task. Contributors include Craig Blomberg, David Pao, I. Howard Marshall, Frank Thielman, Philip H. Towner, and George H. Guthrie. At almost 1,200 pages of text, this volume is a most impressive and helpful body of work. Anyone preaching or teaching on the NT needs to have this book!

*Berding, Kenneth, and Jonathan Lunde. *Three Views on the New Testament Use of the Old Testament*. Counterpoints Bible and Theology. Edited by Stanley N. Gundry. Grand Rapids: Zondervan, 2008.

Contributors to this helpful volume are Walter C. Kaiser Jr. ("Single Meaning, Unified Referents"), Darrell L. Block ("Single Meaning, Multiple Contexts and Referents"), and Peter Enns ("Fuller Meaning, Single Goal"). This volume follows the Counterpoints format of presentation and then robust debate by the other contributors.

Ellis, E. Earle. *The Old Testament in Early Christianity: Canon and Interpretation in the Light of Modern Research*. Grand Rapids: Baker, 1992.

Not reviewed for this edition.

*Goppelt, Leonhard. *Typos: The Typological Interpretation of the Old Testament in the New*. Translated by Donald H. Madvig. Grand Rapids: Eerdmans, 1982.

This highly significant work, first published in German in 1939, was inaccessible to English readers for decades. This welcome edition makes Goppelt's work available to a much broader audience. It focuses on a much misunderstood and often misapplied subject, typology, and how the NT writers interpreted the OT in its light. The bulk of the book is divided into three main sections: "Typology in Late Judaism," "Typology in the New Testament," and "Apocalypticism and Typology in Paul." A masterpiece! See also in chapter 4 under "Hermeneutics."

*Kaiser, Walter C., Jr. *The Uses of the Old Testament in the New*. Chicago: Moody, 1985. Reprint, Eugene, OR: Wipf & Stock, 2001.

> This book explores the question over whether NT writers were accurate in their OT quotations or did they permissively interpret OT texts. The central argument of Kaiser is that NT writers cited OT texts with regard to the intention of the original writer. Thus, each passage has one basic interpretation and not a dual or deeper meaning. Very helpful in sorting out the current debate!

NEW TESTAMENT TEXTUAL CRITICISM

*Aland, Kurt, and Barbara Aland. *The Text of the New Testament: An Introduction to the Critical Editions and to the Theory and Practice of Modern Textual Criticism*. Translated by Erroll F. Rhodes. Grand Rapids: Eerdmans, 1987.

> The "bible" of textual criticism by two of the world's leading authorities on the subject. Indispensable! "Thorough, current, and lucid introduction to all major aspects of textual criticism" (Bauer, 258).

*Black, David Alan. *New Testament Textual Criticism: A Concise Guide*. Grand Rapids: Baker Academic, 1994.

> This book is a very brief overview of the science of textual criticism. It has been superseded by the work by Porter and Pitts.

*Comfort, Philip W. *New Testament Text and Translation Commentary*. Carol Stream, IL: Tyndale, 2008.

> "When an English NT version notes in the margin that there are other manuscript readings for this verse, this is the volume to consult. While it quotes the Greek text for the variants, it then gives an English translation, plus the primary English versions that use that reading, so the pastor who does not know Greek can use this work. Comfort's brief comments on each variant reading are generally very helpful—at least, each comment gives the preacher solid food for thought as he considers which text to use in preaching" (**Stout**).

*Epp, Eldon Jay, and Gordon D. Fee. *Studies in the Theory and Method of New Testament Textual Criticism*. Grand Rapids: Eerdmans, 1974.

> A seminal work on the subject. The compilation of seventeen studies.

*Finegan, Jack. *Encountering New Testament Manuscripts: A Working Introduction to Textual Criticism*. Grand Rapids: Eerdmans, 1974.

> As its title indicates, the approach of this volume is to allow students to learn firsthand the principles of textual criticism by actually reading samples of manuscripts.

*Metzger, Bruce M., and Bart D. Ehrman. *The Text of the New Testament: Its Transmission, Corruption, and Restoration*. 4th ed. Oxford: Oxford University Press, 2005.

> Although this book was intended to be an introduction to the science of NT textual criticism, it goes well beyond that, paying particular attention to the transmission, corruption, and restoration of the text.

Parker, D. C. *An Introduction to the New Testament Manuscripts and Their Texts*. 2nd ed. Cambridge: Cambridge University Press, 1991.

> Not reviewed for this edition.

*Porter, Stanley E., and Andrew W. Pitts. *Fundamentals of New Testament Textual Criticism*. Grand Rapids: Eerdmans, 2015.

> This guidebook is aimed at beginning students of NT Greek. It strikes a reasonable balance between being too simplistic and too detailed in providing a helpful overview of the field. One welcome feature is his chapter on the NT canon.

*Trobisch, David. *The First Edition of the New Testament*. New York: Oxford University Press, 2000.

> "This fascinating study argues that the textual evidence of the Greek manuscripts indicates that the organization of the NT reveals an editorial concept that produced a fairly standard edition of the NT in codex (bound) form by the early second century AD. The implications toward the NT canon are tremendous, as Trobisch argues that the canon was established far earlier than critical scholarship has allowed. This book will give the pastor greater confidence in his understanding of the authority of the NT" (**Stout**).

Wegner, Paul D. *A Student's Guide to Textual Criticism of the Bible: Its History, Methods, and Results*. Downers Grove: InterVarsity, 2006.

> Not reviewed for this edition.

*+Westcott, B. F., and F. J. A. Hort. *Introduction to the New Testament in the Original Greek*. New York: Harper, 1982. Reprint, Peabody: Hendrickson, 1988

> A true classic of textual criticism! Controversial in its day! "Probably the most significant volume ever produced in the history of the field of textual criticism" (Bauer, 259).

NEW TESTAMENT EXEGESIS

*Blomberg, Craig L., and Jennifer Foutz Markley. *A Handbook of New Testament Exegesis*. Grand Rapids: Baker Academic, 2010.

> This handbook is an exceptionally helpful volume for anyone involved in the daunting task of NT exegesis. The authors take the reader from text to application with a well-written and accessible guide that is full of illustrations from the NT. Topics covered are textual criticism, translation and translations, historical-cultural context, literary context, word studies, grammar, interpretive problems, outlining, theology, and application. This is one of the best works on the subject that the writer has read. Being in possession of this book and that of Fee, the student or pastor is well covered in this area of study. Highly recommended!

*Carson, D. A. *Exegetical Fallacies*. 2nd ed. Grand Rapids: Baker Academic, 1996.

> The material contained in this volume had its genesis in the Spring Lectureship sponsored by Western Conservative Baptist Seminary in Portland, Oregon, in 1983. Carson, a noted NT scholar and professor at Trinity Evangelical Divinity School, exposes common sins of interpretation committed by preachers and Bible teachers alike. Reading this book and putting its principles into practice are the cure for sloppiness in exegeting the Scriptures in both the pulpit and the classroom. A must-read for pastors!

*Fee, Gordon D. *New Testament Exegesis: A Handbook for Students and Pastors*. Philadelphia: Westminster John Knox, 2002.

> "This work gives a step-by-step process for doing practical exegesis of the NT-the type of hermeneutical spadework essential for digging out the intended meaning of a passage. Every pastor ought to use the 'Short Guide for Sermon Exegesis' when preparing a sermon. The book also contains excellent leads for additional studies in particular areas" (**Stout**).

*Resseguie, James L. *Narrative Criticism of the New Testament: An Introduction*. Grand Rapids: Baker Academic, 2005.

> This volume is an introduction to the science of narrative criticism of the NT, the exegetical approach that applies literary methods to the study of the Bible.

GREEK GRAMMARS

Introductory

*Bateman, Herbert W., IV. *A Workbook for Intermediate Greek*. Grand Rapids: Kregel, 2008.

> Although the title touts this book as an intermediate workbook, all of the exercises are based upon the grammar, exegesis, and commentary of 1–3 John, which makes it more of a beginner's workbook rather than intermediate. This guide is geared toward Greek students in either the second semester of their first year or the first semester of their second year of study. This workbook is a very helpful tool for helping students learn translation skills and syntax. It includes a CD with exercise answer keys and verse diagrams.

*Decker, Rodney J. *Reading Koine Greek: An Introduction and Integrated Workbook*. Grand Rapids: Baker Academic, 2014.

> Published posthumously, this textbook for teaching NT Greek is the result of the author's many years teaching the subject as professor of Greek and NT at Baptist Bible Seminary in Clarks Summit, Pennsylvania. This volume is Baker's answer to Zondervan's *Basics of Biblical Greek* by William Mounce. It is accessible and quite "user friendly" for both students who are beginning their studies in the Greek NT as well as pastors who would like to review their skills. Unlike many of the older introductory grammars (e.g., Machen, Summers, etc.), this work is up to date and cutting edge, including such issues in Greek linguistics as verbal aspect, voice, lexical semantics, and pronunciation. Decker not only was a consummate scholar and teacher, he began his career as a pastor, which is reflected in his teaching style. One advantage that this book has over that of Mounce is that the author introduces verbs in chapter 5, whereas Mounce waits until chapter 15. In the writer's opinion, that is much too late. This book is highly recommended! One personal note: Rodney and I became friends after meeting in the early 1980s as young pastors in Michigan and discovering a mutual interest in books and scholarly pursuits.

*Hewett, James Allen, C. Michael Robbins, and Steven R. Johnson. *New Testament Greek: A Beginning and Intermediate Grammar*. Rev. ed. Grand Rapids: Baker Academic, 2009.

> First published in 1986 by Hewett, this revised edition of a familiar first-year Greek textbook is a straightforward approach to learning the Greek NT. The authors frame their explanations and illustrations of each Greek concept in terms of its English grammar counterpart. Of particular value to the student is its early introduction to the verb system in chapter 2. A CD-ROM, containing tools for vocalizing the language, Greek vocabulary, and identification of verb forms, accompanies the textbook.

*+Machen, J. Gresham, and Dan G. McCartney. *New Testament Greek for Beginners*. 2nd ed. New York: Pearson, 2003.

> First published in 1923, the revised edition of this classic work is a personal favorite, having been my beginning Greek textbook while in seminary and as a college professor of first-year Greek. It is a basic, no-nonsense approach to learning NT Greek. Its thirty-three lessons carefully and logically take the student through a first-year grammar course. Mastery of this book is an excellent preparation for reading the Greek NT. My first-year Greek class completed this book in three months and proceeded to translate the Johannine Epistles and the Gospel of Mark by the end of the first year. A masterful approach by one of the intellectual giants of the twentieth century!

*Mounce, William D. *Basics of Biblical Greek*. 2nd ed. Grand Rapids: Zondervan, 2003.

> Since its publication in 1993, this seminal work has been the "gold standard" for teaching NT Greek in colleges and seminaries. This second edition endeavors to minimize some of the weaknesses of the first one. For example, the second edition features a two-track approach which offers the option of learning verbs earlier in the course. Track 1 goes through the book in its regular order introducing Greek verbs in lesson 15. Track 2 proceeds directly from chapter 9 to chapter 15 and then from chapter 21 back to chapter 10. Track 2 is a much better approach in that it allows students to learn the Greek verb system much sooner than previously. However, I learned Greek using Machen's *New Testament Greek for Beginners* in which the verbs are introduced in the third chapter. Thus, in my opinion, Mounce waits too long to introduce verbs, which is a weakness of this approach. However, I would be the last person to argue with the monumental success of this book. It includes an interactive study-aid CD-ROM. There is also an accompanying DVD with video lectures that can be obtained separately. In addition, students may access other classroom aids and video lectures at the author's website (www. teknia.com).

*———. *Basics of Biblical Greek Workbook.* 2nd ed. Grand Rapids: Zondervan, 2003.

> This helpful workbook is the companion volume to the author's *Basics of Biblical Greek*.

*———. *Greek for the Rest of Us: The Essentials of Biblical Greek.* 2nd ed. Grand Rapids: Zondervan, 2013.

> This course for beginners in the study of NT Greek is not meant to replace the author's *Basics of Biblical Greek*, but is designed more as a "crash course" on the essentials of the language. The subtitle of the first edition read "Using Greek Tools without Mastering Biblical Greek." This approach is more for those who do not plan to go on to the next level, but are content to know just a little bit of the language and would like to be able to use some of the basic tools. With today's de-emphasis on biblical languages and the fact that some seminary programs do not require them at all, this volume is desperately needed. After all, a little bit of Greek is better than no Greek at all.

Intermediate and Advanced

*Blass, F., and A. Debrunner. *A Greek Grammar of the New Testament and Other Early Christian Literature.* Translated and revised by Robert W. Funk. Chicago: University of Chicago Press, 1961.

> At one time this grammar was considered to be the finest grammar for advanced students of NT Greek. It is thorough, but not to the extent of Moulton or A. T. Robertson and somewhat more difficult to use.

Burton, Ernest DeWitt. *Syntax of the Moods and Tenses in New Testament Greek.* 3rd ed. Edinburgh: T. & T. Clark, 1898.

> This study is a very helpful tool on a limited area of NT Greek grammar. There is a thorough discussion on the relationship of Greek and English past tenses, and a good presentation on Greek direct and indirect discourse. Despite its age, it is still worth obtaining. Moule's *Idiom Book of New Testament Greek* has superseded this work.

*Dana, Harvey Eugene, and Julius R. Mantey. *A Manual Grammar of the Greek New Testament.* New York: Macmillan, 1957.

> At one time, this book was the standard intermediate grammar for New Testament Greek. Unfortunately, there are a large number of typographical errors and some of the examples used are not always the clearest. This is a good book

to master by anyone wanting to read and exegete the NT. However, there are now better, more up-to-date treatments of the subject.

*Moule, C. F. D. *An Idiom Book of New Testament Greek*. 2nd ed. Cambridge: Cambridge University Press, 1963.

This guide is an excellent tool for assistance in selected grammatical areas. Supplements Moulton's *Grammar of New Testament Greek*. "A valuable book on the syntax of the NT with an up-to-date treatment of the idioms" (Barber, 124).

*Moulton, James Hope, William Francis Howard, and Nigel Turner. *A Grammar of New Testament Greek*. 4 vols. Edinburgh: T. & T. Clark, 1906–1976.

An exceptional treatment of NT Greek. Despite its age, still extremely valuable. Vol. 1 on *Prolegomena* was written by Moulton; vol. 2 on *Accidence* was written by Howard; and vol. 3 on *Syntax* and vol. 4 on *Style* were written by Turner. "An extremely worthwhile study" (Barber, 124).

*Mounce, William D. *A Graded Reader of Biblical Greek*. Grand Rapids: Zondervan, 1996.

This helpful inductive approach to learning Greek grammar helps to ease the transition from beginning Greek student to the intermediate stage. This method helps students to learn NT Greek the same way they would any other language: through a graded program. This course is the next step for students who have mastered the author's *Basics of Biblical Greek*.

*Robertson, Archibald Thomas. *A Grammar of the Greek New Testament in the Light of Historical Research*. Nashville: Broadman, 1934.

Affectionately called "Big Bob" by generations of Greek students, this work represents the life-work of arguably the greatest Greek scholar that the United States has ever produced. It is incredibly thorough and comprehensive and a marvel of scholarship. However, it has been superseded by more up-to-date works. "Very full and complete. Covers the history of Greek grammar, accidence, and syntax" (Barber, 124).

*Runge, Steven E. *Discourse Grammar of the Greek New Testament: A Practical Introduction for Teaching and Exegesis*. Peabody: Hendrickson, 2010.

This extremely helpful volume is a guide to discourse analysis in the Greek NT. The author utilizes a function-based approach to linguistics by focusing on how the grammatical conventions in the NT accomplish communication tasks. The linguistic approach is what the author terms *cross-linguistic*, meaning that it looks at how languages in general tend to operate, not just

NT Greek. It is also *function-based*, in the sense that it tends to assist the reader "to conceptualize what is happening in Greek by understanding how the comparable task is accomplished in another language" (from the preface). The reader is able to make the leap from linguistic theory to practical exegetical application. A unique study that is an important resource for Greek students of all levels. It is accessible enough for even first-year students to benefit, but helpful also for seasoned scholars.

*Wallace, Daniel B. *Basics of New Testament Syntax*. Grand Rapids: Zondervan, 2000.

This practical grammar for intermediate Greek students is an abridgment of the author's very popular *Greek Grammar Beyond the Basics: An Exegetical Syntax of the New Testament*.

*————. *Greek Grammar Beyond the Basics: An Exegetical Syntax of the New Testament*. Grand Rapids: Zondervan, 1996.

"The current undisputed leader in Greek grammar, this work, of course, requires knowledge of Greek, but it makes grammar actually enjoyable to study. Its Scripture index makes it handy for the pastor when studying a passage to check how the NT uses various parts of speech, so it should remain in easy reach during sermon preparation" (**Stout**).

GREEK LEXICONS

*Bauer, W., F. Danker, W. Arndt, and F. W. Gingrich. *A Greek-English Lexicon of the New Testament*. 3rd ed. Chicago: University of Chicago Press, 2000.

This essential resource is the standard lexicon for students and scholars of the Greek NT. It is a translation and adaptation of Walter Bauer's *Griechisch-Deutsches Worterbuch zu den Schriften des Neuen Testaments und der ubrigen urchistlichen Literatur* by Arndt and Gingrich and then updated by Danker. This meticulous work has superseded all previous English lexicons.

*Beale, G. K., Daniel J. Brendsel, and William A. Ross. *An Interpretative Lexicon of New Testament Greek*. Grand Rapids: Zondervan, 2014.

At just under one hundred pages, this handy little lexicon really packs a wallop. It functions as both a lexicon and an interpretative handbook. It assists users to quickly and easily determine the range of translation possibilities for prepositions, adverbs, particles, relative pronouns, and conjunctions without having to wade through massive amounts of material in more comprehensive lexicons. This is a useful guide to keep on the desktop. It will be consulted regularly.

Cremer, Hermann. *Biblico-Theological Lexicon of New Testament Greek*. 4th English ed. Translated by William Urwick. Edinburgh: T. & T. Clark, 1895.

> Over a hundred years ago, this valuable study was considered one of the most important tools for the study of NT Greek. It is still particularly valuable in that it demonstrates how extrabiblical usage of Greek words influences their meaning in Scripture. Until the publication of Kittel's *TDNT*, this lexicon was indispensable.

*Kubo, Sakae. *A Reader's Greek-English Lexicon of the New Testament and a Beginner's Guide for the Translation of New Testament Greek*. Grand Rapids: Zondervan, 1975.

> This handy reference lexicon is a very helpful volume to have for those who would like to be able to read Greek quickly with a limited vocabulary. Verse-by-verse definitions are listed for all words in the NT occurring fewer than fifty times so that the reader does not have to take time to look them up in a standard lexicon. This allows for more efficient reading. This book presupposes a knowledge of basic grammar and a basic Greek vocabulary of words occurring more than fifty times. A very helpful quick reference guide.

*Louw, J. P., and E. A. Nida, eds. *Greek-English Lexicon of the New Testament Based on Semantic Domains*. 2nd ed. 2 vols. Stuttgart: United Bible Societies, 1998.

> "This lexicon takes a novel approach by outlining NT words into their semantic domains, such as People, Danger, Help, Value, Time, etc. The reader then has quick access to the synonyms of the NT, an important tool in defining words. Knowledge of Greek is necessary, but with concentrated effort, an English reader can learn to use this important resource" (**Stout**).

*Moulton, James Hope, and George Milligan. *The Vocabulary of the Greek Testament*. Reprint, Grand Rapids: Eerdmans, 1976.

> This very specialized lexicon treats only those NT words that have been illumined by modern papyri discoveries and other nonliterary sources. First published in 1930, this study is still extremely valuable for NT word studies. "Invaluable. . . . A work for the advanced student" (Barber, 123).

*Mounce, William D. *The Analytical Lexicon to the Greek New Testament*. Grand Rapids: Zondervan, 1993.

> Based on the UBS third edition (revised), this handy reference guide was created to aid the study of the Greek NT, utilizing sophisticated computer resources to ensure accurate and in-depth analyses of the word forms that comprise the NT. It is consistent with today's standard Greek lexicons and includes both accepted and variant readings. An important feature is that it is keyed to the author's *Morphology of Biblical Greek*, which explains in detail

the variations that Greek words follow. This book is a very helpful quick-reference guide that also provides the Greek student with an index to another body of literature.

Thayer, Joseph Henry, ed. *Greek-English Lexicon of the New Testament*. Grand Rapids: Zondervan, 1962.

> This old standard is still used in colleges and seminaries. It is a translation of *Clavis Noiv Testamenti*. Although it has been superseded by other more recent works, it is still worth consulting for its excellent word studies. For those who cannot afford to purchase Bauer, Arndt, Gingrich, and Danker's much more expensive lexicon, this book is a fairly serviceable alternative.

GREEK CONCORDANCES

*Aland, Kurt. *Vollstandige Konkordanz zun griechischen Neuen Testament*. Berlin: de Gruyter, 1983.

> This essential tool is the standard concordance for NT Greek. A must-buy for all serious Greek students and scholars.

*Hatch, Edwin, and Henry A. Redpath. See section on LXX.

Moulton, W. F., and A. S. Geden. *A Concordance to the Greek Testament*. 5th ed. Reprint, Edinburgh: T. & T. Clark, 1963.

> First published in 1897, for many decades this was the best concordance on Westcott and Hort's Greek text and an essential tool for students and scholars. Since the completion of Aland's *Vollstandige Konkordanz zun griechischen Neuen Testament*, it has been superseded. It is still worth purchasing if it can be picked up secondhand.

Wigram, G. W. *The Englishman's Greek Concordance of the New Testament*. 9th ed. London: Baxter, n.d. Reprint, Grand Rapids: Zondervan, 1970.

> This handy concordance is a very helpful tool for those who do not read Greek.

GREEK LANGUAGE HELPS

*?Bromiley, Geoffrey W., trans., ed. *Theological Dictionary of the New Testament.* 10 vols. Grand Rapids: Eerdmans, 1964–74.

> After over forty years since the publication of the final volume, this set by Gerhard Kittel and Gerhard Friedrich remains an indispensable tool for the serious Greek student. "Despite its age and deserved criticism, *TDNT* remains the standard for NT word studies, and these days it can be purchased rather reasonably. It is a bit cumbersome for English readers (knowledge of Greek is most helpful), but it can be navigated with a little effort. Some of the articles tend to give theologically liberal interpretations, but the historical and linguistic research is unparalleled. Any serious student in the NT needs to consult *TNDT*" (**Stout**). "This set is without peer" (Bauer, 255).

Brown, Colin, ed. *The New International Dictionary of New Testament Theology.* 3 vols. Grand Rapids: Zondervan, 1975; 1986.

> This set has been superseded by the 2014 revision by Moises Silva. Although the discussions in this set are not up to date with current issues, much of the material is still very valuable. "While this research tool is no longer new, *NIDNTT* remains very valuable for the English reader as most of the main NT terms are discussed under the primary English word, with the Greek and Hebrew transliterated for ease of reading. The words are discussed in their historical usages, especially showing how they are used in the Septuagint, giving the NT its theological terminology. A used copy can be bought for an affordable price" (**Stout**).

*Decker, Rodney J. *Koine Greek Reader: Selections from the New Testament, Septuagint, and Early Christian Writers.* Grand Rapids: Kregel, 2007.

> This excellent Greek resource is unique in that it provides graded readings from the NT, LXX, Apostolic Fathers, and early creeds. The late Rodney Decker, a professor of Greek and NT at Baptist Bible Seminary in Clarks Summit, Pennsylvania, until his death in 2014, fine-tuned these exercises over many years in the classroom and the result is an extremely helpful set of readings for the intermediate Greek student. This book is hands down the best of its kind available today. In addition to being carefully prepared and organized, some of its features include vocabulary lists, references to other resources, translation helps, a review of basic grammar and syntax, and an introduction to *BDAG*. This book is an intermediate Greek course all by itself. Highly recommended!

*Duvall, J. Scott, and Verlyn D. Verbrugge, eds. *Devotions on the Greek New Testament.* Grand Rapids: Zondervan, 2012.

> This interesting devotional book is a unique collection of fifty-two devotional reflections, each of which is based on a brief passage of Scripture from the Greek NT. These reflections span the breadth of the NT from Matthew to Revelation and every book is covered, with the two exceptions of 2 John and 3 John. The list of contributors reads like a who's who of NT evangelical scholarship today, including such noteworthy scholars as Craig Blomberg, Darrell Bock, Lynn Cohick, Scot McKnight, William Mounce, Mark Strauss, and Ben Witherington. This book will assist the busy pastor to sharpen and review his Greek tools as well as warm his heart.

!*Harris, Murray J. *Prepositions and Theology in the Greek New Testament.* Grand Rapids: Zondervan, 2012.

> This informative book is an expanded version of the author's earlier one on the Greek prepositions of the NT. Harris demonstrates how fluid the meanings of Greek prepositions are and how they influence the translation and interpretation of certain problem passages. A must for all Greek exegetes and advanced students!

*Metzger, Bruce M. *Lexical Aids for Students of New Testament Greek.* 3rd ed. Grand Rapids: Baker Academic, 1998.

> This standard Greek reference tools assists students in learning vocabulary quickly by listing words according to their frequency in the NT. The author, one of the most esteemed NT professors of the twentieth century, was the George L. Collard Professor of NT Language and Literature at Princeton Theological Seminary. When I was a seminary student, this handy book rarely left my side.

*Mounce, William D. *The Morphology of Biblical Greek.* Grand Rapids: Zondervan, 1994.

> This excellent guide explains in simple language, geared for intermediate Greek students, how Greek words are formed. The author demonstrates that Greek word formation follows a fixed set of rules that, once understood, help the student to understand how irregular verbs are formed. Mounce organizes this reference book into five parts: (1) The rules that determine how Greek words change; (2) The rules of verb formation, from augment to personal ending; (3) Paradigms for every type of noun and adjective form, with all the words that belong in each category and any peculiarities of a given word; (4) All the verbs and principal parts, with verbs that follow the same rules grouped together; and (5) An index of all words in the NT with their morphological category. An invaluable resource!

!*Porter, Stanley E. *Linguistic Analysis of the Greek New Testament: Studies in Tools, Methods, and Practice*. Grand Rapids: Baker Academic, 2015.

> This helpful volume is comprised of twenty-one essays, most of them from papers already delivered at conferences, on the Greek language and linguistics. Among the many topics covered in the book are discourse analysis, structural linguistics, sociolinguistics, verbal aspect, word order, and hyponymy. Porter brings his readers up to date on the latest advances in NT Greek linguistics.

*Robertson, Archibald Thomas. *Word Pictures in the New Testament*. 6 vols. Nashville: Broadman, 1930–33.

> A work of impeccable scholarship by a master Greek grammarian, this set is essentially a verse-by-verse commentary on the English text of the NT in which Robertson points out those word pictures and nuances in the Greek that are often lost in the translation. Greek words are transliterated so this work can be used by a very broad audience.

*Robinson, Thomas A. *Mastering New Testament Greek: Essential Tools for Students*. Peabody: Hendrickson, 2007.

> This helpful Greek vocabulary resource is meant to be used alongside a beginning grammar to help enlarge the student's knowledge of Greek words. The author's system utilizes cognate groups that link Greek words together by their common roots. A supplementary CD-ROM is included.

*Silva, Moisés, revision editor. *New International Dictionary of New Testament Theology and Exegesis*. 5 vols. Grand Rapids: Zondervan, 2014.

> This indispensible set is a thorough revision of the *New International Dictionary of New Testament Theology* that was edited by Colin Brown and published in three volumes in 1975–78. A fourth volume consisting mostly of indexes was tacked on in the 1986 reissue. Brown's work was itself a translation, revision, and expansion of the 1979–71 *Theologisches Begriffslexikon Neuen Testament*, which was the product of German scholarship. This new edition contains updated bibliographies, correction of inaccuracies and inconsistencies, and biblical quotations which follow the NIV (2011). It is larger than the original Brown edition by about a third and is more than simply a cosmetic updating. This is a major overhaul, and it is most welcome and long overdue. "It brings changes that make it richer and more user-friendly to those interested in detailed exegesis. Not all 'standard reference works' deserve to be standards; this one does" (Carson). Indispensable for NT work!

Trobisch, David. *A User's Guide to the Nestle-Aland 28 Greek New Testament.* Society of
Biblical Literature Text-Critical Series. Atlanta: Society of Biblical Literature, 2013.

> The title of this brief little book (80 pages) would indicate that it is for users
> of the Greek NT. Unfortunately, the preponderance of the book's contents are
> devoted to matters of basic introduction to the Nestle-Aland text for those
> who are approaching it for the very first time and thus, are definitely not
> users. For the beginner, there are even exercises with answers at the back
> of the book. This volume would be helpful for first- or second-year Greek
> students, but seasoned scholars will find themselves skimming over or by-
> passing altogether the first two chapters. Finally, in the third and final chapter,
> Trobisch addresses information to the advanced Greek student and scholar.
> Of particular interest to scholars is his discussion of the differences between
> Aland's Local-Genealogical Method critical approach and the newer Coher-
> ence-Based Genealogical Method approach.

Vincent, Marvin R. *Word Studies in the New Testament.* 4 vols. New York: Scribner, 1887.
Reprint, Grand Rapids: Eerdmans, 1946.

> Similar to Robertson's work, this much older set is of limited value due to
> advances in the study of the Greek NT. Purchase Robertson instead.

GREEK TEXTS

*Aland, Barbara, Kurt Aland, Johannes Karavidopoulos, Carlo M. Martini, and Bruce
M. Metzger. 4th ed. *The UBS Greek New Testament: Reader's Edition with Textual
Notes.* Wheaton: Crossway, 2011.

> This beautiful reader's edition is based on the UBS fourth edition and is
> a delight to read. It offers a crystal clear layout with the Greek text above
> notes that are on every page. Notes include parsing of difficult verb forms
> and translations of Greek words occurring thirty times or less. My copy is an
> absolutely gorgeous leather-bound edition that I treasure and carry to church
> services every Sunday. A treasure!

Goodrich, Richard J., and Albert L. Lukaszewski. *A Reader's Greek New Testament.* 3rd
ed. Grand Rapids: Zondervan, 2015.

> This volume is Zondervan's latest reader's edition of the NT. Like the Cross-
> way edition, a definition is provided for Greek words occurring fewer than
> thirty times in the NT thus allowing the reader to focus on faster reading and
> comprehension. This edition offers footnotes comparing the Greek text with
> the critical text of UBS5/NA28.

The Greek-English New Testament: UBS 5th Revised Edition and NIV. Grand Rapids: Zondervan, 2015.

> This volume combines the UBS5 Greek text (with the full textual apparatus) with the NIV translation. The text is the same as NA28, differing only in matters of punctuation and paragraph configuration. The critical apparatus offers fewer variants than NA28, including only those variants of significance to translators. However, like the standard UBS edition, there is an extensive critical apparatus.

*Nestle, Eberhard, Erwin Nestle, and Kurt Aland. *Novum Testamentum Graece*. 28th ed. Stuttgart: Deutsche Bibelstiftung, 2012.

> This twenty-eighth edition of the famous Nestle-Aland text of the NT is the standard critical version used by scholars, Bible translators, professors, students, and pastors worldwide. This latest edition has some significant improvements such as a revised and improved critical apparatus along with an in-depth revision of the Catholic Epistles. Papyrii 117–127 are included for the first time.

COMMENTARIES

The Entire New Testament

! *+Alford, Henry. *The Greek Testament*. Revised by Everett F. Harrison. 4 vols. Chicago: Moody, 1968.

> This four-volume set by the renowned Dean of Canterbury is a recognized classic. This revision is an update of the original 1894 edition. It is still quite helpful in exegetical matters, but should be supplemented with more recent works. Should be purchased if found in a secondhand store. A real treasure! "He shows great knowledge of the Greek text and faces problems of both a doctrinal and textual nature" (Rosscup, 195). Reformed. Anglican. Premillennial.

*Arnold, Clinton E. *Zondervan Exegetical Commentary on the New Testament*. 20 vols. Grand Rapids: Zondervan Academic, 2008+.

> This promising series began in 2008 with Blomberg and Kamell's volume on the book of James. Each volume in the series endeavors to provide the reader with a discussion of the literary context, main idea, structure, and an exegetical outline. Much of the space of each commentary is devoted to an exegetical explanation of the text. Each passage also includes a section titled "Theology in Application" in which the theological message is summarized and then

placed not only within the context of the book, but also within its "broader biblical-theological context. Finally, each commentator provides some suggestions on what the message of the passage is for the church today" (from the series introduction). An added feature is its "Translation and Graphical Layout," which presents each writer's translation of the text in a diagram format "to help the reader visualize, and thus better understand, the flow of thought within the text" (from the series introduction). The introduction of each commentary, in most instances, is sketchy and substandard in my opinion. However, there is a lot to like in this series. The format is pleasing and easily accessible to even the casual Greek student and pastor. The contributors are highly respected in the field. The quality of scholarship and writing has been of uniformly high quality thus far.

?Barclay, William. *Daily Study Bible*. 17 vols. Reprint, Louisville: Westminster John Knox, 1979.

This hugely popular set of commentaries was originally published by Saint Andrew Press, the Church of Scotland's publishing house. Barclay, professor of divinity and biblical criticism at the University of Glasgow in the middle of the twentieth century, intended to make the best of biblical scholarship available to the average reader. The result was a tremendously popular set of commentaries known for the author's turn of phrase and homiletical insight. His questionable interpretations of the Gospels are quite obviously influenced by critical scholarship and negate the value of this set. However, if it can be obtained secondhand at a reasonable price, this set is worth obtaining if one can sift the wheat from the chaff.

*Hendriksen, William, and Simon Kistemaker. *New Testament Commentary*. 15 vols. Grand Rapids: Baker.

This hugely popular series was begun by William Hendriksen, who produced eleven volumes prior to his death: Matthew, Mark, Luke, John, Romans, Galatians, Ephesians, Philippians, Colossians-Philemon, 1–2 Thessalonians, and 1–2 Timothy-Titus. Upon his death, Simon Kistemaker agreed to complete the series, which is now complete. The series is evangelical and often of great help to students and preachers. The volumes across the board are bedrock conservative, extremely practical, and of great value to preachers. "Although his comments are often helpful to the expositor, the verbosity of his style and the selectivity of his interaction with alternative interpretations demand that he be supplemented with other works. . . . His concern for practical application can make his work useful to some preachers. . . . On the whole, his work is solid but not incisive, with the result that there are usually better alternatives" (Carson, 25). Reformed. Amillennial.

!*Lenski, Richard Charles Henry. *Interpretation of the New Testament*. 14 vols. Minneapolis: Augsburg, 1946.

> "Aims to force the student to think through the Greek text and stimulate exegetical rigor, but his grasp of Greek is mechanical, amateurish, and without respect for the fluidity of Greek in the Hellenistic period. The series is marred by a militant or even angry tone in defense of orthodox Lutheranism" (Carson, 24). To be fair, I purchased this set and used it extensively during my seminary years and found it quite useful and of great help in exegesis. It was my shield at my right hand during my years of Greek study. Lutheran. Amillennial.

!*Marshall, I. Howard, and Donald A. Hagner, eds. *New International Greek Testament Commentary*. Grand Rapids: Eerdmans, 1978–present.

> This promising series has been a godsend for those seeking a technical treatment of the Greek text from an evangelical perspective. Although the Greek words are not transliterated, unfortunately Hebrew and Aramaic words are, which is irritating. As of this writing fourteen volumes are available: Romans, Hebrews, Thessalonians, Colossians and Philemon, Philippians, Mark, Galatians, the Pastoral Epistles, James Revelation, 1 Corinthians, 2 Corinthians, Matthew, and Luke. Contributors include top NT scholars such as F. F. Bruce, I. Howard Marshall, Anthony Thistleton, G. K. Beale, Peter Davids, and George Knight. "Up-to-date, bibliographically almost exhaustive, exegetical, and within the evangelical tradition, broadly understood. . . . For clergy and others well trained in Greek and exegesis, the series is not to be missed" (Carson, 15).

!*+Meyer, Heinrich August Wilhelm. *Meyer's Commentary on the New Testament*. Edited and translated by William P. Dickson et al. 12 vols. Edinburgh: T. & T. Clark, 1884. Reprint, Winona Lake, IN: Alpha, 1979.

> The scholarship of this old standard is rightly considered to be of the highest order. Its approach is fairly evangelical for the most part, but not uniformly. It is most helpful in the exegesis of the text, but should be supplemented with more recent works. "Marked by the finest scholarship. Close attention is paid to critical details, and theology is blended with exegesis in expounding the text" (Barber, 128). "Should not be used independently of more recent ones" (Carson, 23). "One of the finest old works on meticulous exegesis of the Greek verse by verse, informed by much expertise and study" (Rosscup, 196).

!*Nicoll, William Robertson, ed. *The Expositor's Greek Testament*. 5 vols. Grand Rapids: Eerdmans, 1951.

> This set was at one time considered to be one of the standard works on the Greek text. It is a bit weak on theology (e.g., Marcus Dods wrote the section on the Gospel of John.), but unsurpassed on exegetical matters. It is a bit dated now being over sixty years old, but still worth consulting. It is regrettably out of print, but should be purchased if available. "Still worth owning and reading along with more recent works" (Carson, 11).

*Osborne, Grant R., ed. *InterVarsity New Testament Commentary Series*. Downers Grove: InterVarsity.

> This series is designed for the pastor, teacher, or Bible study leader who wants a nourishing commentary without wading through reams of technical data. Contributors come from a "wide of theological traditions" who are committed "to the authority of Scripture for Christian faith and practice" (from the general preface). Contributors include such luminaries as Craig Keener, Gordon Fee, Darrell Bock, I. Howard Marshall, and J. Ramsey Michaels.

Synoptic Problem

*Black, David Alan, and David R. Beck. *Rethinking the Synoptic Problem*. Grand Rapids: Baker Academic, 2001.

> The content of this book is a series of papers that were delivered at Wake Forest in 2000. The objective of this volume is to familiarize students with the main positions held by NT scholars on the matter of priority. Darrell Bock, Scot McKnight, and Craig Blomberg are among the luminaries contributing to the discussion.

?Farmer, William R. *The Synoptic Problem: A Critical Analysis*. Dillsboro, NC: Western North Carolina Press, 1976.

> This book is a scholarly defense of the priority of Matthew.

Porter, Stanley E., and Bryan R. Dyer. *The Synoptic Problem: Four Views*. Grand Rapids: Baker Academic, 2016.

> Not reviewed for this edition. Contributors are Craig A. Evans, Mark Goodacre, David B. Peabody, and Rainer Reisner. It promises to be most enlightening.

*Stonehouse, Ned B. *Origins of the Synoptic Gospels: Some Basic Questions*. Grand Rapids: Baker, 1963.

> This book is an evangelical scholarly defense of the priority of Mark by a noted NT scholar and professor at Westminster Theological Seminary.

+?Streeter, Burnett Hillman. *The Four Gospels: A Study in Origins*. London: Macmillan, 1926.

> Long regarded as the standard work in this discussion, this book is still the starting point for much of the scholarly debate.

The Gospels

*Blomberg, Craig L. *Jesus and the Gospels: An Introduction and Survey*. 2nd ed. Nashville: B & H Academic, 2009.

> This Gold Medallion Award winner from the Evangelical Christian Publishers Association is a wonderful study of Jesus and the Gospels. Blomberg, distinguished professor of NT at Denver Seminary, has contributed a delightful volume that is both introduction and survey as well as rejoinder to some of the fuzzy thinking that has surrounded the Gospels in recent centuries. This book is on the cutting edge of current scholarship, debate, critical methods, and recent discussions on the historical Jesus. Highly recommended! "So eminently sane and readable that it should be on the reading list of anyone who has not perused a serious introduction to the Gospels in some time" (Carson, 41).

*Green, Joel B., ed. *Dictionary of Jesus and Gospels*. 2nd ed. Downers Grove: IVP Academic, 2013.

> An indispensable tool for the study of the Gospels.

Hiebert, D. Edmond. *The Gospels and Acts*. Introduction to the New Testament. Chicago: Moody, 1975.

> This introduction is a helpful guide to the study of the Gospels and the book of Acts. Published in 1975, it is now a bit dated and should be supplemented with more current works. But still very helpful particularly for undergraduate students.

*Jenkins, Philip. *Hidden Gospels: How the Search for Jesus Lost Its Way*. Oxford: Oxford University Press, 2001.

> An incisive critique of Jesus Seminar scholars and their claims that texts outside of the canon of Scripture undermine the historical validity of the Gospels.

*Scroggie, Graham. *A Guide to the Gospels*. Old Tappan, NJ: Revell, n.d.

> This book is an exceptional treatment of the Gospels. It is thorough and extremely helpful. Even after more than half a century of age, it is still worth consulting. Highly recommended! "Worth an entire shelf of books on the same subject" (Barber, 139).

Watson, Francis. *The Fourfold Gospel: A Theological Reading of the New Testament Portraits of Jesus*. Grand Rapids: Baker Academic, 2016.

> Not reviewed for this edition.

Synopsis of the Gospels

*Aland, Kurt, ed. *Synopsis of the Four Gospels*. English ed. Stuttgart: United Bible Societies, 1982.

> This edition is a revision based on Nestle-Aland's twenty-sixth edition and Greek NT third edition. The English text is the second edition of the RSV. "This is the standard Gospel synopsis and ought to be in every pastor's library. It uses the RSV (a Greek version is also available) and puts the parallel Gospel passages in very readable columns for quick comparison, making it an excellent tool for study" (**Stout**).

*Swanson, Reuben J. *The Horizontal Line Synopsis of the Gospels*. Ashville, NC: Western North Carolina Press, 1975.

> "This Synopsis takes a different visual approach to the Four Gospels by printing them in English one book at a time in horizontal lines with the parallel passages in other Gospels printed under the main text with similarities underlined. In this manner, the reader can quickly see what words and phrases are distinct in each Gospel" (**Stout**).

*Thomas, Robert L., and Stanley N. Gundry. *A Harmony of the Gospels*. New York: HarperCollins, 1991.

> "Based on the NAS version, this harmony puts the four Gospels in easy-to-read parallel columns so the reader can easily note the distinctive of each Gospel. This harmony follows an order in the Gospel of Luke, so the reader has to jump around somewhat to follow the order in the other Gospels. It also contains some excellent essays on related subjects" (**Stout**).

Matthew

!?Allen, Willoughby C. *A Critical and Exegetical Commentary on the Gospel according to St. Matthew*. ICC. Edited by Samuel Rolles Driver, Alfred Plummer, and Charles Augustus Briggs. 3rd ed. Edinburgh: T. & T. Clark, 1912.

> This commentary is not one of the stronger offerings in the old ICC series. In any event, it has been thankfully superseded by Davies and Allison's excellent work. "The most helpful part of this work is the introduction. The rest of the comments on the Greek text reflect the writer's liberal theology" (Barber, 141).

*Allison, Dale C., Jr. *Studies in Matthew: Interpretation Past and Present*. Grand Rapids: Baker Academic, 2005.

> This supplemental volume is a series of random essays on subjects that did not make it into the author's magisterial three-volume ICC work. Topics are as diverse as "The Magi's Angel," "Reading Matthew through the Church Fathers," and "Deconstructing Matthew." Interesting and provocative!

*Blomberg, Craig. *Matthew*. NAC. Edited by E. Ray Clendenen. Nashville: B & H, 1992.

> An extremely helpful work by a noted NT scholar. A wonderful resource for pastors! "A work containing great insight" (Evans, 280).

!*?Davies, W. D., and Dale C. Allison. *A Critical and Exegetical Commentary on the Gospel according to Saint Matthew, I–VII*. ICC. Edited by J. A. Emerton, C. E. B. Cranfield, and G. N. Stanton. Edinburgh: T. & T. Clark, 1988.

!*?————. *A Critical and Exegetical Commentary on the Gospel according to Saint Matthew, I–VII*. ICC. Edited by J. A. Emerton, C. E. B. Cranfield, and G. N. Stanton. Edinburgh: T. & T. Clark, 1991.

!*?————. *A Critical and Exegetical Commentary on the Gospel according to Saint Matthew, I–VII*. ICC. Edited by J. A. Emerton, C. E. B. Cranfield, and G. N. Stanton. Edinburgh: T. & T. Clark, 2004.

> These three volumes, published over a sixteen-year period, replace Allen's one-volume work from 1912 in the old ICC series. Although moderately critical, it is still an exceptional effort particularly in the area of exegesis and the presentation of different views on issues. The authors conclude that there is much redaction in the sayings of Jesus. "This work is moderately critical and leaves few stones unturned. Its attention to detail sometimes means the flow of Matthew's argument is less than clear" (Carson, 43). "About the finest exegetical tool available" (Evans, 279).

*France, R. T. *The Gospel of Matthew*. NICNT. Edited by Ned B. Stonehouse, F. F. Bruce, and Gordon D. Fee. Grand Rapids: Eerdmans, 2007.

> An exceptional treatment of Matthew's gospel is this massive commentary in the NICNT series. At over 1,100 pages, France leaves few stones unturned in this magisterial commentary. Particularly helpful is his extensive bibliography which spans more than thirty pages. This is the best general work on Matthew by far. "Judicious, well written, and informed, this is likely to become a standard work on Matthew for some time to come, whether or not one agrees with all of France's positions" (Carson, 43).

*Hagner, Donald A. *Matthew 1–13*. WBC. Edited by David A. Hubbard and Glenn W. Barker. Dallas: Word, 1993.

*———. *Matthew 14–28*. WBC. Edited by David A. Hubbard and Glenn W. Barker. Dallas: Word, 1995.

> This massive study of almost nine hundred pages offers a wealth of exegetical detail. The author, the George Eldon Ladd Chair of NT at Fuller Theological Seminary, has produced an impressive work of careful scholarship that is particularly helpful for its excellent bibliographies. "Tends to be cautious and understated on many points" (Carson, 43).

Haurerwas, Stanley. *Matthew*. BCTB. Edited by R. R. Reno. Grand Rapids: Brazos, 2006.

> As are the other volumes in Baker's Brazos Theological Commentary on the Bible series, this study is not a commentary as such, but rather an investigation into what the Gospel of Matthew has to say about today's enduring theological issues. Hauerwas, a brilliant theologian, delves into this gospel by grappling with what it has to say about the implications of Christian discipleship and how a believer should live in today's world. Along the way, the author deals with such important issues as wealth and power, marriage, homosexuality, and abortion, to name just a few, while interacting with the writings of seminal theologians such as Karl Barth and Dietrich Bonhoeffer.

Mounce, Robert H. *The Gospel of Matthew*. New International Biblical Commentary. Edited by W. Ward Gasque. Peabody: Hendrickson, 1991.

> This short study is a helpful, albeit brief, volume in many respects. It is highly regarded by many. Unfortunately the introduction is only five pages, much too brief to cover the issues required in the study of this gospel. Mounce was the president of Whitworth College in Spokane, Washington, and father of the noted Greek scholar William Mounce. Premillennial.

!*Nolland, John. *The Gospel of Matthew: A Commentary on the Greek Text*. NIGTC. Edited by I. Howard Marshall and Donald A. Hagner. Grand Rapids: Eerdmans, 2005.

> This volume is a massive commentary with much to commend it. At 1,481 pages including indexes, it is huge and comprehensive. There is an extensive general bibliography at the very beginning of the book as well as a specialized bibliography at the end of each section of commentary. One weakness is the introduction which at forty-nine pages is much too brief for such a comprehensive work. He concludes that authorship of the book by the Apostle Matthew "is most unlikely" (4). "The annotated structural outline of the book is superb and the exegesis of the Greek text more accessible than some other volumes in this series. Nolland deploys a restrained redaction criticism and a fair bit of narrative criticism" (Carson, 43). "Clearly one of the best commentaries on the Greek text" (Evans, 280).

*Osborne, Grant R. *Matthew*. Zondervan Exegetical Commentary on the New Testament. Edited by Clinton E. Arnold. Grand Rapids: Zondervan, 2010.

> This study is a massive commentary at just over 1,100 pages. As are the other volumes in this series, it is strong on exegesis of the Greek text and weak on introductory matters. The introduction is a sparse nineteen pages not including the seven-page outline of the book and the seven-page select bibliography on Matthew. That is just too sketchy for a book in a series of this magnitude. "Little attention devoted to such matters as the narrative flow or antecedent Jewish parallels" (Carson, 43).

Ridderbos, H. N. *Matthew*. Bible Student's Commentary. Translated by Ray Togtman. Reprint, Grand Rapids: Zondervan, 1987.

> This reprint edition was originally published in 1950–51 in Dutch under the title *Korte Verklaring der Heilege Schrift—Matthew* in the Netherlands. The author was a highly regarded Dutch Reformed scholar from the mid-twentieth century. This commentary is a helpful treatment of the English text that is of particular help to preachers and beginning students. "Offers expositors quite a lot of help" (Rosscup, 217). Amillennial.

*Turner, David L. *Matthew*. BECNT. Edited by Robert W. Yarbrough and Robert W. Stein. Grand Rapids: Baker Academic, 2008.

> This volume is a massive commentary that is very helpful to the scholar and advanced student. As part of the excellent BECNT, it is based on the Greek text and is very detailed. "He rejects any appeal to redaction criticism . . . but is sensitive to the demands of narrative criticism" (Carson, 44). Premillennial. Progressive dispensational.

*Wilkins, Michael J. *Matthew*. NIVAC. Edited by Terry Muck. Grand Rapids: Zondervan, 2004.

> An extremely helpful and practical volume.

The Sermon on the Mount

*Lloyd-Jones, D. Martyn. *Studies in the Sermon on the Mount*. 2 vols. Grand Rapids: Eerdmans, 1959–60.

> These two volumes contain an exceptional compilation of sermons preached at Westminster Chapel in London on successive Sunday mornings. The form of the messages in the book is just as they were preached. They were not edited for a reading audience, but dictated as is. This is expository preaching at its very best. My heart was warmed and my mind challenged as I worked through both volumes. "This is one of the finest expositions of the sermon by an evangelical preacher of the modern era, a deeply perceptive man relevant to his age and a man of scholarly awareness. He is stimulating, practical, often wise in his interpretations of problem verses. It is well worth the money" (Rosscup, 215). "A lengthy, reverent, penetrating exposition, which deserves a place on every pastor's shelf" (Evans, 288)!

*McKnight, Scot. *Sermon on the Mount*. Story of God Bible Commentary. Edited by Tremper Longman III and Scot McKnight. Grand Rapids: Zondervan, 2013.

> This study is a scholarly treatment of the Sermon on the Mount that is also eminently readable. In the SGBC series, each passage of Scripture is examined from three angles: "Listen to the Story," "Explain the Story," and "Live the Story." It is in the third section of each chapter that McKnight really shines. The author examines the text and seeks to apply it to today's world, how the text might be lived out in the contemporary life of the church. McKnight is especially helpful in his discussion on the divorce question that is both scholarly in its examination of the many different views while, at the same time, pastoral in its application. The bibliographic notations are found in the footnotes which can be annoying if one is looking for a separate bibliography. Anabaptist.

*Palmer, Earl F. *The Enormous Exception: Meeting Christ in the Sermon on the Mount*. Waco, TX: Word, 1986.

> A tremendously practical and insightful compilation of fifteen studies by a leading Presbyterian preacher.

*Quarles, Charles. *Sermon on the Mount: Restoring Christ's Message to the Modern Church*. NAC Studies in Bible & Theology. Edited by E. Ray Clendenen. Nashville: B & H Academic, 2011.

> This study is a commentary that combines scholarship with exposition and application. It is engaging and readable. It seeks to bridge the gap between the ancient Jewish context of the sermon and its modern twenty-first-century application and in this it succeeds. The author's conclusions are based on sound exegesis. "More important yet for the diligent pastor" (Carson, 51). Baptist.

*Stott, John R. W. *The Message of the Sermon on the Mount (Matthew 5–7)*. BST. Edited by John R. W. Stott. Downers Grove: InterVarsity, 1978.

> This book is an outstanding exposition of the Sermon on the Mount by one of the leading evangelical writers of the twentieth century. Any book written by Stott is well worth obtaining. This book suffers from the lack of an index and bibliography.

Mark

*+Alexander, J. A. *Commentary on the Gospel of Mark*. New York: Scribner, 1864. Reprint, Minneapolis: Klock & Klock, 1980.

> This commentary is a classic study by a nineteenth-century Princeton professor. It is massive and very detailed. "A heartwarming study which does not adequately explain the theme of Mark's Gospel" (Barber, 144). "The author's learning and care have made it invaluable" (Spurgeon, 158). Reformed.

Cole, Alan. *The Gospel according to St. Mark*. TNTC. Edited by R. V. G. Tasker. Grand Rapids: Eerdmans, 1961.

> Though now rather dated, this volume is still fairly serviceable for pastors and laypersons.

!*Cranfield, C. E. B. *The Gospel according to St. Mark*. Cambridge Greek Testament Commentary. Edited by C. F. D. Moule. London: Cambridge University Press, 1959.

> Although this study by the late University of Durham NT scholar is now over a half-century old, it is a tribute to its enduring excellence that it remains one of the best treatments of the Greek text. A masterful treatment! "A valuable exegetical study" (Barber, 144). "Now very dated, but it says something for the quality of his work and the reverent and understated nature of his prose that this relatively short commentary is still in print" (Carson, 52). "Clear, insightful, and refreshing" (Rosscup, 220).

*Edwards, James R. *The Gospel according to Mark*. PNTC. Edited by D. A. Carson. Grand Rapids: Eerdmans, 2001.

> An excellent commentary in an impressive series. More accessible than the works by Cranfield, Stein, and France. Very good for pastors with limited Greek skills. It is interesting that Bauer does not even list this commentary. "Clearly written, good and solid, offering a satisfying exegetical treatment and theological discussion" (Evans, 290).

!*Evans, Craig. *Mark 8:27—16:20*. WBC. Edited by David A. Hubbard and Glenn W. Barker. Waco, TX: Word, 2001.

> Ably completes the commentary that Guelich began. Of great assistance in working with the Greek text.

*France, R. T. *The Gospel of Mark*. NIGTC. Edited by I. Howard Marshall and Donald A. Hagner. Grand Rapids: Eerdmans, 2002.

> Pride of place as the best commentary available on this gospel is France's laudable study. It is based on the Greek text, but is not too technical for the average reader. At 688 pages of text, it is quite thorough. "Remarkably accessible and includes a healthy mix of history, theology, social context, even warmth" (Carson, 51).

*Garland, David E. *Mark*. NIVAC. Edited by Terry Muck. Grand Rapids: Zondervan, 1996.

> An excellent and very helpful offering in a very practical series.

!?Gould, Ezra P. *A Critical and Exegetical Commentary on the Gospel according to St. Mark*. ICC. Edited by Samuel Rolles Driver, Alfred Plummer, and Charles Augustus Briggs. Edinburgh: T. & T. Clark, 1896.

> As are all of the ICC volumes, this old commentary is extremely helpful for its exegetical insights, but at over 120 years of age it has been superseded by more recent works. It is quite technical and only for those pastors with a scholarly bent. It is worth obtaining if it can be purchased secondhand, but it should not be the student or pastor's first choice. "Can safely be ignored" (Evans, 293).

!*Guelish, Robert A. *Mark 1—8:26*. WBC. Edited by David A. Hubbard and Glenn W. Barker. Waco, TX: Word, 1989.

> An exhaustive and extremely detailed scholarly work that was not completed due to the author's untimely death. The commentary was completed by Craig Evans.

Healy, Mary. *The Gospel of Mark*. CCSS. Edited by Peter S. Williamson and Mary Healy. Grand Rapids: Baker Academic, 2008.

> This offering in the Catholic Commentary on Sacred Scripture, by a noted professor of Sacred Scripture at Sacred Heart Major Seminary, is particularly well done and moderately critical. "Well written and tries to link literary observations with the 'living tradition' of the Catholic Church" (Carson, 53).

Hendriksen, William. *Exposition of the Gospel according to Mark*. New Testament Commentary. Grand Rapids: Baker, 1975.

> This study is a helpful volume that is accessible to the layperson, yet still helpful for pastors and students. One criticism is that it does very little interaction with the scholarly literature of the author's time. "Making its own unique contribution to the study of Mark's Gospel, this work will be eagerly sought after by preachers of all persuasions" (Barber). "One of the better works of a less technical nature" (Rosscup, 222). Reformed.

*Hiebert, David Edmond. *Mark: A Portrait of the Servant*. Chicago: Moody, 1974.

> A conservative commentary that focuses thematically on Christ as the servant. A popular treatment that is quite dated, but is still tremendously helpful to the preacher. "A reverent and insightful treatment which deserves the attention of the Bible teacher and expository preacher" (Barber).

Martin, Ralph. *Mark: Evangelist and Theologian*. Contemporary Evangelical Perspectives. Grand Rapids: Academie, 1972.

> A companion volume to Marshall's *Luke: Historian and Theologian*, this book is a scholarly treatment of discussions that were trending in the early 1970s on this gospel.

*+Morison, James. *A Practical Commentary on the Gospel according to St. Mark*. 4th ed. London: Hodder and Stoughton, 1884. Reprint, Minneapolis: Klock & Klock, 1981.

> This classic study is a very rich treatment based upon the English text. "A very full, devotional treatment. The overall strength of this exposition far outweighs its syntactical deficiencies" (Barber, 145). "A deeply learned work; we know of none more thorough. . . . Set a high price upon this production" (Spurgeon, 158).

!*?+Plummer, Alfred. *The Gospel according to St. Mark*. Cambridge: Cambridge University, 1914. Reprint, Grand Rapids: Baker, 1982.

> This commentary is a classic treatment of the Greek text, first published in 1914, by the master of University College, Durham in the late nineteenth century. It is especially helpful on exegesis, but, as with all older commentaries, should be supplemented with more recent works. Anglican.

Robertson, A. T. *Studies in Mark's Gospel*. Revised and edited by Heber F. Peacock. Nashville: Broadman, 1958.

> First published in 1919 in book form under the title *Making Good in the Ministry*, the essays in this compilation first appeared in print in such publications as the *Biblical World*, the *Expositor*, the *Homiletic Review*, and the *Sunday School Times*. They deal with diverse topics such as the person of John Mark, the influence of Peter upon him, and the person and work of Christ in miracles, parables, teaching, and preaching. Robertson was a first-rate Greek scholar who knew his topic well.

*Strauss, Mark L. *Mark*. Zondervan Exegetical Commentary on the New Testament. Edited by Clinton E. Arnold. Grand Rapids: Zondervan, 2014.

> In keeping with the series objective, this commentary, by a professor of NT at Bethel Seminary in San Diego, is an excellent treatment of the Greek text of this gospel for those with a working knowledge of Greek. It is not overly technical and quite accessible even to those with no knowledge of Greek. At 747 pages of text, it is thorough, without being cumbersome. The author holds to Markan priority with John Mark having the strongest claim to authorship. The two main themes of this gospel, according to Strauss, are Jesus as the Mighty Messiah and Son of God and Jesus as the suffering servant of the Lord. Highly recommended!

!*+Swete, Henry Barclay. *Commentary on Mark*. London: Macmillan, 1913. Reprint, Grand Rapids: Kregel, 1977.

> First published in 1898, this fine exegetical work is moderately conservative and a true classic of scholarly endeavor. Swete was the Regius Professor of Divinity at Cambridge University prior to retiring in 1915. It is now dated and should be supplemented with more recent works. "Long regarded as one of the finest exegetical treatments available" (Barber, 145). "Dull and stodgy in spite of its thorough scholarship" (Carson, 54). Anglican.

Luke

*+Arndt, William F. *Luke*. Concordia Classic Commentary Series. St. Louis: Concordia, 1956.

> This commentary, by a conservative Lutheran NT scholar and professor at Concordia Seminary, is thorough and exhaustive and has rightly been regarded as a classic by many. The author is well known for his work on the standard *A Greek English Lexicon of the New Testament and Other Early Christian Literature*. Surprisingly recommended by Danker.

*Bock, Darrell. *Luke*. BECNT. Edited by Robert W. Yarbrough and Robert H. Stein. 2 vols. Grand Rapids: Baker Academic, 1994–96.

> Vies with Garland's work as the best evangelical works for the pastor. Bock is a top-notch NT scholar and a prolific and clear writer. "None can match his thoroughness" (Evans, 298). Premillennial. Progressive dispensational.

*———. *Luke*. NIVAC. Edited by Terry Muck. Grand Rapids: Zondervan, 1996.

> A most practical and accessible work which distills the essence of the author's BECNT work.

?Creed, John Martin. *The Gospel according to St. Luke*. London: Macmillan, 1930.

> A radically critical work that was a first choice by Danker. Outdated and of little use to preachers today. "Can be safely ignored" (Evans, 300).

*Edwards, James R. *The Gospel according to Luke*. PNTC. Edited by D. A. Carson. Grand Rapids: Eerdmans, 2015.

> Not reviewed for this edition.

Erdman, Charles R. *The Gospel of Luke*. Philadelphia: Westminster, 1956.

> This brief study is helpful to the layperson. "A devotional and practical exposition of the theme of Luke's Gospel. Excellent as a study guide" (Barber, 147). Reformed.

!*?Fitzmyer, Joseph A. *The Gospel according to Luke*. AB. Edited by William F. Albright and David Noel Freedman. 2 vols. Garden City: Doubleday, 1981–85.

> An exceptional commentary by an internationally recognized expert on the Aramaic and Semitic background of the NT. Roman Catholic.

*Garland, David E. *Luke*. Zondervan Exegetical Commentary on the New Testament. Edited by Clinton E. Arnold. Grand Rapids: Zondervan, 2011.

In keeping with the series objective, this commentary, by the dean and William B. Hinson Professor of Christian Scriptures at George W. Truett Seminary, Baylor University, is an excellent treatment of the Greek text of this gospel for those with a working knowledge of the language. It is also extremely helpful to those with no knowledge of Greek. At 983 pages of text, the length of this treatment is about right for a work of this magnitude. Unfortunately, the introduction is a sketchy twenty pages, including over three pages of outline. "Quite strong at the exegetical level and helpful at the homiletical level. . . . This commentary is a tad verbose, but at 1039 pages Garland has space to address most issues" (Carson, 58).

*Geldenhuys, Norval. *Commentary on the Gospel of Luke*. NICNT. Edited by F. F. Bruce. Grand Rapids: Eerdmans, 1951.

Now retired and replaced by the volume by Green, this commentary was the first offering in the NICNT. Still helpful for pastors. Reformed. Amillennial.

*+Godet, F. *The Gospel of St. Luke*. 2 vols. 5th ed. Reprint, Edinburgh: T. & T. Clark, 1976.

There are many good reasons why this superb commentary has remained in print for over a century since its original publication. This is a superlative treatment of Luke's gospel and a well-deserved classic. Purchase it if it can be found, but supplement it with the works of Bock, Green, Fitzmyer, Marshall, and/or Garland. This massive commentary, originally published in 1870, has long been considered a classic in its treatment of the Greek text. It is exhaustive and detailed and of particular assistance in exegesis of the text. "An exhaustive, technical commentary that ably defends the cardinal doctrines of the Christian faith while expounding the text. Deserves a place on the shelf of every pastor" (Barber, 147). "Godet is virtually pre-critical but can be valuable. Apart from his digressions on old and forgotten controversies, he is consistently clear and to the point. He is still worth using in conjunction with a more recent work" (Carson, 62).

*Green, Joel B. *The Gospel of Luke*. NICNT. Edited by Ned B. Stonehouse, F. F. Bruce, and Gordon D. Fee. Grand Rapids: Eerdmans, 1997.

This volume replaces the one by Geldenhuys, which is now retired after more than sixty years of service. Although this is a very fine commentary in many respects, it is not nearly as conservative as its predecessor and it is sometimes difficult to nail down just what Green believes on a particular topic. Not the strongest NICNT offering. "Its forte is narrative historiography or discourse analysis" (Carson, 58).

*Hendriksen, William. *Exposition of the Gospel of Luke*. New Testament Commentary. Grand Rapids: Baker, 1978.

> At 1,082 pages of text, this massive commentary is the author's longest and up to his high standards of scholarship. It was published in 1978 and needs to be supplemented with more recent works. It is particularly helpful and accessible to preachers. "Fills a long-felt need for a comprehensive, scholarly exposition of this neglected Gospel. Structures Luke's thematic presentation around Christ's words, 'the work Thou gavest Me to do,' and then treats Christ's ministry in terms of its inauguration, continuation, and consummation. Recommended" (Barber)! "Freely engages in homiletical whimsy" (Carson, 62). Reformed.

*+Kelly, William. *An Exposition of the Gospel of Luke*. London: Pickering and Inglis, n.d. Reprint, Minneapolis: Klock & Klock, 1981.

> This commentary is a devotional classic. It is nontechnical, easy to read, and characterized by evangelical warmth. "A clear readable exposition.... Readers will find themselves blessed and enriched" (Barber). "Useful" (Carson, 62).

!*Marshall, I. Howard. *The Gospel of Luke*. NIGTC. Edited by I. Howard Marshall and W. Ward Gasque. Grand Rapids: Eerdmans, 1978.

> This wonderful volume is an exceptionally detailed and learned commentary on the Greek text by a leading NT scholar and professor at the University of Aberdeen. It is a work of impeccable scholarship and one of the better evangelical treatments available. "Unfortunately the prose is so densely packed, owing not least to the fact that the notes are incorporated into the text, that some will find it hard going. Moreover, it presupposes reasonable proficiency in the Greek text. Those with the requisite skills will benefit greatly from reading it" (Carson, 58). "It is a serious attempt to explain verses in detail, with a keen perception of problems and different recent views, and an attempt to take a stand on most issues.... The author has sought to provide for serious evangelical scholars a technically and exegetically-based answer to Bultmanian-type theories that are destructive to the Gospel's real authority" (Rosscup, 229).

*————. *Luke: Historian and Theologian*. Contemporary Evangelical Perspectives. Grand Rapids: Zondervan, 1970.

> An important, but dated, work that places Luke's theology on an equal footing with his work as a historian. "An admirable and even invaluable study in its time but is now very dated" (Carson, 63).

*+Morgan, G. Campbell. *The Gospel according to Luke*. Old Tappan, NJ: Revell, 1931.

> This volume is one of Morgan's stronger offerings. A masterful exposition by the predecessor of Lloyd-Jones at Westminster Chapel in London. "A carefully reasoned exposition which adheres quite closely to Luke's argument and provides an example of expository preaching at its best" (Barber, 147). Premillennial.

*Morris, Leon. *The Gospel according to St. Luke*. TNTC. Edited by R. V. G. Tasker. Grand Rapids: Eerdmans, 1974.

> This volume is an excellent commentary that is surprisingly detailed in light of the limitations of the series. Morris is a careful and lucid NT scholar and always worth reading. "A clear, forthright presentation of the facts surrounding the authorship and date of this Gospel. . . . A handy and helpful volume" (Barber). "Good value, one of the better volumes in the series . . . he skates over some difficult questions and skirts some contemporary issues" (Carson, 61).

*Parsons, Mikeal C. *Luke*. Paideia. Edited by M. C. Parsons, C. H. Talbert, and B. W. Longenecker. Grand Rapids: Baker Academic, 2013.

> This is a very fine commentary with regard to its treatment of the text. However, the introduction at just seventeen pages is much too brief for a work of this nature. Having said that, it is still worth acquiring.

*+?Plummer, Alfred. *A Critical and Exegetical Commentary on the Gospel according to St. Luke*. ICC. Edited by Samuel Rolles Driver, Alfred Plummer, and Charles Augustus Briggs. 5th ed. Edinburgh: T. & T. Clark, 1901.

> This moderately liberal work was long considered to be the best treatment of the Greek text. It is still a masterful treatment that well deserves to be considered a classic, but its age mandates that it be supplemented with more recent works such as that by Marshall, Bock, or Green. "A most exhaustive and helpful treatment of the Greek text" (Barber, 148). "Was once good on the Greek text, but its reputation lingers on after later writers have superseded the work" (Carson, 61).

John

!*? Barrett, C. K. *The Gospel according to St. John*. Philadelphia: Westminster, 1955.

> This volume is a moderately liberal work of great scholarship by a noted NT scholar and professor at the University of Durham. This treatment is primarily for advanced students with good Greek tools. "This is probably the best

critical commentary on the Greek text, especially the grammar, where he is superior to Westcott, Godet, and others" (Rosscup, 230). "This work is nevertheless not only elegantly and lucidly written but also usually profound in its grasp of John's theological message and rightly skeptical about many modern literary and historical reconstructions" (Carson, 66). "Indispensable for the student and scholarly pastor doing exegesis of the Greek text" (Evans, 304).

!Beasley-Murray, George R. *John*. WBC. Edited by David A. Hubbard and Glenn W. Barker. Rev. ed. Nashville: Nelson, 1999.

There are very few substantive changes from the original 1987 volume published by Word to this one. This commentary appears to be quite a bit weaker in the area of exegesis than other offerings in the series. This work is moderately critical as are many in the WBC series. Beasley-Murray denies Johannine authorship, but argues against Bultmann's rearrangement of the text. At just over four hundred pages, this volume appears to be a bit "thin" to be able to do the fourth gospel justice. The author's treatment of the Passion Narrative is a strength of this work. "Some readers will be less than convinced by the source-critical 'solution' to the challenges of chapter 20" (Carson, 66).

!?Bernard, J. H. *A Critical and Exegetical Commentary on the Gospel according to St. John*. ICC. Edited by A. H. McNeile. 2 vols. New York: Scribner, 1929.

This highly respected commentary is the product of early twentieth-century liberal scholarship from an Irish archbishop. It offers good exegetical insights, but at over eighty-six years of age is very outdated and out of touch with recent scholarly discussions. "The work is thoroughly uneven, occasionally good, but the best of his material has inevitably been culled" (Carson, 69). Recommended by Danker.

*Brown, Raymond E. *The Gospel according to John*. AB. Edited by William Foxwell Albright and David Noel Freedman. 2 vols. Garden City: Doubleday, 1966.

This volume is an exceptional commentary by a noted Roman Catholic NT scholar. It is one of the better commentaries on this gospel written in the past fifty years. It is also one of the very best in the AB series. "Brown brings immense learning to the task, and leaves few stones unturned" (Rosscup, 232). "Of particular value to serious and discerning students of the NT. Brown's moderate historiography ably complements Barrett's scholarly volume" (Barber, 148). "A fine representative of moderate NT Roman Catholic scholarship" (Carson, 64).

*Bruce, F. F. *The Gospel of John*. Grand Rapids: Eerdmans, 1983.

F. F. Bruce was one of the evangelical world's leading NT scholars of the twentieth century. Any book by him is well worth obtaining. This commentary is no exception. It is very readable and not overly technical. "Probably the best of the 'popular' commentaries" (Carson, 71). "Overall, it is a very fine commentary by one of the leading evangelicals of recent decades" (Rosscup, 232).

*Burge, Gary M. *John*. NIVAC. Edited by Terry Muck. Grand Rapids: Zondervan, 2000.

A capable and practical treatment based upon solid scholarship that is highly recommended for pastors. "Bold, thought-provoking application" (Evans, 304).

*Carson, D. A. *The Gospel according to John*. PNTC. Edited by D. A. Carson. Grand Rapids: Eerdmans, 1991.

Although about a quarter century old, this remains one of the very best midlevel commentaries on this gospel from an evangelical perspective. The author staunchly defends apostolic authorship.

Erdman, Charles R. *The Gospel of John*. Philadelphia: Westminster, 1944.

This study is a devotional treatment based upon the ASV primarily for the nonspecialist. Ideal for laypersons.

!*+Godet, Frederic Louis. *Commentary on John's Gospel*. New York: Funk & Wagnalls, 1886. Reprint, Grand Rapids: Kregel Publications, 1978.

This massive commentary, based on the Greek text by a noted nineteenth-century Swiss Protestant Reformed scholar, is a model of impeccable scholarship. At over one thousand pages, this is a most comprehensive and impressive effort. "A monumental work by a great theologian and an able defender of the faith. Thorough and exhaustive without being elaborate and verbose" (Barber, 149).

*Keener, Craig S. *The Gospel of John*. 2 vols. Peabody: Hendrickson, 2003. Reprint, Grand Rapids: Baker Academic, 2010.

As usual, Keener has written an amazingly comprehensive (and long) commentary from a reliable evangelical perspective. Includes a plethora of background data! "Indispensable for the serious student" (Carson, 64). "Students willing to work through the astonishing amount of detail will find this set a masterful guide" (Evans, 305).

*Klink, Edward W., III. *John*. Zondervan Exegetical Commentary on the New Testament. Edited by Clinton E. Arnold. Grand Rapids: Zondervan, 2016.

Not reviewed for this edition.

*Köstenberger, Andreas J. *John*. BECNT. Edited by Robert W. Yarbrough and Robert H. Stein. Grand Rapids: Baker Academic, 2004.

> A solid, dependable commentary that is bedrock conservative by a noted NT professor at Southeastern Baptist Theological Seminary. Extensive bibliography.

*Michaels, J. Ramsey. *The Gospel of John*. NICNT. Edited by Gordon Fee. Grand Rapids: Eerdmans, 2010.

> A massive treatment that ably replaces the volume by Morris in the series. Many pastors may not be inclined to wade through the roughly 1,100 pages of detail, but there is much to commend this impressive commentary. It is a first choice of Carson with good reason. "The writing style is superb, and insights abound on just about every page" (Carson, 64).

*Morris, Leon. *The Gospel according to John*. NICNT. Edited by F. F. Bruce. Grand Rapids: Eerdmans, 1971.

> This study is an outstanding commentary in the usually reliable NICNT series by the noted NT scholar and principal of Ridley College, Melbourne. This is one of the best volumes in the series and should be purchased if available. It has been replaced by Michaels in the series. "A work of superlative scholarship which not only replaces the majestic work by Westcott, but surpasses Barrett as well" (Barber, 149). "An encyclopedic treatment from the strictly 'earthly-historical' view of Jesus's ministry. . . . One of the major conservative commentaries on John, and its footnotes are a mine of quotable material" (Carson, 66).

*Palmer, Earl F. *The Intimate Gospel: Studies in John*. Waco, TX: Word, 1978.

> This delightful study is not a verse-by-verse commentary, but rather is comprised of forty-two brief sequential chapters of expositions on this gospel. This book by a Presbyterian pastor and master preacher is highly recommended.

!Plummer, Alfred. *The Gospel according to St. John*. Cambridge: Cambridge University Press, 1882. Reprint, Grand Rapids: Baker, 1981.

> This commentary was originally published as part of the Cambridge Bible for Schools and Colleges in 1882. It is based on the Greek text and consists primarily of brief notes on the text rather than a detailed full treatment. Not Plummer's best work. Anglican.

*Ridderbos, Herman. *The Gospel of John: A Theological Commentary*. Translated by John Vriend. Grand Rapids: Eerdmans, 1997.

> Ridderbos, a master theologian who was professor of NT at the Theological School of the Reformed Churches of the Netherlands in Kampen until his

death in 2007, sees the gospel as a profoundly theological book. In this unusual commentary originally written in Dutch, he interacts with the myriad twentieth-century interpretations of John and establishes his own understanding of the theology of this gospel. "A major contribution" (Carson, 67).

*?Schnackenburg, Rudolf. *The Gospel according to St John*. 3 vols. Herder: Freiburg, 1965. Reprint, New York: Crossroad, 1987.

This work is a standard critical commentary by a liberal Roman Catholic NT scholar and professor at the University of Wurzburg. This commentary is a massive treatment of the gospel combined with impeccable scholarship. "Moderate critical stance" (Carson, 65). Roman Catholic.

Tenney, Merrill C. *John: The Gospel of Belief*. Grand Rapids: Eerdmans, 1948.

This study does not pretend to be a verse-by-verse commentary, but is rather an analytical study of the text utilizing alliterative outlines. "It is very good in helping the student to see the movement in the book though it should not be expected to get down into exegetical detail as the verse-by-verse studies can" (Rosscup, 238–39).

Thomas, David. *The Gospel of John: Expository and Homiletical Commentary*. London: Dickson, 1885. Reprint, Grand Rapids: Kregel, 1980.

This old study can still be used by preachers with profit. The homiletical outlines can help to prime the preacher's pump when the well is almost dry. Very devotional.

!*+Westcott, B. F. *The Gospel according to St. John*. Speaker's Commentary. Cambridge, 1881. Reprint, Grand Rapids: Eerdmans, 1975.

For many decades this commentary was considered the standard treatment of the Greek text of the Gospel of John. Despite its age, it remains one of the best exegetical studies of the Greek text. His writing is difficult to follow sometimes and the argument becomes submerged in the details. Still, any student or preacher studying this gospel should consult this volume. "This is a good work to consult in any thorough study of John, and the student who wants to build his library with the best will not pass it by" (Rosscup, 239). "Westcott offers thorough exegesis with hints at applications that are there for the discerning reader, but the reputation of the commentary grew when there was little better. Moreover, his exegesis was done when scholars were more tightly tied to classical Greek than to Hellenistic Greek. His works are worth consulting but no longer the first priority" (Carson, 70).

Acts of the Apostles

*+Alexander, Joseph Addison. *Commentary on the Acts of the Apostles*. New York: Scribner, Armstrong, 1875. Reprint, Minneapolis: Klock & Klock, 1980.

> This commentary is, at 960 pages, an exhaustive and satisfying treatment of the text. Originally published in 1875, it is hopelessly out of date with respect to critical research and needs to be supplemented with modern works. However, it is a true classic and useful to pastors and students alike. Purchase if found. "An exhaustive, thorough exposition which gives valuable help on the meaning of Greek words . . . and provides preachers with an abundance of usable material" (Barber, 151). "In all respects a work of the highest merit" (Spurgeon, 162). Reformed.

!*?Barrett, C. K. *Acts*. ICC. 2 vols. Edited by J. A. Emerton, C. E. B. Cranfield, and G. N. Stanton. London: T. & T. Clark, 1994–98.

> A monument of towering scholarship, this massive moderately critical work is a *tour de force* capping a brilliant career. This offering is from the new ICC series and is prohibitively expensive in hardcover, but a paperback edition came out in 2004 costing a relatively cheaper $60 per copy. For those not willing to wade through the mounds of exegetical detail, try the author's *Acts: A Shorter Commentary*, published in 2002, a condensed and much cheaper version. "One must not ignore the magnum opus of C. K. Barrett" (Carson, 76).

*Bock, Darrell. *Acts*. BECNT. Edited by Robert W. Yarbrough and Robert H. Stein. Grand Rapids: Baker Academic, 2007.

> An excellent follow-up to the author's two-volume set on the Gospel of Luke. One cannot go wrong with this commentary. "A thorough and competent commentary" (Carson, 76).

!*Bruce, F. F. *The Acts of the Apostles*. Grand Rapids: Eerdmans, 1952.

> This very scholarly volume is the first of two commentaries by the author on the Acts of the Apostles. This commentary, first published in 1951, is based solely on the Greek text and should not be confused with the author's work in the NICNT series. It is entirely exegetical and more technical than the NICNT volume. It was revised and enlarged in 1990 by the author prior to his death. "Offers substantial technical information" (Carson, 77).

*———. *Commentary on the Book of Acts*. NICNT. Edited by F. F. Bruce. Grand Rapids: Eerdmans, 1954.

> Until the publication of the works by Peterson and Bock, this commentary remained the default study for pastors and students who wanted a general

work that was not too technical. It too was revised and enlarged by the author prior to his passing. However, this volume and the preceding one need to be supplemented with more recent works. "Perhaps the best expository work for the pastor. Sound exposition based upon careful exegesis and a thorough knowledge of the historical background" (Barber, 152). "Very influential in the past, but . . . now largely outstripped by Peterson and Bock" (Carson, 77). "It remains the finest commentary on Acts as to exposition in detail. . . . He shows a fine grasp of pertinent history, a sound explanation of most passages, and insights on many of the problems" (Rosscup, 241).

Erdman, Charles R. *The Acts: An Exposition*. Philadelphia: Westminster, 1919.

This commentary is a brief, but helpful, exposition of the text based on the ASV. It is geared toward the nonspecialist. "A devotional and practical commentary of great help to preachers" (Barber, 152).

*Fernando, Ajith. *Acts*. NIVAC. Edited by Terry Muck. Grand Rapids: Zondervan, 1998.

A capable and practical exposition by the National Director of Youth for Christ in Sri Lanka. "Very good indeed" (Carson, 78).

!*+?Foakes-Jackson, F. J., and Kirsopp Lake. *The Beginnings of Christianity*. 5 vols. London: Macmillan, 1939.

This monumental study is a very detailed and thorough work on Acts. It is a true classic and regrettably OP. It should be purchased if found. I was fortunate to pick up my copy when a friend had to sell part of his library due to space limitations. A first choice of Danker. "A technical, theologically liberal work which does contain valuable information on the background of the first century AD in volumes 1 and 2, a reconstruction of the text in volume 3, and a commentary with notes in volumes 4 and 5" (Barber, 152).

!*Gasque, W. Ward. *A History of the Criticism of the Acts of the Apostles*. Grand Rapids: Eerdmans, 1975.

This study began as a doctoral thesis at the University of Manchester under F. F. Bruce. It is not a commentary and thus would be of limited value to the pastor and casual student. The author centered his discussion around the central problems of criticism and introduction that came to light during the nineteenth and twentieth centuries in Acts studies. He upholds the essential historical reliability of Luke's account. "Beginning with F. C. Baur and the Tubingen school, Gasque traces the *Actaforschung* down to the present time. His coverage is remarkably full, and he provides an important basis for the future study of Luke's writings" (Barber). "Invaluable for the serious student" (Carson, 81).

*+Gloag, Paton J. *A Critical and Exegetical Commentary on the Acts of the Apostles.* 2 vols. Edinburgh: T. & T. Clark. Reprint, Minneapolis: Klock & Klock, 1870.

> This masterful exposition is based on careful exegesis of the Greek text and remains, after almost a century and a half, a true classic. It is regrettably out of print again, but should be purchased if found. "Dr. Gloag's expository studies are his finest monument. In his treatment of the Book of Acts, he reveals his mastery of the subject matter, his practical, pastoral insights, and his ability to bridge the centuries with relevant application of principles which are pertinent to the needs of the Church today" (Barber, 152). "For my purposes, I have found it unsurpassed by any similar work in the English language. It shows a thorough mastery of the material, philology, history, and literature pertaining to this range of study, and a skill in the use of this knowledge, which places it in the first class of modern expositions" (Spurgeon, 164). Reformed.

Harrison, Everett F. *Acts: The Expanding Church.* Chicago: Moody, 1975.

> This commentary is a readable treatment of the English text geared to the pastor, layperson, or student. It is weak on its approach to problem passages. "A well-organized and non-technical commentary by a fine evangelical scholar. . . . The commentary reads easily and comes directly to the point" (Rosscup, 243).

*Keener, Craig S. *Acts: An Exegetical Commentary: Introduction and 1:1—2:47.* Grand Rapids: Baker Academic, 2012.

*———. *Acts: An Exegetical Commentary: Introduction and 3:1—14:28.* Grand Rapids: Baker Academic, 2013.

*———. *Acts: An Exegetical Commentary: Introduction and 15:1—23:35.* Grand Rapids: Baker Academic, 2014.

*———. *Acts: An Exegetical Commentary: Introduction and 24:1—28:31.* Grand Rapids: Baker Academic, 2015.

> At 4,459 pages including bibliographies and indexes, it is probably safe to conclude that this four-volume monster of a commentary is the longest commentary on Acts, or any other book of the NT for that matter, ever written. A remarkably prolific writer, Keener churned out a volume per year from 2012 through 2015. The result is an incredible body of work on which future and past commentaries on the Acts will be judged. This treatment of the book is full of detailed exegesis of the text, minute historical detail from the classical world, and meaningful interaction with current Acts scholarship. The number of works cited and bibliographies are exhaustive. In addition, more than forty-five thousand extrabiblical ancient references are cited in the text. The final volume includes a searchable CD-ROM version of the bibliography

and indexes. No serious student or scholar of Acts should be without this set. A remarkable scholarly achievement! A huge commentary at an equally huge price! "The range of topics is impressive. . . . The commentary has the Keener earmarks: deceptively straightforward prose, great learning, and impressive bibliography" (Carson, 76–77).

Kurz, William S. *Acts of the Apostles*. CCSS. Edited by Peter S. Williamson and Mary Healy. Grand Rapids: Baker Academic, 2013.

This offering in the Catholic Commentary on Sacred Scripture series is by a respected Roman Catholic NT scholar and professor at Marquette University. In line with the goals of the series, this commentary blends the best of current Roman Catholic scholarship with the richness of that church's tradition.

*Marshall, I. Howard. *The Acts of the Apostles*. TNTC. Edited by R. V. G. Tasker. Grand Rapids: Eerdmans, 1980.

This volume replaces the 1959 offering by E. M. Blaiklock. It is an excellent treatment of the text and much more detailed than one might expect in the TNTC series, which has a deserved reputation for brevity. Published in 1980, it should be supplemented with more recent works. "Very useful" (Carson, 77). "This, with Bruce's NIC work, is one of the finer, more often helpful evangelical commentaries on Acts in recent times" (Rosscup, 246).

*Morgan, G. Campbell. *The Acts of the Apostles*. Old Tappan, NJ: Revell, 1924.

This study is a fine exposition of the English text by the "prince of expositors." It is not a verse-by-verse commentary. It is almost a century old and not much help on critical matters, but its application of the text is second to none. "By many regarded as being *the* most important single expository work for the pastor" (Barber, 14). "One of Morgan's better commentaries and one which the student can profitably consult" (Rosscup, 246).

Ogilvie, Lloyd J. *Acts*. CC. Edited by Lloyd J. Ogilvie. Waco, TX: Word, 1983.

This volume is more of an exposition than a commentary. It can be useful to the preacher who has done his exegetical work on the text and has supplemented it with more substantial works. "Contains useful material but is sometimes more interested in communication than in careful understanding of the material to be communicated" (Carson, 80).

*Peterson, David G. *The Acts of the Apostles*. PNTC. Edited by D. A. Carson. Grand Rapids: Eerdmans, 2009.

This helpful commentary is perhaps the best mid-level commentary available. This volume, at over seven hundred pages of text, is a serious contribution that does not get bogged down in details and is accessible to nonspecialists. "The first choice today for pastors and students. . . . It reflects careful work across the gamut of integral disciplines: text criticism, grammatical exegesis, historical considerations, literary criticism, and, above all, robust theological reflection" (Carson, 75).

*Pohill, John B. *Acts*. NAC. Edited by E. Ray Clendenen. Nashville: Holman Reference, 1992.

A solid commentary that will particularly benefit pastors by a professor of NT at the Southern Baptist Theological Seminary in Louisville. "Well worth buying" (Evans, 323).

Ryrie, Charles Caldwell. *The Acts of the Apostles*. Chicago: Moody, 1961.

This commentary is so brief as to be of assistance only to the layperson or other nonspecialist. "A brief, popular and genuinely helpful exposition. Ideal for home Bible classes and Bible study groups" (Barber, 153). Premillennial. Dispensational.

*Schnabel, Eckhard J. *Acts*. Zondervan Exegetical Commentary on the New Testament. Edited by Clinton E. Arnold. Grand Rapids: Zondervan Academic, 2012.

In keeping with the series objective, this commentary, by the Mary French Rockefeller Distinguished Professor of NT Studies at Gordon-Conwell Theological Seminary, is an excellent treatment of the Greek text of this gospel for those with a working knowledge of Greek. It is exegetically quite good and very helpful for those working through the Greek text. However, one weakness of this book and indeed of this entire series is the sketchy introduction. At thirty-three pages, including about seven pages devoted to structure and outline, this is just too brief to be of much value. On the plus side, it abounds with excellent historical data and insights. Also, the translation and graphical layout of the books in this series is very helpful in finding information and in visualizing "the flow of thought within the text" (8). "At 1,162 pages, it is very thorough. Considering it works with the Greek text, it is very accessible, clearly written, and very strong on the theme of mission and on Greco-Roman history and sources" (Carson, 76).

Thomas, David. *Acts of the Apostles: Expository and Homiletical Commentary*. London: R. D. Dickson, 1870. Reprint, Grand Rapids: Kregel, 1980.

This study is a homiletical commentary consisting of 111 sermons from different passages in the book of Acts. The exegete will find little of value here. For pastors only.

The Pauline Epistles

*Bird, Michael F. *Four Views on the Apostle Paul. Counterpoints.* Edited by Stanley N. Gundry. Grand Rapids: Zondervan, 2012.

> In recent decades, the Apostle Paul has received increasing scrutiny. This helpful volume, using the Counterpoints format, explores the Apostle Paul, his historical and religious context, and its effects on his theology. Four scholars provide their own positions and then receive response for one another. Thomas R. Schreiner presents the Reformed View, Luke Timothy Johnson the Roman Catholic view, Douglas A. Campbell the post-new perspective view, and Mark D. Nanos the Jewish view.

*+Bruce, F. F. *Paul: Apostle of the Heart Set Free.* Grand Rapids: Eerdmans, 1977.

> A recognized modern classic, this volume explores the life of the Apostle Paul and the main themes of his letters.

*————. *The Pauline Circle.* Grand Rapids: Eerdmans, 1985.

> This slim volume (100 pages) examines the closest friends and associates of the Apostle Paul. Included are Ananias, Barnabas, Silas, Timothy, Luke, Priscilla and Aquila, Apollos, Titus, Onesimus, and Mark.

*Campbell, Constantine R. *Paul and Union with Christ: An Exegetical and Theological Study.* Grand Rapids: Zondervan, 2012.

> This seminal work won *Christianity Today's* 2014 Book Award in Biblical Studies. The author, a noted Greek scholar, examines in the writings of Paul every occurrence of the phrases "in Christ," "through Christ," "into Christ," etc., to create a holistic theology of Paul on the topic of union with Christ.

*+Conybeare, W. J., and J. S. Howson. *The Life and Epistles of Saint Paul.* Cincinnati: National, 1871.

> First published in 1852, this classic is truly a gem. The authors make an excellent attempt to harmonize the life of the Apostle Paul with the Acts of the Apostles and provide a chronological framework for his epistles. "Excellent background material" (Barber, 159).

*+Eadie, John. *Paul the Preacher: A Popular and Practical Exposition of His Discourses and Speeches.* London: Griffin, 1859. Reprint, Minneapolis: James Family, 1979.

> Again out of print, this classic is an examination of the speeches of the Apostle Paul from the Acts of the Apostles by the noted NT scholar John Eadie.

Goodwin, Frank J. *A Harmony of the Life of St. Paul*. Grand Rapids: Baker, 1951.

> Long out of print, this book is a helpful attempt to harmonize the life of the
> Apostle Paul using the epistles and the Acts of the Apostles as points of refer-
> ence. Dated.

*Harvey, John D. *Interpreting the Pauline Letters: An Exegetical Handbook*. Handbooks
for New Testament Exegesis. Edited by John D. Harvey. Grand Rapids: Kregel
Academic, 2012.

> This book is the inaugural volume in the HNTE series. It is intended for pas-
> tors and students with a familiarity of NT Greek. The author walks the reader
> through the exegetical process with the end in mind of moving from text to
> sermon. Very helpful!

*Hawthorne, Gerald F., Ralph B. Martin, and Daniel G. Reid, eds. *Dictionary of Paul and
His Letters*. Downers Grove: IVP Academic, 1993.

> An indispensable work for those engaged in Pauline studies. Not as up to date
> on recent scholarship as it needs to be so an updated edition is in order.

Hiebert, D. Edmond. *An Introduction to the Pauline Epistles*. Chicago: Moody, 1954.

> This book is a rather dated introductory guide to the Pauline Epistles. It is
> intended for college students approaching this body of literature for the first
> time. "Among the best introductory studies available. Thoroughly conserva-
> tive" (Barber, 157).

!*+Lightfoot, J. B. *Notes on the Epistles of St Paul*. Reprint, Winona Lake, IN: Alpha, 1904.

> Published posthumously in 1904, these notes contain what was intended to be
> commentaries on the Greek text of 1 and 2 Thessalonians, 1 Corinthians, Ro-
> mans, and Ephesians as part of a collaborative effort with Westcott and Hort on
> the entire NT. The work on 1 and 2 Thessalonians was completed, but Lightfoot
> contributed only Romans 1–7, 1 Corinthians 1–7, and Ephesians 1:1–14. Light-
> foot was a first-rate Greek scholar and this volume is a real treasure.

*Longenecker, Bruce W., and Todd D. Still. *Thinking Through Paul: A Survey of His Life,
Letters, and Theology*. Grand Rapids: Zondervan, 2014.

> This well-written volume is an engaging survey of Paul's life, letters, and the-
> ology. It is intended to be a textbook for university and seminary students.
> The beginning of each chapter includes a chapter overview as well as a section
> titled "Key Verses." At the end of each chapter, there is a listing of key people,
> places, and terms, questions for review and discussion, and contemporary
> theological reflection questions to enhance further thinking. Finally, there

is a helpful bibliography concluding each chapter divided into two sections: "Commentaries" and "Special Studies."

Longenecker, Richard N. *The Ministry and Message of Paul*. Contemporary Evangelical Perspectives. Grand Rapids: Zondervan, 1971.

This book is a very brief introduction to the ministry and message of the Apostle Paul aimed at the beginning theology student or layperson.

————. *Paul, Apostle of Liberty*. Grand Rapids: Baker, 1964.

Long out of print, this book is an enlightening examination of the two main dynamic tensions in Paul's life and ministry: the law and legality and liberty. The author maintains that Paul cannot be rightly understood apart from an understanding of these two forces in his life. "An exacting study of the origin and nature of Paul's message" (Barber, 158).

*+Ramsay, W. M. *The Cities of St. Paul: Their Influence on His Life and Thought*. New York: Armstrong, 1908. Reprint, Minneapolis: James Family, n.d.

This out of print classic examines the life and culture of five cities from the life of the Apostle Paul—Tarsus, Psidian Antioch, Iconium, Derbe, and Lystra—and seeks to determine how their culture and social milieu influenced his thought and writings. Ramsay was the greatest Pauline expert of his day and deserves to be read today over a century later.

*+————. *St. Paul the Traveler and the Roman Citizen*. London: Hodder and Stoughton, 1897. Reprint, Grand Rapids: Baker, 1962.

Again out of print, this classic examines the cities that the Apostle Paul visited in the Acts of the Apostles.

*Schreiner, Thomas R. *Interpreting the Pauline Epistles*. 2nd ed. Grand Rapids: Baker Academic, 2011.

The author is a reliable guide in the world of Pauline studies. In this volume, he has provided an excellent brief handbook on how to conduct exegetical work in the Pauline Epistles. Chapter 5 on diagramming and conducting a grammatical analysis is extremely helpful for those wanting to see the relationships of words and ideas in Paul's thought.

*————. *Paul, Apostle of God's Glory in Christ*. Downers Grove: IVP Academic, 2001.

An accessible guide to Pauline theology. "Well worth buying as an introductory study" (Evans, 326).

*+Smith, James. *The Voyage and Shipwreck of St. Paul.* 4th ed. Revised and corrected by Walter E. Smith. Reprint, Minneapolis: James Family, n.d.

> First published in 1848, this volume is a reproduction of the 1880 fourth edition and is most helpful in understanding Acts 27 and 28. "Indispensable background material" (Barber).

Stalker, James. *The Life of St. Paul.* Westwood, NJ: Revell, 1950.

> A popular biography of the Apostle Paul that is particularly suited for laypersons.

*Theilman, Frank. *Paul and the Law: A Contextual Approach.* Downers Grove: IVP Academic, 1995.

> A careful investigation of Paul's perspective on the law. An important correction to the "new perspective" on Paul.

Romans

*Barnhouse, Donald Grey. *Expositions of Bible Doctrines Taking the Epistle to the Romans as the Point of Departure.* 4 vols. Grand Rapids: Eerdmans, 1952–63.

> This set, by the late editor of *Eternity Magazine* and pastor of 10th Presbyterian Church in Philadelphia, is a masterful examination of Bible doctrines using the Epistle to the Romans as his point of departure. It is not a commentary, but will reward careful reading. "Very rich. His many striking illustrations help make the series especially valuable to the pastor as well as the teacher" (Rosscup, 248). "An exposition of Bible doctrine which is very full, well-illustrated and appropriately applied" (Barber, 162).

*+Brown, John. *Analytical Exposition of the Epistle of Paul the Apostle to the Romans.* Edinburgh: Oliphant, Anderson, & Ferrier, 1883. Reprint, Minneapolis: James Family, 1979.

> This wonderful commentary is a masterful exposition of Paul's greatest epistle. It is regrettably out of print again, but should be purchased if found. It represents John Brown at his very best. "Of all the works by John Brown of Edinburgh, this exposition is without a doubt one of the best. It was out of print for so long a time that many Bible students were unaware of its existence. Now, in the providence of God, it has been made available again. Buy it" (Barber)! "Dr. Brown's work must be placed among the first of the first-class. He is a great expositor" (Spurgeon, 170).

*Bruce, F. F. *The Epistle to the Romans*. TNTC. Edited by R. V. G. Tasker. Grand Rapids: Eerdmans, 1963.

> This brief study is now dated and uneven in spots mostly due to the limitations of the TNTC series. It was revised in 1986 prior to the author's death, but the revision was not as extensive as warranted. However, any book by Bruce is certainly worth acquiring. "Draws upon a wide knowledge of literature, frequently cites theological writers, and provides an understandable, and, in many ways, significant exposition of this epistle. Occasionally the comments are too brief to be of help to the pastor and at other times exceptionally full" (Barber, 162).

!*Cranfield, C. E. B. *A Critical and Exegetical Commentary on the Epistle to the Romans*. ICC. Edited by J. A. Emerton and C. E. B. Cranfield. 2 vols. Edinburgh: T. & T. Clark, 1975.

> These two volumes replace the one by Sanday and Headlam in the ICC series. This massive commentary is perhaps the best treatment of the Greek text available providing an excellent discussion of the various exegetical problems found in Romans. This book is for the specialist and the pastor with solid Greek skills. "Occasionally Cranfield seems more influenced by Barth than by Paul, but for thoughtful exegesis of the Greek text, with a careful weighing of alternative positions, there is nothing quite like it. It is rare that a commentary provides students with an education in grammatical exegesis" (Carson, 83). "An exceptionally good commentary" (Rosscup, 250). "Magisterial! Indispensable for close exegesis" (Evans, 335).

!?Dunn, James D. G. *Romans*. WBC. Edited by David A. Hubbard and Glenn W. Barker. 2 vols. Dallas: Word, 1988.

> This controversial volume by the University of Durham Professor of Divinity is a learned work that brings a wealth of exegetical insights to this epistle. The bibliographies are extensive and Dunn's interaction with other scholarly views is commendable. However, his critical theories will not convince most conservative traditionalists. If you want insight into the new perspective on Paul, this commentary is a good place to start. "Certainly worthy of diligent study. Nonetheless, one of its controlling foci, viz. the thesis that Paul and his readers are wrestling over the 'signs' of membership in the people of God, is rather overdone and is in general too indebted to E. P. Sanders" (Carson, 83).

*+Gifford, E. H. *The Epistle of St. Paul to the Romans*. London: John Murray, 1886. Reprint, Minneapolis: James Family, 1977.

> This commentary is a classic exposition of the Greek text by a nineteenth-century Archdeacon of London and Canon of St. Paul's. "Should be purchased if found because of its exegetical insights" (Barber, 162). "A careful

work which traces the argument closely and states it well. . . . One of the top older commentaries" (Rosscup, 251). Amillennial. Anglican.

*+Godet, Frederic Louis. *Commentary on Romans*. 1883. Reprint, Grand Rapids: Kregel, 1977.

> This commentary is a classic work first translated into English from French in 1864. Although it is now dated and not up to date on scholarship from the past 150 years, it is still worth consulting and a gold mine for the pastor who preaches on this epistle. "This exhaustive and technical commentary provides an excellent treatment of the argument of the epistle. The author surveys the varying theories, refutes theological liberals who differ with him on important points of doctrine, and adequately defends his views. A valuable addition to the pastor's library" (Barber, 162)! "The thoughtful reader will always discern practical applications" (Carson, 88). Arminian.

*+Haldane, Robert. *An Exposition of the Epistle to the Romans*. Reprint, McLean, VA: MacDonald, n.d.

> This fine work, first published between 1835–39, is a compilation of lectures given by a Christian layman in Geneva that provoked a great movement of the Holy Spirit. Although this book is greatly respected, its usefulness is greatly hampered by a lack of any outline or indices as well as age. "The work has much gold if one has time to read voluminously to dig out the many nuggets. . . . This is one of the greatest of the older commentaries, almost always offering solid help and much to stimulate the heart" (Rosscup, 252). "An exposition full of heart" (Evans, 339). Reformed.

*Hendriksen, William. *Exposition of Paul's Epistle to the Romans*. New Testament Commentary. 2 vols. Grand Rapids: Baker, 1980.

> This commentary, like all of Hendriksen's works in this series, is helpful primarily for pastors and students. It is a warm, pastoral, and practical exposition. However, at just twenty-eight pages, the introduction is too brief in my judgment. This book must be supplemented with more detailed exegetical works that interact with recent trends in Pauline scholarship. "Lacks some of the vigor of earlier works" (Evans, 339). Amillennial. Reformed.

*+Hodge, Charles. *A Commentary on Romans*. 1835. Reprint, Carlisle, PA: Banner of Truth, 1972.

> This commentary by a leading Princeton professor of the nineteenth century is a true classic. This work's strength is its superb doctrinal emphasis. "Good theological perspective. . . . It is a good, solid evangelical commentary helpful to a teacher, preacher, or layman on the problems because it delves into

them with a zest" (Rosscup, 253). "Hodge's method and matter make him doubly useful in commenting. He is singularly clear, and a great promoter of thought" (Spurgeon, 171). Reformed.

*Kruse, Colin G. *Paul's Letter to the Romans*. PNTC. Edited by D. A. Carson. Grand Rapids: Eerdmans, 2012.

A fine mid-level treatment, not quite in the class of Moo and Schreiner, but capable nonetheless. Particularly helpful for pastors. "Writes with clarity, verve, and good judgment" (Carson, 83).

!*+Liddon, H. P. *Explanatory Analysis of St. Paul's Epistle to the Romans*. London: Longmans, Green, 1899; Minneapolis: James and Klock, 1977.

A work of immense scholarship! For those with solid Greek skills. "A thorough, technical commentary which provides preachers with a comprehensive outline of the epistle. Frequently serves to give readers useful insights into the trend of Paul's thought" (Barber, 163). "Though Liddon lays out immense detail, he does it in a point-by-point, systematic order that analyzes the text verse by verse as to grammar, logic, and doctrine. Serious readers can follow his clear outline and trace the argument of Paul's epistle. Liddon treats Greek words, views on problems, and pertinent details of syntax, history, and connection with other Scripture. This meticulous effort and Stifler's briefer work are models to help an expositor pursue the chain of argument" (Rosscup, 254–55).

!*+Lightfoot, J. B. See section on the Pauline Epistles.

!*Longenecker, Richard. *The Epistle to the Romans*. NIGTC. Edited by I. Howard Marshall and W. Ward Gasque. Grand Rapids: Eerdmans, 2016.

Not reviewed for this edition, but it promises to be an evangelical standard for decades. Finally, a technical treatment from a conservative perspective!

*Moo, Douglas J. *The Epistle to the Romans*. NICNT. Edited by Ned B. Stonehouse, F. F. Bruce, and Gordon D. Fee. Grand Rapids: Eerdmans, 1996.

This commentary is one of the very best on this epistle from any time period and certainly the top of the line from the past twenty years. It is a detailed, cautious, and rich offering by a highly respected NT scholar who teaches at Wheaton College. Despite this, the book is not without its limitations. It is now almost twenty years old and its introduction is a sparse thirty-five pages, but its careful exegesis and overall excellence in most other areas give it pride of place among general works for the pastor or student. It is a replacement volume for Murray. "The best Romans commentary for pastors available in English. . . . Moo exhibits extraordinary good sense in his exegesis. No less important, his is the first commentary to cull what is useful from the new perspective on Paul while nevertheless offering telling criticisms of many of its exegetical and theological stances. The combination of the strong exegesis and the rigorous interaction makes the work superior" (Carson, 82–83). "Shows shrewd exegetical judgment and understands the theology of the epistle" (Evans, 336).

*———. *Romans*. NIVAC. Edited by Terry Muck. Grand Rapids: Zondervan, 2000.

What Bock has done for students of the Gospel of Luke, Moo has done for students of Romans. This volume distills the essence of his NICNT commentary and makes it accessible for general audiences. "Great for pastors" (Evans, 342).

Moule, H. C. G. *Studies in Romans*. Cambridge: Cambridge University Press, 1892. Reprint, Grand Rapids: Kregel, 1977.

This capable exegetical study was originally published in 1892 as a part of the series the Cambridge Bible for Schools and Colleges. Moule was a leading Calvinist of the nineteenth century. His verse-by-verse treatment of the text is both warmly devotional and practical. Reformed.

*Mounce, Robert H. *Romans*. NAC. Edited by E. Ray Clendenen. Nashville: Holman Reference, 1995.

A well-written mid-level commentary aimed primarily at pastors. Premillennial. Baptist.

*Murray, John. *The Epistle to the Romans*. NICNT. Edited by F. F. Bruce. Grand Rapids: Eerdmans, 1959–65.

This commentary is a magnificent treatment of the book particularly in the areas of exegesis and theology. For decades it has been one of the standard conservative works on this epistle. It has now been replaced by Moo in the NIC series, but hardly eclipsed. Though this work is now dated, it still stands as one of the outstanding commentaries on this epistle. "Murray deals with problem verses with careful scholarship and good insight, leaving few stones unturned. It is one of the most helpful works on the epistle for the teacher or pastor who is serious about his Bible study" (Rosscup, 257). "A superb theological commentary which shows good exegetical judgment" (Evans, 342). Reformed. Postmillennial.

!*+Olshausen, Hermann. *Studies in the Epistle to the Romans*. Edinburgh: T. & T. Clark, 1849. Reprint, Minneapolis: Klock & Klock, 1983.

This commentary, by a noted nineteenth-century German NT scholar, is over 160 years old, but still worth consulting. It is a learned work that demonstrates the fruit of tireless and independent scholarship. Olshausen was staunchly conservative and his commentary reflects that evangelical bias.

"Offers independent interpretations that are worth pondering" (Carson, 88). "Many prize, and all respect him" (Spurgeon, 172). Lutheran.

!*+Sanday, William, and Arthur C. Headlam. *A Critical and Exegetical Commentary on the Epistle to the Romans.* ICC. Edited by S. R. Driver, A. Plummer, and C. A. Briggs. Edinburgh: T. & T. Clark, 1895.

> This volume has been replaced by Cranfield's two-volume masterpiece in the ICC series. Since its publication in 1895, this commentary has been regarded as one of the better technical commentaries on the Greek text. Although it is still useful, it has been superseded by more recent works. "Because of its thoroughness in matters of the Greek text, some have regarded this as the best of the older Greek works on Romans" (Rosscup, 257). "Not as dull as is often supposed; they are still worth perusing, even though now eclipsed by Cranfield" (Carson, 86). Arminian.

*Schreiner, Thomas R. *Romans.* BECNT. Edited by Moisés Silva. Grand Rapids: Baker Academic, 1998.

> Along with Moo, this work is probably the best fairly recent mid-level conservative work available. Not as strong as the Moo volume, but still a very capable treatment.

!*+Shedd, William G. T. *A Critical and Doctrinal Commentary on the Epistle of St. Paul to the Romans.* New York: Scribner, 1879. Reprint, Minneapolis: Klock & Klock, 1978.

> This commentary is a thorough exegetical study of the Greek text designed primarily for the theologian. "His use of the Greek text is most satisfying, and his exegesis does not impede his exposition of the writer's theme. . . . A model of sound research, clear thinking, and careful application" (Barber). Reformed.

Stifler, James M. *The Epistle to the Romans.* Chicago: Moody, 1960.

> This brief commentary, by the late longtime professor of Greek at Crozier Theological Seminary, is geared to the English reader and is still useful to the preacher or layperson. "Traces the argument of the epistle very well so that the reader receives help in a nutshell form in thinking his way through Paul's profound reasoning" (Rosscup, 258). Premillennial. Dispensational.

Thomas, W. H. Griffith. *St. Paul's Epistle to the Romans: A Devotional Commentary.* Grand Rapids: Eerdmans, 1946.

> As the title indicates, this study is a devotional commentary useful mainly to the nonspecialist and layperson. Griffith was very helpful to me as a baby Christian. "Excellent outlines and illustrations" (Barber, 164).

Wiersbe, Warren W. *Be Right: An Expository Study of Romans*. Wheaton: Victor, 1977.

> As are the other volumes in this series, this study is particularly helpful for laypersons and nonspecialists.

1 Corinthians

*? Barrett, C. K. *A Commentary on the First Epistle to the Corinthians*. Harper's New Testament Commentaries. Edited by Henry Chadwick. New York: Harper & Row, 1968.

> This book is an excellent scholarly commentary that is fairly accessible to nonspecialists. Be aware that Barrett is no evangelical. "A wealth of useful material, and those with no Greek can follow the argument" (Carson, 93–94). "A valuable modern treatment which makes a vital contribution to the study of this epistle. The writer does not believe in inspiration and has a weak theological system. However, he is a capable exegete and his handling of this letter deserves attention" (Barber, 165).

*Blomberg, Craig L. *1 Corinthians*. NIVAC. Edited by Terry Muck. Grand Rapids: Zondervan, 1995.

> A capable and eminently practical work that is of great value to pastors. Blomberg is one of the evangelical luminaries writing today and this volume is not to be missed! "A thoughtful, suggestive work" (Evans, 345).

*Ciampa, Roy E., and Brian S. Rosner. *The First Letter to the Corinthians*. PNTC. Edited by D. A. Carson. Grand Rapids: Eerdmans, 2010.

> At 867 pages of text, this commentary is massive and seems to cover all the bases. The authors include an extensive bibliography and there is evidence of substantial interaction with modern scholarship. Very helpful in the introduction is a lengthy section on how to interpret the epistle. "Very full, but on occasion not easy to follow and not very plausible" (Carson, 93).

!*+Edwards, Thomas Charles. *A Commentary on the First Epistle to the Corinthians*. Hamilton, Adams, 1885. Reprint, Minneapolis: Klock & Klock, 1979.

> This technical exegetical commentary based on the Greek text is an acknowledged classic. The author, a nineteenth-century lecturer at Lincoln College, Oxford, and later principal of the University College of Wales in Aberystwyth, has produced an enduring work that is still of value for exegetes today. Regrettably, it is again out of print, but should be purchased if found. "Demonstrates his awareness of the writings of others—ancient, medieval and modern—and

quotes their contributions in a way that enlarges our understanding of Paul's theology and its application to the needs of the church" (Barber).

*Fee, Gordon D. *The First Epistle to the Corinthians*. NICNT. Edited by Ned B. Stonehouse, F. F. Bruce, and Gordon D. Fee. Grand Rapids: Eerdmans, 1987.

This is an exceptional commentary and along with Garland vies for supremacy as the very best general-purpose commentaries on the text. Of course, Garland's work is more recent by sixteen years. But both should be obtained if possible. The author's denominational affiliation is Assemblies of God, so the reader may disagree with his positions on some issues. For example, Fee views 14:34–35 as a textual gloss essentially dismissing those arguments against a limited role for women in the church. "This is the all-around best evangelical commentary on the epistle at this time. Fee is well-organized, clear, and perceptive on issues. . . . He is thorough verse by verse, skilled in Greek details, and keeps the argument of the epistle in view. His grasp of literature on I Corinthians is masterful, and he takes up more matters than other commentaries on the letter, looking at various views and reasons, supporting his views, applying truth to the church and the Christian life" (Rosscup, 262). "Fee's commentary is lucid, informed, sensible, and written with great verve. Occasionally the passion that marks this commentary is grating, especially when Fee is passionate about a position with which one disagrees" (Carson, 93)!

*Garland, David E. *1 Corinthians*. BECNT. Edited by Robert W. Yarbrough and Robert H. Stein. Grand Rapids: Baker Academic, 2003.

This study is one of the very best general commentaries on this epistle. At 775 pages of text, it is massive and thorough. Because of the comparative newness of this treatment and its interaction with current scholarship, it belongs on the shelf of every pastor who preaches on this epistle. "Thorough and praise-worthy" (Evans, 346).

*+Godet, Frederic Louis. *Commentary on First Corinthians*. Edinburgh: T. & T. Clark, 1889. Reprint, Grand Rapids: Kregel, 1977.

As are all of Godet's exegetical commentaries, this is a classic study that has stood the test of time and should still be consulted today. "One of the outstanding treatments of all time" (Barber, 165). "A mine of exposition" (Evans, 348).

Grosheide, F. W. *Commentary on the First Epistle to the Corinthians*. NICNT. Edited by F. F. Bruce. Grand Rapids: Eerdmans, 1953.

Despite Rosscup's glowing recommendation, this commentary is one of the weaker volumes in the NICNT series. It has since been replaced by Fee's impressive work. "This is a lucid evangelical work of capable scholarship which ranks among the top commentaries from the standpoint of the Greek and dealing with problems" (Rosscup, 263). "Below par and can be safely skipped" (Carson, 96). Reformed.

*Hays, Richard B. *First Corinthians*. Interp. Edited by James Luther Mays, Patrick D. Miller, and Paul J. Achtemeier. Louisville: John Knox, 1997.

This brief commentary is a nontechnical work that is particularly well done. It is strong on application. "Overdoes the apocalyptic emphasis" (Carson, 94).

Hodge, Charles. *A Commentary on 1 & 2 Corinthians*. Reprint, Carlisle, PA: Banner of Truth, 1974

This book is a one-volume compilation of two commentaries originally published in 1857 and 1860. It is a very helpful doctrinal treatment of both letters. Hodge was a master theologian who taught for many years at Princeton Theological Seminary. "A doctrinal commentary of considerable merit" (Barber). "Much assistance in thinking through issues consistently with Scripture" (Rosscup, 263). "The more we use Hodge, the more we value him" (Spurgeon, 174). Reformed.

*Kistemaker, Simon J. *1 Corinthians*. New Testament Commentary. Grand Rapids: Baker Academic, 1993.

A capable exposition well-suited for pastors. Kistemaker has proven to be a worthy successor to Hendriksen in this series. "A sure-footed theological guide" (Evans, 349).

!*+Lightfoot, J. B. See section on the Pauline Epistles.

*+Morgan, G. Campbell. *The Corinthian Letters of Paul*. Old Tappan, NJ: Revell, 1956.

G. Campbell Morgan, who lived from 1863–1945, was highly regarded as a preacher and was rightly known as the "prince of expositors" throughout the English-speaking world. Although this book is not an exegetical commentary, any book by Morgan is well worth reading. Of particular value to preachers. "A renowned pulpiteer addresses himself to the problems which plague the church. His statements are timely and show a mastery of the subject matter" (Barber, 166).

*+Olshausen, Hermann. *A Commentary on Paul's First and Second Epistles to the Corinthians*. Edinburgh: T. & T. Clark, 1855. Reprint, Minneapolis: Klock & Klock, 1984.

This fine commentary was written by the nineteenth-century German exegete who taught at Konigsberg and then at Erlangen until his death at age forty-three in 1839. "Well deserving of continued reading today" (Barber). "Varies between the insightful and the eccentric" (Carson, 95). "Highly esteemed for its happy combinations of grammatico-historical exegesis, with spiritual insight into the meaning of the sacred writers" (Spurgeon, 175).

*Prior, David. *The Message of 1 Corinthians: Life in the Local Church*. BST. Edited by J. A. Motyer and John R. W. Stott. Downers Grove: InterVarsity, 1985.

This middle level popular treatment is by a practitioner who has pastored churches in South Africa and Oxford, England. It is not a verse-by-verse treatment, but rather paragraph-by-paragraph. It is well written and eminently practical. "Many will appreciate his insightful strokes that are relevant today on areas such as divorce, remarriage, and tongues" (Rosscup, 265).

Redpath, Alan. *The Royal Route to Heaven: Studies in First Corinthians*. Old Tappan, NJ: Revell, 1960.

This book is not a commentary, but rather a compilation of sermons delivered from the pulpit at the Moody Memorial Church in Chicago. These sermons are warm, devotional, and pastoral expositions that would benefit any pastor who plans to preach from this epistle. Of course, this work needs to be supplemented by scholarly commentaries as his exegesis is weak, but these messages will help to prime the homiletical pump. "They rebuke shallowness and ineffectiveness in the church, expose the tragedy of living in sinfulness and worldliness, and vigorously apply the message of this epistle to the lives of believers today" (Barber, 166). "Remarkably practical" (Carson, 96).

!*+Robertson, Archibald, and Alfred Plummer. *A Critical and Exegetical Commentary on the First Epistle of St Paul to the Corinthians*. ICC. Edited by S. R. Driver, A. Plummer, and C. A. Briggs. Edinburgh: T. & T. Clark, 1914.

This commentary is an exceptional treatment of the Greek text. At more than one hundred years old, it is now dated, but still extremely helpful especially on exegetical matters. "A monumental work which has earned for itself a deserved place on the Bible teacher's book shelf" (Barber, 166). "This work is one of the better ones in the series" (Carson, 94). "This, after Fee, is the most detailed and the best critical commentary on the epistle. Though not as readable as works by Godet, Grosheide, Johnson, and Morris, it is more detailed in discussing possibilities for a given passage" (Rosscup, 265). "A magnificent piece of work which is still widely consulted today" (Evans, 350).

*+ Stanley, Arthur Penrhyn. *The Epistles of St. Paul to the Corinthians*. London: John Murray, 1858. Reprint, Minneapolis: Klock & Klock, 1981.

> This excellent commentary is a scholarly critical study on the Greek text by a nineteenth-century Regius Professor of Ecclesiastical History at Oxford University. Although Stanley wrote numerous highly regarded books and was a revered preacher, this is his only exegetical commentary. Interestingly, Spurgeon did not recommend the purchase of this book, questioning both its value and soundness.

*Taylor, Mark. *1 Corinthians*. NAC. Edited by E. Ray Clendenen. Nashville: Homan Reference, 2014.

> A capable nontechnical commentary by a Southern Baptist. Most helpful for pastors.

!*Thiselton, Anthony C. *The First Epistle to the Corinthians*. NIGTC. Edited by I. Howard Marshall and Donald Hagner. Grand Rapids: Eerdmans, 2000.

> At 1,353 pages of text, this massive commentary is magisterial and full of exceptional exegetical work. This volume is hands down the best technical commentary on the Greek text. It is deep and penetrating. Highly recommended for those with good Greek skills! "Very impressive. . . . It provides not only detailed exegesis but also a tracing of the main issues of interpretation from the church fathers to the present. This work will doubtless prove too difficult for poorly trained pastors, but for those with the requisite skills this commentary will prove an invaluable resource" (Carson, 93).

*Thrall, Margaret E. *The First and Second Letters of Paul to the Corinthians*. CBC. Edited by P. R. Ackroyd, A. R. C. Leaney, and J. W. Packer. Cambridge: Cambridge University Press, 1965.

> This very brief commentary is based on the English text of the NEB, but is very good for laymen and Bible study leaders, and at over fifty years of age, has not outlived its usefulness. Do not confuse this nontechnical study with the author's exceptional two-volume ICC set on 2 Corinthians. "One of the best of the brief commentaries" (Carson, 96).

Wiersbe, Warren W. *Be Wise*. Wheaton: Victor, 1983.

> This little study guide is primarily intended for laypersons and Bible study groups. Wiersbe is always practical and engaging.

Witherington, Ben, III. *Conflict and Community in Corinth: A Socio-Rhetorical Commentary on 1 and 2 Corinthians*. Grand Rapids: Eerdmans, 1995.

> This interesting commentary examines these two books in terms of Greco-Roman rhetoric. Witherington is always interesting and frequently charming. "Like all his work, it is accessible and talks good sense" (Carson, 92).

2 Corinthians

*Barnett, Paul. *The Second Epistle to the Corinthians*. NICNT. Edited by Edited by Gordon D. Fee. Grand Rapids: Eerdmans, 1997.

> Published in 1997, this handy volume is still the best nontechnical work available to pastors and students. It replaces the highly regarded Hughes commentary in the old series, which still packs quite a punch. "A joy to read" (Evans, 99).

*?Barrett, C. K. *A Commentary on the Second Epistle to the Corinthians*. Harper's New Testament Commentaries. Edited by Henry Chadwick. New York: Harper & Row, 1973.

> See comments on the author's commentary on 1 Corinthians. "This is one of the top commentaries in usually getting at key issues and bringing quality comments on these based on broad research and awareness" (Rosscup, 268). "Quite outstanding" (Carson, 99).

Best, Ernest. *Second Corinthians*. Interp. Edited by James Luther Mays, Patrick D. Miller, and Paul J. Achtemeier. Louisville: John Knox, 1987.

> This slender volume has some good practical insights, but there are better works available. The author, a professor of divinity at the University of Glasgow, shares nothing new in this brief commentary. Not one of the better volumes in this series.

!*?Furnish, Victor Paul. *II Corinthians*. AB. Edited by William Foxwell Albright and David Noel Freedman. New York: Doubleday, 1984.

> This study, by a professor of NT at the Perkins School of Theology in Dallas, is a marvelously detailed and comprehensive treatment. It is one of the standard technical works on this epistle and highly regarded by many scholars. It is particularly strong in the area of exegesis. A bit wordy, but highly recommended. "This one leaves few stones unturned and on many points offers sane and thoughtful exegesis" (Carson, 99). "Has much to offer serious students. He writes clearly, discussing each section with its structure and themes, gives detail on text, word study, grammar, geography, history etc. . . . His richness

in many aspects such as grammar provides much for mature users trained to discern, and for translators" (Rosscup, 269). "Still among the best scholarly commentaries available" (Evans, 353).

*Garland, David E. *2 Corinthians*. NAC. Edited by E. Ray Clendenen. Nashville: Holman Reference, 1999.

An exceptional nontechnical work by a Baylor University NT scholar. "Deserves serious consideration as a priority purchase for evangelical pastors" (Evans, 351).

Guthrie, George. *2 Corinthians*. BECNT. Edited by Robert W. Yarbrough and Robert H. Stein. Grand Rapids: Baker Academic, 2015.

Not reviewed for this edition.

*Hafemann, Scott J. *2 Corinthians*. NIVAC. Edited by Terry Muck. Grand Rapids: Zondervan, 2000.

One of the best in the series, this volume is of immense value to pastors. "A superior entry" (Carson, 99).

*Hodge, Charles. See section on 1 Corinthians.

*Hughes, Philip Edgcumbe. *Paul's Second Epistle to the Corinthians*. NICNT. Edited by F. F. Bruce. Grand Rapids: Eerdmans, 1962.

At over fifty years of age, this commentary still retains its value. It is one of the stronger contributions to the original NICNT series and is quite helpful to both scholars and pastors. At 490 pages of text, it is very detailed and while, based on the English ASV text, it carefully uses the Greek. "May well be regarded as the finest conservative exposition of this epistle" (Barber, 166)!

*Kruse, Colin G. *2 Corinthians*. TNTC. Edited by Eckhard J. Schnabel. 2nd ed. Downers Grove: IVP Academic, 2015.

Originally published in 1987, this work capably replaces the quite serviceable volume by Tasker with stronger exegesis.

!*?Martin, Ralph P. *2 Corinthians*. WBC. Edited by Nancy L. deClaissé-Walford and Lynn Allan Losie. 2nd ed. Grand Rapids: Zondervan, 2014.

Originally published in 1986, this revision appeared posthumously after the author's death in 2013. It is a highly technical and detailed work that is moderately critical. Carson's criticism is of the original work. "A little disappointing, too speculative at many junctures and occasionally wrong-headed" (Carson, 99).

Morgan, G. Campbell. See section on 1 Corinthians.

*?Plummer, Alfred. *A Critical and Exegetical Commentary on the Second Epistle of St Paul to the Corinthians*. ICC. Edited by S. R. Driver, A. Plummer, and C. A. Briggs. Edinburgh: T. & T. Clark, 1915.

> The author's exceptional work on the Greek text makes this one of the very best of the older technical commentaries on this epistle. Whereas the treatment of the Greek text is exceptional, the author's views on the unity of the epistle detract from its usefulness. However, it is one of the stronger offerings in the old ICC series. "This is one of the best older commentaries on the epistle from the standpoint of the Greek text and critical study" (Rosscup, 272–73). "Tends to be pedestrian" (Carson, 100).

*Seifrid, Mark A. *The Second Letter to the Corinthians*. PNTC. Edited by D. A. Carson. Grand Rapids: Eerdmans, 2014.

> This fine offering in the PNTC series approaches this epistle as a unified letter, rather than, as many modern scholars argue, a composite of fragments and excerpts. The author has produced a well-written and exegetically sound commentary that is theologically rich. The introduction is disappointingly sparse (13 pages).

*+Stanley, Arthur Penrhyn. See section on 1 Corinthians.

Tasker, R. V. G. *The Second Epistle of Paul to the Corinthians*. TNTC. Edited by R. V. G. Tasker. Grand Rapids: Eerdmans, 1963.

> At 192 pages, this is a brief, but well-written, treatment of the epistle that is most helpful to pastors and laypersons. Like the other volumes in this series, this book would benefit from an index and a bibliography. Replaced by Kruse.

!*?Thrall, Margaret. *A Critical and Exegetical Commentary on the Second Epistle of St Paul to the Corinthians: I–VII*. ICC. Edited by J. A. Emerton, C. E. B. Cranfield, and G. N. Stanton. Edinburgh: T. & T. Clark, 1994.

!*?———. *A Critical and Exegetical Commentary on the Second Epistle of St Paul to the Corinthians: VIII–XIII*. ICC. Edited by J. A. Emerton, C. E. B. Cranfield, and G. N. Stanton. Edinburgh: T. & T. Clark, 2000.

> These two volumes replace Plummer's 1915 offering in the old ICC series. Thrall's treatment of the Greek text is rivaled only by Harris's NICTC work. This commentary is a fairly critical work that argues for a partition theory. It is technical and thorough, but does not offer much for the pastor with weak Greek skills. "Thrall's treatment of the Greek text is always thorough and thought provoking but often less convincing" (Carson, 98).

*————. See section on 1 Corinthians.

Wiersbe, Warren W. *Be Encouraged*. Colorado Springs: Cook, 1994.

> This is a helpful little study primarily intended for laypersons and Bible study groups. Particularly helpful are the study questions for each chapter in the back of the book.

Witherington, Ben, III. See section on 1 Corinthians.

Galatians

!*Betz, Hans Dieter. *A Commentary on Paul's Letter to the Churches in Galatia*. Hermeneia. Edited by Helmut Koester. Philadelphia: Fortress, 1979.

> This commentary, by the renowned professor of NT at the Claremont School of Theology and Claremont Graduate School and the University of Chicago, is considered by many to be the best modern treatment of the Greek text. It is weighty and substantial with detailed and copious footnotes. Some are not so enamored by his approach. One such critique is *Rhetoric and Galatians: Assessing an Approach to Paul's Epistle to the Galatians* by Philip H. Kern (1998). Betz endorses the North Galatia Theory and holds to early Pauline authorship. "Serious students looking for vigorous critical comments on interpretation of the Greek with heavy awareness and use of critical studies will gain much help here. . . . He provides excellent indices on references in the Old Testament and Apocrypha, Old Testament Pseudepigrapha, other Jewish literature, New Testament, early Christian writings, Greek and Latin authors, Greek words, subjects, and names of commentators and other authors of ancient and modern times" (Rosscup, 273). "Provides voluminous parallels from the Greco-Roman world, including almost endless comment on the kinds and style of argument Paul deploys. Betz's use of Jewish background is disappointingly thin, and the salvation-historical structure of parts of Paul's argument is sometimes overlooked. Ostensible parallels cannot substitute for accurate exegesis. I do not think he has gotten to the bottom of Paul's understanding of the relationships between law and grace" (Carson, 102).

*+Brown, John. *An Exposition of the Epistle of Paul the Apostle to the Galatians*. Edinburgh: Oliphant, 1853. Reprint, Minneapolis: James Family, 1979.

> Again out of print, this is a very rare classic indeed and should be purchased if found. The author was a noted Presbyterian pastor and seminary professor in Scotland. His expositions are comprehensive, warmly devotional, and first rate. "Perhaps one of the most satisfactory commentaries for the expository preacher" (Barber, 167). "Brown is a modern Puritan. All his expositions are of the utmost value" (Spurgeon, 175). Reformed.

!*Bruce, F. F. *The Epistle to the Galatians: A Commentary on the Greek Text*. NIGTC. Edited by I. Howard Marshall and W. Ward Gasque. Grand Rapids: Eerdmans, 1982.

> This commentary, by the late professor of NT at the University of Manchester in England, is based on the Greek text and is perhaps the finest treatment of the Greek text published since the latter part of the twentieth century. Many consider Bruce to have been the finest NT scholar of the twentieth century and this study lives up to the high standards of scholarship that he set. "A work of first rank treating technical questions. . . . This takes its place as one of the truly great commentaries . . . on the technical thorough side for students intense about their study" (Rosscup, 274). "Evenhandedly weighs virtually all of the relevant literature up to the time of writing and presents the flow of the argument with a deft touch and readable prose" (Carson, 102). "Showing wise exegetical judgment and providing expert discussion of the historical background" (Evans, 358). Evangelicals would do well to read the "Review of Burton on Galatians," by J. Gresham Machen in the *Princeton Theological Review* 20 (1922) 142ff., which has been reproduced in *Machen's Notes on Galatians*, by John H. Skilton (see below).

!*+Burton, Ernest De Witt. *A Critical and Exegetical Commentary on the Epistle to the Galatians*. ICC. Edited by S. R. Driver, A. Plummer, and C. A. Briggs. Edinburgh: T. & T. Clark, 1921.

> For decades this commentary was the standard treatment of the Greek text. It is still outstanding and helpful for the scholar, but no longer has pride of place as the very best technical work on this book. "Many regard it as the best technical commentary on the text" (Rosscup, 274). "A most extensive, satisfactory commentary based on the Greek text" (Barber, 167). "Remains a monument to thoroughness and concern with detail" (Carson, 105). "A number of his theological conclusions are fundamentally wrong-headed" (Evans, 358).

Cole, Alan. *The Epistle of Paul to the Galatians: An Introduction and Commentary*. TNTC. Edited by R. V. G. Tasker. Grand Rapids: Eerdmans, 1965.

> This helpful little commentary was revised in 1989. It offers help with the Greek text, but is not technical and is aimed at the general reader. Not one of the better volumes in the series, but serviceable. "It is a good evangelical commentary, well-informed, solid, clear with good help at times on problem verses" (Rosscup, 274). "Readable, informative, and suggestive" (Barber, 167).

*?Cousar, Charles B. *Galatians*. Interp. Edited by James Luther Mays, Patrick D. Miller, and Paul J. Achtemeier. Louisville: John Knox, 1982.

> This slim volume, by a professor of NT language, literature, and exegesis at Columbia Theological Seminary in Decatur, Georgia, contains some excellent application and insights, making it one of the better efforts in this series.

!*+Eadie, John. *Commentary on the Epistle of Paul to the Galatians*. Edinburgh: T. & T. Clark, 1884. Reprint, Minneapolis: James and Klock, 1977.

> At 480 pages, this commentary is a massive work of scholarship. It has long been a classic work and standard treatment of the Greek text. It is weighty, yet written with devotional warmth. Again, out of print, it should be purchased if found. "Scholarly, practical, and designed for those with a knowledge of Greek" (Barber, 167). "This is a most careful attempt to ascertain the meaning of the Apostle by a painstaking analysis of his words. The author is not warped by any system of theology, but yet he does not deviate from recognized evangelical truth. As a piece of honest grammatical exegesis the value of this commentary is very great" (Spurgeon, 176). "Grapples with problems in an energetic fashions, presenting various views and coming to conclusions" (Rosscup, 275).

*Fung, Ronald Y. K. *The Epistle to the Galatians*. NICNT. Edited by F. F. Bruce. Grand Rapids: Eerdmans, 1988.

> This volume supersedes the 1953 one in this series by Ridderbos and is itself scheduled for replacement. It is a real improvement over the former. He advocates the South Galatian theory, is solid in his interpretations, and is thoroughly evangelical. "It is thorough, usually with traditional conservative views and many satisfactory explanations, some even excellent" (Rosscup, 275). "Workmanlike and a substantial improvement over its predecessor" (Carson, 103). "Has not aged well" (Evans, 360).

*George, Timothy. *Galatians*. NAC. Nashville: Holman Reference, 1994.

> This well-done study, by the founding dean of Beeson Divinity School, is rich theologically and will benefit pastors. "There is much to appreciate about this theologically astute, traditionally-styled commentary" (Evans, 360).

Gromacki, Robert G. *Stand Fast in Liberty: An Exposition of Galatians*. Grand Rapids: Baker, 1979.

> This little guide is a popular commentary for the nonspecialist by a professor of Greek and New Testament at Cedarville College (now Cedarville University). It is practical and competent and ideal for Bible study groups. The questions for discussion at the end of each chapter are especially thought provoking.

*Hendriksen, William. *Exposition of Galatians*. New Testament Commentary. Grand Rapids: Baker, 1968.

> With good reason, Hendriksen has earned a wide following among pastors. His commentaries are based on the Greek text, but not technical and practical and devotional in spirit. This commentary is no exception. The author provides arguments for both the North and South Galatian theories in his introduction, but the book is not up to date on the latest scholarship. "Warm-hearted but too frequently misses the historical and theological nuances of the text" (Carson, 105). "A conservative exposition which deserves a place on every pastor's bookshelf" (Barber, 167). "Rich detail on verses, documented views, reasons, and a warmth of practical comment, all of this helpful to expositors" (Rosscup, 276). Reformed.

Hogg, C. F., and W. E. Vine. *The Epistle to the Galatians*. Fincastle, VA: Scripture Truth, 1921.

> This little volume is a helpful commentary by two Plymouth Brethren scholars for the nonspecialist and preacher looking for sermonic material. Published in 1921, it is seriously dated and not up to date on scholarship. "A doctrinal commentary which continues the development of Paul's thought begun in his Epistle to the Romans. Holds to a late date for the writing of this letter, deals quite ably with the chronological problems and provides a practical exposition" (Barber, 167). Premillennial. Dispensational.

!*+Lightfoot, J. B. *The Epistle of St. Paul to the Galatians*. London: Macmillan, 1865. Reprint, Grand Rapids: Zondervan, 1957.

> This commentary is a true classic treatment on this epistle, legendary for its exegesis of the Greek text. It has been hugely influential to generations of commentators and still retains its value. The author was a staunch defender of the North Galatia view. "Mined . . . thoroughly by others" (Carson, 105). "Lightfoot is highly regarded for his work on the Greek text, top notch exegesis verse by verse, special notes on key problems, giving of views and reasons, etc." (Rosscup, 276). "An important study which cannot be overlooked or ignored. Without question one of the greatest commentaries on the Greek text of this epistle" (Barber, 167).

!*Longenecker, Richard N. *Galatians*. WBC. Edited by Bruce M. Metzger. Nashville: Nelson, 1990.

> An outstanding, technical offering by a noted evangelical that is surprisingly accessible to nonspecialists. The introduction really shines. "Especially strong on the Jewish roots of the debate" (Carson, 103).

*+Luther, Martin. *Commentary on Galatians*. Edited by John Prince Fallowes. Translated by Erasmus Middleton. Reprint, Grand Rapids: Kregel, 1979.

> This commentary is an abridgment of Luther's lecture notes. Over thirty English editions of this commentary have been published over the years depending upon which lecture notes were used. This version provides the meat and power of Luther's thought. Those wishing to read a fuller treatment should consult volumes 26 and 27 of *Luther's Works* published by Concordia Publishing House. There you will find the substance of lectures delivered to his students in 1519 and 1539. This commentary is a condensed version of that thought. According to Spurgeon, John Bunyan preferred this commentary to all other books except the Bible. "This is a great historic work, and is beyond criticism on account of its great usefulness" (Spurgeon, 176–77).

!?Martyn, J. Louis. *Galatians*. AB. Edited by William Foxwell Albright and David Noel Freedman. New York: Doubleday, 1997.

> This commentary is a monumental scholarly achievement, but is not without interpretive flaws. Scholars and students will want to obtain it for its help with the text, but pastors seeking homiletical assistance might want to give it a pass. "A major tome . . . rich in suggestive insights and in the idiosyncratic interpretations that mark most of Martyn's work. But it requires a fair bit of knowledge to spot the serious breaches and interpretations that abound in it" (Carson, 103).

*McKnight, Scot. *Galatians*. NIVAC. Edited by Terry Muck. Grand Rapids: Zondervan, 1995.

> A lucid and accessible treatment that abounds in practical insights.

*Moo, Douglas J. *Galatians*. BECNT. Edited by Robert W. Yarbrough and Robert H. Stein. Grand Rapids: Baker Academic, 2013.

> This exceptional treatment of the Greek text by the revered Kenneth T. Wessner Professor of NT at Wheaton College Graduate School is a major contribution to the commentary literature on this book. The author interacts with the New Perspective on Paul, which is completely absent from earlier commentaries. Of particular value to the scholar is the extensive Works Cited as well helpful indices of subjects, authors, Greek words, and Scripture and other ancient writings. It promises to be the top commentary on this epistle for years to come.

*+Ramsay, William Mitchell. *A Historical Commentary on St. Paul's Epistle to the Galatians*. New York: Putnams, 1900. Reprint, Minneapolis: Klock & Klock, 1978.

> This classic work, first published in 1900, is a unique treatment totally unlike any other works on this epistle. The author was a recognized authority on the travels of the Apostle Paul. His work is still widely quoted in modern commentaries. Ramsay advocates the South Galatia view. This book is again out of print, but should be purchased if found. It is a true classic. "From a century ago, for matters of technical introduction, it is still worth reading" (Carson, 108). "Readers of Professor Ramsay's work will find that it contains a good deal more than historical argument. As an archaeologist he includes a considerable amount of first-hand data gleaned from his exploration in the area. Furthermore, his commentary is based upon the original text and is replete with important references to local situations, social and political trends, informative word studies, and geographical details. It also contains abundant evidence of the author's sensitivity to the Apostle Paul's physical weakness, sense of mission, and love for his converts" (Barber).

Ridderbos, Herman N. *The Epistle of Paul to the Churches of Galatia*. NICNT. Edited by F. F. Bruce. Grand Rapids: Eerdmans, 1953.

> This brief commentary by a noted professor of NT at Kampen Theological Seminary, Kampen, The Netherlands, is based on the English text and can still be helpful and a bargain if picked up secondhand. However, it has totally been superseded by Fung as the series is undergoing a complete revision. Reformed.

*Schreiner, Thomas R. *Galatians*. Zondervan Exegetical Commentary on the New Testament. Edited by Clinton E. Arnold. Grand Rapids: Zondervan Academic, 2010.

> This volume is an excellent treatment of the Greek text by the James Buchanan Harrison Professor of NT at the Southern Baptist Theological Seminary in Louisville. It upholds the author's high standards of scholarship. It is "user friendly" and well written. Includes an excellent select bibliography. Although this book is intended for those with a working knowledge of Greek, it is not necessary to be a Greek scholar to benefit from Schreiner's insights. "Simply written but enables pastors and students to see what the exegetical options are and to work through the Greek text without too much technical detail" (Carson, 102). Baptist.

Skilton, John H. *Machen's Notes on Galatians*. International Library of Philosophy and Theology. Edited by Robert L. Raymond. Philadelphia: Presbyterian and Reformed, 1973.

> This volume is a compilation of the renowned J. Gresham Machen's teaching notes. The results are often spotty, but with some excellent exegetical and expositional insights. Covers only 1:1—3:14. Machen was one of the towering evangelical figures of the twentieth century and a noted Greek scholar. Reformed.

Tenney, Merrill C. *Galatians: The Charter of Christian Liberty*. Rev. ed. Grand Rapids: Eerdmans, 1957.

> This interesting little volume is a brief treatment of the book using different methods of Bible study. This is definitely for the beginning student, but can be helpful to the pastor in approaching the book. It gives little exegetical assistance. "Designed to help students of the Word grapple with the text firsthand. Approaches the epistle from synthetic, critical, biographical, and devotional points of view. Excellent" (Barber, 168)!

Wiersbe, Warren W. *Be Free: An Expository Study of Galatians*. Wheaton: Victor, 1975.

> This study is a helpful little book ideal for laymen and Bible study groups.

Ephesians

*Arnold, Clinton E. *Ephesians*. Zondervan Exegetical Commentary on the New Testament. Edited by Clinton E. Arnold. Grand Rapids: Zondervan Academic, 2010.

> In keeping with the series objective, this commentary, by the dean and professor of NT at Talbot School of Theology in La Mirada, California, is an excellent treatment of the Greek text of this gospel for those with a working knowledge of Greek. The strength of this book, as with all of the volumes in this series, is its emphasis on exegesis of the Greek text. It is quite accessible even to those with little or no knowledge of Greek. The introduction, in line with the other works with this series, is fairly brief, although at forty pages it is more detailed than most. Arnold holds that this epistle is a genuine Pauline letter. His discussion of the historical background of the epistle is also quite good. At 508 pages, its detail and comprehensiveness feels about right. "Helps students to work through the Greek text and provides numerous pastoral asides, but it is not as rich as O'Brien and Thielman" (Carson, 109).

!*?Barth, Markus. *Ephesians*. AB. Edited by William Foxwell Albright and David Noel Freedman. 2 vols. Garden City: Doubleday, 1974.

> A massive critical commentary, this is certainly one of the major works on this epistle of the past fifty years. It is a rigorous and full work, comprehensive in scope, and yet very practical. It will be much appreciated by evangelicals as it adheres to several conservative positions such as Pauline authorship. "An extensive, critical exposition, combining a careful blend of historical-grammatical exegesis with a down-to-earth application to the condition of the church today. A work of real quality which expository preachers will find most helpful" (Barber). "Painstakingly detailed. . . . More advanced students can scarcely afford to be without it" (Carson, 110).

*+Calvin, John. *Sermons on the Epistle to the Ephesians*. Translated by Arthur Golding in 1577. Revised translation, 1973. Reprint, Edinburgh: Banner of Truth, 1973.

> This gem is a true classic of the Christian faith. First published in French in 1562, this collection of sermons, by the eminent Swiss reformer, is a gold mine of sermonic material that serves as a homiletical textbook for conveying Christian doctrine. These forty-eight sermons were preached at Geneva on consecutive Sundays in 1558–59 when Calvin was forty-nine years of age. Reading this book is a cure for superficial preaching. "The sermons are priceless" (Spurgeon, 177). "One should certainly not overlook . . . which can still be marvelously suggestive to preachers" (Carson, 112). Reformed.

!*+Eadie, John. *Commentary on the Epistle to the Ephesians*. Edinburgh: T. & T. Clark, 1883. Reprint, Minneapolis: James and Klock, 1977.

> Although now over 130 years have passed since its initial publication, it is still of great value on the Greek text. A true classic! I bought this and other Eadie works while a student in seminary and have never ceased to be impressed by the careful scholarship of his work. "A very full exposition which deals with all the exegetical problems, pays careful attention to the development of Paul's theme, and provides important digressions on the theological truths of the epistle" (Barber, 168). "This book is one of prodigious learning and research. The author seems to have read all, in every language, that has been written upon the Epistle. It is also a work of independent criticism, and casts much new light upon many passages" (Spurgeon, 177).

*Hendriksen, William. *Exposition of Ephesians*. New Testament Commentary. Grand Rapids: Baker, 1967.

> This commentary, by the late noted professor of NT at Calvin Theological Seminary, like all of his commentaries, is extremely well done, scholarly, and warmly devotional. A worthy acquisition to any student or pastor's library. "A

well-written commentary which is both scholarly and practical and of great value to preachers" (Barber, 169). Reformed.

*+Hodge, Charles. *Commentary on the Epistle to the Ephesians*. Reprint, Old Tappan, NJ: Revell, n.d.

> Based on the Greek text, this is a masterful exposition by the nineteenth-century Princeton giant, both practical and doctrinal. "Solid and often theologically very suggestive" (Carson, 112). "Most valuable. With no writer do we more fully agree" (Spurgeon, 178). Reformed.

*Hoehner, Harold W. *Ephesians: An Exegetical Commentary*. Grand Rapids: Baker Academic, 2002.

> A scholarly, exegetical treatment that has much to commend it. At about nine hundred pages, it is marvelously detailed and comprehensive. "Unsurpassed on many fronts" (Carson, 109).

Kent, Homer. *Ephesians: The Glory of the Church*. Chicago: Moody, 1971.

> Like all of the author's works, this book is a concise and lucid treatment of the main themes of the book with an emphasis on the practical. At 127 pages this book is not as detailed or as helpful as his commentary on the Pastoral Epistles. This book is mainly for the beginning student and nonspecialist. Ideal for laypersons.

!*+Lightfoot, J. B. See section on the Pauline Epistles.

*+Moule, H. C. G. *Grace and Godliness: Studies in the Epistle to the Ephesians*. London: Seeley, 1895. Reprint, Minneapolis: Klock & Klock, 1983.

> This brief devotional gem was published together in one volume along with Pattison's *Exposition of Ephesians: Lessons in Grace and Godliness* by Klock & Klock. It is now regrettably out of print. This volume came about in 1894 when ministers gathered at Cambridge for the "Long Vacation" and requested Professor Moule, at that time principal of Ridley Hall, to provide them with a series of Bible readings. These studies are the result of that request.

*+————. *Studies in Ephesians*. Cambridge: Cambridge University Press, 1893. Reprint, Grand Rapids: Kregel, 1977.

> This handy little commentary was originally published in 1893 in the Cambridge Bible for Schools and Colleges series. This is one of several works the author penned on this epistle. One was a commentary on the Greek text in the Cambridge Greek Testament and the other a devotional work titled *Grace and Godliness: Studies in the Epistle to the Ephesians*. All of Dr. Moule's works

exhibit tremendous insight into the meaning of the text as well as devotional warmth. This book is well worth obtaining if it can be purchased secondhand.

*O'Brien, Peter T. *The Letter to the Ephesians*. PNTC. Grand Rapids: Eerdmans, 1999.

This substantial commentary, at close to five hundred pages of text, leaves few stones unturned and is a major contribution to the study of this epistle. Belongs on the shelf of every pastor who is preaching or teaching through this book. "Perhaps the best English-language commentary" (Carson, 108).

*+Pattison, Robert Everett. *A Commentary on the Epistle to the Ephesians*. Boston: Gould and Lincoln, 1859. Reprint, Minneapolis: Klock & Klock, 1983.

This book is a rich exposition of the text by a noted nineteenth-century preacher and president of Waterville College. It was reprinted by Klock & Klock along with Moule's *Grace and Godliness: Studies in the Epistle to the Ephesians*. "A book to instruct intelligent, experienced believers. It is a model for a class-book, plain and yet profound" (Spurgeon, 178).

*+Robinson, J. Armitage. *Commentary on Ephesians*. 2nd ed. London: Clark, 1903. Reprint, Grand Rapids: Kregel, 1979.

Along with Westcott, this treatment of the Greek text vies for supremacy among older commentaries. This book is actually two commentaries in one volume. The first part has a brief introduction followed by translation and exposition. The second part is perhaps the finest exegetical treatment of the Greek text ever written. "The venerable classic on the Greek text" (Carson, 112). "One of the finest exegetical treatments to be found anywhere" (Barber, 169).

Simpson, E. K., and F. F. Bruce. *Commentary on the Epistles to the Ephesians and the Colossians*. NICNT. Edited by F. F. Bruce. Grand Rapids: Eerdmans, 1957.

Simpson wrote the portion on Ephesians and Bruce did Colossians. The work by Bruce is of much greater substance than that by Simpson, which tends to be flowery and sermonic. Although Bruce revised this commentary in 1984 adding a section on Philemon, this work still deserves to be consulted, particularly the work by Bruce which is quite substantial. Of the Simpson writing, "On the whole the work is an erudite disappointment. His vocabulary is impressive, but not much else is" (Carson, 111).

*Snodgrass, Klyne. *Ephesians*. NIVAC. Edited by Terry Muck. Grand Rapids: Zondervan, 1996.

One of the better volumes in the series, this is an eminently practical guide to the epistle that pastors will greatly appreciate. Please note that Snodgrass has a weak view of election.

Talbert, Charles H. *Ephesians and Colossians*. Paideia. Edited by Mikeal C. Parsons and Charles H. Talbert. Grand Rapids: Baker Academic, 2007.

> At 247 pages the author covers both the Ephesian and Colossian epistles. In my opinion, each epistle deserved as much detail and deserved an individual volume. He devotes barely twenty-five pages of introduction covering both epistles, much too scanty in my judgment. The author holds that both epistles are pseudonymous. "Talbert's strength is invariably in his close reading of the text and in the attention he pays to its structure" (Carson, 111). "The exegesis is compact and well-informed" (Evans, 369).

!*Thielman, Frank. *Ephesians*. BECNT. Edited by Robert W. Yarbrough and Robert H. Stein. Grand Rapids: Baker Academic, 2010.

> This volume is a comprehensive and well-done commentary on the Greek text by a first-rate NT scholar and professor at Beeson Divinity School. A superior work! Highly recommended! "Remarkably accessible—even in a commentary like this that uses a lot of Greek and in-text citations. The simplicity of his style masks remarkably deep learning" (Carson, 109).

!*+Westcott, Brooke Foss. *Saint Paul's Epistle to the Ephesians*. London: Macmillan, 1906. Reprint, Minneapolis: Klock & Klock, 1906.

> This venerable classic is still worth consulting on exegetical matters. Among older commentaries, this is almost as good as the one by Robinson, according to Carson. Westcott's handling of the Greek text is masterful. "Detailed and scholarly" (Rosscup, 284). "Will always be consulted as a careful, dependable work" (Evans, 369).

Philippians

Boice, James Montgomery. *Philippians: An Expositional Commentary*. Grand Rapids:

> This work is similar to most of the author's other works on books of the Bible in that it is a series of expositions on the text. It is particularly well suited to laypersons and beginning students. He is extremely practical and does not get bogged down in technical details. Preachers will find Boice to be quite suggestive. "A lucid and very readable simple exposition that is helpful and competent on many of the issues. . . . The exposition is practical and sermonic, with sometimes good background and comparison with relevant passages from other Scripture. He illustrates heavily from literature, history, and contemporary life" (Rosscup, 285).

*Bruce, F. F. *Philippians*. New International Biblical Commentary. Edited by W. Ward Gasque. Peabody: Hendrickson, 1989.

> This commentary, based on the NIV by the esteemed NT scholar and professor at the University of Manchester, is concise, very accessible to the nonspecialist, and well worth acquiring. The serious student will want to supplement it with more detailed works.

Cohick, Lynn H. *Philippians*. The Story of God Bible Commentary. Edited by Tremper Longman III and Scot McKnight. Grand Rapids: Zondervan, 2013.

> Although the series' intentions are laudable and this volume does a good job of highlighting the Bible's grand story in Philippians, it is not strong on the details. For example, the introduction at twenty-one pages is much too brief and it lacks a bibliography.

!*+Eadie, John. *A Commentary on the Greek Text of the Epistle of Paul to the Philippians*. Edinburgh: T. & T. Clark. Reprint, Minneapolis: James & Klock, 1977.

> Originally published in 1857, this is still a most valuable treatment especially for its treatment of the Greek text. "Gives excellent definitions of Greek words, contains a very comprehensive discussion of the *kenosis* passage, and presents the writings of leading men of all schools of thought" (Barber, 170). "A standard work. Essential to the scholarly student" (Spurgeon, 180).

*Fee, Gordon D. *Paul's Letter to the Philippians*. NICNT. Edited by Gordon D. Fee. Grand Rapids: Eerdmans, 1995.

> One of the top NT scholars of the past generation, Fee has written what is arguably the best mid-level commentary on this epistle. It is beautifully written and accessible. This commentary replaces the 1955 volume by Müller, which was one of the weakest in the old series. This update is a huge improvement and will prove to be invaluable to pastors and students. With this volume and O'Brien, pastors and students are well served. "Fee could not be boring if he tried. The zest of his prose makes him exciting to read, and his scholarship is always rigorous" (Carson, 114).

Getz, Gene A. *A Profile of Christian Maturity: A Study of Philippians*. Grand Rapids: Zondervan, 1976.

> This little book is not a verse-by-verse commentary, but rather a series of studies "With 20th Century Lessons for Your Church." Each chapter begins with "Something to Think About" and ends with "A Personal Life Response." Very practical for laypersons and pastors.

*Hansen, G. Walter. *The Letter to the Philippians*. PNTC. Edited by D. A. Carson. Grand Rapids: Eerdmans, 2009.

> I have been impressed by the generally high level of scholarship and production values of this series. This volume is no exception. It is extremely well written and irenic in spirit. Hansen is a professor for global theological education at Fuller Theological Seminary.

!*Hawthorne, Gerald F. *Philippians*. WBC. Edited by David A. Hubbard and Glenn W. Barker. Waco, TX: Word, 1983.

> There is good news and there is bad news regarding this commentary by a respected professor of NT at Wheaton College. The good news is that this is one of the very best technical commentaries produced on this epistle in the past forty years. "Some rank this as the top commentary on Philippians due to the wide reading and masterfully good survey on introductory questions and its carefulness on grammar, philology, capture of the epistle's flow and handling of difficult passages" (Rosscup, 287). The bad news is that it is now over thirty years old and not up to date on recent scholarship. Also, there are some idiosyncratic exegetical interpretations. The book was revised and enlarged by Ralph P. Martin in 2004, adding about a hundred pages to the original with mixed results. "The bibliography is thoroughly updated, but the added explanations are sometimes not integrated with Hawthorne, making for a disjointed work" (Carson, 114). "Solid and informed, though not particularly original" (Bauer, 361).

*+Johnstone, Robert. *Lectures on the Epistle to the Philippians*. Edinburgh: T. & T. Clark, 1875. Reprint, Minneapolis: Klock & Klock, 1977.

> This delightful book is a collection of thirty lectures on the epistle that were delivered from the pulpit in successive Sunday services. Johnstone, late professor of NT literature and exegesis, United Presbyterian College, Edinburgh, shares the insights he learned as a student of the law and a NT scholar in these brilliant expositions. I read this book during my devotions while a student in seminary almost forty years ago and was enthralled and greatly blessed. I felt as if I were in the presence of pulpit royalty. It is true that preachers do not preach this way in the twenty-first century, but perhaps the church would be less superficial if they did. "A thorough, practical, and homiletical exposition, which warns against the fallacies of churchianity, strongly defends the preexistence of Christ, and remains one of the leading expository works on the subject" (Barber, 170). "A noble volume. A real boon to the man who purchases it" (Spurgeon, 180). Presbyterian.

*+Lightfoot, J. B. *St. Paul's Epistle to the Philippians.* London: Macmillan, 1913. Reprint, Grand Rapids: Zondervan, 1953.

> This classic, first published in 1868, is a masterful exposition of the book based on the Greek text. Its treatment of the text is unsurpassed and should be purchased if found. "A thorough exposition which discusses every grammatical and interpretive problem imaginable" (Barber, 171). "Still one of the most valuable works on Philippians" (Evans, 373).

*Martin, Ralph P. *The Epistle of Paul to the Philippians.* TNTC. Edited by R. V. G. Tasker. Grand Rapids: Eerdmans, 1959.

> This volume is not to be confused with the author's Philippians volume in the New Century Bible series published in 1976. In 1987 he revised this commentary to bring its views more into line with the other with not altogether satisfying results. The revision is more up to date on scholarly issues and literature, but the writer prefers the earlier edition for its evangelical fidelity. "An exposition particularly well adapted to Christians living under tension and facing the pressures of life" (Barber, 171). "It is packed with useful interaction with the secondary literature, but by this point Martin was influenced by Kasemann's 'odyssey of Christ' approach to the Philippians hymn and related material. I find this interpretation exegetically weak" (Carson, 116).

?———. *Philippians.* New Century Bible. Edited by Ronald E. Clements and Matthew Black. Grand Rapids: Eerdmans, 1980.

> This treatment, published almost twenty years after his TNTC volume, shows a tendency to stray from accepted evangelical positions. See my discussion on the author's *The Epistle of Paul to the Philippians* above. "Here Martin shows more use of critical sources and must be studied with discernment since he has been inclined away from some of his older, some will feel more defensible positions" (Rosscup, 289).

*Melick, Richard R. *Philippians, Colossians, Philemon.* NAC. Edited by E. Ray Clendenen. Nashville: Holman Reference, 1991.

> A helpful volume particularly for pastors by a professor of NT at Golden Gate Theological Seminary in Mill Valley, California. "Workmanlike but not outstanding" (Carson, 115). Baptist.

Moule, H. C. G. *Studies in Philippians.* Cambridge: Cambridge University Press, 1893. Reprint, Grand Rapids: Kregel, 1977.

> This brief treatment was originally published in 1893 in the series, Cambridge Bible for Schools and Colleges. Although now quite dated on technical matters, it is still worth obtaining for its devotional emphasis. "A beautifully

written, deeply devotional treatment which expounds the affectionate character of this epistle and relates its message to the lives of believers" (Barber, 171). "Warm devotional tone that bathes his exegesis" (Carson, 117).

Müller, Jacobus J. *The Epistles of Paul to the Philippians and to Philemon*. NICNT. Edited by F. F. Bruce. Grand Rapids: Eerdmans, 1955.

This offering, by the professor of NT at the Theological Seminary, Stellenbosh, South Africa, is one of the weakest in the series. Why Philemon was even paired with Philippians is still a mystery to me as it is usually treated with Colossians. Whereas, it was not a very strong commentary to begin with, it has not shown its age well and is now quite dated. "Concise and helpful. Defends the unity of the epistle and the preexistence and deity of Christ. Praiseworthy treatment of the Greek text. Pedantic style" (Barber, 171).

!*O'Brian, Peter T. *The Epistle to the Philippians*. NIGTC. Edited by I. Howard Marshall and W. Ward Gasque. Grand Rapids: Eerdmans, 1991.

Although now a quarter century old, this comprehensive study remains the best exegetical commentary on the Greek text. The author accepts Pauline authorship of the epistle and argues for its unity. Students and pastors doing exegetical work on the text will find this to be indispensable. Highly recommended! "The best exegetical work on the letter. . . . The commentator is thorough and clear on key problem verses (2:6–7; 2:13, etc.), and one comes away confident of seeing a masterful sifting" (Rosscup, 290). "The best technical commentary on the Greek text. . . . O'Brien read and thought through everything of importance up to his date, with the result that he gives *reasons* for his exegetical decisions. At the same time, this commentary is theologically rich, even if its prose is sometimes pedestrian. The treatment of the so-called Christ hymn (2:5–11) is superb" (Carson, 114).

*Robertson, A. T. *Paul's Joy in Christ: Studies in Philippians*. Old Tappan, NJ: Revell, 1917. Reprint, Grand Rapids: Baker, 1979.

This little volume, by perhaps the foremost Greek grammarian the United States has ever produced, is a sheer delight to read. It is not a detailed commentary, but rather a series of expositions on the text. It is not technical and easily accessible to the beginning student or layperson. "He is rich in word studies and in the explanation of the text" (Rosscup, 291).

*Silva, Moisés. *Philippians*. BECNT. Edited by Robert Yarbrough and Robert H. Stein. 2nd ed. Grand Rapids: Baker Academic, 2005.

For such a brief work (just over 200 pages), this is an outstanding commentary quite strong on exegesis. Definitely a must purchase! "Especially strong in tracing the flow of the argument. . . . Attention to semantics and syntax are wholly admirable. One constantly feels he is not so much trying to master the text as to be mastered by it" (Carson, 115).

*Theilman, Frank. *Philippians.* NIVAC. Edited by Terry Muck. Grand Rapids. Zondervan, 1995.

> An outstanding nontechnical commentary by a noted NT scholar. Perhaps the best NT treatment in the series. A real joy to read!

Colossians

!?Barth, Markus, and Helmut Blanke. *Colossians.* AB. Edited by William Foxwell Albright and David Noel Freedman. New York: Anchor Bible, 1994.

> Regrettably, this commentary is not one of the stronger NT offerings in the AB series. I do not recommend it for purchase.

Carson, H. M. *The Epistles of Paul to the Colossians & Philemon.* TNTC. Edited by R. V. G. Tasker. Grand Rapids: Eerdmans, 1960.

> One of the older volumes in the old series, this commentary has been honorably retired by Wright.

*+Daille, Jean. *An Exposition of the Epistle of Paul to the Colossians.* Reprint, Minneapolis: Klock & Klock, 1983.

> This welcome addition to Klock & Klock's LCRL series is the compilation of a series of sermons preached in 1639 by the noted seventeenth-century French pulpiteer Jean Daille and first published in 1648. Regrettably, it is again out of print and should be purchased if found. "Written in a deliciously florid style. Very sweet and evangelical after the French manner" (Spurgeon, 179).

*+Davenant, John. *An Exposition to the Epistle of St. Paul to the Colossians.* 2 vols. Translated by Josiah Allport. Birmingham: Hamilton, Adams, 1831. Reprint, Lynchburg, VA: James Family, 1979.

> This classic was originally written in Latin and appeared first in 1627. It is the 1831 translation into English that is reprinted here. This version is a very substantial treatment by the seventeenth-century Lord Bishop of Salisbury, president of Queen's College, and Lady Margaret's Professor of Divinity, Cambridge. Again out of print, it should be purchased if available.

!*?Dunn, James D. G. *The Epistles to the Colossians and to Philemon*. NIGTC. Edited by I. Howard Marshall, W. Ward Gasque, and Donald A. Hagner. Grand Rapids: Eerdmans, 1996.

> This commentary is an excellent treatment of the Greek text. However, Dunn's apparent waffling over the authorship issue is at times infuriating. He denies Pauline authorship, but concedes that it was likely someone within the Pauline circle written during Paul's lifetime. This issue aside, this book is a very fine study, but now a bit dated at twenty years of age. "Rivals O'Brien as a first-rate technical work on these epistles" (Evans, 377).

!*+Eadie, John. *Commentary on the Epistle of Paul to the Colossians*. Richard Griffin, 1856. Reprint, Minneapolis: James and Klock, 1977.

> This volume is another classic reprint of an outstanding commentary by a noted nineteenth-century Scottish Presbyterian scholar and churchman. The author's meticulous detail and thoroughness are a joy to behold. However, it is not for the layperson or nonspecialist. Apparently, this valuable work is back in print again (Wipf & Stock, 1998). "A rich and inspiring exposition which preachers who have a knowledge of Greek will appreciate for its insights and detailed explanations" (Barber, 172). "Very full and reliable. A work of the utmost value" (Spurgeon, 182). Reformed.

*Garland, David E. *Colossians, Philemon*. NIVAC. Edited by Terry Muck. Grand Rapids: Zondervan, 1998.

> This volume is the rare practical commentary that has substantial interaction with scholarly writings. It is also quite helpful for pastors.

Harrison, Everett F. *Colossians: Christ All-Sufficient*. Chicago: Moody, 1971.

> This book is an extremely brief treatment by a former professor of NT at Dallas Theological Seminary and Fuller Theological Seminary. It is well written, but its brevity makes it of interest only to the beginning students and other nonspecialists. "Good things frequently come in small packages. This is one of them" (Barber, 172).

*Hendriksen, William. *Exposition of Colossians and Philemon*. New Testament Commentary. Grand Rapids: Baker, 1964.

> This volume is a devotional gem based on the Greek text, but accessible to the general reader. This work upholds the high standards of the series. "Contains an extensive introduction, a new translation of the text, an informative commentary, a valuable summary of the data covered in the book, and a series of critical notes dealing with problems which are of a more specialized nature" (Barber, 172).

!*+Lightfoot, J. B. *Saint Paul's Epistles to the Colossians and to Philemon*. London: Macmillan, 1879. Reprint, Grand Rapids: Zondervan, 1959.

> This volume is a classic treatment of the Greek text. It is extremely strong in exegesis and still deserves to be consulted. Out of print again, but should be purchased if found. "Valuable studies which admirably illuminate the text of both epistles" (Barber, 172).

!*?Lohse, Eduard. *Colossians and Philemon*. Hermeneia. Edited by Helmut Koester. Translated by William R. Poehlmann and Robert J. Karris. Philadelphia: Fortress, 1971.

> This entry in the Hermeneia series was translated from the 1968 German edition *Die Briefe an die Kolosser und an Philemon*. Although the author denies Pauline authorship, this is still a very useful commentary for the advanced student or scholar. "An exacting inquiry into the text and possible background. . . . Wide acquaintance with literature on or related to Colossians. Good use of Jewish and Hellenistic backgrounds, references to Qumran material" (Rosscup, 294). "Contains a wealth of clear and useful comment" (Carson, 119).

Lucas, R. C. *The Message of Colossians and Philemon*. BST. Edited by John R. W. Stott. Downers Grove: IVP Academic, 1984.

> A popular treatment of these epistles that will help preachers prime the homiletical pump.

*Melick, Richard R. See section on Philippians.

*Moo, Douglas J. *The Letters to the Colossians and to Philemon*. PNTC. Edited by D. A. Carson. Grand Rapids: Eerdmans, 2008.

> This commentary is a mid-level work by a front-rank evangelical scholar that is a top choice for pastors. Highly recommended!

Moule, H. C. G. *Studies in Colossians & Philemon*. Cambridge: Cambridge University Press, 1893. Reprint, Grand Rapids: Kregel, 1977.

> This volume is a devotional commentary on these epistles first published in 1877 by the noted Cambridge professor of the late nineteenth / early twentieth century. It is for general audiences and should be supplemented with more substantial works. "Moule was known for his saintliness and evangelical fervor. These studies bear testimony to his ability as an expositor. They deal adequately with the text and deftly apply the message of these epistles" (Barber, 172).

!*O'Brien, Peter T. *Colossians, Philemon.* WBC. Edited by David A. Hubbard and Glenn W. Barker. Waco, TX: Word, 1982.

> This excellent commentary is much like Hawthorne's fine treatment on Philippians in this same series in that it is now over thirty years old and not up to date on the latest scholarship. That being said, this is an excellent treatment of the Greek text that is not overly technical and accessible to nonspecialists. At one time, this was the best technical commentary on the epistle. "The best exegetical work on the letter. . . . The commentator is thorough and clear on key problem verses (2:6–7; 2:13, etc.) and one comes away confident of seeing a masterful sifting" (Rosscup, 294).

*Pao, David W. *Colossians and Philemon.* Zondervan Exegetical Commentary on the New Testament. Edited by Clinton E. Arnold. Grand Rapids: Zondervan Academic, 2012.

> In keeping with the series objective, this commentary, by a professor of NT and chairman of the NT Department at Trinity Evangelical Divinity School, is an excellent treatment of the Greek text of this gospel for those with a working knowledge of Greek. Its strength is in exegesis of the text; its glaring weakness, as in many of the volumes in this series, is the sketchiness of the introduction. At just sixteen pages, it is much too brief to do the complex issues much justice. Kudos again to the editors of this series for the Translation and Graphical Layout. It makes everything so much more accessible and readable. "The most recent exegetical commentary on the Greek text that is remarkably accessible—so accessible it will help pastors review their Greek. . . . It is careful, understated, reliable, and nuanced" (Carson, 118).

Simpson, E. K., and F. F. Bruce. See section on Ephesians.

Talbert, Charles H. See section on Ephesians.

*+Westcott, Frederick Brooke. *Colossians: A Letter to Asia.* London: Macmillan, 1914. Reprint, Minneapolis: Klock & Klock, 1981.

> This offering in Klock & Klock's LCRL was written by the son of the illustrious B. F. Westcott. His writing is less technical and more pastoral than that of his father. "Expounds the epistle with clarity and insight. His exegesis provides a solid basis for his comments on the text" (Barber, 173).

*Wright, N. T. *Colossians and Philemon.* TNTC. Edited by Leon Morris. Downers Grove: IVP Academic, 1986.

> An exceptional brief treatment by the controversial and prolific NT scholar who was formerly the Bishop of Durham in the Church of England. This commentary retires Carson's 1960 work in the series.

1 and 2 Thessalonians

*Beale, G. K. *1–2 Thessalonians*. InterVarsity New Testament Commentary series. Edited by Grant Osborne. Downers Grove: InterVarsity, 2003.

This nontechnical commentary provides a good mix of exegesis, theology, OT background, and application of the text to the modern reader. As usual, Beale's work is meticulous and well worth reading. "Very well done" (Evans, 381). Reformed. Amillennial.

Bruce, F. F. *1 & 2 Thessalonians*. WBC. Edited by David A. Hubbard and Glenn W. Barker. Waco: Word, 1982.

This commentary was the first volume published in the WBC series. It is surprisingly brief for a work of this nature. The introduction is barely twenty pages. As always, what Bruce does have to say is first rate. Carson is more enamored with this commentary than I am. "Characterized by Bruce's thoroughness and care for detail, the work is especially valuable in its introductory remarks, its careful delineation of the background, and its useful excursus on 'The Antichrist'" (Carson, 124).

!*+Eadie, John. *A Commentary on the Greek Text of the Epistle of Paul to the Thessalonians*. Edited by William Young. London: MacMillan, 1877. Reprint, Minneapolis: James and Klock, 1977.

This volume is a true classic and for many decades a standard work on the Greek text. James and Klock has done a tremendous service by making this work available to another generation of students and scholars. Very helpful on matters of the text! Purchase if available. "A rich and inspiring exposition which preachers who have a knowledge of Greek will appreciate for its insights and detailed explanations" (Barber, 173).

*Fee, Gordon D. *The First and Second Letters to the Thessalonians*. NICNT. Edited by Gordon D. Fee. Grand Rapids: Eerdmans, 2009.

This excellent treatment replaces the 1959 volume in the series by Leon Morris. As usual with Fee, the writing is exceptional, the exegesis first-rate, and his insights often profound. The only problem that I found with this book is the extremely brief introduction. With the NICNT series, I expect a much fuller and more comprehensive treatment of introductory issues. Despite that, this is the best mid-level commentary available that is up to date. "A disciplined focus on the text and sober, thorough, penetrating exegesis" (Evans, 380).

!Frame, James Everett. *A Critical and Exegetical Commentary on the Epistles of St. Paul to the Thessalonians*. ICC. Edited by S. R. Driver, A. Plummer, and C. A. Briggs. Edinburgh: T. & T. Clark, 1912.

> This commentary at one time was the standard treatment of the Greek text. It is still helpful on grammatical and other technical areas, but weak in the area of theological interpretation.

*Green, Gene. *The Letters to the Thessalonians*. PNTC. Edited by D. A. Carson. Grand Rapids: Eerdmans, 2002.

> An excellent mid-level commentary by an evangelical. Vies with Fee for supremacy as the best nontechnical works.

*Hendriksen, William. *Exposition of I and II Thessalonians*. New Testament Commentary. Grand Rapids: Baker, 1955.

> This volume, though slim and now dated, having been published in 1955, is still very helpful for students and preachers. It is based on the Greek text and is a careful study, but should be supplemented with more modern treatments. "As usual, the author is detailed, careful in word meanings and background, lucid and warm in application. He always has considerable usefulness for an expositor" (Rosscup, 296). Amillennial.

*Hiebert, D. Edmond. *The Thessalonian Epistles: A Call to Readiness*. Chicago: Moody, 1971.

> This commentary by the late professor of Greek and New Testament at the Mennonite Brethren Biblical Seminary in Fresno, California, is user friendly, warm, and quite readable. Now somewhat dated, it sets forth the pretribulational, premillennial viewpoints in an exemplary fashion. "An outstanding exposition based upon unusually comprehensive and complete exegesis. A leader among commentaries for accuracy and reliability" (Barber, 173). "Many features make this volume valuable: background information, extensive bibliography up to its day, numerous footnotes, and a rich use of the original Greek" (Rosscup, 296).

· Hogg, C. F., and W. E. Vine. *The Epistles to the Thessalonians*. Fincastle, VA: Scripture Truth, 1914.

> This slim volume is a rudimentary commentary for the nonspecialist. There are some attempts to deal with the meanings of Greek words and nuances. Premillennial. Dispensational.

*Holmes, Michael W. *1 and 2 Thessalonians*. NIVAC. Edited by Terry Muck. Grand Rapids: Zondervan, 1998.

> A practical commentary that is exceedingly helpful for pastors. "Judicious in its pastoral application" (Carson, 125).

!*+Lightfoot, J. B. See section on the Pauline Epistles.

!*?Malherbe, Abraham J. *The Letters to the Thessalonians*. AYB. Edited by William Foxwell Albright and David Noel Freedman. New Haven: Yale University Press, 2004.

> An excellent technical commentary by the Buckingham Professor Emeritus of NT Criticism and Interpretation at Yale University, this work is well done and surprisingly conservative in several respects. For example, the author argues for the authenticity of the both epistles and Pauline authorship. It is somewhat weak theologically. "Very rich on the Greco-Roman background and its bearing on the interpretation of these two epistles" (Carson, 124). "Scholarly standards are exceedingly rigorous" (Evans, 383).

*Martin, D. Michael. *1, 2 Thessalonians*. NAC. Edited by E. Ray Clendenen. Nashville: Holman Reference, 1995.

> A workmanlike study by a professor at Golden Gate Baptist Seminary. Helpful for pastors. Premillennial. Posttribulational. Baptist.

*+Milligan, George. *St Paul's Epistles to the Thessalonians*. London: Macmillan, 1908. Reprint, Minneapolis: Klock & Klock, 1980.

> At one time, many regarded this commentary as the best treatment of the Greek text, but it has been superseded by more recent works. It is still a wonderful resource and worth obtaining if available and should be consulted. "A brilliantly written, critical study which must of necessity take second place to more recent works" (Barber, 173).

*Morris, Leon. *The First and Second Epistles to the Thessalonians*. NICNT. Edited by F. F. Bruce. Grand Rapids: Eerdmans, 1959.

> This treatment of these letters is more comprehensive than his volume on the same epistles in the TNTC series. It is based on the English text, but throughout demonstrates the author's grasp of exegetical issues. It was revised in 1984, updating the scholarly literature and reflecting a change from the KJV to the NIV. "A wealth of learning" (Barber, 173). Premillennial. Posttribulational.

!*Shogren, Gary S. *1 and 2 Thessalonians*. Zondervan Exegetical Commentary on the New Testament. Edited by Clinton E. Arnold. Grand Rapids: Zondervan Academic, 2012.

> This study is a first-rate treatment of the Greek text of these epistles. Its introduction to the two epistles, at just over twenty-three pages, while a bit fuller than some of the other volumes in this series, is still disappointing. "May well become the pastor's first recourse to a Greek-language commentary on these epistles" (Carson, 124).

!*Wanamaker, Charles A. *The Epistles to the Thessalonians*. NIGTC. Edited by I. Howard Marshall and W. Ward Gasque. Grand Rapids: Eerdmans, 1990.

> This commentary is an exceptional treatment of the Greek text of these epistles. It is the best work available for the serious student with good Greek skills. "Has to rate among the top works" (Rosscup, 299). "The best commentary on the Greek text. . . . Wanamaker is thorough and usually sensitive to both literary and theological flow. For students and pastors who can handle Greek, this commentary falls into the 'must' column" (Carson, 123–24).

!*Weima, Jeffrey A. D. *1–2 Thessalonians*. BECNT. Edited by Robert Yarbrough and Robert Stein. Grand Rapids: Baker Academic, 2014.

> A standout technical commentary by an evangelical and a respected Pauline scholar who teaches at Calvin Theological Seminary. This work fills what up to now has been a real void.

Wiersbe, Warren W. *Be Ready*. Wheaton: Victor, 1979.

> This brief work is another in the author's popular *Be* series. Like all volumes in the series, this book is a popular treatment of these epistles helpful mainly for pastors and beginning students.

The Pastoral Epistles

!?Dibelius, Martin, and Hans Conzelmann. *The Pastoral Epistles*. Hermeneia. Edited by Helmut Koester. Translated by Philip Buttolph and Adela Yarbro. Philadelphia: Fortress, 1972.

> This book is a technical, critical commentary in the notoriously liberal Hermeneia series. The authors deny Pauline authorship and are heavily influenced by form criticism. This commentary was long the standard technical work and is still frequently cited in scholarly literature, but has now been superseded by more recent works. "Somewhat overrated. It was far too committed

to an unbelievable reconstruction of early church history to be very useful to most pastors" (Carson, 129).

*+Ellicott, Charles J. *The Pastoral Epistles of St. Paul.* 3rd ed. London: Longman, 1864.

"Ellicott wrote at the beginning of the modern challenges to a Pauline interpretation of the Pastorals. He properly raised objections to what has unfortunately become the major critical position on authorship, and he saw clearly the ad hoc nature of the Pastorals, interpreting Paul's thought and even vocabulary in light of the false teaching in Ephesus. It is a rare author who can critique a movement when it is just beginning without the benefit of hindsight. His handling of the text is concise and exact, and requires a comfortable working knowledge of Greek. If you can find this volume, by all means get it" (**Mounce**).

!*+Fairbairn, Patrick. *Pastoral Epistles.* Edinburgh: T. & T. Clark, 1874. Reprint, Minneapolis: James & Klock, 1976.

This helpful commentary, by a former professor at both Aberdeen College and Glasgow College, was first published in 1874. It is based on the Greek text and represents the very best of nineteenth-century Scottish scholarship. "A fine example of the use of exegesis in the exposition of the text. . . . His methodology is worthy of emulation. Designed for pastors" (Barber). "This volume is about as complete a guide to the smaller epistles as one could desire" (Spurgeon, 184).

*Fee, Gordon D. *1–2 Timothy, Titus.* Good News Commentary. San Francisco: Harper & Row, 1984.

"Fee's work was the first of the modern commentaries to emphasize the ad hoc nature of the Pastorals, not just in 1 Tim 2:8–15 but throughout the entire corpus. He also emphasizes that Timothy was not a pastor but an apostolic delegate, standing outside of the normal church structure. While the volume is unfortunately short, it does the best job at orienting the reader to a proper understanding of the Pastorals as a whole" (**Mounce**).

Getz, Gene A. *A Profile for a Christian Life Style: A Study of Titus with 20th-Century Lessons for Your Church.* Grand Rapids: Zondervan, 1978.

This little book is an interesting compilation of expositions on this epistle with helpful sermonic outlines at the beginning of each chapter and pointed questions at the end of them to aid in review and internalization of the material. This is a general treatment for the nonspecialist.

*Guthrie, Donald. *The Pastoral Epistles: An Introduction and Commentary*. TNTC. Edited by R. V. G. Tasker. Grand Rapids: Eerdmans, 1957.

> This commentary is a good basic treatment of the text for the nonspecialist by the former tutor in NT language and literature at London Bible College. This commentary is brief, but is very helpful on introductory matters particularly with summaries of conflicting interpretations.

*Hendriksen, William. *Exposition of the Pastoral Epistles*. New Testament Commentary. Grand Rapids: Baker, 1957.

> Now over fifty years old, this helpful treatment is still very useful for pastors and serious students. His New Testament Commentary series as a whole has offered a high standard of exegesis and has stood well the test of time. "As usual, Hendriksen is detailed and offers much aid in word meanings, possible views which he documents, and full discussion of the passages. His commentary is one of the finer works for serious students" (Rosscup, 301). Reformed. Amillennial.

Hughes, R. Kent, and Bryan Chapell. *1 & 2 Timothy and Titus: To Guard the Deposit*. Preaching the Word. Edited by R. Kent Hughes. Wheaton: Crossway, 2000.

> Hughes wrote the 1 and 2 Timothy sections and Chapell wrote the Titus portion. Both are noted masters of the homiletical craft and offer much here of value for pastors, teachers, and students. Illustrations abound.

*Johnson, Luke Timothy. *The First and Second Letters to Timothy*. AB. Edited by William Foxwell Albright and David Noel Freedman. New York: Doubleday, 2001.

> This commentary is a very good surprisingly conservative treatment of these epistles in a very liberal series. The author, a noted professor of NT at the Candler School of Theology in Atlanta, has written a valuable commentary that packs a lot into a volume that is just shy of five hundred pages. He accepts Pauline authorship and offers much in the way of assistance to the exegete. "Well worth reading. . . . This one brims with insight in relatively short compass" (Carson, 129). "The work is quite worthwhile in opening up many parts of the book" (Rosscup, 301). Roman Catholic.

*———. *Letters to Paul's Delegates*. New Testament in Context. Harrisburg, PA: Trinity, 1996.

> Unlike the author's AB volume, this commentary includes the epistle to Titus. This pithy volume upholds the author's high scholarly standards. "Luke Timothy Johnson at his best: for its length, the work is both a model of clarity and packed with useful information" (Carson, 130). Roman Catholic.

*Kelly, J. N. D. *A Commentary on the Pastoral Epistles*. BNTC. Edited by Henry Chadwick. London: Black, 1963.

> This work is one of the better commentaries in this series. It is very well done, but not as exhaustive as those by Marshall, Towner, Mounce, and Knight. "Able defense of the Pauline authorship. Presents a vivid picture of first-century church life. Thorough" (Barber, 174–75). "This is one of the better commentaries of recent decades. Held in high respect by scholars, the effort concludes for authenticity of the epistles and carries on a judicious exegesis while often being quite instructive in reasoning" (Rosscup, 301).

*Kent, Homer A., Jr. *The Pastoral Epistles*. Chicago: Moody, 1958.

> This is an outstanding commentary for the nonspecialist. Very helpful especially in comparing different views. I used it extensively many years ago and found it to be quite helpful for preaching. "A work of quality and reliability. Admirably bridges the gap between a laborious, technical treatment and a superficial, popular one" (Barber, 175).

*Knight, George W., III. *The Pastoral Epistles: A Commentary on the Greek Text*. NIGTC. Edited by I. Howard Marshall and W. Ward Gasque. Grand Rapids: Eerdmans, 1992.

> This commentary on the Greek text is a personal favorite. At just under five hundred pages of text, it is not as massive as the works by Marshall, Towner, and Mounce, but his treatment of the text feels "just right." It is clearly one of the two or three best works on these epistles published in the past quarter century. It is a well-done scholarly work and a first-rate piece of work. "This has to rate near the top in terms of the most frequently helpful exegetical works that grapple with the meaning at length. It is also quite worthwhile theologically. Knight provides judicious material illumining issues, views, reasons for choices, etc. He is often quite well-balanced in use of various channels to decide what is taught, and able to weigh matters before the readers. He looks alertly at near context, overall context, grammar, word study, Pauline and other thought in Scripture's unity, and offers much insight. Those seriously studying these letters need to give this work much attention" (Rosscup, 302). "It is cautious, conservative, and thoughtful" (Carson, 128). Highly recommended!

Köstenberger, Andreas J., and Terry L. Wilder. *Entrusted with the Gospel: Paul's Theology in the Pastoral Epistles*. Nashville: B & H Academic, 2010.

> This interesting book is not a commentary on the text, but rather a collection of articles by top NT scholars on the theology of these books. In addition to the editors, contributors include F. Alan Tomlinson, Ray Van Neste, Greg A. Couser, Daniel L. Akin, George M. Wieland, Benjamin L. Merkle, B. Paul Wolfe, Thorvald B. Madsen II, Chiao Ek Ho, and I. Howard Marshall. "A trustworthy exploration of the theology of the Pastorals" (Carson, 133).

!*+Liddon, H. P. *Explanatory Analysis of St. Paul's First Epistle to Timothy*. London: Longmans, Green, 1897. Reprint, Minneapolis: Klock & Klock, 1978.

> This commentary, first published in 1897 by a former professor of NT exegesis at Oxford University, is a grammatical analysis of the Greek text and is particularly valuable for the specialist. "Deals faithfully with the text and, through his perceptive analysis of Paul's theme, lays bare the purpose and development of the apostle's wise counsel" (Barber, 175).

*Liefeld, Walter L. *1 and 2 Timothy, Titus*. NIVAC. Edited by Terry Muck. Grand Rapids: Zondervan, 1999.

> A very helpful work for preachers.

!Lock, Walter. *A Critical and Exegetical Commentary on the Pastoral Epistles*. ICC. Edited by Samuel Rolles Driver, Alfred Plummer, and Charles Augustus Briggs. Edinburgh: T. & T. Clark, 1924.

> For decades this esteemed commentary was the standard work on the Greek text. It has been retired in the series by the 1999 volume by Marshall. It can still be consulted on exegetical matters with great profit.

!*Marshall, I. Howard. *A Critical and Exegetical Commentary on the Pastoral Epistles*. *International Critical Commentary*. Edited by J. A. Emerton, C. E. B. Cranfield, and G. N. Stanton. London: T. & T. Clark International, 2004.

> Published in the new ICC series, this is the critical commentary to own on these epistles. Marshall wrote this commentary in collaboration with Philip Towner. It is a massive treatment with 831 pages of text. Along with the similar works by Mounce and Knight, these would serve as all that a diligent scholar would need on these three epistles. It is probably the best technical work on the Greek text with Mounce and Knight coming in second and third. For all its strengths, this book is weak on the authorship question with Marshall questioning the authorship of Paul. "It is packed with thoughtful, well-written reflection on every issue of importance. For academically gifted pastors who can handle the Greek, the learned and careful exegesis will be a joy to pore over" (Carson, 127).

Montague, George T. *First and Second Timothy, Titus*. CCSS. Edited by Peter S. Williamson and Mary Healy. Grand Rapids: Baker Academic, 2008.

> "The Catholic Commentary on Sacred Scripture aims to serve the ministry of the Word of God in the life and mission of the Church" (from editor's preface). This is a worthy addition to this series within the Roman Catholic tradition. It adheres to Pauline authorship.

Moule, H. C. G. *Studies in II Timothy*. London: Religious Tract Society, n.d.; Grand Rapids: Kregel, 1977.

> This little book is a brief devotional study for the nonspecialist. The author, who lived from 1841–1920, served as principal of Ridley Hall, Cambridge, for nineteen years and was a popular speaker at Keswick Conventions and church conferences. He was well-known for his piety and practical application.

!*Mounce, William D. *Pastoral Epistles*. WBC. Edited by Bruce M. Metzger, David A. Hubbard, and Glenn W. Barker. Nashville: Nelson, 2000.

> Though not quite up to the level of Marshall in the area of exegesis, this still is a formidable work. Mounce is more conservative than Marshall and favors Pauline authorship of these epistles. However, the format of the WBC is irritating and a trial to the reader. I read this commentary from cover to cover for a doctoral class on the Pastoral Epistles with Dr. Mounce and, while the writing is well done, instructive, and always edifying, the book's format drove me to distraction. At just over six hundred pages of text, it is a weighty tome that investigates many issues of a pastoral nature. For example, the author believes that the weight of evidence forbids women from preaching/teaching men in the church setting. The deciding factor in this debate is the sin of Adam and Eve in the garden of Eden. Highly recommended! This is one of the few commentaries in the WBC series that did not earn a "?" for critical biases.

*Stott, John R. W. *Guard the Gospel: The Message of 2 Timothy*. BST. Edited by John R. W. Stott. Downers Grove: InterVarsity, 1973.

> This little commentary is a brief, but rich, exposition that will be particularly helpful for preachers. Anything written by Stott is worth purchasing and consulting regularly. "Will be treasured by preachers" (Carson, 132). "Deserves to be read by all who are interested in living dynamically for Christ in this present era" (Barber). "Stott has quite good insight into the meaning of verse, and has a rare ability to state truth succinctly" (Rosscup, 304).

*+Taylor, Thomas. *Exposition of Titus*. Cambridge, 1619. Reprint, Minneapolis: Klock & Klock, 1980.

> This commentary is a classic exposition by a Puritan writer. First published in 1619, it is rich, thorough, and warm. "This commentary will well repay the reader" (Spurgeon, 185).

*Towner, Philip H. *The Letters to Timothy and Titus*. NICNT. Edited by Ned B. Stonehouse, F. F. Bruce, and Gordon D. Fee. Grand Rapids: Eerdmans, 2006.

> The Pastoral Epistles have been blessed by a cornucopia of riches in recent years with the publication of major works by Marshall, Mounce, Knight, and

Towner. This is an outstanding treatment based on the English text and quite massive at just over eight hundred pages. Towner collaborated with Marshall on his ICC contribution and published a shorter commentary on these epistles, but this is the one to purchase. This is my first choice for a mid-level commentary. Upholds Pauline authorship. "This is perhaps the best commentary on the Pastorals based on the English text. . . . Often very insightful" (Carson, 128).

Wiersbe, Warren W. *Be Faithful*. Colorado Springs: Cook, 1981.

This little book is a popular commentary on the Pastoral Epistles and Philemon by the *Back to the Bible* speaker and former pastor of Moody Memorial Church in Chicago. This book is excellent for beginning students, laypersons, and pastors.

Woychuk, N. A. *An Exposition of Second Timothy: Inspirational and Practical*. Old Tappan, NJ: Revell, 1973.

This brief commentary, by the founder of Bible Memory Association, is for the nonspecialist. "An original and creative exposition which abounds in illustrative material" (Barber).

Philemon

Usually included with commentaries on other books such as Colossians.

Carson, H. M. See section on Colossians.

*+Cox, Samuel. *The Epistle to Philemon*. Reprint, Minneapolis: Klock & Klock, 1982.

This brief classic was reprinted and bound together with Drysdale's famous devotional commentary by Klock & Klock thus making available to a new generation the treasures of a past one. "Such exposition as this adds interest to the epistles, and makes their writings live again before our eyes. . . . Happy are the people who are thus instructed" (Spurgeon, 185).

*+Drysdale, A. H. *The Epistle to Philemon*. 3rd ed. London: Religious Tract Society, 1924. Reprint, Minneapolis: Klock & Klock, 1982.

See comments under Cox.

*?Dunn, D. G. See section on Colossians.

!*?Fitzmyer, Joseph A. *The Letter to Philemon*. AYB. Edited by William Foxwell Albright and David Noel Freedman. New Haven: Yale University Press, 2000.

A first-rate technical treatment of this the briefest of Paul's epistles.

*Garland, David E. See section on Colossians.

*Hendriksen, William. See section on Colossians.

!*+Lightfoot, J. B. See section on Colossians.

!*?Lohse, Eduard. See section on Colossians.

Lucas, R. C. See section on Colossians.

*Melick, Richard R. See section on Philippians.

*Moo, Douglas J. See section on Colossians.

Moule, H. C. G. See section on Colossians.

!*O'Brien, Peter T. See section on Colossians.

*Pao, David W. See section on Colossians.

*Wright, N. T. See section on Colossians.

The General Epistles

*Bateman, Herbert W., IV. *Interpreting the General Letters: An Exegetical Handbook*. Handbooks for New Testament Exegesis. Edited by John D. Harvey. Edited by John D. Harvey. Grand Rapids: Kregel Academic, 2012.

This helpful guide was designed as a step-by-step methodology for analyzing and preaching/teaching the letters of the General Epistles. There are nine steps outlined here for moving from the task of interpretation to that of communication. The author provides ample assistance in how to do exegesis as well as textual criticism with examples from the biblical text. Provides a very helpful bibliography on each epistle as well as on such varied topics as biblical theology, textual problems, syntax, and semantics.

Hiebert, D. Edmond. *An Introduction to the Non-Pauline Epistle*. Chicago: Moody, 1962.

This helpful book is a well-done, but dated, introduction to the general epistles. Hebrews is not included. Each section deals with such introductory matters as canonicity and authorship. There is an outline for each book and a brief bibliography, which sorely needs updating. Good for the general reader, but should be supplemented with a more recent volume such as Jobes's new work.

Jobes, Karen H. *Letters to the Church*. Grand Rapids: Zondervan Academic, 2015.

> This book was not reviewed for this edition. However, in view of Jobes's reputation, this promises to become the standard textbook on this body of literature for some years.

Hebrews

*+Brown, John. *Hebrews*. Reprint, Edinburgh: Banner of Truth, 1961.

> First published in 1862, this commentary was treasured by Spurgeon for its thorough exposition, boldness, and evangelical warmth. Reformed.

*+Bruce, Alexander Balmain. *The Epistle to the Hebrews*. Edinburgh: T. & T. Clark, 1899. Reprint, Minneapolis: Klock & Klock, 1980.

> This commentary is a welcome addition to Klock & Klock's LCRL by the former professor of apologetics and NT exegesis at Free Church College, Glasgow. Bruce's books are always thorough and thought provoking. "An exhaustive interpretation of the epistle based on the premise that it is a formal defense of the Christian faith. Readers will not always agree with Bruce, but they will find that he has made a valuable contribution to the overall study of the epistle" (Barber, 176).

*Bruce, F. F. *The Epistle to the Hebrews*. NICNT. Edited by F. F. Bruce. Grand Rapids: Eerdmans, 1964.

> F. F. Bruce was the Rylands Professor of Biblical Criticism and Exegesis at the University of Manchester, England, and editor of the *Evangelical Quarterly*. He was the author of dozens of books and one of the evangelical world's shining scholarly lights of the twentieth century. Upon its publication in 1964, this commentary assumed pride of place as the finest evangelical commentary on this epistle. Prior to his death, Bruce revised his work that was published in 1997, but the differences are marginal at best. This still remains one of the very finest expositions of the Epistle to the Hebrews. Retired in the series by the volume by Cockerill. "A thorough, reverent exposition" (Barber, 176). "The best of Bruce's many commentaries" (Bauer, 373).

!?Buchanan, George Wesley. *To the Hebrews*. AB. Edited by William Foxwell Albright and David Noel Freedman. Garden City: Doubleday, 1972.

> A weak volume that has been replaced in the series by the one by Koester.

*Cockerill, Gareth Lee. *The Epistle to the Hebrews*. NICNT. Edited by Gordon D. Fee. Grand Rapids: Eerdmans, 2012.

A worthy successor to Bruce's 1964 commentary is this fine volume by the research professor of NT and biblical theology at Wesley Biblical Seminary. Since I am Reformed, I found myself disagreeing with many of Cockerill's positions particularly in chapter 6. In fact, because of his Arminian positions, I would choose O'Brien as my first-choice for a mid-level work. However, there is much to like in this stimulating and fresh treatment. "His treatment of the use of the Old Testament in Hebrews is frequently disappointing" (Carson, 134). Wesleyan.

!*+Delitzsch, Franz. *Commentary on the Epistle to the Hebrews*. 2 vols. Translated by Thomas L. Kingsbury. Edinburgh: T. & T. Clark, 1871. Reprint, Minneapolis: Klock & Klock, 1978.

This commentary is a classic treatment of the epistle by the renowned Lutheran scholar best known for his contributions to the OT commentary set coauthored by J. K. F. Keil. This commentary has all the trademarks that have been associated with his OT work such as a high standard of careful exegesis and thoroughness. "Another older work that is still worth a close reading. . . . It is too dense and dated for most preachers, but scholars should not overlook it" (Carson, 139). "An extremely fine exposition which uses Talmudic source material to highlight the meaning of the text. A valuable acquisition" (Barber, 176)!

*+Edwards, Thomas Charles. *The Epistle to the Hebrews*. London: Hodder & Stoughton, 1911. Reprint, Minneapolis: Klock & Klock, 1982.

First published in 1911 and long out of print, this brief volume was reprinted as part of Klock & Klock's LCRL in 1982. It is not an exhaustive commentary, but rather a collection of sixteen expositions on different themes or topics from the epistle by the eighteenth-century Oxford professor and principal of University College of Wales in Aberystwyth. Such topics as the Great High Priest, the Impossibility of Renewal, the Impossibility of Failure, the New Covenant, and Conflict are ably treated in this volume.

!*Ellingworth, Paul. *The Epistle to the Hebrews*. NIGTC. Edited by I. Howard Marshall and W. Ward Gasque. Grand Rapids: Eerdmans, 1993.

At 736 pages of text, this massive study vies for supremacy as the "go-to" commentary for scholars and advanced students looking for a first-rate treatment of the Greek text. It really is an impressive work of scholarship that still holds up after more than twenty years. The author's treatment of the authorship question, which he leaves open, is quite thorough. "Complex, almost encyclopedic detail verse by verse. . . . For the extremely patient, the work often has a mass of discussion from which many benefits can be sifted, and in listing scholars' sources for studying Hebrews, this prolific book rates with Altridge and Lane. It is unfortunate here that so fine a mind has not been too widely user friendly" (Rosscup, 307). "A massive, erudite work . . . will definitely be of interest to the pastor wanting a first-class exegetical library" (Evans, 397).

English, E. Schuyler. *Studies in the Epistle to the Hebrews*. Neptune, NJ: Loizeaux, 1955.

This commentary is a popular treatment of the epistle for the nonspecialist. "A capable exposition of the theme of this epistle" (Barber, 176).

*Guthrie, George H. *Hebrews*. NIVAC. Edited by Terry Muck. Grand Rapids: Zondervan, 1998.

This volume is one of the strongest in the series and is great help to both pastors looking for homiletical assistance and students seeking exegetical insight. A real treat!

Hewitt, Thomas. *The Epistle to the Hebrews: An Introduction and Commentary*. TNTC. Edited by R. V. G. Tasker. Grand Rapids: Eerdmans, 1960.

This volume was one of the weakest offerings in the TNTC series. The author sees Silas as the likely author and takes a bizarre position on the warning passages. Replaced in the series by Guthrie. Reformed.

*Hughes, Philip Edgcumbe. *A Commentary on the Epistle to the Hebrews*. Grand Rapids: Eerdmans, 1977.

This commentary is one of the finest treatments of the epistle published within the past forty years. It is especially well written, but is weak on exegesis and strong on theology. In the authorship debate he favors Barnabas. "Focuses less attention on lexical matters and contemporary secondary literature, but is better than most modern commentaries at surveying the history of interpretation across the entire span of the church, not just the last few decades or centuries" (Carson, 135).

Kent, Homer A., Jr. *The Epistle to the Hebrews*. Grand Rapids: Baker, 1972.

This volume is an excellent commentary for the nonspecialist by the former dean and professor of NT and Greek at Grace Theological Seminary. It is well organized, like all of Kent's works, quite readable, and is easily accessible to the layperson. "A helpful evangelical commentary, especially from the standpoint of clarity on the Greek where this is crucial to the interpretation, without being technical" (Rosscup, 310). "A work which the pastor or seminary student will welcome. Adequately explains the theme of the epistle, builds exposition upon a very capable exegesis of the text, and ably elucidates the theological facets of the epistle" (Barber, 177).

*Kistemaker, Simon J. *Exposition of the Epistle to the Hebrews*. New Testament Commentary. Grand Rapids: Baker, 1984.

> After the death of William Hendriksen, Simon Kistemaker began the project of completing the series. Although this treatment is quite helpful and is very detailed, it is not his strongest work. This commentary is based on the Greek text, but is easily accessible to the nonspecialist. Reformed.

!*?Koester, Craig R. *Hebrews*. AYB. Edited by William Foxwell Albright and David Noel Freedman. New Haven: Yale University Press, 2001.

> This volume thankfully replaces the weak 1972 one by Buchanan and is a must-buy for those pastors wanting to build a first-rate reference library. This is one of the stronger works in the series. "A major work of scholarship" (Carson, 134).

!*Lane, William L. *Hebrews*. WBC. Edited by David A. Hubbard and Glenn W. Barker. 2 vols. Dallas: Word, 1991.

> This helpful commentary is one of the better NT offerings in the WBC series. It is detailed in its exegesis and sound in its theology. The bibliographies are extensive, but at twenty-five years of age, need to be updated and brought into line with current scholarship. "This has been the best piece of scholarship from the evangelical perspective, arguably the best piece of scholarship from any perspective" (Evans, 395).

!?Moffatt, James. *A Critical and Exegetical Commentary on the Epistle to the Hebrews*. ICC. Edited by S. R. Driver, A. Plumer, and C. A. Briggs. Edinburgh: T. & T. Clark, 1924.

> This volume is a critical commentary that is very helpful on technical aspects of the Greek text, but has been superseded by later works. For decades it was the standard work on the Greek text. It is still worth consulting, but it is no longer a first choice. "One of the better commentaries on *theme* of Hebrews" (Barber, 177). "A work of considerable learning" (Carson, 136).

*+Owen, John. *An Exposition of the Epistle to the Hebrews*. 7 vols. Edited by W. H. Goold. London: Johnstone & Hunter, 1855. Reprint, Grand Rapids: Baker, 1980.

> The Baker edition is a beautiful reprint of this classic Puritan commentary first published from 1668–74. The treatment of the text is exhaustive and voluminous and also makes for some tedious reading, but the results far outweigh the effort. Kregel has distilled the essence of Owen's work into a one volume work edited by M. J. Tyron and titled *The Epistle of Warning*. "Here, the patient will meet with ponderous discussions of connections between

New Testament fulfillments in Christ and Old Testament preparation for Him. Much is rich and worthwhile if one has time to sort through the laborious discussions. . . . Theologically Owen has a lot to contribute" (Rosscup, 312). "All the rigor, theological profundity, and verbosity you would expect from the greatest scholar among the Puritans" (Evans, 400). This is a true masterpiece and treasure!

?Thompson, James W. *Hebrews*. Paideia. Edited by Mikeal C. Parsons and Charles H. Talbert. Grand Rapids: Baker Academic, 2008.

This commentary is a moderately critical, nontechnical treatment. "Well focused and compact. He favors Hellenistic and philosophical background over Jewish background and is sometimes weak on the actual exegesis of the text" (Carson, 135).

*+Westcott, Brooke Foss. *The Epistle to the Hebrews*. London: Macmillan, 1889. Reprint, Grand Rapids: Eerdmans, 1977.

This commentary, along with Moffatt, has long been regarded as a standard older work on the Greek text. It is still useful for its exegetical notes, but has been superseded by more recent works. More conservative than Moffatt. Anglican.

Wiersbe, Warren W. *Be Confident*. Colorado Springs: Chariot Victor, n.d.

This little volume is a popular exposition of the theme of the epistle for the nonspecialist.

James

*Adamson, James B. *The Epistle of James*. NICNT. Edited by F. F. Bruce. Grand Rapids: Eerdmans, 1976.

This commentary provides an excellent treatment of the text with excellent discussions at the end of each major section. The excursus, for example, titled "The Prayer of a Righteous Man," is extremely helpful in its explanation of the verbal form in 5:16. Has been replaced in the series by McKnight. "Fully abreast of the latest scholarship, this careful treatment combines exegesis with exposition and emphasizes the cohesion of James's thought. Recommended" (Barber). "One of the very best commentaries" (Rosscup, 314). "Disproportionately dependent on Hellenistic parallels at the expense of Jewish sources" (Carson, 143).

!?Allison, Dale C., Jr. *James*. ICC. Edited by J. A. Emerton, C. E. B. Cranfield, and G. N. Stanton. London: Bloomsbury T. & T. Clark, 2013.

> If you are looking for a technical commentary on James that is both critical and comprehensive, this is the volume to purchase. At roughly seven hundred pages, it is a massive tome that seemingly covers every area of inquiry and interacts with current scholarship. If you are a pastor looking for a quick sermon outline, give this book a pass. So far I have seen it only in hardcover with a list price of $136. Gulp! This replaces Ropes in the series.

*Blomberg, Craig L., and Mariam J. Kame. *James*. Zondervan Exegetical Commentary on the New Testament. Edited by Clinton E. Arnold. Grand Rapids: Zondervan Academic, 2008.

> At first glance, this 263-page commentary appears to be too brief to do justice to this epistle. However, upon further investigation, it is apparent that the authors cover all of the bases in this excellent treatment. Blomberg, a distinguished professor of NT at Denver Seminary, is a name that needs no introduction in the evangelical scholarly world. His work always adheres to the very highest standards of scholarship and this commentary is no exception. He is also a leading figure in the discussion of the place of wealth and material possessions in the Christian's life. This book contains excellent material on this topic as well as adding to the discussion on poverty. Highly recommended! "The first to appear in the ZECNT series and set a high standard. Its combination of patient exegesis, theology, and application will appeal to many pastors. In some ways, the ordered pedagogy implicit in this series, doubtless appreciated by many readers, makes the work seem more comprehensive than it is. Its treatment of the structure of James is not to be missed" (Carson, 140).

*Davids, Peter H. *The Epistle of James: A Commentary on the Greek Text*. NIGTC. Edited by I. Howard Marshall and W. Ward Gasque. Grand Rapids: Eerdmans, 1982.

> Though slightly dated now, this commentary remains an impressive treatment of the book based on the Greek text. It is not as detailed as some commentaries on this epistle coming in at just over two hundred pages of text. It devotes sixty-one pages to introductory matters. "Writes in a style that often refreshes" (Rosscup, 315).

*Hiebert, D. Edmond. *The Epistle of James: Tests of a Living Faith*. Chicago: Moody, 1979.

> This volume is a helpful treatment of the English text by a professor of NT at Mennonite Brethren Biblical Seminary in Fresno, California. "A lucid evangelical work that looks at every verse, discussing exegetical matters, views, supports, and the relevance to a practical spiritual life" (Rosscup, 315). "The product of mature scholarship" (Barber). "A bit stodgy, but worth skimming" (Carson, 144).

*Johnson, Luke Timothy. *The Letter of James*. AB. Edited by William Foxwell Albright and David Noel Freedman. Garden City: Doubleday, 1995.

> The author, professor of NT at the Candler School of Theology at Emory University, is one of the foremost interpreters of the NT writing today. This fine commentary does nothing to lessen his stature. The superb introduction is 163 pages and leaves few stones unturned. Included in this section is a fascinating survey of the history of the interpretation of this epistle. Johnson's exegetical work is detailed and precise. This commentary is a major contribution to the study of this epistle. "Johnson is always incisive, although I am less persuaded by some of his exegetical decisions" (Carson, 140). "Brilliant" (Evans, 402)! "Lucid, elegantly written, and theologically profound" (Bauer, 378).

*+Johnstone, Robert. *A Commentary on James*. Edinburgh: Banner of Truth, 1871. Reprint, Edinburgh: Banner of Truth, 1977.

> This volume is a reprint edition of a book first published in 1871 by a minister in the United Presbyterian Church in Scotland who had a well-deserved reputation for scholarship. This book is a compilation of lectures on this epistle. Dr. Johnstone succeeded the eminent John Eadie to the chair of NT Literature and Exegesis at the University of Edinburgh in 1876. "A very useful, scholarly, and readable book" (Spurgeon, 191).

*Kistemaker, Simon J. *Exposition of the Epistle of James and the Epistles of John*. New Testament Commentary. Grand Rapids: Baker, 1986.

> This volume is another offering in the Hendriksen commentary series begun in 1953. It is scholarly without being pedantic, and is easily accessible to the pastor, beginning student, or layperson. Reformed.

*+Manton, Thomas. *The Epistle of James*. Reprint, Mobile, AL: R E Publications, n.d.

> This book was first published in 1693 and still packs a punch. It is encyclopedic and an example of the finest of Puritan scholarship of that day. "In Manton's best style. An exhaustive work as far as the information of the period admitted. Few such books are written now" (Spurgeon, 191).

!*?Martin, Ralph P. *James*. WBC. Edited by Bruce M. Metzger. Nashville: Nelson, 1988.

> An impressive work of scholarship, this commentary is now somewhat dated but still useful. The extensive bibliographies need to be updated as well as interaction with James scholarship over the last quarter century. I also disagree with his two-stage theory of the composition of the epistle, which I find to be a stretch. Yet, for a technical commentary, this is accessible and helpful to the pastor. "A masterpiece of condensed writing" (Carson, 141).

!*+Mayor, Joseph B. *The Epistle of St James*. New York: Macmillan, 1913. Reprint, Minneapolis: Klock & Klock, 1977.

> This massive work of scholarship by an emeritus professor of King's College, London, and honorary fellow of St. John's College, Cambridge, was first published in 1882. The Klock & Klock reprint is itself a reprint of the Zondervan reprint of the revised third edition published by Macmillan in 1913. It is based on the Greek text and is quite technical with almost three hundred pages devoted to the introduction alone. It can be daunting for the student with inadequate Greek tools. For over a hundred years it was the standard, but its work has been superseded by others. "An encyclopedic work on the Greek text regarded by many as being the most important critical commentary on this portion of God's word" (Barber, 179). "The thoroughness of Mayor's work is quite breathtaking, but he is not always as helpful on the practical side as one might desire" (Carson, 142). "It is a work of towering scholarship and exhaustive detail. From the standpoint of the Greek text it is the best older and one of the best at any time on James" (Rosscup, 318). "Contains massive compilation of technical historical, linguistic, and text-critical information that is often simply adopted by later commentators" (Bauer, 379).

*McCartney, Dan G. *James*. BECNT. Grand Rapids: Baker Academic, 2009.

> This volume is a very fine offering in the BECNT series. Based on the Greek text, it is well written and comprehensive without being overly long. It devotes seventy-six pages to introductory matters and an excellent bibliography. "In the very first rank, combining rigorous exegesis and carefully worded and probing theological reflection" (Carson, 140). Reformed.

*McKnight, Scot. *The Letter of James*. NICNT. Edited by Gordon D. Fee. Grand Rapids: Eerdmans, 2011.

> This excellent offering replaces the anemic 1954 volume by Ross in the series. McKnight is an accomplished NT scholar who provides a significant upgrade over Ross, particularly in the area of exegesis. "This work is admirably researched, written with verve and clarity, and focuses more attention than most on the likely historical setting that ostensibly calls it into being" (Carson, 140).

*Moo, Douglas J. *James*. TNTC. Edited by Eckhard J. Schnabel. 2nd ed. Downers Grove: InterVarsity, 2015.

> The second edition of this commentary was not evaluated for this edition. The first edition, which was published in 1986, was a fine offering ably superseding the brief volume by Tasker (1957). Moo is a fine writer and top-drawer NT scholar who always exercises good judgment and sound exegesis. Suffice

it to say that any work by Moo is uniformly excellent in its quality and worth acquiring. Do not confuse this book with the author's 2000 PNTC volume.

*————. *The Letter of James*. PNTC. Edited by D. A. Carson. Grand Rapids: Eerdmans, 2000.

> This volume, not to be confused with the author's TNTC volume, is an excellent contribution to this series. Moo, the Kenneth T. Wessner Professor of NT at Wheaton Graduate School, is one of the top evangelical NT scholars writing today. He concludes that James, the Lord's brother, was the author and is sound on his other judgments. One of the very best, if not the best, mid-level works on this epistle available today. "A lovely blend of good judgment, good writing, good theology, and sometimes good application. His established competence in Romans means that while he rightly wants James to be read on his own terms, he includes some especially incisive discussion of the similarities and differences between the two books" (Carson, 140).

Motyer, J. A. *The Tests of Faith*. London: InterVarsity, 1970.

> This book is a very brief but helpful volume that deals primarily with the themes running through this epistle. Excellent for laypersons. Very well done. Anglican.

Nystrom, David P. *James*. NIVAC. Edited by Terry Muck. Grand Rapids: Zondervan, 1997.

> Not one of the stronger volumes in the series. The homiletical applications are fine, but the exegesis is weak. Though they are dated, Motyer and Hiebert would be more helpful. "Singularly poor at the level of exegesis" (Carson, 143).

!?Ropes, James Hardy. *A Critical and Exegetical Commentary on the Epistle of St. James*. ICC. Edited by S. R. Driver, A. Plummer, and C. A. Briggs. Edinburgh: T. & T. Clark, 1916.

> This commentary offers an excellent treatment of the Greek text. Along with Mayor, this has been the standard critical treatment for decades. The author denies that the Lord's brother was the author. "Useful for . . . classical and Hellenistic parallels" (Carson, 142).

Ross, Alexander. *The Epistles of James and John*. NICNT. Edited by F. F. Bruce. Grand Rapids: Eerdmans, 1954.

> Very dated, of limited usefulness, and honorably retired in the series and replaced by McKnight.

*+Stier, Rudolf. *Commentary on James*. Edinburgh: T. & T. Clark, 1864. Reprint, Lynchburg, VA: James Family, n.d.

> This volume is not a commentary, but rather a series of thirty-two sermons on the book. Though first published over 150 years ago, these discourses are still useful and challenging and the book should be obtained if available. "No one can be expected to receive all that Stier has to say, but he must be dull indeed who cannot learn much from him. Read with care he is a great instructor" (Spurgeon, 149).

Tasker, R. V. G. *The General Epistle of James: An Introduction and Commentary*. TNTC. Edited by R. V. G. Tasker. Grand Rapids: Eerdmans, 1956.

> This slim volume is a well written, albeit brief, exposition of the book for the nonspecialist. Moo's updated volume in the same series supersedes this commentary. "Introductory data is carefully outlined, and the verse-by-verse exposition is practical and helpful" (Barber, 179).

Wiersbe, Warren W. *Be Mature*. Colorado Springs: Chariot Victor, 1978.

> This little book is a popular exposition of the theme of the epistle for the nonspecialist. Wiersbe's writing is always warm and practical.

1 Peter

!?Achtemeier, Paul J. *1 Peter*. Hermeneia. Edited by Eldon Jay. Philadelphia: Fortress, 1996.

> A formidable technical commentary that will be mostly of use to students and scholars, but can be safely bypassed by most evangelical pastors. "A masterpiece of careful scholarship" (Carson, 145).

!?Bigg, Carl. *A Critical and Exegetical Commentary on the Epistles of St. Peter and St. Jude*. ICC. Edited by Samuel Rolles Driver, Charles Augustus Briggs, and Alfred Plummer. Edinburgh: T. & T. Clark, 1901.

> For many decades a standard work along with Selwyn that still deserves to be consulted for its exegetical and technical insights. Takes a standard view on 1 Peter, but rejects 2 Peter as inauthentic and thus pseudonymous.

*+Brown, John. *Expository Discourses on 1 Peter*. 2 vols. Reprint, Edinburgh: Banner of Truth, 1975.

> First published in three volumes in 1848, this is a collection of warmly devotional discourses on 1 Peter from a Reformed perspective by the well-known John Brown of Haddington. They are over two hundred years old, but still

worth reading for the good they can provide one's soul. "Dr. Brown produced what is substantially a commentary, and one of the best. It affords us a grammatical interpretation, together with an exposition, at once exegetical, doctrinal, and practical. It is a standard work, and the indices increase its value" (Spurgeon, 192). "Rich and suggestive theologically" (Evans, 410). Reformed.

*Davids, Peter H. *The First Epistle of Peter*. NICNT. Edited by R. K. Harrison. Grand Rapids: Eerdmans, 1990.

An exceptional commentary that is very well written and accessible. This is the one mid-level commentary that will be of the most use to the average pastor. "Combines informed exegesis and probing theological reflection" (Carson, 145).

!?Elliott, John H. *I Peter*. AB. Edited by William Foxwell Albright and David Noel Freedman. New Haven: Yale University Press, 2001.

A massive critical commentary that rivals Achtemeier and is a must-buy for students and pastors of a scholarly bent.

*Grudem, Wayne. *1 Peter*. TNTC. Edited by Leon Morris. Downers Grove: IVP Academic, 1988.

A fine commentary that replaced Stibbs in the series. Perfect for pastors and motivated laypersons. Reformed.

Hiebert, D. Edmond. *First Peter: An Expositional Commentary*. Chicago: Moody, 1984.

This book is a helpful treatment of the English text that would particularly benefit the pastor or nonspecialist. It is well written and very readable. "Gentle, cautious, and pious (in the best sense), but essentially a distillation of older work" (Carson, 147).

!*Jobes, Karen H. *1 Peter*. BECNT. Edited by Robert W. Yarbrough and Robert H. Stein. Grand Rapids: Baker Academic, 2005.

A first-rate exegetical work from the evangelical camp, this is an exceptional technical commentary that has the added benefit of being accessible to the average pastor. "Strong on every front, including careful exegesis of the Greek text" (Carson, 145).

!*+Johnstone, Robert. *The First Epistle of Peter*. Edinburgh: T. & T. Clark, 1888. Reprint, Minneapolis: James Family, 1978.

This volume is a massive commentary of impressive scholarship on the Greek text regarded as a classic for over a century. "These concise studies faithfully expound the Greek text and provide a solid foundation for a series of relevant messages. Works of this nature are rare and should be obtained and used by every Bible-teaching preacher" (Barber).

?Keating, Daniel. *First and Second Peter, Jude.* CCSS. Grand Rapids: Baker Academic, 2011.

> This book is another offering in Baker's promising CCSS series offering the best of contemporary Roman Catholic scholarship along with Catholic tradition and teaching. There is much to commend Protestant evangelicals who wish to mine the rich veins of Roman Catholic thought. This book is moderately critical and easily accessible for laypersons.

*Kistemaker, Simon J. *Exposition of the Epistles of Peter and the Epistle of Jude.* New Testament Commentary. Grand Rapids: Baker, 1987.

> A dependable and workmanlike commentary by a bedrock conservative who accepts the authenticity of both Petrine epistles. Pastors will find this volume particularly helpful. Reformed.

*+Leighton, Robert. *Commentary on First Peter.* London: Bohn, 1853. Reprint, Grand Rapids: Kregel, 1972.

> Kregel reprint by a nineteenth-century Anglican has been regarded as a classic for over 150 years. It is a warm and devotional exposition of the text and will be very helpful for pastors. "One of the best expository works on 1 Peter. Leighton provides his reader with the results of his vast learning without ostentation; and his eloquence unmatched" (Barber, 180). "A thorough discussion of the text with an exceptionally warm spirit. Among older works, it is easily one of the most helpful" (Rosscup, 323).

*+Lillie, John. *Lectures on the First and Second Epistles of Peter.* New York: Scribner, 1869. Reprint, Minneapolis: Klock & Klock, 1978.

> This volume is comprised of a series of lectures by the nineteenth-century Presbyterian minister and scholar published posthumously. This book represents the best scholarship of the time and is warmly devotional in spirit. Reformed.

!*?Michaels, J. Ramsey. *1 Peter.* WBC. Edited by Bruce M. Metzger. Nashville: Nelson, 1988.

> An important technical work that is moderately critical, this commentary was once considered by many to be the best available work on this epistle. While that is no longer the case, this commentary is still a quite impressive work of scholarship that deserves to be consulted. "A remarkably learned work" (Evans, 413).

*+Nisbet, Alexander. *An Exposition of 1 & 2 Peter*. Reprint, Edinburgh: Banner of Truth, 1982.

> This volume is a warmly devotional exposition. "A judicious and gracious Scotch commentary, after the style of Dickson and Hutcheson" (Spurgeon, 192).

*Schreiner, Thomas. *1, 2 Peter, Jude*. NAC. Edited by E. Ray Clendenen. Nashville: Holman Reference, 2003.

> An outstanding work that for some reason is not even listed by Bauer as either recommended or significant, this commentary was written by one of the evangelical world's top NT scholars and it rightly towers over most of the other mid-level offerings. The writings of Schreiner have greatly impressed me over the years and this volume is no exception. It is well written and eminently practical, a top choice for pastors. "This is one of most impressive volumes in the series, nicely displaying Schreiner's combination of exegesis and theological reflection coached in admirable clarity" (Carson, 145). Baptist.

!*+?Selwyn, Edward Gordon. *The First Epistle of Peter*. London: Macmillan, 1947.

> This commentary is an exceptional treatment of the Greek text. It is no longer the first choice on the Greek text, but still a formidable work of scholarship. Added features are the extensive sections at the back of the book titled "Additional Notes" (65 pp.) and "Essays" (175 pp.). Selwyn believes that water baptism is being discussed in 3:21f. A first choice of Danker. "A brilliant work which is regarded by many as the finest treatment of the Greek text extant" (Barber, 180). "This is one of the monumental pieces of industry that characterized the earlier Macmillan series. Most later commentaries have depended heavily on Selwyn" (Carson, 147).

*Stibbs, Alan M. *The First Epistle General of Peter*. TNTC. Edited by R. V. G. Tasker. Grand Rapids: Eerdmans, 1959.

> Though dated now and superseded by other works of this nature, this remains an excellent exposition of the English text that is surprisingly comprehensive considering the limitations of the Tyndale series. It contains an outstanding introduction and for the most part is extremely helpful for the nonspecialist. "The exposition is representative of the finest evangelical scholarship" (Barber, 180).

2 Peter

!*?Bauckham, Richard J. *Jude–2 Peter*. WBC. Edited by David A. Hubbard and Glenn W. Barker. Waco, TX: Word, 1983.

> A moderately critical work of immense scholarship that has been highly regarded as the best technical commentary available. The paucity of conservative exegetical treatments on 2 Peter and Jude makes commentaries such as this one and Neyrey all the more important. Considers 2 Peter to be pseudonymous. "By far the best work on 2 Peter and Jude" (Carson, 149). "The most authoritative and current commentary on these books" (Bauer, 381).

!?Bigg, Carl. See section on 1 Peter.

!*Green, Gene L. *Jude and 2 Peter*. BECNT. Edited by Robert W. Yarbrough and Robert H. Stein. Grand Rapids: Baker Academic, 2008.

> This commentary is another strong offering in the ongoing BECNT series which purpose is "to provide, within the framework of informed evangelical thought, commentaries that blend scholarly depth with readability, exegetical detail with sensitivity to the whole, and attention to critical problems with theological awareness" (series preface). This is a solidly conservative evangelical treatment of the text. Because of the paucity of technical works of an evangelical nature, this is a must-buy for conservative pastors. "Especially strong on the Hellenistic content in which it was written" (Carson, 149–50).

?Keating, Daniel. See section on 1 Peter.

*Kistemaker, Simon J. See section on 1 Peter.

*+Lillie, John. See section on 1 Peter.

*Lloyd-Jones, D. M. *Expository Sermons on 2 Peter*. Edinburgh: Banner of Truth, 1983.

> These twenty-five sermons, by the matchless English preacher D. M. Lloyd-Jones, were preached on consecutive Sunday mornings at Westminster Chapel in London during 1946–47 and were first compiled in the *Westminster Record* from 1948–50. It is my opinion that anything published by Lloyd-Jones is worth acquiring. His insights are penetrating and he pulls no punches in his preaching. "One is soon aware that Lloyd-Jones has much insight, explaining the essentials of the text adeptly and developing how these have vital force for living in this world. This book is a primer for expositors and refreshing for Christians in general" (Rosscup, 327).

!*+Mayor, Joseph B. *The Epistle of St. Jude and the Second Epistle of St. Peter.* New York: Macmillan, 1907; Minneapolis: Klock & Klock, 1978

> This huge volume is a massive critical commentary on the Greek text long regarded as a classic. This book is only for those with good Greek skills. A true classic of scholarly achievement! "A brilliant, technical treatment. Denies the Petrine authorship of II Peter, but is inclined to accept its canonicity and fully appreciates its intrinsic spiritual value and practical worth" (Barber).

*Moo, Douglas J. *2 Peter, Jude.* NIVAC. Edited by Terry Muck. Grand Rapids: Zondervan, 1996.

> This exceptional work builds upon a solid exegetical base and is tremendously helpful for pastors. Moo is a well-respected NT scholar who teaches at Wheaton College and is best known for his work on Romans and Galatians.

!?Neyrey, Jerome H. *2 Peter, Jude.* AB. Edited by William Foxwell Albright and David Noel Freedman. New York: Doubleday, 1993.

> A technical commentary that is highly regarded by some, but dismissed for its frivolous flights of fancy by others. Evangelicals will find much of this commentary to be unreliable and would do well to avoid it. "Neyrey's reconstruction of the settings of these epistles, though entertaining, is too speculative to be very useful to the serious preacher. . . . This sometimes yields thought-provoking insight; more commonly, it builds castles out of thin air" (Carson, 150).

*+Nisbet, Alexander. See section on 1 Peter.

*Schreiner, Thomas. See section on 1 Peter.

1, 2, and 3 John

Akin, Daniel L. *1, 2, 3 John.* NAC. Edited by E. Ray Clendenen. Nashville: Holman Reference, 2001.

> A workmanlike commentary that is of particular value to pastors. Baptist.

Boice, James Montgomery. *The Epistles of John.* Grand Rapids: Zondervan, 1979.

> This well-written and informative volume is a popular compilation of expositions of the text by a noted Presbyterian pastor. This commentary is very helpful for the pastor or general reader. Reformed.

!?Brooke, Alan England. *A Critical and Exegetical Commentary on the Johannine Epistles.* ICC. Edited by Samuel Rolles Driver, Alfred Plummer, and Charles Augustus Briggs. New York: Scribner, 1928.

> A critical work that still retains some value for its exegetical insights and comments on the Greek text. However, its theology is extremely suspect and totally out of touch with evangelical biblical theology. "A standard in its day" (Carson, 154).

!*?Brown, Raymond E. *The Epistles of John.* AB. Edited by William Foxwell Albright and David Noel Freedman. New York: Doubleday, 1982.

> The author, like Schnackenburg, is a highly respected Roman Catholic Johannine scholar who has produced a major work on John's gospel. This work shows that he has leaned a bit to the left since publishing the gospel commentary over a decade earlier. "The exegetical comments are often incisive" (Carson, 152).

!?Bultmann, Rudolf. *The Johannine Epistles.* Hermeneia. Edited by Robert W. Funk. Translated by R. Philip O'Hara. Philadelphia: Fortress, 1973.

> This commentary is one of the very worst volumes in the notoriously liberal Hermeneia series. Bultmann's critical presuppositions place his conclusions so far beyond the pale so as to render this commentary almost useless for evangelicals. It has even lost its influence among non-evangelicals and has been rendered totally obsolete. Replaced in the series by Strecker. "So brief and so concerned with improbable source criticism that its remaining exegetical comments were never worth the price. Mercifully, it has now been replaced" (Carson, 155).

*Burge, Gary M. *Letters of John.* NIVAC. Edited by Terry Muck. Grand Rapids: Zondervan, 1996.

> A fine addition to the series, this volume shines on application with an exegetical foundation that is equally strong.

*+Candlish, Robert S. *First Epistle of John.* Edinburgh: Black, 1877. Reprint, Grand Rapids: Kregel, 1979.

> This classic treatment by a nineteenth-century Scottish churchman is not a commentary as such, but rather a series of expository messages. They are warm and eminently readable and eminently practical. "A moving portrait of Christ, and the believer's relationship to Him" (Barber, 181).

*+Cox, Samuel. *The Epistles of John*. Reprint, Minneapolis: Klock & Klock, 1982.

> This slender volume of commentary on the second and third epistles of John were published in one volume in 1982 together with Morgan's more substantial exposition. "Such exposition as this adds interest to the epistles, and makes their writers live again before our eyes. . . . Happy are the people who are thus instructed" (Spurgeon, 185).

*+Findlay, George G. *Fellowship in the Life Eternal: An Exposition of the Epistles of St. John*. New York: Hodder & Stoughton, 1909. Reprint, Minneapolis: James & Klock, 1977.

> This classic work, first published in 1909 by a renowned English Methodist educator and biblical scholar who died about a century ago, is based on the Greek text and still retains its usefulness though it has been superseded by more recent commentaries. Still it remains an outstanding treatment of the text as well as a practical exposition. "An outstanding exposition. . . . Dedicated scholarship combined with rare spiritual insight makes this a first-rate work" (Barber, 182). "A devotional classic, justly famous, to which pastors have turned again and again" (Evans, 422). Wesleyan.

*Jobes, Karen H. *1, 2, & 3 John*. Zondervan Exegetical Commentary on the New Testament. Edited by Clinton E. Arnold. Grand Rapids: Zondervan, 2014.

> This study is outstanding in its treatment of the Greek text. However, its introduction to 1, 2, and 3 John at eleven pages is very skimpy, not what one would expect from a major work such as this. Barely two pages are devoted to the subject of Gnosticism as it might relate to 1 John. Despite these flaws, this is still a very fine commentary that is quite accessible to the average pastor with seminary training. Supplement this volume with that of Kruse.

*Kistemaker, Simon. See section on James.

*Kruse, Colin G. *The Letters of John*. PNTC. Grand Rapids: Eerdmans, 2000.

> This is one of the very finest commentaries published over the past two decades and is geared at the student and pastor with limited Greek skills. Kruse argues for apostolic authorship of all three epistles. Throughout the commentary there are useful discussions on topics of interest as the meaning of different terms such as "fellowship," "propitiation," or "antichrist." These helpful discussions enhance the value of this commentary. "Displays independent judgment, obvious reliance upon primary sources, clarity, and good judgment" (Carson, 151).

*+Law, Robert. *The Tests of Life*. 3rd ed. Edinburgh: T. & T. Clark, 1909. Reprint, Grand Rapids: Baker, 1968.

> This classic, originally published the same year as Findlay's similar work, is now regrettably out of print and almost unobtainable except online. It covers only the first epistle and should be purchased if found. Its treatment of the book is really exceptional and has influenced generations of pastors and scholars alike. "This unique contribution covers a major portion of the first epistle, provides timely discussion on theological and Christological themes, and includes the doctrine of sin, the account of propitiation, and the tests of righteousness, love, and belief" (Barber, 182).

*+Lias, John James. *An Exposition of the First Epistle of John*. LCRL. London: Nisber, 1887; Minneapolis: Klock & Klock, 1982.

> This book is a scholarly, but not technical, commentary that is a masterpiece of exposition. The chapters of this book appeared originally serially in *Homiletical Magazine*. It is a welcome addition to Klock & Klock's LCRL. "A conservative and scholarly exposition defending the genuineness of the epistle and containing some valuable exegetical insights" (Barber, 182).

*Marshall, I. Howard. *The Epistles of John*. NICNT. Edited by F. F. Bruce. Grand Rapids: Eerdmans, 1978.

> This commentary is a very fine treatment of these epistles by the senior lecturer in NT exegesis at the University of Aberdeen, Scotland, and one of the finest NT scholars of the twentieth century. Marshall's approach is scholarly, but also accessible to the nonspecialist. An excellent effort! "Keen ability to follow the thought of a book and articulate it with clarity" (Rosscup, 331). "Much . . . value to the preacher. The book is simply written and ably brings together a good deal of previous scholarship without getting bogged down in minutiae. . . . A very good commentary" (Carson, 153). "Characterized by careful augmentation, balanced judgment, and clear and understandable presentation of current scholarly discussions and of complex exegetical issues" (Bauer, 387). Arminian.

*+Morgan, James. *The Epistles of John*. Edinburgh: T. & T. Clark, 1865. Reprint, Minneapolis: Klock & Klock, 1982.

> The reprinting of this rare volume in Klock & Klock's LCRL is a welcome addition to the corpus of Johannine literature. It has been much esteemed since its initial publication in 1865. "Dr. Candlish says that this is a work 'of great practical interest and value,' and that had it appeared at an earlier date, 'he might have abstained from issuing' his own Lectures on this Epistle. We are glad to possess both works" (Spurgeon, 196).

Parsenios, George L. *First, Second, and Third John*. Paideia. Edited by Mikeal C. Parsons, Charles H. Talbert, and Bruce W. Longenecker. Grand Rapids: Baker Academic, 2014.

> This volume in Baker's Paideia series, by a noted Johannine scholar and former professor at Princeton Theological Seminary, explores cultural context and theological meaning in these books. This is a fairly brief volume of 164 pages of text with the introductory matters comprising almost a third of that. Readers will not find detailed exegesis of the text, but they will discover concise discussions of theological issues in each section.

!Plummer, Alfred. *The Epistles of St. John*. Cambridge: Cambridge University Press, 1886. Reprint, Grand Rapids: Baker, 1980.

> This commentary, based upon the Greek text, is by a nineteenth- and early twentieth-century Anglican scholar and theologian who taught at University College, Durham, for almost thirty years. This volume is marked by an extensive introduction and careful critical notes. This is for the advanced student who possesses good command of Greek. "Not his finest hour" (Carson, 156).

!?Schnackenburg, Rudolf. *The Johannine Epistles*. New York: Crossroad, 1992.

> This commentary, first published in German in 1984, is by a respected Roman Catholic Johannine scholar who also has written a major work on John's gospel. Schnackenburg is a careful and detailed scholar. "Provides richer theological reflection than any other commentary on these letters" (Bauer, 387). "The reasoning is constantly exegetical, historical, and theological" (Carson, 152). Roman Catholic.

Smalley, Stephen S. *1, 2, 3 John*. WBC. Edited by David W. Hubbard and Glenn W. Barker. Waco, TX: Word, 1984.

> This volume is a moderately conservative offering in the uneven WBC series by the Canon Residentiary and Precentor of Coventry Cathedral in England. Smalley is a Johannine scholar who has provided particularly good bibliographies at the beginning of each major section according to the series' protocol. This commentary was revised in 2007. "At his best when he is summarizing and interacting with the positions of others" (Carson, 152).

?Smith, D. Moody. *First, Second, and Third John*. Interp. Edited by James Luther Mays, Patrick D. Miller, and Paul J. Achtemeier. Louisville: John Knox, 1991.

> This brief volume, unlike most commentaries in this series, appears to focus more on interpretation and less on application. The author, the George Washington Ivey Professor of NT at the Divinity School, Duke University, argues that John the Elder, not John the Apostle, is the likely author of these epistles.

*Stott, John R. W. *The Epistles of John: An Introduction and Commentary*. TNTC. Edited by R. V. G. Tasker. Grand Rapids: Eerdmans, 1964.

> This volume, which was revised in 1988, is one of the finest offerings in the TNTC series. Stott, an Anglican and one of the elder statesmen of the evangelical world in the twentieth century has written an outstanding commentary that, in spite of its age, has continued to hold its own alongside other more recent works. Any book written by Stott is worth obtaining. Age has not tarnished its luster. This is a nontechnical work that can be used by both pastors and laypersons. "A beautiful blending of Bible teaching and practical theology" (Barber, 182). "One of the most useful conservative commentaries on these epistles, so far as the preacher is concerned" (Carson, 154).

!?Strecker, Georg. *The Johannine Letters*. Hermeneia. Edited by Harold W. Attridge. Translated by Linda M. Maloney. Philadelphia: Fortress, 1996.

> A highly technical, highly critical commentary that replaces Bultmann in the series, written by one of his students at Marburg. Scholars, and students will find this volume extremely helpful, pastors much less so. Overall, a marked improvement over Bultmann!

*+Westcott, Brooke Foss. *The Epistles of St John*. Reprint, Grand Rapids: Eerdmans, 1966.

> First published in 1883, this commentary has long been regarded as the classic treatment of the Greek text. In this 1966 edition, F. F. Bruce has updated the introductory materials and other important information and writings over the eighty-three years since its publication. "Detailed, thorough, and very useful for its incisive, definitive statements on problem areas as well as grammatical matters" (Rosscup, 333). Anglican.

*Yarbrough, Robert W. *1–3 John*. BECNT. Edited by Robert W. Yarbrough and Robert H. Stein. Grand Rapids: Baker Academic, 2008.

> This fine commentary in the excellent BECNT series is by a noted NT scholar and professor at Trinity Evangelical Divinity School. The introduction is a bit brief for a work of this nature, but overall this is a substantial addition to the Johannine literature. "He writes with color and verve; he is never leaden or boring. More important, he combines good exegesis, theological reflection, interaction not only with the most recent Johannine scholars but with two or three major figures in the past (notably Augustine, Calvin, and Schlatter), pastoral insight, and an independent judgment that means his work is always fresh. This is the place to start for pastors with functioning Greek" (Carson, 151).

Jude

Usually included with commentaries on 2 Peter.

!*?Bauckham, Richard J. See section on 2 Peter.

!?Bigg, Carl. See section on 1 Peter.

!*Green, Gene L. See section on 2 Peter.

*+Jenkyn, William. *An Exposition upon the Epistle of Jude.* Revised by James Sherman. London: James Nisbet, 1653. Reprint, Minneapolis: James & Klock, 1976.

> This massive Puritan commentary is the compilation of a series of lectures delivered at Christ Church in London in 1652. It has rightly achieved classic status. James & Klock have done a wonderful service to the Christian church by reprinting this jewel. "Very full, and profoundly learned. A treasure-house of good things" (Spurgeon, 197). "This work preceded Manton's monumental treatment. Manton regarded this exposition with such awe that he purposely avoided duplicating any of its material in his own work. Should be purchased if found" (Barber, 183).

Keating, Daniel. See section on 1, 2 Peter.

*+Manton, Thomas. *An Exposition on the Epistle of Jude.* London, 1658. Reprint, Minneapolis: Klock & Klock, 1978.

> This massive volume is a monumental treatment of the text by a noted Puritan writer. Manton was one of the most prolific writers of his day and his writing style is characterized by clarity and simplicity. "Manton's work is most commendable" (Spurgeon, 197). "Manton has an ease and clarity of style which immediately alerts the reader to the fact that he so thought through the issues as to be able to make even the most complex thoughts clear and understandable" (Barber).

!*+Mayor, Joseph B. See section on 1 Peter.

*Moo, Douglas J. See section on 2 Peter.

!?Neyrey, Jerome H. See section on 2 Peter.

*Schreiner, Thomas. See section on 1 Peter.

Revelation

!?Aune, David E. *Revelation*. WBC. Edited by Bruce M. Metzger, David Allen Hubbard, and Glenn W. Barker. 3 vols. Nashville: Nelson, 1997–98.

> Coming out just prior to Beale's seminal work, this massive technical work is a very useful scholarly resource which should be used alongside of Beale. However, it will likely be of little use to the average pastor. "The prose is accessible, the arguments often elegant" (Carson, 157).

Bauckham, Richard. *The Theology of the Book of Revelation*. Cambridge: Cambridge University Press, 1993.

> Not reviewed for this edition.

!*Beale, G. K. *The Book of Revelation*. NIGTC. Edited by I. Howard Marshall and Donald A. Hagner. Grand Rapids: Eerdmans, 1999.

> Although over seventeen years old, pride of place for the very best commentary for advanced students and pastors with still intact Greek skills is this magisterial volume. At 1,157 pages of text, it is a massive work of scholarship that is exceptionally well done and thorough. "The commentary that best combines comprehensiveness with biblical fidelity, exegesis with theology, and literary sensitivity with historical awareness. . . . The prose is sometimes dense, and, inevitably (not the least in a book like this!), readers will want to disagree with him from time to time—but there are few significant things that Beale has not thought deeply about. He is especially good at untangling how the Apocalypse incorporates Old Testament passages and themes" (Carson, 156–57). Amillennial.

*Beasley-Murray, George. *Revelation*. New Century Bible. Grand Rapids: Eerdmans, 1974.

> An excellent mid-level work that is now dated. Premillennial. Posttribulational.

*+Beckwith, Isbon T. *The Apocalypse of John*. New York: Macmillan, 1919. Reprint, Grand Rapids: Baker, 1979.

> This monumental effort is an outstanding critical and exegetical commentary first published in 1919. It is considered a classic by many and is considered first rate. The approximately four hundred pages of introductory material make it a worthy acquisition to any theological library. At almost eight hundred pages, this is a massive work of scholarship. "A work of impeccable scholarship" (Barber, 183). "One of the better older scholarly commentaries" (Evans, 429). Amillennial.

Caird, G. B. *A Commentary on the Revelation of St. John the Divine*. Harper New Testament Commentaries. Edited by Henry Chadwick. New York: Harper & Row, 1966.

> This offering in the HNTC series by a senior tutor of Mansfield College, Oxford University, will disappoint some evangelicals. This is a good commentary that has some real strengths, but it also has its flaws such as the annoying tendency to skip over verses in the exposition. It is also quite dated now. "One of the major strengths of this work is the reconstruction of the first-century AD setting with continuous emphasis upon a present understanding of what the Spirit might be saying to churches in our own day" (Barber, 183).

!*+Charles, R. H. *A Critical and Exegetical Commentary on the Revelation of St. John*. ICC. 2 vols. Edited by Samuel Rolles Driver, Alfred Plummer, and Charles Augustus Briggs. Edinburgh: T. & T. Clark, 1920.

> This excellent work is a comprehensive, detailed technical commentary that contains an exhaustive exegetical treatment of the Greek text. Though now dated, it still is considered the granddaddy of all commentaries on Revelation by many. It belongs in the library of the serious student and scholar. "This work and Swete's vie for supremacy" (Barber, 183). "Should not be overlooked, in view of the immense scholarship it represents. In one sense it has not been surpassed, but the preacher should not set too much hope on it, as the two volumes are very technical and only rarely practical" (Carson, 162). "The most comprehensive" (Danker, 272). "An enduring classic" (Carson, 430). Amillennial.

Cohen, Gary G. *Understanding Revelation: An Investigation of the Key Interpretational and Chronological Questions Which Surround the Book of Revelation*. Chicago: Moody, 1968.

> This book, by the former president of Graham Bible College in Bristol, Tennessee, is not a commentary, but rather attempts to provide a basic chronological framework for understanding the book of Revelation. It outlines six basic approaches (critical, allegorical, preterit, historical, topical, and futuristic) and then attempts to wrestle with the chronological problems in chapters 2–3, 4–5, 6–19, and 20–22. "A definitive work which develops a chronological framework for the interpretation of John's Apocalypse" (Barber). Premillennial.

!?Ford, J. Massyngberde. *Revelation*. AB. Edited by William Foxwell Albright and David Noel Freedman. New York: Doubleday, 1975.

> I list this commentary only in the sense of fairness and completeness. I do not recommend it. If the reader wants to read a work of fiction, I can supply a list of great works. "Wild and woolly ideas" (Evans, 431)!

*Hendriksen, W. *More Than Conquerors: An Interpretation of the Book of Revelation.* Grand Rapids: Baker, 1939.

> Although somewhat dated, this volume is still an excellent popular treatment of the book. It was at one time regarded the standard conservative commentary on the book by many pastors, particularly from a Reformed perspective. I found the prose to be a bit annoying. "In some circles this book has been assigned almost legendary value, but one must assume that the reason lies primarily in the combination of sober interpretation and evangelical fervor, all of it easily accessible, at a time when evangelicals were not producing much of worth on Revelation" (Carson, 161). Amillennial.

*Keener, Craig S. *Revelation.* NIVAC. Edited by Terry Muck. Grand Rapids: Zondervan, 1999.

> At 576 pages, this commentary is longer than some exegetical commentaries. Of course, Keener is well-known for producing prodigious works. This book is no exception. Although this is an "application" commentary, there is ample scholarly interaction with other works and Keener treats fairly different views of interpretation. Carson feels that this volume is uncharacteristically weak on exegesis and theological reflection (157). Pastors will find much to like here.

*Kistemaker, Simon J. *Revelation.* New Testament Commentary. Grand Rapids: Baker, 2001.

> An excellent mid-level commentary that completes the project he inherited from William Hendriksen. In my judgment, it is a major upgrade over Hendriksen's *More Than Conquerors.* Reformed. Amillennial.

!?Koester, Craig R. *Revelation.* AYB. Edited by John J. Collins. New Haven: Yale University Press, 2014.

> A major scholarly work that is massive in size along with a huge price tag. Hardcover will cost over $120 with the 2015 paperback version slightly over half that. It is an impressive work of scholarship that is technical, detailed, and comprehensive. However, the average evangelical pastor will find little use for this book. Replaces (thankfully) Ford.

*Ladd, George Eldon. *A Commentary on the Revelation of John.* Grand Rapids: Eerdmans, 1972.

> This excellent scholarly commentary, by a noted NT professor at Fuller Theological Seminary, is well done but not exhaustive in its analysis. "Its chief value lies in the coverage of all viewpoints, analysis of interpretative problems, and attempt to adhere to a consistent hermeneutic" (Barber, 184). "A sharp eye for theological themes" (Evans, 433). Premillennial. Posttribulational.

*Mounce, Robert. *The Book of Revelation*. NICNT. Edited by F. F. Bruce. Grand Rapids: Eerdmans, 1977.

> This volume is an especially well-done commentary by the former president of Whitworth College in Spokane, Washington. Its prose is easily accessible to both student and layperson. This book is the very best nontechnical commentary available. "A learned and well-written work that not only explains the text satisfactorily in most instances but also introduces the student to the best of the secondary literature" (Carson, 157). "A full and detailed commentary containing a great deal of information that will be of particular interest to those who preach on prophetic themes" (Barber). Premillennial.

Newell, William R. *The Book of the Revelation*. Chicago: Moody, 1935.

> This commentary, based on the English text by an American Bible teacher and evangelist who worked closely with Dwight L. Moody, is aimed primarily at laypersons and beginning Bible students. "A careful unfolding of the theme and purpose of the Revelation" (Barber, 184). Premillennial. Dispensational.

!*Osborne, Grant R. *Revelation*. BECNT. Edited by Moises Silva. Grand Rapids: Baker Academic, 2002.

> For an exegetical commentary, this fine effort by Grant Osborne, noted NT professor at Trinity Evangelical Divinity School, is accessible and "reader friendly." It is useful both to the scholar and advanced student as well as to those who have no background in NT Greek. Highly recommended! Premillennial.

Patterson, Paige. *Revelation*. NAC. Edited by E. Ray Clendenen. Nashville: Holman Reference, 2012.

> Patterson is the president of the Southwestern Baptist Theological Seminary and a towering figure in Southern Baptist circles. This commentary presents a more progressive dispensational stance toward the interpretation of the prophecy rather than the more militant approach of Walvoord. Premillennial. Dispensational.

Phillips, John. *Exploring Revelation*. Chicago: Moody, 1974.

> This commentary, like Newell's book, is aimed primarily at laypersons and beginning Bible students. It is not detailed and is rather superficial in approach. "Here is a light dispensational work, often alliterative, picturesque, with frequent illustrations (some quite good), but scant in supporting interpretation. Often Phillips shows no real attempt to grapple with meaning. . . . The work as a whole offers minimal light to help any but elemental readers grasp some points" (Rosscup, 347). Premillennial. Dispensational.

*+Ramsay, William. *The Letters to the Seven Churches of Asia*. New York: Armstrong, 1904. Reprint, Minneapolis: James Family, 1978.

> Although dated, this remains an outstanding treatment on the historical background of the seven churches in chapters 2–3. The scholarly discussions have been updated by more recent scholars, but this still remains a true classic. "The student will obtain much rich detail here to lend colorful vividness to his preaching and teaching" (Rosscup, 348). "A brilliant study of the historical and archaeological material relating to these churches" (Barber, 185). Preterist.

Ramsey, James B. *The Book of Revelation*. Richmond, VA: Presbyterian Committee of Publication, 1873. Reprint, Edinburgh: Banner of Truth, 1977.

> This commentary, originally published posthumously under the title *The Spiritual Kingdom*, by a noted nineteenth-century Presbyterian minister does not cover the entire book, but rather is an exposition of the first eleven chapters. This volume consists of twenty-eight lectures on those eleven chapters. It was not completed due to the author's deteriorating health. This work is pastoral and eminently practical.

Seiss, J. A. *The Apocalypse: Lectures on the Book of Revelation*. Cook, 1900. Reprint, Grand Rapids: Zondervan, 1964.

> This commentary by a noted nineteenth-century Lutheran writer is actually comprised of fifty-two lectures on the book. "An exhaustive . . . exposition" (Barber, 184). Premillennial. Dispensational.

Smith, J. B. *A Revelation of Jesus Christ: A Commentary on the Book of Revelation*. Scottdale, PA: Herald, 1961.

> This commentary, by a former professor of NT at Hesston College in Hesston, Kansas, was completed by J. Otis Yoder after the death of Smith in 1951. It is based on the Greek text and is considered in dispensational circles to be one of the better older commentaries on the Revelation. "Based on careful exegesis and providing rich source material. Well-substantiated conclusions" (Barber, 184). Premillennial. Dispensational.

Stott, John R. W. *What Christ Thinks of the Church: Insights from Revelation 2–3*. Grand Rapids: Eerdmans, 1958.

> The contents of this slender volume began in embryo form as a series of sermons at All Souls Church in London during the Lenten season 1957. Stott's applications are needed today. It is the writer's experience that anything published by Stott is well worth reading and should be purchased if available. "Characteristic of the writer's penetrating insight and usual brilliant

exposition, these messages on Revelation 2 and 3 set forth the ideal qualities of the church" (Barber, 185).

*+Swete, Henry Barclay. *Commentary on Revelation*. New York: Macmillan, 1911; Grand Rapids: Kregel, 1977.

This magisterial work, based upon the Greek text, rightly has achieved classic status and is matched only by Charles among older treatments. "A masterful exposition of the Greek text" (Barber, 184). "Swete is normally stodgy and often dull, but although he never shakes off his pedestrianism, in this commentary, there is some really useful and thorough material that helps the reader to see the depth of this book" (Carson, 162). Amillennial.

*+Trench, Richard Chenevix. *Commentary on the Epistles to the Seven Churches in Asia*. 6th ed. Kegan, Paul, Trench, Trubner, 1897. Reprint, Minneapolis: Klock & Klock, 1978.

Published prior to Ramsey's seminal work on the same subject, this book lacks some of the historical data included therein. However, this does not negate the value of Trench's important work. "Exemplary treatment of the Greek text" (Barber).

Walvoord, John F. *The Revelation of Jesus Christ*. Chicago: Moody, 1966.

This commentary, based upon the English text, by the former president of Dallas Theological Seminary, is considered a classic by many in dispensational circles. One weakness of the book is that little exegetical support is offered in support of the positions advanced. This was one of the first books that I purchased while a seminary student, but I cannot now recommend it as a faithful guide to interpreting the prophecy. "This book is a lucid exposition of the Revelation which combines textual exposition with theological orientation" (Rosscup, 349). "Illustrates what old-style dispensationalists do with the book" (Evans, 437). Premillennial. Dispensational.

Chapter 4

Systematic Theology, Church History, and Theological Topics

CHURCH HISTORY

*+Armitage, Thomas. *A History of the Baptists*. 2 vols. New York: Bryan, Taylor, 1887. Reprint, Minneapolis: James and Klock, 1977.

> This classic treatment is a history of the Baptists from John the Baptist to 1886. A comprehensive study.

*Cross, F. L., and E. A. Livingstone, eds. *The Oxford Dictionary of the Christian Church*. 3rd ed. New York: Oxford University Press, 2005.

> Indispensable for anyone doing work on the subject.

*Douglas, J. D. *The New International Dictionary of the Christian Church*. Rev. ed. Grand Rapids: Zondervan, 1978.

> At well over one thousand pages, this massive work contains 4,800 articles written by 180 Protestant scholars. It truly is a magnificent achievement and deserves to be on the shelf of every pastor. However, at almost forty years of age, it needs to be updated.

*Douglas, J. D., Walter A. Elwell, and Peter Toon, eds. *The Concise Dictionary of the Christian Tradition: Doctrine, Liturgy, History*. Grand Rapids: Regency Reference Library, 1989.

> An indispensable reference tool. Over three thousand terms and names, some hard to find in other works of this kind.

*Ferguson, Everett. *Church History: From Christ to the Pre-Reformation.* 2nd ed. Grand Rapids: Zondervan, 2013.

> This provocative book is a revision of the author's original 2003 work. It is the first volume of the two-volume work completed by John D. Woodbridge and Frank A. James III. This set's goal is to offer "a unique contextual view of how the Christian church spread and developed. It did so not in a vacuum, but in a setting of times, cultures, and events that both influenced and were influenced by the church" (from the back cover). Volume 1 covers from the time of Christ to just prior to the Reformation. Volume 2 picks up where volume 1 ends and brings it up to the present day. This work also provides an excellent overview of church history, but at five hundred-plus and eight hundred-plus pages, these two volumes do little more than skim the details and provide an overview. However, both volumes are well written and easy reading, and the format is easy on the eyes.

*Hill, Jonathan. *Zondervan Handbook to the History of Christianity.* Oxford: Lion Hudson, 2007.

> This volume is an excellent "bird's eye" look at Christian history. At 560 pages, it is highly selective offering forty-two feature articles.

*Latourette, Kenneth Scott. *Christianity in a Revolutionary Age: A History of Christianity in the 19th and 20th Centuries.* 5 vols. Grand Rapids: Zondervan, 1958–62.

> The five volumes of this brilliant work cover the nineteenth century in Europe (2 vols.) and outside Europe (1 vol.). The fourth and fifth volumes outline the twentieth century in Europe and Outside Europe. The author convincingly interweaves the different threads of global Christianity into a unified whole as he surveys the ecclesiastical and theological trends of these two centuries.

*———. *A History of Christianity.* 2 vols. Rev. ed. New York: Harper & Row, 1975.

> An exceptional work that should be on the shelf of every pastor. This revised edition is expanded to include the years 1950–1975. Interesting and well written! "A superb work which embraces both occident and orient, treats at length the history of Eastern Christianity, is fair and objective in handling developments within Catholicism, and provides a brilliant synthesis of trends in the church for students of church history" (Barber, 338).

*———. *A History of the Expansion of Christianity.* 7 vols. Grand Rapids: Zondervan, 1937–45.

> This brilliant set covers the first centuries of Christianity and concludes with the year 1914 and its aftermath. "No one can afford to ignore this monumental work" (Barber, 338).

*+Lindsay, Thomas M. *The Church and the Ministry in the Early Centuries*. New York: Doran, 1902. Reprint, Minneapolis: James Family, 1977.

> This compilation of eight lectures represents the eighteenth series of the Cunningham Lectures in Scotland. This book is often quoted on issues of church polity in the early church.

*+———. *A History of the Reformation*. 2 vols. Edinburgh: T. & T. Clark, 1906.

> This classic history is a comprehensive account of the Reformation and its effects in Germany and beyond.

*Littell, Franklin H. *The Macmillan Atlas History of Christianity*. New York: Macmillan, 1976.

> This essential resource portrays through maps the crucial aspects of Christian history that can be rendered in cartographic interpretation. This impressive achievement contains 197 maps and 162 illustrations.

*+Neal, Daniel. *The History of the Puritans*. 3 vols. London: Tegg, 1837. Reprint, Minneapolis: Klock & Klock, 1979.

> This massive history was originally conceived by John Evans and was intended to be a history of nonconformity from the Reformation to the Act of Uniformity. Neal, who lived from 1678–1743, took over the project and extended it to include the Act of Toleration (1689). The resulting work first appeared in 1732. This edition of Neal's famous work was updated and edited after his death by Joshua Toulmin, a respected historian and theologian, and it was published in 1797. It has since had many editions and reprinting over the past two hundred or so years. It has earned a well-deserved reputation as a true classic and is now regrettably out of print.

*+Schaff, Philip. *History of the Christian Church*. 8 vols. New York: Scribner, 1910. Reprint, Grand Rapids: Eerdmans, 1975.

> This set is the most comprehensive treatment of the subject available up until the time of the Swiss Reformation. A particular delight to read! "A brilliant, detailed account of the history of Christianity up to and including the continental Reformation. Well-written and easy to read. One of the most informative and valuable treatments available" (Barber, 339).

*Shelley, Bruce L. *Church History in Plain Language*. Waco, TX: Word, 1982.

> This book is the author's attempt to simplify the story of church history. He divides church history into eight ages. If there is a weakness, it is that he devotes more than half the book on the period ranging from the Reformation until 1980. Engagingly written and fun to read!

Vos, Howard F. *An Introduction to Church History*. Rev. ed. Chicago: Moody, 1984.

> This brief treatment of the subject is now over thirty years of age and dated. It
> is best suited as an undergraduate introduction.

*Woodbridge, John D., and Frank A. James III. *Church History: From Pre-Reformation to
the Present Day*. Grand Rapids: Zondervan, 2013.

> See review of Ferguson, Everett. *Church History: From Christ to the Pre-Refor-
> mation*. 2nd ed. Grand Rapids: Zondervan, 2013.

GENERAL STUDIES

Protestant

!*+?Barth, Karl. *Church Dogmatics*. 14 vols. 2nd ed. Edited by G. W. Bromiley and T. F.
Torrance. Translated by G. W. Bromiley. Edinburgh: T. & T. Clark, 1975. Reprint,
Peabody: Hendrickson, 2010.

> This massive study is Barth's magnum opus, covering a lifetime of theological
> thought. Four topics are covered in fourteen volumes. The first two volumes
> focus on "The Doctrine of the Word of God." The next two are devoted to
> "The Doctrine of God." Four volumes focus on "The Doctrine of Creation"
> and five on "The Doctrine of Reconciliation." The final volume is an index. To
> understand theological developments in the twentieth century, one must be
> aware of Barth's thought. His writings might not be agreed with, but he can-
> not be ignored. "This epochal theology by a great Neo-orthodox theologian
> records the stages through which Barth's theology went during his long and
> fruitful lifetime" (Barber, 199). "German Neo-Orthodox theologian who had
> a life changing encounter with Christ after he was already a professor. As
> such, he was described as being like a bomb dropped on the liberal theolo-
> gians' playground! This is a massive work. Barth is verbose and can be tedious
> to twenty-first-century readers; yet it has profound treasures available for the
> mature reader. Of special note is the final volume that follows the last volume
> titled *Index with Aids for the Preacher*. Don't go into the pulpit before check-
> ing the material of this volume. Advanced" (**Olsen**).

———. *Church Dogmatics: A Selection with Introduction*. Translated by G. W. Bromiley.
Louisville: Westminster John Knox, 1994.

> "Very helpful digest of the *Dogmatics*, and as much of Barth as is needed
> by most. But for those who wish to go deeper, this digest serves as a map
> with which the reader can navigate the appropriate sections within the larger
> work" (**Olsen**).

*Bavinck, Herman. *Reformed Dogmatics*. 4 vols. Edited by John Bolt. Translated by John Vriend. Grand Rapids: Baker Academic, 2003–8.

> "Many regard Bavinck's four volume summary of theology to be the best synthesis of Dutch Reformed theology available. Bavinck moves with ease from biblical exegesis to historical debates and finally to theological construction. His work is invaluable as it develops a distinctly Dutch theology in the context of his day. It is no less applicable today. Few books are as deep and readable as these books" (**Brandt**). "This is truly an outstanding work" (**Olsen**). Reformed.

*Berkhof, L. *Systematic Theology*. 4th ed. Grand Rapids: Eerdmans 1939.

> This work is an outstanding evangelical treatment of the subject. I read it with great profit during my first year of seminary. The writing is clear, engaging, and often profound. "This book is one of the standards of reformed theology. The book is especially useful for introductory students. Berkhof has a gift for summarizing doctrinal points with a concise and clear prose. His book is therefore especially helpful to consult. While he is short and concise, his theology still stands on its own today. There are many lost gems throughout this work. The reader should be especially aware of his succinct summary of points in prolegomena" (**Brandt**). "This particularly capable treatment is perhaps the best one-volume work available" (Barber, 189). Reformed.

Bird, Michael F. *What Christians Ought to Believe: An Introduction to Christian Doctrine through the Apostle's Creed*. Grand Rapids: Zondervan, 2016.

> Not reviewed for this edition.

Boettner, Loraine. *Studies in Theology*. 2nd ed. Grand Rapids: Eerdmans, 1951.

> This book is comprised of a series of independent books or magazine articles that first appeared in *Christianity Today* in 1937 and the *Evangelical Quarterly* in 1938–39. Reformed.

*Buswell, James Oliver, Jr. *A Systematic Theology of the Christian Religion*. Grand Rapids: Zondervan, 1962.

> This book is an excellent one-volume summary of Christian doctrine by a professor at Covenant Theological Seminary. "Gives evidence of a thorough knowledge of Greek and Hebrew. Frequently shows how this knowledge may be used to good advantage" (Barber, 189). Reformed. Premillennial.

*+Calvin, John. *Institutes of the Christian Religion*. 2 vols. Edited by John T. McNeill. Translated by Ford Lewis Battles. Library of Christian Classics. Edited by John Baillie, John T. McNeill, and Henry P. Van Dusen. Louisville: Westminster John Knox, 1960.

> One of the seminal works of the Christian faith. "This book is a classic of the faith. While controversial on many points, Calvin is regarded as one of the greatest theologians in the history of the church. This book is an excellent summary of his doctrine. It is not structured like systematic theologies today. In fact, many suggest that his theological topics are structured biblically. He begins with God and creation, moves to consider redemption, and then explores the church and eschatology. Calvin is most concerned with being biblical, forming piety into his readers, and staying away from speculative endeavors. Calvin's greatest contribution can be found in book 1, where he incessantly correlates the knowledge of God and humans. His work is recommended for readers at all levels, though an introductory student might find some of his discussions challenging" (**Brandt**). Reformed.

Chafer, Lewis Sperry. *Systematic Theology*. 8 vols. Dallas: Dallas Seminary Press, 1947.

> This set has been for decades the standard systematic theology from a dispensational perspective. The author was the founder and first president of Dallas Theological Seminary and editor of *Bibliotheca Sacra* for over ten years. Reading this set was my first introduction to Christian doctrine in a systematic fashion as a first-year seminary student at a dispensational institution. I found it to be very readable and clear. "A comprehensive manual of Christian doctrine. Remarkable for its clarity, brevity, and accuracy" (Barber, 189).

*Erickson, Millard J. *Christian Theology*. 3rd ed. Grand Rapids: Baker Academic, 2013.

> "This text is one of the standard systematic theology texts for undergraduate and graduate students. It is more in-depth but less readable than Grudem's comparable theology textbook. While Erickson is committed to the Baptist perspective, his discussions often transcend the denominational divide. Erickson can be faulted for failing to exegete as often as he should, but his historical discussions are especially helpful and intriguing" (**Brandt**).

*Grudem, Wayne. *Systematic Theology: An Introduction to Biblical Doctrine*. Leicester: InterVarsity, 1994.

> "Grudem's book is readable and clear. Because of this, his book is often the standard for undergraduate studies in the Baptist world. While there is little original in the text, it is an excellent overview for the beginning student. Grudem can be faulted for ignoring the historical context of most doctrines. His book is a good biblical introduction, but it fails to do systematic theology in this

sense. Grudem's book should be consulted alongside Allison's *Historical Theology* (2012) in order to show the full contour of systematic doctrines" (**Brandt**). "Although this work is faithful to its Reformed tradition, it is a remarkable work that intends to be useful for readers of various points of view. Each chapter concluded with a bibliography containing references to parallel systematic theologies listed by denomination and/or point of view, other important works, memory verses, and hymns. Excellent Scripture, author, and subject indices that enhance the volume's usefulness. Evangelical, Reformed, and eminently biblical. A large work that is accessible to the trained pastor" (**Olsen**). Reformed.

Gundry, Stanley N., and Alan F. Johnson, eds. *Tensions in Contemporary Theology*. Chicago: Moody, 1976.

This book is an evangelical attempt to survey contemporary theology up to the date of publication in 1976. The first 104 pages are devoted to the history of theology from Schleiermacher's early modernism to Tillich's radical views. Separate chapters trace religious language, secular theology, theology of hope, process theology, recent Roman Catholic theology, liberation theology, and the conservative option. Though it is now outdated, it is helpful and informative.

*+Hall, Francis J. *Introduction to Dogmatic Theology*. 10 vols. Reprint, New York: American Church Publications, 1970.

This massive work was first published in 1912. "The only full-blown systematic theology by an American Episcopalian from early in the last century. Hall was a 'High Church' orthodox believer. Deep, rich, philosophically, historically, and exegetically based work of profound learning" (**Olsen**).

*———. *Theological Outlines*. 3rd ed. Revised by Frank Hudson Hallock. New York: Morehouse-Barlow, 1933.

"This is an extremely helpful condensation of the author's ten volume *Summa*. Footnotes are noteworthy. This work should not be ignored, especially by a pastor or parish priest" (**Olsen**).

*+Henry, Carl F. H. *God, Revelation, and Authority*. 6 vols. Waco, TX: Word, 1976–83.

This six-volume work covers most of the topics included under the broad topic, systematic theology and is Carl Henry's magnum opus. The author was one of the twentieth century's leading evangelical theologians and thinkers. This set covers not only theology, but also philosophy, ethics, and contemporary culture. A seminal work that is must reading for every Christian leader!

Heppe, Heinrich. *Reformed Dogmatics: Set Out and Illustrated from the Sources*. London: Allen & Unwin, 1950.

> "A technical, rich work that brings together voluminous material from many of the church's great theologians, who are now long forgotten, and who are helpfully resurrected in this volume. Sometimes reading like a telephone book, it is a 'secret weapon' for the professional theologian. It was one of Karl Barth's favorite volumes, and referenced in every chapter of Grudem's *Systematic Theology*. Out of print and getting hard to find" (**Olsen**).

*+Hodge, Charles. *Systematic Theology*. 3 vols. Reprint, Grand Rapids: Eerdmans, 1952.

> Though now dated having been originally published 1871–73, this set has long been regarded as the standard for Reformed theology. This is Hodge's *magnum opus*. "A comprehensive theological treatment by one of the greatest nineteenth-century Princeton theologians" (Barber, 190). Reformed.

*Horton, Michael. *The Christian Faith: A Systematic Theology for Pilgrims on the Way*. Grand Rapids: Zondervan, 2011.

> "Has been called the finest systematic theology since that of Louis Berkhof. It is a huge volume (over a thousand pages) that is as weighty as it is large, and very much worth the effort of the reader. Does a noteworthy job of weaving together the biblical and historical development of doctrinal theology. He deftly distinguishes between the various points of view, all the while offering mature judgment and providing full, rich footnotes running along with the text (rather than the cheaper and less convenient end notes). It is accessible to the trained pastor. Reformed" (**Olsen**).

———. *Pilgrim Theology: Core Doctrines for Christian Disciples*. Grand Rapids: Zondervan, 2012.

> "This book describes itself as being based in part on Horton's much larger work, *The Christian Faith*. But let us be clear that this is no simple abridgement; rather, it seeks to reach a larger audience of Christians. It is truly a stand-alone volume that has a clearly defined purpose of seeking to take theology in the direction of *why it all matters*. In this sense, it may be regarded as a compliment to the larger work" (**Olsen**).

!*+Kuyper, Abraham. *Principles of Sacred Theology*. Translated by Hendrik de Vries. Grand Rapids: Eerdmans, 1954.

> Originally published in Dutch in 1898 as part of the author's *Encyclopedia of Sacred Theology*, this classic Reformed work grapples with the science of theology. "This classic book documents Kuyper's theology from a scientific standpoint. Of particular interest is the author's definition of theology in

relation to the scientific field. Theology is a science, according to Kuyper. While considered a classic among reformed folk, this book is generally overlooked in contemporary systematic theology. The book is an especially valuable tool for a master level student or above" (**Brandt**).

!*Lints, Richard. *The Fabric of Theology: A Prolegomenon to Evangelical Theology*. Grand Rapids: Eerdmans, 1993.

"This book is one of the more valuable resources in understanding the relationship between biblical and systematic theology. Lints helpfully captures how the reader of Scripture ought to frame Scripture in its context (whether literal, epochal, or canonical) and then move to systematic theology. His book is not for beginners, though a well-read beginning student would have no difficulty picking up the concepts" (**Brandt**).

*McGrath, Alister E. *Christian Theology: An Introduction*. 5th ed. Hoboken, NJ: Wiley-Blackwell, 2011.

*———. *The Christian Theology Reader*. 4th ed. Hoboken, NJ: Wiley-Blackwell, 2011.

*———. *Historical Theology*. Hoboken, NJ: Wiley-Blackwell, 2012.

"This evangelical Anglican, longtime professor of Historical Theology at the University of Oxford, has authored scores of books and given the believing church one of the richest introductions to the Christian faith extant. A real must" (**Olsen**)!

*McKim, Donald K. *The Westminster Dictionary of Theological Terms*. 2nd ed. Louisville: Westminster John Knox, 2014.

"The best, most up to date, comprehensive dictionary of its kind. A must for all pastors and teachers" (**Olsen**).

*Morris, Thomas V. *Our Idea of God: An Introduction to Philosophical Theology*. Notre Dame: University of Notre Dame Press, 1991.

This book demonstrates how the use of philosophical methodologies can help to illuminate complex theological doctrines. "Great book by a fine conservative philosophical theologian. Very helpful work" (**Olsen**).

!Mueller, John Theodore. *Christian Dogmatics*. St. Louis: Concordia, 1934.

"The author, a Missouri Synod Lutheran, trained under Francis Pieper. This work is a very biblical, moderately technical work of genuine value, and a must for professors of any persuasion" (**Olsen**).

*Muller, Richard A., ed. *Dictionary of Latin and Greek Theological Terms*. 2nd ed. Louisville: Westminster John Knox, 2014.

"Extremely useful in looking up Latin and Greek theological words that are often encountered in theological and philosophical literature" (**Olsen**).

*———. *Post-Reformation Dogmatics: The Rise and Development of Reformed Orthodoxy, ca. 1520 to ca. 1725*. 2nd ed. 4 vols. Grand Rapids: Baker, 2003.

"This series of books is the standard for understanding reformed dogmatics in the post-reformation period. The series is truly momentous. It is intended as a reference. The series is recommended for those deeply interested in post-reformation dogmatics. Muller's discussion of the prolegomena and *principia* in theology is of particular interest to the contemporary theologian" (**Brandt**).

!*?Pannenberg, Wolfhart. *Systematic Theology*. 3 vols. Translated by Geoffery W. Bromiley. Grand Rapids: Eerdmans, 1994.

"While not orthodox, Pannenberg's three volume text stands as one of the most monumental systematic theologies written in the twentieth century. His engagement with the historical record is especially strong. While not a strong biblical exegete, his discussions are illuminating—if not sometimes mistaken. Of particular interest is his argument that Christianity's early flourishing is proof that the resurrection actually and historically took place. He also argues that the doctrine of God ought to be treated before Scripture. His book is not very readable, so I would not recommend this book for beginners or undergraduates" (**Brandt**).

*Schaeffer, Francis A. *The Complete Works of Francis A. Schaeffer: A Christian Worldview*. 5 vols. Westchester, IL: Crossway, 1982.

This collection contains all of the twenty-one books written by Schaeffer between 1968 and 1981. Volume 1 is titled *A Christian View of Philosophy and Culture*, volume 2 is *A Christian View of the Bible as Truth*, volume 3 is *A Christian View of Spirituality*, volume 4 is *A Christian View of the Church*, and volume 5 is *A Christian View of the West*. Schaeffer was one of the most influential evangelical voices of the twentieth century and deserves to be read today. Not to be missed! Reformed.

+?Schleiermacher, Friedrich. *The Christian Faith*. Edited by H. R. MacKintosh and J. S. Stewart. London: T. & T. Clark, 1999.

"Often seen as the father of theological liberalism, Schleiermacher re-wrote orthodox theology in this influential text. It represents his mature thought. While evangelicals will disagree with his theology, he should be commended for holding to devout, devotional piety throughout his career. This text shows how he re-reads theology through personal piety. The human-centered dimension should be evident throughout this book. Schleiermacher believed that one should move from religious feeling to theologizing. This idea accounts for why many doctrines are redefined, as he explains throughout this work" (**Brandt**).

Shedd, William G. T. *Dogmatic Theology*. 3 vols. 2nd ed. Reprint, Nashville: Nelson, 1980.

> This outstanding treatment, first published in 1888–94 by the eminent Roosevelt Professor of Systematic Theology at Union Theological Seminary in New York, is still considered a standard work. "An eminently readable, thoroughly Biblical work, which contains a most extensive and satisfactory treatment of the doctrine of endless punishment" (Barber, 190).

*+Strong, Augustus Hopkins. *Systematic Theology*. 3 vols. in 1. Old Tappan, NJ: Revell, 1907.

> The author was a late nineteenth- / early twentieth-century Baptist minister and theologian whose most magnum opus was a mainstay of Reformed Baptist theological education for several generations. He does make accommodations to Darwinism.

Thiessen, Henry Clarence. *Introductory Lectures in Systematic Theology*. Grand Rapids: Eerdmans, 1956.

> Although dated, this book is still a good basic introduction to the subject of systematic theology. Dispensational.

*Thiselton, Anthony C. *Systematic Theology*. Grand Rapids: Eerdmans, 2015.

> This important new work, by a professor emeritus of Christian theology at the University of Nottingham, England, is an accessible and readable introduction to Christian theology that is designed for students and pastors, rather than professional theologians. Thiselton does not approach theology as an abstract system as so many theologians do, but rather sees theology as a living, organic whole. This book, as well as the author's *Thiselton Companion to Christian Theology*, constitutes the capstone of a more than half century of teaching and research. Both books are affordable and highly recommended.

*———. *The Thiselton Companion to Christian Theology*. Grand Rapids: Eerdmans, 2015.

> See my review of the author's *Systematic Theology* above. This book, building upon and drawing from the author's earlier work *Concise Encyclopedia of the Philosophy of Religion*, is an encyclopedia of Christian theology including just over six hundred articles ranging from A–Z, from *Abba* to *Zwingli*. Unlike most encyclopedias, this volume was written by one author, rather than having multiple contributors. The articles are well written and interesting.

*Vardy, Peter. *The Puzzle of God*. Oxford: Clarendon, 1994.

> "Outstanding clear introduction to Theology Proper by an evangelical. A must have book" (**Olsen**)!

Roman Catholic

Allen, Michael, and Scott R. Swain. *Reformed Catholicity: The Promise of Retrieval for Theology and Biblical Interpretation*. Grand Rapids: Baker Academic, 2015.

> "In this recent book, Allen and Swain argue for a retrieval method of theology. Coming from a reformed Catholic perspective, they suggest that theology is best seen within the ecumenical context of the church as a whole. While remaining consistent with evangelicalism, the book shows how their retrieval method might be helpful in our modern context, especially in circles that underplay tradition. Each chapter shows how their method would contribute to systematic theology in different subjects. The first three chapters are particularly helpful and original" (**Brandt**).

*+Aquinas, Thomas. *Summa Theologica*. Translated by the Fathers of the English Dominican Province. Rev. ed. New York: Benziger, 1920.

> "Thomas's work is often seen as the standard of Catholic theology. He is also regarded as one of the most significant theologians in history. Of particular interest is his discussion on the relationship between faith and reason, his understanding of God, and his development of virtue ethics" (**Brandt**).

!+Bonaventure. *Breviloquium*. Translated and edited by Dominic V. Monti. *Works of St. Bonaventure*. Vol. 9. Saint Bonaventure, NY: Franciscan Institute Publications, 2005.

> "In this classic work, Bonaventure develops a deductive approach to theology. He includes an unusually large section on prolegomena and method in the Middle Ages. While his acquaintance, Thomas Aquinas, receives more attention today, Bonaventure was one of the most influential theologians of the time. One can sense the depth of his thinking throughout this work. His work is dense and harmonious, attempting to synthesize the whole of theology under the triune God" (**Brandt**).

SPECIAL SUBJECTS

Anthropology and Harmartiology

*Berkouwer, G. C. *Man: The Image of God.* Studies in Dogmatics. Translated by Dirk W. Jellema. Grand Rapids: Eerdmans, 1962.

> This book is a brilliant and incisive critique of the different views of the image of God. "More a discussion of contemporary views of man than a systematic theological treatment" (Barber, 216).

*———. *Sin.* Studies in Dogmatics. Translated by Phillip C. Holtrop. Grand Rapids: Eerdmans, 1971.

> This study is a work of massive scholarship. At 567 pages of text, it is comprehensive and thought-provoking. "Destined to take its place as one of the most authoritative works of its kind" (Barber, 217).

*+Laidlaw, John. *The Biblical Doctrine of Man.* Edinburgh: T. & T. Clark, 1895. Reprint, Minneapolis: Klock & Klock, 1983.

> This book is a compilation of the Cunningham Lectures on "The Bible Doctrine of Man" delivered at the New College in Edinburgh in the late nineteenth century.

*+MacDonald, Donald. *The Biblical Doctrine of Creation and the Fall.* Edinburgh: Constable, 1856. Reprint, Minneapolis: Klock & Klock, 1984.

> This classic study is a detailed examination of Genesis 1–3. "We do not hesitate to designate this volume as the most complete examination of the literature and the exegesis of the Creation and the Fall which has appeared in England" (Spurgeon, 53). Reformed.

Apologetics

!*+Aquinas, Thomas. *Summa Contra Gentiles.* 3 vols. Reprint, Notre Dame & London: University of Notre Dame Press, 1991.

> "Perhaps one of the greatest and most under-read and under-appreciated apologetic classics of the middle ages, and maybe of all time, Aquinas' *Summa Contra Gentiles* was written specifically for Christian missionaries who would be working in regions of Europe and abroad with a strong intellectual Muslim-Arab presence. Aquinas organized his *SCG* into four 'books,' and his method is two-fold: (1) to provide demonstrable as well as probable arguments for truthfulness of the Christian faith to the skeptic, and (2) to answer

arguments leveled against the truth of the Christian faith by skeptics. In doing so, Aquinas covers nearly every major apologetic topic beginning with God, creation, man, the Trinity and the Incarnation as well as the end of the universe. Using Scripture as well as a balanced use of Aristotelian philosophical principles, he provides a sound and careful defense of Christian truth to an unbelieving and skeptical world. In the corpus of Thomistic works, the *SCG* is one the most accessible and practical" (**Wright**).

*Brown, Colin. *Miracles and the Critical Mind*. Grand Rapids: Eerdmans, 1984.

This excellent study is an examination of the arguments about the miracles of Jesus and their place in the faith of the believer. The author, professor of systematic theology at Fuller Theological Seminary, provides a detailed examination of David Hume's attack on miracles and evaluates it within the framework of the ongoing controversy over Christ's miracles that began during his lifetime and continues on into the present. Brown then reappraises the role of miracles in Christian apologetics focusing particularly on the writings of B. B. Warfield, C. S. Lewis, and Alan Richardson as well as other evangelical and Roman Catholic writers. This helpful volume provides a comprehensive account of the controversy surrounding the miracles of Christ from the early church to the time of the book's writing.

Carnell, Edward John. *An Introduction to Christian Apologetics*. Grand Rapids: Eerdmans, 1948.

For decades, this book was a standard evangelical work on Christian apologetics. Carnell was the president of Fuller Theological Seminary and also a professor of apologetics there. This seminal book is divided into three parts: The Need for a Christian World-View, The Rise of the Christian World-View, and the Implications of the Christian World-View. "A thought-provoking, but disappointing work. Makes many concessions to science, and persistently detracts from or stretches the intent of Scripture in an attempt to satisfy the present-day claims of scientists" (Barber, 227).

*Collins, Francis S. *The Language of God: A Scientist Presents Evidence for Belief*. New York: Free Press, 2006.

This provocative book was *Christianity Today* magazine's Book of the Year in the category of Apologetics and Evangelism in 2007. Collins is head of the Human Genome Project and a world-respected scientist. In this book, he answers the question of whether it is possible to achieve harmony between a scientific and a spiritual worldview. He traces his own spiritual pilgrimage from atheism to faith and then examines modern science to demonstrate how it fits together with belief in God and the Bible. A must-read!

Cowan, Steven B., ed. *Five Views on Apologetics*. Counterpoints. Edited by Stanley N. Gundry. Grand Rapids: Zondervan, 2000.

> Not reviewed for this edition, but the other volumes in this series are of uniformly high quality and recommended.

!*Dembski, William, and Thomas Shirrmacher. *Tough Minded Christianity: Honoring the Legacy of John Warwick Montgomery*. Nashville: B & H Academic, 2009.

> "This book contains a collection of excellent apologetics essays honoring one of the most prolific apologists and theologians of the twentieth century, John Warwick Montgomery. Montgomery, a Lutheran theologian, has earned eleven degrees including a PhD and a ThD and is a barrister (lawyer), historian, and theologian. His work has influenced countless Christian apologists in the twentieth century, including Francis Beckwith, Gary Habermas, and many others. The essays touch on nearly every major apologetic topic including chapters on miracles, arguments for God's existence, intelligent design, natural law theory, evangelism, and social theory as well as Montgomery's unique use of evidentialist apologetic approach" (**Wright**).

Dulles, Avery. *A History of Apologetics*. Eugene, OR: Wipf and Stock, 1999.

> The author writes in his preface, "Apologists came to recognize that every Christian harbors within himself a secret infidel." With this in mind, this book traces the history of apologetics from the New Testament times to the twentieth century. Extensive and helpful bibliographies for each chapter.

*Dyrness, William. *Christian Apologetics in a World Community*. Downers Grove: InterVarsity, 1983.

> This book describes the efforts of Christians to do apologetics in the past and then sketches a model for doing them in the twentieth century in a multicultural world. He specifically relates his model to several non-Christian philosophies as well as to Christian concerns such as suffering. There are helpful questions for review at the end of each chapter. Thought provoking.

!*Feser, Edward. *The Last Superstition: A Refutation of the New Atheism*. South Bend, IN: St. Augustine's, 2010.

> "Feser is a Roman Catholic philosopher who writes from an Aristotelian-Thomistic tradition. This book provides one of the most robust defenses of classical theism and its philosophical foundations in print today. Feser's book takes direct aim at the arguments set forth by the 'new atheists' such as Richard Dawkins, Sam Harris, and the late Christopher Hitchens. Feser is a brilliant communicator and his wit is as sharp as his mind. Evangelicals should not be put off by Ferer's Catholic background. His main thesis in the book is

to answer the arguments (a loose term when applied to the new atheists). This book should be read and studied by every Christian thinker and defender who wishes to engage with the new atheism with rigorous philosophical arguments for God's existence" (**Wright**).

*Geisler, Norman L., ed. *Baker Encyclopedia of Christian Apologetics*. Grand Rapids: Baker, 1999.

This handy reference tool is both extensive and comprehensive in its treatment of topics relating to the field of Apologetics from Anselm to Zen.

*———. *Christian Apologetics*. 2nd ed. Grand Rapids: Baker Academic, 2013.

"It could be argued that Norman Geisler is one of the most prolific and influential apologists of the late twentieth and early twenty-first century. His *Christian Apologetics* is perhaps his most influential book. It was originally published in 1976. Since then it has become a benchmark in the classical approach to classical Christian apologetics—an approach Geisler has gleaned, distilled, organized, and translated for modern audiences, from Augustine, Thomas Aquinas, and C. S. Lewis. The classical approach to Christian apologetics consists of a few simple, but foundational questions, each building on the other. These questions form the basic three-part outline of the book. In Part I (**Methodology**) Geisler covers the fundamental questions of how one approaches the question of truth, and whether or not truth is, or is not relative. In Part II (**Theistic Apologetics**), Geisler analyzes the question of whether God exists and the various approaches to god: no God (atheism), one God (theism), many gods (polytheism), an all wise but aloof, universe-making God (deism), or a god who is limited in either goodness, power, or both (finite godism). In Part III (**Christian Apologetics**), Geisler tackles the question of whether miracles are possible. In this chapter, Geisler argues that since classical theism is true, then miracles and the supernatural are possible (on this point, see also C. S. Lewis's *Miracles*). In the final few chapters, Geisler evaluates the claims in the NT from Christ, that He was God in human flesh, as well as miracles and their meaning. He concludes with possibility of objectivity in historical knowledge, and that the NT is historically trustworthy and reliable, as well as inspired and infallible. From beginning to end, *Christian Apologetics* is a methodical, comprehensive, and meticulous defense of, and case for Christianity. If one is looking for an intelligently argued, academic, and philosophically informed volume on Christian apologetics, then look no further than this excellent and time-tested book" (**Wright**).

*Geisler, Norman L., and Frank Turek. *I Don't Have Enough Faith to Be an Atheist*. Wheaton: Crossway, 2004.

> "This work is perhaps one of the best and most accessible apologetics books in print today. Geisler and Turek present the classical apologetic approach from the ground up. The classical approach to apologetics combines classical arguments for God's existence (the cosmological argument, the teleological argument, and the moral argument) with the evidential/historical approach. The book is arranged around twelve main apologetics points, which can be summarized into five basic questions: Does truth exist? Does God exist? Are miracles possible? Is the New Testament historically reliable? and Did Jesus rise from the dead? The book is relentlessly methodical as it gives numerous examples from reason, science, and history to support its claims. Presents a comprehensive case for Christianity beginning with the existence of truth, and ending with the resurrection of Christ and the reliability of the Bible" (**Wright**).

*Geivett, R. Douglas, and Gary R. Habermas, eds. *In Defense of Miracles: A Comprehensive Case for God's Action in History*. Downers Grove: IVP Academic, 1997.

> Some of the most noteworthy evangelical philosophers, writing in the latter part of the twentieth century, have banded together to produce this excellent collection of essays about the philosophical issues surrounding miracles. The book takes as its starting point the fact that miracles in the Bible have been questioned for centuries. It begins with an examination of the arguments by David Hume and twentieth-century atheist philosopher Anthony Flew. The list of contributors is impressive, including Ronald Nash, Norman Geisler, Francis Beckwith, William Craig, and J. P. Moreland. Compelling!

*Groothuis, Douglas. *Christian Apologetics: A Comprehensive Case for Biblical Faith*. Downers Grove: InterVarsity, 2011.

> "Douglas Groothuis, who teaches apologetics at Denver Seminary, has provided a large and comprehensive apologetics textbook geared toward the seminary student or advanced layman. In his book, Groothuis covers nearly every major apologetic topic and sub-topic. As a textbook, Groothuis' massive tome is a welcome addition to any apologetics library as a competent source in defending the Christian faith. In contrast to the 'Classical Apologetics' approach of Norman Geisler, R. C. Sproul, John Gerstner, et al., Groothuis' work is grounded in the analytic philosophical tradition, and an evidentialist apologetic approach" (**Wright**).

Habermas, Gary R., and Michael R. Licona. *The Case for the Resurrection of Jesus*. Grand Rapids: Kregel, 2004.

> This interesting study offers a comprehensive argument for the historical veracity of the resurrection of Jesus Christ. Although there is an attempt to offer a variety of evidentiary materials that evangelicals can utilize to argue for the historical foundation of their faith, the book tries to do too much and cover too much ground. For example, criticisms have been leveled at the authors' tendency to go down rabbit holes such as Elvis sightings, alien sightings, and Mormonism. Another criticism is that the book appears to have been put together hastily, which results in an often poorly written work.

House, H. Wayne. *Charts of Apologetics and Christian Evidences*. Grand Rapids: Zondervan, 2006.

> Not reviewed for this edition.

———. *Reasons for Our Hope: An Introduction to Christian Apologetics*. Nashville: B & H Academic, 2011.

> Not reviewed for this edition.

!*Keener, Craig. *Miracles: The Credibility of the New Testament Accounts*. 2 vols. Grand Rapids: Baker Academic, 2011.

> Craig Keener is a careful and meticulous NT scholar who teaches at Asbury Theological Seminary in Louisville. Anything he publishes is certainly worth reading and careful study. He is particularly well known for his magisterial work on the Acts of the Apostles. "Monumental is one word that could be used to describe Keener's epic two-volume work on miracles. Since the crowning jewel of the Christian faith is the resurrection of Jesus Christ from the dead (a grand miracle indeed!), a thorough and comprehensive defense of the viability of miracles is essential to any Christian apologetic approach. Keener, however, does not restrict his work only to the resurrection. He examines ancient as well as contemporary miracle accounts found in various cultures around the world using anthropological, philosophical and sociological lenses. Essentially, Keener's work can be broken down into two essential components: (1) The philosophical objection to miracles via David Hume, and the response to Hume philosophically, and (2) Keener's response to one of the main premises to Hume's argument, i.e.—'that uniform experience reveals that miracles are impossible' (paraphrase). In response, Keener documents countless miracle claims throughout history and well into the modern world in cultures around the world. Keener's work is by far, the most thorough response to the objection to miracles and the supernatural in print today. This book should be consulted by every Christian engaged in apologetics today" (**Wright**).

*+Lewis, C. S. *Mere Christianity*. New York: Macmillan, 1944.

This book is a classic defense of Christianity and Christian behavior by argu-ably the foremost apologist of the twentieth century. C. S. Lewis, who taught at both Oxford and Cambridge Universities, wrote for the educated layperson as well as seminary student. This brilliant work is highly recommended and not to be missed! "Between 1942–44 C. S. Lewis gave a series of talks which were broadcasted on the BBC at the height of Britain's engagement in WWII. Lewis, who was at Oxford at the time, was invited by Rev. James Welch, the director of religious broadcasting. The book is a transcript of the original broadcasts that were initially published as a series of shorter individual pamphlets. One of the main arguments that Lewis sets forth in the book and in his original BBC talks is taken from the moral argument for God's existence. Lewis argued that an objective moral law must exist or else what Hitler did (and was wrong at the time) is not morally wrong. Every law must have a 'lawgiver,' so Lewis argues that the moral law (the objective standard of right and wrong that all cultures all time inherently know), must have a moral law giver whom he identifies as God. Another important contribution that Lewis put forward is the now fa-mous 'tri-lem-ma' of Christ, now known as the 'Lewis trilema.' In the trilema, Lewis reduces the identity of Christ into three contradictory notions—either Christ was insane, or He was deliberately lying, or He was telling the truth. The first two options, Lewis argues, are inconsistent with Christ's character, and so he concludes that Christ was indeed telling the truth about His claim to be God incarnate. It is no exaggeration to say that nearly every apologetic book in print today has been either directly or indirectly influenced by arguments in *Mere Christianity*. It should be essential reading for every Christian apolo-gist" (**Wright**). An eight-session video group study is available from Zondervan titled *Discussing Mere Christianity: A DVD Study* by Eric Metaxas.

*+———. *Miracles*. New York: Macmillan, 1947.

"Certainly one of the most important and influential apologetics books in the twentieth century is Lewis's *Mere Christianity*. Perhaps Lewis's second most im-portant philosophical and apologetic work is his book, *Miracles*. Is the universe an open or closed system? Are miracles and the supernatural possible? These questions are evaluated in depth by Lewis in this book. Since the core truth of Christianity centers on the deity of Jesus Christ (in the incarnation) and His resurrection from the dead, a defense of miracles against anti-supernatural bias is essential. *Miracles* is Lewis's answer to the most robust critique of the mi-raculous since the eighteenth-century Enlightenment (via David Hume, et al.). *Miracles* is a glowing example of Lewis's laser sharp intellect, signature wit, and unique literary style in a way that his other books and novels do not bring out. In this book, Lewis charges skeptics, and those who reject miracles *a priori* with being more anti-intellectual and closed minded than those who do believe in miracles. Logic and reason, Lewis argues, do not preclude the miraculous. On the contrary, they are pointers and indicators of it and to it. Rational thought and logic themselves argue very strongly for the existence of the supernatural. Since the principles of logic are nonmaterial, it follows that there must exist a nonmaterial entity (i.e., God and/or a Mind/Intelligent) to explain them. Lewis's book, *Miracles*, should be essential reading for every Christian apologist who will encounter entrenched anti-supernaturalism, both in academia and in everyday encounters with nonbelievers. For well over sixty years, Lewis continues to teach and instruct Christians how to defend the Faith, and to love God with our souls as well as our minds" (**Wright**).

*Licona, Michael. *The Resurrection of Jesus: A Historiographical Approach*. Downers Grove: IVP Academic, 2010.

"This book is a look at Christ's resurrection from an historian's perspective. How would a modern historian investigate the claims of the resurrection of Jesus as they are recorded in the New Testament? This is the question that associate professor of theology at Houston Baptist University, Michael Licona (PhD, University of Pretoria), explores in his extensively researched book, *The Resurrection of Jesus*. As the title says, Licona's book looks at the resurrection from a purely historiographical approach. There are some pros and cons to this approach. One of the potential pitfalls is that there are numerous assumptions and intramural arguments among contemporary historians that are not fully agreed upon. Secondly, apologists should be cautious not to put all of one's 'apologetic eggs' in the historian's basket. The case for the resurrection of Christ is cumulative (utilizing arguments from philosophy, science, history, and archaeology) and should be built on a foundation of classical theism. The truth that God exists means that miracles and the miraculous is a logical and actual possibility. It is certainly true that historical texts (within a degree of probability), can record miraculous events (such as the resurrection, etc.). But, if miracles are *de facto*, not possible, then all the historical arguments one could marshal will not convince the hardened atheist and skeptic of the truth of the resurrection. That being said, Licona's historiographical research on the contemporary, cultural background and milieu of the New Testament is impeccable. In the book, he systematically dismantles and eliminates contemporary criticism of the historical reliability of the New Testament document as a first rate historical document. A must read and a valuable contribution to contemporary 'historical Jesus' studies" (**Wright**).

McDowell, Josh, and Bill Wilson. *He Walked Among Us: Evidence for the Historical Jesus*. Nashville: Nelson, 1993.

This book is a popular study of the historical evidence for the existence of Jesus. Written in an engaging, readable style, the authors examine the NT writings as well as those of the early Church leaders, martyrs, and ancient rabbis along with historical geography and archaeology to prove the historicity of

Jesus of Nazareth. They evaluate the teachings of liberal scholarship such as higher criticism and find their arguments lacking.

McGrath, Alister E. *Mere Apologetics: How to Help Seekers and Skeptics Find Faith*. Grand Rapids: Baker, 2012.

> Not reviewed for this edition.

Meister, Chad V., and Khaldoun A. Sweis. *Christian Apologetics: An Anthology of Primary Sources*. Grand Rapids: Zondervan Academic, 2012.

> Not reviewed for this edition.

*Sproul, R. C., Arthur Lindsley, and John Gerstner. *Classical Apologetics: A Rational Defense of the Christian Faith and a Critique of Presuppositional Apologetics*. Grand Rapids: Zondervan, 1984.

> This book is divided into three parts. Section 1 is titled "Classical Natural Theology: An Overview of Problem and Method." This section is a prolegomenon outlining the problems and methods of apologetics. Section 2 is titled "Classical Apologetics: The Theistic Proofs, the Deity of Christ, and the Infallibility of Scripture." This section develops theistic proofs and the authority of Scripture. Section 3 is titled "A Classical Critique of Presuppositional Apologetics." This section deals particularly with the thought of Van Til. Highly recommended!

Strobel, Lee. *The Case for Christ*. Grand Rapids: Zondervan, 1998.

> "Strobel, a reporter, has done a terrific job of laying out the case for why we believe Christ is the Son of God. His book has done for this generation what C. S. Lewis and Josh McDowell did for previous generations—set down a popular, timely argument for the deity of Christ and the veracity of Scripture" (**Fleming**).

*Wallace, J. Warner. *Cold Case Christianity*. Colorado Springs: Cook, 2013.

> "This is an excellent book to give to skeptics and/or introduce laymen to Christian apologetics. J. Warner Wallace is a retired cold-case homicide detective from California, who utilizes his forensic research skills (think CSI) to investigate the claims of the resurrection of Christ as it is recorded in the New Testament. The book is very well organized, the arguments are easy to follow and it contains numerous, helpful illustrations and charts. Wallace follows and 'interrogates' all relevant leads and sources, leaving no stone unturned for clues, including the four Gospel writers, contemporary historical accounts, and the early Church fathers" (**Wright**).

*————. *God's Crime Scene*. Colorado Springs: Cook, 2015.

"*God's Crime Scene* is Wallace's second book in which he utilizes his forensic research skills as a cold-case homicide detective. In Wallace's first book, *Cold Case Christianity*, he investigates the claims of the resurrection of Christ. In *God's Crime Scene* he investigates the universe (on the small and large scale) and the evidence *for* and *against* a Creator. In his research, Wallace utilizes his forensic research skills to uncover compelling scientific evidence. This book would be an excellent introduction to two of the most convincing arguments in contemporary Christian apologetics: the argument from design (the teleological argument), and the argument from the beginning of the universe (the cosmological argument)" (**Wright**).

!*Wright, N. T. *The Resurrection of the Son of God*. Minneapolis: Fortress, 2003.

"This book is the third volume in Wright's series on the life of Christ and is an in-depth, scholarly treatment of the resurrection from the perspective and assumption of contemporary critical scholarship. Wright is the former Bishop of Durham of the Church of England, and currently as Chair of NT and Early Christianity at St. Andrews University (UK) at the Divinity School. The primary focus of this volume is what really happened on Easter morning. Ever since the earliest apostles, Christians have maintained that Jesus literally rose from the dead. But since the time of the European Enlightenment, scholars have been critical, if not downright skeptical of the factual nature of Christ's resurrection as it appears in the NT. In more recent times, 'historical Jesus' studies have come back into vogue with the *Jesus Seminar* as well as wide public interest in scholars such as John Dominick Crossan, Bart Ehrman, and others. In this lengthy volume (740 pages), Wright explores the literary, historical, and cultural context of the resurrection claim, focusing on the Jewish and Greco-Roman (religious and nonreligious) aspects of such a claim. Herein lies the strength of Wright's book—a literary and exegetical defense of the historical resurrection of Jesus against a mythological or spiritualized account, proposed by such writers as Bultmann, Crossan, and others writing today. Wright is a top-rate biblical exegete whose mastery of the literary, cultural, and historical context of the NT and early Christian documents is unparalleled. For those who wish to interact with mainline scholarship on the historical Jesus and the resurrection of Jesus, this book is tops in the field. It will be considered a standard and landmark book on the subject for years to come" (**Wright**).

Biblical Theology

*Gentry, Peter J., and Stephen J. Wellum. *God's Kingdom through God's Covenants.* Wheaton: Crossway, 2015.

> This welcome book is an abridgement of the authors' 2012 work, *Kingdom through Covenant: A Biblical-Theological Understanding of the Covenants.* The earlier book, which some readers found difficult and ponderous, attempted to present a mediating position between dispensational and covenant theology. This abridgement is a much easier read and more user friendly.

!*———. *Kingdom through Covenant: A Biblical-Theological Understanding of the Covenants.* Wheaton: Crossway, 2012.

> This book is an impressive attempt to provide a framework for understanding the meta-narrative of Scripture. The authors present what they coin "New Covenant Theology" or progressive covenantalism as a middle ground between dispensationalism and covenant theology. Their conclusions are certainly thought-provoking and will be a part of the discussion on biblical theology for some decades, but they probably will not wind up pleasing either the dispensationalists or the covenant theologians. For example, they reject the Reformed teaching on the continuity of circumcision and baptism, but reject many of the dispensationalist's teachings on the land and the Jewish people. The book consists of three parts. Part 1, "Prolegomena," was written by Wellum, as was part 3, "Theological Integration." Part 2, "Exposition of Biblical Covenants," was written by Gentry. A major work on biblical theology!

*Robertson, O. Palmer. *The Christ of the Covenants.* Phillipsburg, NJ: Presbyterian and Reformed, 1980.

> This important study of the covenantal structure of Scripture, by a former professor of OT at Westminster Theological Seminary and Covenant Theological Seminary, ably presents the Reformed understanding of covenant theology, but with an emphasis on the overarching theme of all the covenants, Jesus Christ. Reformed.

*Treat, Jeremy R. *The Crucified King: Atonement and Kingdom in Biblical and Systematic Theology.* Grand Rapids: Zondervan, 2014.

> This book expounds the doctrine of two of the seminal themes presented in Scripture and demonstrates the relationship between the two. Kingdom and atonement are often presented in the church and the academy as almost mutually exclusive constructs. This work beautifully interweaves the two.

*+Vos, Geerhardus. *Biblical Theology: Old and New Testaments*. Grand Rapids: Eerdmans, 1948.

> A brilliant treatment of the subject following a historical approach. This book is the fruit of the author's thirty-nine years of teaching the subject at Princeton. Reformed.

Ecclesiology

*Allison, Gregg R. *Sojourners and Strangers: The Doctrine of the Church*. Foundations of Evangelical Theology. Edited by John S. Feinberg. Wheaton: Crossway, 2012.

> This book is hands down the best and most comprehensive treatment of the doctrine of the church in the past quarter century. The book is divided into seven parts: "Foundational Issues"; "The Biblical Vision—Characteristics of the Church"; "The Vision Actualized—The Growth of the Church"; "The Government of the Church"; "The Ordinances of the Church"; "The Ministries of the Church"; and "Conclusion." In the first section of the book, Allison explains his methodology for approaching the doctrine of ecclesiology. He identifies himself as one who stands in between those adherents of the contrasting views of continuity and discontinuity between the testaments and considers himself to embrace a moderate discontinuity. Baptist. Progressive dispensational.

*+Bannerman, James. *The Church of Christ*. 2 vols. Reprint, Carlisle, PA: Banner of Truth, 1960.

> This comprehensive work, first published in 1869, outlines the nature, powers, ordinances, discipline, and government of the church. A true classic! Reformed.

*Berkouwer, G. C. *The Church*. Studies in Dogmatics. Translated by James E. Davison. Grand Rapids: Eerdmans, 1976.

> This seminal work examines four facets of the church: its unity, catholicity, apostolicity, and holiness.

*Kuiper, R. B. *The Glorious Body of Christ: A Scriptural Appreciation of the One Holy Church*. Reprint, Carlisle, PA: Banner of Truth, 1967.

> This book is a comprehensive and popular presentation of the doctrine of the church. It is well written and totally engaging. Each of its brief chapters is meant to be read in a single sitting. "A masterful treatment of the nature and function of the church" (Barber). Reformed.

Saucy, Robert L. *The Church in God's Program*. Chicago: Moody, 1972.

> My ecclesiology textbook while in seminary. "Deals with the church in both its universal and local aspects, emphasizes the Biblical pattern for the organization, ministry, and worship of the church. Provides one of the most readable and extensive treatments available today" (Barber). Dispensational.

Eschatology

*Archer, G., Jr., P. D. Feinberg, D. J. Moo, and R. R. Reiter. *The Rapture: Pre-, Mid-, or Post-Tribulational?* Contemporary Evangelical Perspectives. Grand Rapids: Zondervan Academie Books, 1984.

> This book examines the question of the timing of the Rapture from three premillennial positions by three evangelical scholars. Feinberg argues for the pretribulational rapture, Archer for the midtribulational position, and Moo for the posttribulational one. Each writer presents his case, which in turn is followed by critical responses by the two others. The quasi-dialogue format allows the reader to understand the distinctive characteristics of each position as well as their strengths and weaknesses.

*Berkouwer, G. C. *The Return of Christ*. Studies in Dogmatics. Translated by James Van Oosterom. Grand Rapids: Eerdmans, 1972.

> This brilliant study is the final volume in the esteemed professor of systematic theology's Studies in Dogmatics. "A learned treatise on the doctrine of the second advent. Valuable for the thorough way the writer presents the teaching and position of contemporary theologians" (Barber). Amillennial.

*Blaising, Craig A., Douglas J. Moo, and Alan Hultberg. *Three Views on the Rapture: Pretribulation, Prewrath, or Posttribulation*. Counterpoints. 2nd ed. Grand Rapids: Zondervan, 2010.

> This book examines the question of the timing of the Rapture from three premillennial positions by three evangelical scholars. It covers much of the same territory that Archer, Feinberg, and Moo's 1984 book, *The Rapture: Pre-, Mid-, or Post-Tribulational?* did, but with a fresh appraisal due to the recent prominence of the Pre-Wrath (midtribulational) view. The introduction gives a historical overview of the doctrine of the Rapture. The counterpoint format allows for robust clash of contributors allowing readers to understand each position as well as each one's strengths and weaknesses.

Blomburg, Craig L., and Sung Wook Chung, eds. *A Case for Historic Premillennialism: An Alternative to "Left Behind" Eschatology*. Grand Rapids: Baker Academic, 2009.

> As the title indicates, this volume is a defense of classic premillennialism and a refutation of dispensational premillennialism with contributions by Oscar Campos, Helene Dallaire, Donald Fairbairn, Richard Hess, Don Payne, and Timothy Weber.

Boettner, Loraine. *The Millennium*. Philadelphia: Presbyterian and Reformed, 1957.

> Postmillennialism is probably the least understood of the three major millennial views. This book, originally published in 1957 by a Reformed scholar, is a critical analysis of those views: premillennialism, amillennialism, and postmillennialism. Postmillennial.

*Clouse, Robert G., ed. *The Meaning of the Millennium: Four Views*. Downers Grove: InterVarsity, 1977.

> This book examines the three major views on the millennium (historic premillennialism, amillennialism, and postmillennialism), as well as dispensational premillennialism, in point and counterpoint format. The format allows for a clear presentation of each view as well as robust debate. Very helpful!

Feinberg, Charles L. *Millennialism: The Two Major Views*. 3rd ed. Chicago: Moody, 1980.

> The author, a dispensational premillennialist, examines and compares the Premillennial and Amillennial systems of eschatology. A major weakness of the book is that it does not consider either historic premillennialism or the postmillennial position.

*Gundry, Robert H. *The Church and the Tribulation: A Biblical Examination of Posttribulationism*. Grand Rapids: Zondervan, 1973.

> This book is a powerful apologetic for the postribulational position. Gundry argues that Christ will return again to the earth after the end of the Tribulation and that the first resurrection will occur at that time. A powerful argument! "A vigorous and technical rejection of pretribulationalism by a NT scholar who is convinced of the Posttribulationism position. While weak in dealing with the material in the Gospels, Gundry places his emphasis on data from the Epistles" (Barber). Premillennial. Postribulational.

*Hoekema, Anthony A. *The Bible and the Future*. Grand Rapids: Eerdmans, 1979.

> This is the best work available on the Amillennial position of eschatology. It is scholarly, comprehensive, thorough, and convincing. Hoekema argues that the coming of God's kingdom is both present and future. He structures

his book into two major sections: "Inaugurated Eschatology" (the "already") and "Future Eschatology" (the "not yet"). Highly recommended! "A scholarly reconstruction of the history of eschatology with a deft application of biblical teaching to future events" (Barber). Amillennial.

Hoyt, Herman A. *The End Times*. Chicago: Moody, 1969.

An older work from a dispensational premillennial perspective.

Kik, J. Marcellus. *An Eschatology of Victory*. Phillipsburg, NJ: Presbyterian and Reformed, 1975.

This book is comprised of expositions of Matthew 24 and Revelation 20 from the postmillennial perspective. There is also a discussion of the history of the Reformed position.

*Ladd, George Eldon. *The Blessed Hope: A Biblical Study of the Second Advent and the Rapture*. Grand Rapids: Eerdmans, 1956.

George Eldon Ladd was one of the foremost evangelical NT scholars of the twentieth century. In this user-friendly book, he examines the premillennial position and concludes that the rapture of the church will be after the tribulation period. This is a classic apologetic for that position easily accessible to both scholar and layperson.

*Middleton, J. Richard. *A New Heaven and a New Earth: Reclaiming Biblical Eschatology*. Grand Rapids: Baker Academic, 2015.

This seminal new work argues that the ultimate blessed hope of the believer is a participation in a new heaven and a new earth, rather than an otherworldly heaven. He calls his position "holistic eschatology" and calls for a biblical understanding of cosmic renewal. It is provocative and paradigm changing.

Pentecost, J. Dwight. *Things to Come: A Study in Biblical Eschatology*. Grand Rapids: Zondervan, 1958.

A defense of dispensational premillennialism by a professor at Dallas Theological Seminary. "An exhaustive, well-outlined, clear, comprehensive presentation of premillennial eschatology" (Barber, 223).

Walvoord, John F. *The Blessed Hope and the Tribulation: A Historical and Biblical Study of Posttribulationism.* Contemporary Evangelical Perspectives. Grand Rapids: Zondervan, 1976.

> This volume examines the four main postribulational positions, critiques their positions and presuppositions, and questions their hermeneutics. Pretribulational. Dispensational.

————. *The Millennial Kingdom.* Grand Rapids: Zondervan, 1959.

> This book is a defense of the dispensational premillennial view by one of its leading proponents. John F. Walvoord was, until his death, president of Dallas Theological Seminary. "An exceptionally fine, Biblical evaluation of the various schools of thought" (Barber, 226). Premillennial. Dispensational.

Wood, Leon J. *The Bible and Future Events: An Introductory Survey of Last-Day Events.* Grand Rapids: Zondervan Academie Books, 1973.

> As the title indicates, this book is an introductory treatment and is not meant to be comprehensive in its scope. It is helpful in that it surveys the major themes in eschatology from a premillennial perspective. "An overview of God's prophetic program. Significant because it deals with eschatology from the viewpoint of a Semitic scholar. Provides an entirely new perspective on many old, timeworn themes" (Barber). Premillennial.

Ethics

*Bloesch, Donald G. *Freedom for Obedience: Evangelical Ethics for Contemporary Times.* San Francisco: Harper & Row, 1987.

> In this excellent book, the author argues for the recovery of the moral dualistic motif in ethics and theology. He differentiates between theological and philosophical types of ethics as opposed to the more standard deontological and teleological. He identifies the theological as evangelical ethics and the philosophical as humanistic ethics.

*Davis, John Jefferson. *Evangelical Ethics: Issues Facing the Church Today.* 3rd ed. Phillipsburg, NJ: Presbyterian and Reformed, 2004.

> Since its initial publication in 1985, this helpful book has served the evangelical world as a good basic textbook in Christian ethics. It included chapters on contraception, reproductive technologies, divorce and remarriage, homosexuality, abortion, infanticide and euthanasia, capital punishment, civil disobedience and revolution, and war and peace. For the most part, those

topics remain important ones for conversation today. However, with medical research and technology advancing at a rapid pace, this book was in great need of an infusion particularly in the area of biotechnology. This third edition does just that in that it includes chapters on genetic engineering and environmental ethics, two areas of concern crying out for evangelical reflection.

*Feinberg, John S., and Paul D. Feinberg. *Ethics for a Brave New World*. Wheaton: Crossway, 1993.

> The authors contend that Aldous Huxley's frightening vision as encapsulated in *Brave New World* has come close to fulfillment. We now live in a world in which technological advances have all but destroyed morality and freedom. They write, "Life is manufactured and controlled from beginning to end by modern technology" (xiii). Topics discussed include moral decision-making and the Christian, abortion, euthanasia, capital punishment, sexual morality, birth control, homosexuality, genetic engineering and reproductive technologies, divorce and remarriage, the Christian and war, and the Christian and the secular state.

Geisler, Norman L. *Ethics: Alternatives and Issues*. Grand Rapids: Zondervan, 1971.

> This book is an introduction and analysis of some of the theories and issues involved in the field of ethics. It is divided into two parts. Part 1 explores ethical alternatives such as antinomianism, generalism, situationalism, absolutism, and hierarchicalism. Part 2 then looks at the flip coin, ethical issues, such as the Christian and self-love, war, social responsibility, sex, birth control and abortion, mercy-killing, suicide, capital punishment, and ecology. "Contains a complete introduction and analysis of the theories and issues involved in ethics. Seeks to make situation ethics *acceptable* to evangelicals by changing the terminology and stressing 'hierarchicalism.' Some of his conclusions are certain to be rejected by evangelicals" (Barber, 234).

Grabill, Stephen J. *Rediscovering the Natural Law in Reformed Theological Ethics*. Emory University Studies in Law and Religion. Edited by John Witte Jr. Grand Rapids: Eerdmans, 2006.

> This book demonstrates that natural revelation, theology, and moral law are important elements of Christian teaching and should not be abandoned. The author traces the history of natural law in Protestant theology and argues for the recovery of the catholicity of Protestant theological ethics.

*Harrison, R. K. *Encyclopedia of Biblical and Christian Ethics*. Nashville: Nelson, 1987.

> This book is a must for Christians who are concerned with ethical issues. It is not only descriptive, but also prescriptive, in that it provides guidelines for

behavior. There are two helpful indexes at the back of the book that give this volume added value as a reference tool. There is a personalities index helping readers locate all articles that mention specific persons or ethical thinkers, such as Thomas Aquinas or Aristotle. There is also a Scripture index that should provide assistance to preachers and teachers. The list of contributors is impressive.

*+Henry, Carl F. H. *Christian Personal Ethics*. Grand Rapids: Baker, 1957.

This volume is a massive and scholarly work on Christian ethics. Although it is now over a half-century old, it is a recognized classic and should be on the shelf of every pastor. "A learned treatise on speculative philosophy, the moral quest, and the application of redemption to the moral issues" (Barber, 234).

*Hughes, Philip Edgcumbe. *Christian Ethics in Secular Society*. Grand Rapids: Baker, 1983.

This study, by a renowned NT scholar, is an attempt to demonstrate that Christian ethics is basically theological in nature and that Christian theology must be expressed by application. The author lays down the theological foundation of ethics in chapters titled "Knowing and Doing," "Conscience, and Law" and "Love." He then argues that there is a basic dichotomy between Christian and secular ethics in chapters titled "The New Morality," "The New Confessional," "The Ethics of Humanism," and "Eugenic Utopianism." He concludes by outlining the ethical implications of Christian theology in chapters titled "Sexual Ethics" and "The Christian and the State." An important apologetic for the theocentric focus of Christian ethics!

*Kaiser, Walter C., Jr. *Toward Old Testament Ethics*. Grand Rapids: Zondervan Academie Books, 1983.

This book is an important study of ethics in the OT. At its publication in 1983, it filled a much-needed gap in that there were few books written on the subject in the past hundred years. It is composed of four main parts and a conclusion. Part 1 is titled "Definition and Method," in which Kaiser attempts to define and describe OT ethics and models of approach, their nature and task, the use of the Bible in establishing ethical norms, and exegetical and theological principles in OT ethics. Part 2 examines case studies from the Decalogue, the Book of the Covenant (Exod 20:22—23:33), the Law of Holiness (Lev 18–20), and the Law of Deuteronomy. Part 3 examines the subject of holiness and how it is applied as a way of life in family and society, marriage and sex, wealth and possessions, and truth to name just a few. Part 4 explores the subject of moral difficulties in the OT. Highly recommended!

*Murray, John. *Principles of Conduct: Aspects of Biblical Ethics*. Grand Rapids: Eerdmans, 1957.

> This book began as the Payton Lectures delivered in 1955 at Fuller Theological Seminary. The material in those lectures was expanded to create this volume. The author deals with such important topics as marriage, labor, capital punishment, truth, and law and grace. In all discussions, he directs the reader back to the Scriptures, particularly the Ten Commandments, as the final arbiter of conduct in Christian ethics. "A serious, scholarly attempt to build a Christian ethic squarely upon the Scriptures" (Barber, 233). Reformed.

Payne, Franklin E. *Biblical/Medical Ethics: The Christian and the Practice of Medicine*. Milford, MI: Mott, 1985.

> This book is a study of medical ethics from a biblical, Christian perspective. When it was published in 1985, it was sorely needed by the evangelical community. However, it is now badly outdated and needs to be revised reflecting current discussions particularly in the area of biotechnology.

Rae, Scott. *Moral Choices: An Introduction to Ethics*. 3rd ed. Grand Rapids: Zondervan, 2009.

> Not reviewed for this edition.

Robinson, N. H. G. *The Groundwork of Christian Ethics*. Grand Rapids: Eerdmans, 1971.

> This interesting treatment of Christian ethics addresses the question of what they really are. The author argues that morality exists independently of Christianity. He contends that Christian ethics cannot be understood until the doctrine of neutral morality is accepted.

Sproul, R. C. *Ethics and the Christian: Right and Wrong in Today's World*. Wheaton: Tyndale, 1983.

> This handy little volume is a brief overview of Christian ethics written primarily for the layperson. Sproul, as always, is engaging and informative.

The Future State

*Braun, Jon E. *Whatever Happened to Hell?* Nashville: Nelson, 1979.

> In an engaging and readable style, the author examines the conditions that have led the current age to ignore the biblical teaching on hell. This book is a popular introduction to an important subject.

*Crockett, William. *Four Views on Hell*. Counterpoints: Bible and Theology. Edited by Stanley N. Gundry. Grand Rapids: Zondervan, 1997.

> This book was the first to present four views on hell. The scholars writing essays are John F. Walvoord: Literal; William V. Crockett: Metaphorical; Zachary J. Hayes: Purgatorial; and Clark H. Pinnock: Conditional. This treatment has been superseded by the second edition edited by Preston Sprinkle. One major difference between this book and its successor is that the editor here is also one of the essayists, whereas Sprinkle is more of an objective evaluator of the four views presented in his book. This is a good introduction to the subject, but the 2016 edition should also be considered to understand the past twenty years of discussions and refinements.

Date, Christopher M., Gregory G. Stump, and Joshua W. Anderson. *Rethinking Hell: Readings in Evangelical Conditionalism*. Eugene, OR: Cascade, 2014.

> This book makes a strong biblical case for annihilationism.

Fudge, Edward W. *The Fire That Consumes: A Biblical and Historical Study of the Doctrine of Final Punishment*. 3rd ed. Eugene, OR: Wipf & Stock, 2011.

> This book is an updated and revised edition of the author's seminal defense of the doctrine of annihilationism.

———. *Hell: A Final Word*. Leafwood, 2012.

> This book is a popular distillation of the author's views first presented in the author's 1981 *The Fire That Consumes*. Fudge argues that annihilationism or conditional immortality has the most biblical support of all the views on the subject of hell.

Gregg, Steve. *All You Want to Know about Hell: Three Christian Views of God's Final Solution to the Problem of Sin*. Nashville: Nelson, 2013.

> This volume is a popular examination of the subject by a single author. The three views that he presents are Traditionalism (eternal torment), Annihilationism (conditional immortality), and Restorationism (Christian universalism).

*Morgan, Christopher W., and Robert A. Peterson, eds. *Hell Under Fire: Modern Scholarship Reinvents Eternal Punishment*. Grand Rapids: Zondervan, 2004.

> This interesting book is a collection of essays by some of the most influential Christian thinkers and biblical scholars of this generation on the subject of hell. There are ten chapters. R. Albert Mohler Jr. writes on "Modern Theology: The Disappearance of Hell." Daniel Block writes on "The Old Testament on Hell." Robert W. Yarbrough writes on "Jesus on Hell," and Douglas J. Moo on

"Paul on Hell." Gregory K. Beale's assignment was "The Revelation on Hell," and Christopher W. Morgan's contribution was twofold: "Biblical Theology: Three Pictures of Hell" and "Annihilationism: Will the Unsaved Be Punished Forever?" Robert A. Peterson's chapter was "Systematic Theology: Three Vantage Points on Hell," and J. I. Packer answers the question, "Universalism: Will Everyone Ultimately Be Saved?" Finally, Sinclair B. Ferguson looks at the topic from a pastoral perspective, "Pastoral Theology: The Preacher and Hell." Anyone surprised by the disappearance of the subject of hell from the church and society of the past fifty or so years should read this book.

Peterson, Robert A. *Hell on Trial: The Case for Eternal Punishment.* Phillipsburg, NJ: Presbyterian & Reformed, 1995.

This book, by a professor of systematic theology at Covenant Theological Seminary in St. Louis, Missouri, was not reviewed for this edition.

*Sprinkle, Preston, ed. *Four Views on Hell.* Counterpoints: Bible and Theology. Edited by Stanley N. Gundry. 2nd ed. Grand Rapids: Zondervan, 2016.

This second edition, featuring all new contributors using the familiar counterpoint format, brings the discussions on this important topic up to date. Contributors and views are Denny Burk, Eternal Conscious Torment; John G. Stackhouse Jr., Terminal Punishment; Robin A. Parry, Universalism; and Jerry L. Walls, Purgatory. The editor, Preston Sprinkle, concludes the book by evaluating each view, reviewing important points of clash between participants. This allows the reader to evaluate the most significant issues and arguments in the current debate.

*Toon, Peter. *Heaven and Hell: A Biblical and Theological Overview.* Nashville: Nelson, 1986.

This helpful volume is a sequel to the author's 1984 *The Ascension of Our Lord.* It is a brief introduction to the subject of one's destination after death. It is brief and intended not as a contribution to scholarly debate, but rather as a basic introductory textbook for college and seminary students. Engaging and readable!

*Walls, Jerry L. *Heaven, Hell, and Purgatory: A Protestant View of the Cosmic Drama.* Grand Rapids: Brazos, 2015.

In this seminal work, the author provides a biblical framework for thinking about heaven, hell, and purgatory. Although Walls is a Protestant, he argues that the doctrine of purgatory is not just a Roman Catholic position, but that it is defensible for Protestants as well. One might not agree with all that he says, but this book will stretch one's thinking.

The Godhead: Christology

*+Andrews, Samuel J. *Life of Our Lord upon the Earth*. New York: Scribner, 1906. Reprint, Minneapolis: James Family, 1978.

> Originally published in 1862, this book is a massive, scholarly study of the life of the Lord Jesus Christ that has stood the test of time and is a true classic. Purchase if found! An absolute jewel!

*Berkouwer, G. C. *The Person of Christ*. Translated by John Vriend. Grand Rapids: Eerdmans, 1954.

> This study is a classic work by the late professor of systematic theology at the Free University of Amsterdam, written "by a theologians' theologian whose writings are all of utmost importance. Examines the historical pronouncements of the ecumenical councils and the Christian confessions, the nature, unity, and sinlessness of Christ, together with a consideration of the other teachings which center in a study of His person" (Barber, 205). Reformed.

*———. *The Work of Christ*. Studies in Dogmatics. Translated by Cornelius Lambregtse. Grand Rapids: Eerdmans, 1965.

> This study followed the author's book on the person of Christ. "An in-depth discussion of the Biblical teaching on the theological development of the doctrine of Christ as seen in His birth, suffering, resurrection, ascension, heavenly session, and second advent. Fully abreast of the latest theological literature" (Barber, 205). Reformed.

*Bird, Michael F., et al. *How God Became Jesus: The Real Origins of Belief in Jesus' Divine Nature—A Response to Bart Ehrman*. Grand Rapids: Zondervan, 2014.

> This book is a response by five biblical scholars to Bart Ehrman's claims in *How Jesus Became God: The Exaltation of a Jewish Preacher from Galilee* that neither Jesus nor his disciples claimed that he was God. These scholars contend that Jesus' identity in the early church was always as God and that this was not simply an invention of the church in later centuries.

*+Edersheim, Alfred. *The Life and Times of Jesus the Messiah*. 2 vols. Reprint, Grand Rapids: Eerdmans, 1943.

> Alfred Edersheim was a Viennese Jewish convert to Christianity, who was educated in the Talmud and Torah at a Hebrew school. He later lectured on the LXX at Oxford University. He is best known for this classic work, which is a massive piece of scholarship. "The classic work to which all modern treatments are indebted" (Barber, 209).

*Foster, Rupert Clinton. *Studies in the Life of Christ*. Reprint, Grand Rapids: Baker, 1971.

> This massive study was originally published in four volumes over a roughly thirty-year period ending in 1968. It covers the entire period of the life of Christ. The book is well written and a particular delight to read. "A scholarly study that rivals Edersheim for thoroughness and informative background" (Barber, 209).

*Gromacki, Robert G. *The Virgin Birth: Doctrine of Deity*. Grand Rapids: Baker, 1974.

> This book is a well-written and readable defense of the classic evangelical position on the virgin birth. Of particular value are the author's two chapters on popular misconceptions about the virgin birth and its physical and biological implications. "A masterful statement dispelling popular misinterpretations of Christ's conception and birth, adequately answering critics of the doctrine, and soundly trouncing the liberal views of J. A. T. Robinson, William Barclay, and others. This important contribution deserves a place alongside the magisterial works of Machen" (Barber).

*+!Hengstenberg, Ernst Wilhelm. *Christology of the Old Testament*. 2 vols. Reprint, McLean, VA: MacDonald, n.d.

> This two-volume reprint is an unabridged edition of the classic study originally published between 1872–78. At 1,396 pages, it is a massive treatment of the subject and comprehensive in scope. Its liberal use of both Greek and Hebrew will quickly leave linguistic novices behind. It is also available in a one-volume abridgement if not again OP. "A first-rate study of Christ as He appears in type and prophecy in the OT. Of great value to preachers" (Barber, 206).

*Hoehner, Harold W. *Chronological Aspects of the Life of Christ*. Contemporary Evangelical Perspectives. Grand Rapids: Zondervan, 1977.

> From a detailed study of biblical and extrabiblical sources, the meaning of Greek words, Roman law, and Jewish customs and prophecy, the author carefully documents his conclusions. Among the key dates in the life of Christ are his birth, the commencement of his ministry, the duration of his ministry, and the day and year of his crucifixion. An extremely important study! "A brilliant, reverent treatise which unravels many perplexing problems relating to the life of Christ" (Barber).

*+Liddon, H. P. *The Divinity of Our Lord and Saviour Jesus Christ*. 18th ed. London: Rivingtons, 1867. Reprint, Minneapolis: Klock & Klock, 1978.

> This monumental study is an unabridged compilation of eight lectures preached at the University of Oxford in 1866. Although 150 years old, these

lectures may still be read with great profit today. Lecture 7 contains a history of the important doctrine of *homoousion*.

*+Machen, John Gresham. *The Virgin Birth of Christ*. Reprint, Grand Rapids: Baker, 1967.

First published in 1930, this volume is a classic defense of the supernatural birth of Jesus Christ. Machen was a brilliant NT scholar and theologian, and this book is one of his seminal works.

*Marshall, I. Howard. *Jesus the Savior: Studies in New Testament Theology*. Downers Grove: InterVarsity, 1990.

This helpful book is largely a compilation of essays that have been published over the years in different journals and in *Festschriften* concerning the person and work of Christ. These essays fall into three sections: "The Aims and Methods of NT Theology," "The Person of Jesus," and "The Works of Jesus." Very helpful are the author's two essays in part 2 on the use of the title for Jesus "Son of Man" as it was used in the Gospels and the early church. Marshall is perhaps the foremost NT evangelical scholar writing today, and his work is always challenging and provocative.

*+Orr, James. *The Virgin Birth of Christ*. New York: Scribner, 1907.

This classic work is comprised of lectures that were delivered in April 1907 in the Chapel of the Fifth Avenue Presbyterian Church, under the auspices of the Bible Teachers' Training School. A brilliant defense of the virgin birth of Christ!

*Stout, Stephen O. *The "Man Christ Jesus."* Eugene, OR: Wipf & Stock, 2011.

This exceptional study examines Paul's description of the "Man Christ Jesus" as found in 1 Tim 2:5 and argues "that this title fulfills the OT expectation of God appearing in human history as a man" (from the back cover). Further, Stout investigates the vexing question of the relationship between Jesus and Paul and affirms the humanity of Jesus in Pauline writing. This book is a revision of the author's PhD dissertation from Southeastern Baptist Theological Seminary.

Walvoord, John F. *Jesus Christ Our Lord*. Chicago: Moody, 1969.

This study is now fairly dated, but still a good introduction to the subject for undergraduates. "Scholarly, evangelical presentation of Christology. A valuable work" (Barber, 206).

*+Warfield, Benjamin Breckinridge. *The Person and Work of Christ*. Edited by Samuel G. Craig. Reprint, Philadelphia: Presbyterian and Reformed, 1970.

> This important book is a true classic by the great nineteenth-century Princeton theologian. Should be in every minister's library. "A work of massive scholarship. Ably combines exegetical skills with polemic ability" (Barber, 206).

Wright, N. T. *The Challenge of Jesus: Rediscovering Who Jesus Was and Is*. Downers Grove: InterVarsity, 1999.

> Whatever one thinks of Wright's conclusions in the area of biblical studies, he is a top-flight NT scholar and his views must be weighed and considered.

The Godhead: God the Father

*+Charnock, Stephen. *The Existence and Attributes of God*. Reprint, Minneapolis: Klock & Klock, 1977.

> Originally published in 1797, this massive 801-page Puritan tome is a true classic of the Christian faith. This reprint edition contains Charnock's complete discourses on both the attributes and existence of God. Omitted from this edition are his discourses on providence, practical atheism, and God as a Spirit, which have often been included in previous editions. As is true of most Puritan works, this book is long and tends to be wordy, but it rewards the diligent. "A classic work" (Barber, 203)!

*Feinberg, John S. *No One Like Him: The Doctrine of God*. Wheaton: Crossway, 2001.

> "This text is one of the standard evangelical discussions on the doctrine of God. Feinberg excels at philosophical theology, as this text makes evident. His synthesis of divine sovereignty and free will is especially helpful and influential. This text is not recommended for beginning students" (**Brandt**).

*+Henry, Carl F. H. *God, Revelation, and Authority*. See General Studies: Protestant

*Nash, Ronald H. *The Concept of God*. Grand Rapids: Zondervan, 1983.

> "Outstanding introduction to the existence and attributes of God. Absolutely worth owning" (**Olsen**). Reformed.

*Oliphint, K. Scott. *God With Us: Divine Condescension and the Attributes of God*. Wheaton: Crossway, 2012.

> This engaging volume is for those seeking to understand the nature of God, how he can be both independent and infinite while also being an interactive

force in the finite plane of creation. Oliphint argues that the Son of God is both the quintessential revelation of God's character as well as the explanation of how God relates to us. "This book is a good discussion of God for today. Oliphint is quotable and engaging. Of particular interest is his assertion that humility ought to be understood as an attribute of God" (**Brandt**).

Pink, Arthur W. *Gleanings in the Godhead*. Chicago: Moody, 1975.

This book focuses on God the Father and God the Son. As always, Pink's insights are warm and edifying. Particularly helpful for laypersons.

The Godhead: Pneumatology

Barbeau, Jeffrey W., and Beth Felker Jones, eds. *Spirit of God: Christian Renewal in the Community of Faith*. Downers Grove: IVP Academic, 2015.

These essays constitute the highlights of the 2014 Wheaton Theology Conference, which was an exploration of the person and work of the Holy Spirit.

Bruner, Frederick Dale. *A Theology of the Holy Spirit: The Pentecostal Experience and the New Testament Witness*. Grand Rapids: Eerdmans, 1970.

This important study is comprised of two sections: "The Holy Spirit in Pentecostal Experience" and "The Holy Spirit in New Testament Witness." "Focuses attention on the Pentecostal experience of Acts and the Pentecostal movement within Pentecostalism. Grounds his work in the theological development of the twentieth century and the dramatic turning to a charismatic experience. . . . A documentary section probes the teachings of Wesley on perfection, Finney on justification, Torrey on the baptism of the Holy Spirit, and Andrew Murray on absolute surrender. Concludes with a brief critique of A. J. Gordon and F. B. Meyer" (Barber, 201).

*Ferguson, Sinclair B. *The Holy Spirit*. Contours of Christian Theology. Downers Grove: InterVarsity, 1997.

This excellent work, by a noted Presbyterian pastor and theologian, is a capable exposition of the Reformed understanding of the person and work of the Holy Spirit. It is well written and readable on several levels, scholar, pastor, or layperson. A very necessary corrective to some contemporary muddled thinking on the doctrine of the Holy Spirit. Reformed.

*Holmes, Christopher R. J. *The Holy Spirit*. New Studies in Dogmatics. Grand Rapids: Zondervan Academic, 2015.

> This work is the first volume in Zondervan's new series New Studies in Dogmatics. This volume argues that the immanent Trinity explains and gives rise to the economic Trinity. The book has four sections: part 1, "Engaging Augustine: The Divinity of the Holy Spirit"; part 2, "Engaging Thomas: The Hypostatic Subsistence of the Holy Spirit"; part 3, "Engaging Barth: The Other-Directed Spirit"; part 4, "Correlates: Regeneration, Church, and Tradition." An important new work!

*+Kuyper, Abraham. *The Work of the Holy Spirit*. Translated by Henri De Vries. London: Funk & Wagnalls, 1900. Reprint, Grand Rapids: Eerdmans, 1975.

> This classic study first appeared in the late nineteenth century as 123 articles in the *Heraut*, a Dutch religious weekly of which Kuyper served as editor. "This extensive, scholarly, and exhaustive study gives the Holy Spirit His rightful place in Christian theology" (Barber, 201). Reformed.

Lindsell, Harold. *The Holy Spirit in the Latter Days*. Nashville: Nelson, 1983.

> In this controversial book, Lindsell, the former editor of *Christianity Today*, "explores the roots of the modern charismatic movement, discusses the work of the Holy Spirit in Old and New Testaments, and encourages readers to seek a holy, Spirit-filled life" (from the dust jacket). The author takes a conciliatory approach toward the charismatic movement and its adherents.

*Lloyd-Jones, Martyn. *Joy Unspeakable: Power and Renewal in the Holy Spirit*. Edited by Christopher Catherwood. Wheaton: Shaw, 1984.

> Published posthumously, this book of sermons, by the gifted preacher and evangelical leader who served as the pastor of Westminster Chapel in London for twenty-five years, sounds a clarion call to the church that it is definitely in need of revival by the renewing power of the Holy Spirit. He challenges Christians to examine the teaching of the Scriptures concerning the baptism of the Holy Spirit. Lloyd-Jones is always worth hearing and heeding.

Ryrie, Charles Caldwell. *The Holy Spirit*. Chicago: Moody, 1965.

> This brief study is a concise summarization of the major ministries of the Holy Spirit. "A brilliantly written, brief, complete study of pneumatology. Ideal for Bible study" (Barber, 202). Dispensational.

*+Smeaton, George. *The Doctrine of the Holy Spirit*. Reprint, Edinburgh: Banner of Truth, 1958.

> This volume is reprinted from the original 1882 edition. It is a classic study of the both the doctrine of the Trinity and the Holy Spirit along with a historical survey of the doctrine of the Holy Spirit from the apostolic age. This book is the final volume of a trilogy along with the author's *Doctrine of the Atonement as Taught by Christ Himself* and *Doctrine of the Atonement as Taught by the Apostles*. "Combining theological accuracy with practical teaching" (Barber, 202). Reformed.

*+!Swete, Henry Barclay. *The Holy Spirit in the New Testament*. London: Macmillan, 1910. Reprint, Grand Rapids: Baker, 1976.

> This book is a brilliant study of the subject of pneumatology in the New Testament. A true classic!

Unger, Merrill F. *The Baptizing Work of the Holy Spirit*. Chicago: Scripture Press, 1953.

> This is a helpful, but at some sixty years of age, dated, study of the baptizing work of the Holy Spirit in the New Testament. The author attempts to clear up some of the misconceptions surrounding this doctrine. "An important, reliable study of a much misunderstood subject" (Barber, 202). Dispensational.

The Godhead: The Doctrine of the Trinity

*+Bickersteth, Edward Henry. *The Trinity*. Reprint, Grand Rapids: Kregel, 1976.

> This important study was originally published as *The Rock of Ages; or, Three Persons but One God* in 1859. It clarifies the true nature of the Trinity and clears up misconceptions. "An important contribution" (Barber, 200).

*Erickson, Millard J. *Making Sense of the Trinity*. Grand Rapids: Baker, 2000.

> This book attempts to establish the biblical foundation of the doctrine of the Trinity. It also tries to demonstrate the logical nature of the doctrine and its importance.

*Fairbairn, Donald. *Life in the Trinity: An Introduction to the Theology with the Help of the Church Fathers*. Downers Grove: InterVarsity, 2009.

> This book is a scholarly, yet deeply devotional and eminently practical, look at the doctrine of the Trinity with reflections from the church fathers. It makes primary use of the writings of four Patristic writers, Ireneus of Lyons, Athanasius of Alexandria, Augustine of Hippo, and Cyril of Alexandria.

*Gunton, Colin E. *Father, Son, and Holy Spirit: Towards a Fully Trinitarian Theology*. Edinburgh: T. & T. Clark, 2003.

> This seminal work develops themes that the author first introduced in his book *The Promise of Trinitarian Theology*, in 1992. It is a thoughtful examination of both ancient and current discussions on Trinitarian theology.

!———. *The Promise of Trinitarian Theology*. 2nd ed. Edinburgh: T. & T. Clark, 2003.

> A brilliant introduction to Trinitarian thought and the implications of the doctrine in everyday life.

*+Hodgson, Leonard. *The Doctrine of the Trinity*. London: Nisbet, 1943.

> "Hodgson, former Regius Professor of Divinity at Oxford University, was a prolific writer of massive historical, philosophical, and theological learning, and a genuine believer. There has been a considerable body of literature generated of late concerning the Trinity, but this might top the list from the recent past" (**Olsen**).

*Letham, Robert. *The Holy Trinity*. Phillipsburg, NJ: Presbyterian and Reformed, 2004.

> This important work examines the doctrine's biblical foundations and then traces the historical development of the doctrine through the twentieth century. The author focuses on four issues in Trinity studies: the incarnation, worship and prayer, creation and missions, and the persons of the Trinity. This is a comprehensive and satisfying examination of the doctrine that ties in the doctrine with the implications that it ought to have in the believer's life.

*Sexton, Jason S. *Two Views on the Doctrine of the Trinity. Counterpoints Bible and Theology*. Edited by Stanley N. Gundry. Grand Rapids: Zondervan, 2014.

> Although the title suggests that only two views on the Trinity are considered in this volume, in reality four models and approaches are argued: (1) Classical Trinity: Evangelical Perspective, (2) Classical Trinity: Catholic Perspective, (3) Relational Trinity: Creedal Perspective, and (4) Relational Trinity: Radical Perspective. After each contributor's article, there are three responses by each of the other three contributors with a final rejoinder and clarification by the writer of that article. For those who have become a bit confused by the proliferation of books about the Trinity, this book will help to clarify some of the issues.

Toon, Peter, and James D. Spiceland, eds. *One God in Trinity*. Westchester, IL: Cornerstone, 1980.

> This book is a collection of eleven essays by scholars from five different countries examining how the doctrine of the Trinity has been and was being discussed at

the time of publication. Contributors range from Roger Nicole ("The Meaning of the Trinity") to Gerald Bray ("The Patristic Dogma") to Brian Hebblethwaite ("Recent British Theology"). There are essays on the views of Karl Barth, Bernard Lonergan, and Jurgen Moltmann by Richard Roberts, Hugo Meynell, and Richard Bauckham, respectively. Of course, the collection is now thirty-five years old and does not reflect recent discussions on the subject.

Ware, Bruce A. *Father, Son, and Holy Spirit: Relationships, Roles, and Relevance*. Wheaton: Crossway, 2005.

This study is a very readable and user friendly guide to the Trinity and the roles and relationships within it. Ideal for laypersons and undergraduates.

Hermeneutics

*Bartholomew, Craig G. *Introducing Biblical Hermeneutics: A Comprehensive Framework for Hearing God in Scripture*. Grand Rapids: Baker Academic, 2015.

This fine hermeneutics textbook integrates together the disciplines of theology, philosophy, history, and exegesis to create a first-rate treatment of the science of hermeneutics. At well over five hundred pages, it is not a quick read, but it is always helpful and informative. The bibliography is exhaustive. The book is comprised of five parts: approaching biblical interpretation, biblical interpretation and biblical theology, the story of biblical interpretation, biblical interpretation and the academic disciplines, and the goal of biblical interpretation. Recommended!

*Bray, Gerald. *Biblical Interpretation: Past and Present*. Downers Grove: InterVarsity, 1996.

This book is a massive study of the history of biblical interpretation beginning with the period between the Testaments through the latter part of the twentieth century. The author traces those factors that have remained constant throughout the history of biblical interpretation: divine revelation, the nature of the biblical canon, the relation of the Bible to the life of the Christian church, and tensions in the interpretative process. An impressive scholarly contribution!

*Fee, Gordon D., and Douglas Stuart. *How to Read the Bible for All Its Worth*. 4th ed. Grand Rapids: Zondervan, 2014.

This book is an indispensable tool for Bible study useful to everyone from the layperson to the scholar. Of particular value in this new edition is the updated list of recommended commentaries. Highly recommended!

*Gignilliat, Mark S. *Old Testament Criticism: From Benedict Spinoza to Brevard Childs.* Grand Rapids: Zondervan, 2012.

> This brief overview provides a concise survey of the representative figures of OT criticism and their theories and shows how they led to modern trends in OT interpretation. This book is engaging and informative and serves as a good introduction to the background and issues of modern OT interpretation.

*Goppelt, Leonard. *Typos: The Typological Interpretation of the Old Testament in the New.* Grand Rapids: Eerdmans, 1982.

> "The importance of this study would be hard to overestimate, as Goppelt shows how the OT images and allusions (such as Temple, Passover, Propitiation, Adam, Elijah, David, etc.) that are used abundantly in the NT provide the theological foundation of NT hermeneutics. Goppelt carefully explains how typology differs from allegory in that it is rooted in the realities of OT history. It is crucial that the Christian interpreter watch for the ways that the NT treats the OT in terms of fulfillment. *Typos* comes highly recommended in helping the parish preacher to establish a hermeneutical link from the OT to the NT" (**Stout**).

*Kaiser, Walter C., Jr., and Moisés Silva. *Introduction to Biblical Hermeneutics: The Search for Meaning.* Rev. ed. Grand Rapids: Zondervan, 2007.

> Walter Kaiser, distinguished professor emeritus of OT and president emeritus of Gordon-Conwell Theological Seminary in South Hamilton, Massachusetts, is one of the most revered evangelical OT scholars of the past generation. Silva, who has taught at Westmont College, Westminster Theological Seminary, and Gordon-Conwell Theological Seminary, is also one of the evangelical world's shining lights whose reputation rivals that of Kaiser. The collaborative effort of these two legends is a brilliant, highly readable, and informative volume on the science of hermeneutics.

*Klein, William W., Craig L. Blomberg, and Robert L. Hubbard, Jr. *Introduction to Biblical Interpretation.* Rev. ed. Nashville: Nelson, 2004.

> This book is a very well-written and comprehensive guide to the science of biblical hermeneutics. The three writers are thoroughly evangelical and highly respected scholars in the field of biblical studies. One of the best works available on the subject!

*Köstenberger, Andreas J., and Richard D. Patterson. *Biblical Interpretation: Exploring the Hermeneutical Triad of History, Literature, and Theology*. Grand Rapids: Kregel Academic, 2011.

"This excellent work, designed as a seminary textbook, advances the ideas of the hermeneutical circle and spiral espoused by Grant Osbourne to the design of a triad, "that history, literature, and theology form the proper grid for biblical interpretation"; thus, it deals with the big picture of hermeneutics more than the specifics, such as one would find in Terry's standard but older work *Biblical Hermeneutics*. Still, *Invitation to Biblical Hermeneutics* is packed with resources and examples, making it a first choice for the preacher in honing his interpretive skills" (**Stout**).

*Longman, Tremper, III. *Literary Approaches to Biblical Interpretation*. Foundations of Contemporary Interpretation. Edited by Moises Silva. Grand Rapids: Academie Books, 1987.

This book is a corrective against the type of biblical scholarship that attempts to reduce the Bible to literature alone. Very helpful!

*McKnight, Scot. *The Blue Parakeet: Rethinking How You Read the Bible*. Grand Rapids: Zondervan, 2008.

Beginning with the premise that the Bible is essentially story and that it is not just a book for theologians and scholars to debate *ad infinitum*, McKnight has written a creative and eminently readable book that makes hermeneutics understandable to the average person. A lot of fun to read!

*McQuilkin, Robertson. *Understanding and Applying the Bible*. Rev. ed. Chicago: Moody, 2009.

This book by the president emeritus of Columbia International University is an excellent resource suitable for a textbook on both the undergraduate and graduate levels. Readable and informative!

*Osborne, Grant R. *The Hermeneutical Spiral: A Comprehensive Introduction to Biblical Interpretation*. Downers Grove: InterVarsity, 1991.

Winner of *Christianity Today* magazine's 1993 Critics Choice Award, this seminal work argues that the work of hermeneutics is a spiral from text to context—a movement between the horizon of the text and the horizon of the reader that spirals nearer and nearer toward the text's intended meaning and significance for today. A paradigm-changing work!

*Stein, Robert H. *A Basic Guide to Interpreting the Bible: Playing by the Rules*. 2nd ed. Grand Rapids: Baker Academic, 2011.

> This book is one of those rare volumes that can serve both as a textbook for graduate and undergraduate students. It is accessible enough for lay audiences, too. Takes a difficult subject and simplifies it!

!*+Terry, Milton S. *Biblical Hermeneutics: A Treatise on the Interpretation of the Old and New Testaments*. Reprint, Grand Rapids: Zondervan, 1974.

> Originally published in 1883, this massive work served as the standard scholarly textbook on the subject well into the twentieth century. "An exhaustive work which, despite its age, contains valuable material for those who will take the time to read it" (Barber, 59).

*Thomas, Robert L. *Evangelical Hermeneutics: The New Versus the Old*. Grand Rapids: Kregel Academic and Professional, 2002.

> The goal of this book is fourfold: "to discuss the recent changes in evangelical hermeneutics, to show new meanings being attached to grammatical-historical interpretation, to compare traditional grammatical-historical interpretation with new evangelical hermeneutics, to identify the dominant principles of new evangelical hermeneutics" (from the back cover). The author argues convincingly for a return to the properly applied grammatical-historical principles of interpretation. He documents the dangers of the new methodologies and the negative effects on the Christian world.

Virkler, Henry A. *Hermeneutics: Principles and Processes of Biblical Interpretation*. Grand Rapids: Baker, 1981.

> This volume is interesting, readable, and suitable as an undergraduate textbook. Virkler advocates a five-step hermeneutical method suitable for all genres of biblical literature: historical-cultural analysis, lexical-syntactical analysis, theological analysis, genre identification and analysis, and application. Very user friendly!

!*Yarchin, William. *History of Biblical Interpretation: A Reader*. Peabody: Hendrickson, 2004.

> This valuable volume is a great help for scholars, pastors, and advanced students who wish to go beyond reading about the history of biblical interpretation. This work includes primary source material including writings from the Dead Sea Scrolls, Philo, Justin Martyr, Augustine, the early Syrian Church, the Palestinian Talmud, John Calvin, as well as more modern interpreters, thus allowing the reader to experience directly the thought processes of these earlier interpreters.

Zuck, Roy B. *Basic Bible Interpretation: A Practical Guide to Discovering Biblical Truth.* Wheaton: Victor, 1991.

> This volume is one of the many hermeneutics textbooks that have been published in recent decades. Zuck, the vice president of academic affairs and professor of Bible exposition at Dallas Theological Seminary, has written a book that is informative, easy to read, and very user friendly. His chapters on bridging the cultural gap, the literary gap, and the grammatical gap are particularly helpful. He argues for a threefold pattern of biblical hermeneutics that includes observation, interpretation, and application.

Historical Theology

*Allison, Gregg R. *Historical Theology: An Introduction to Christian Doctrine.* Grand Rapids: Zondervan, 2011.

> "Allison's book parallels Grudem's *Systematic Theology* (1994). Allison treats the same basic doctrines in order. Each chapter reflects a similar chapter from Grudem's book. Each chapter begins with a biblical summary of the doctrine. Then, it summarizes the doctrine in the early church, middle ages, reformation, and modern age, paying special attention to primary sources. This method and purpose makes Allison's book especially accessible and clear. It is an excellent introduction to historical theology for an undergraduate or master level student. It is considered to be the best topical introduction to historical theology among evangelicals" (**Brandt**).

*Berkhof, L. *The History of Christian Doctrines.* Carlisle, PA: Banner of Truth, 1937.

> This helpful volume is a supplement to the author's excellent *Systematic Theology.*

*Bromiley, Geoffrey W. *Historical Theology: An Introduction.* Grand Rapids: Eerdmans, 1978.

> This volume is an excellent introduction to the historical development of the major Christian doctrines. The book is divided into three parts: patristic theology, medieval and reformation theology, and modern theology. This book packs a lot of information into just over four hundred pages. "An outstanding introduction to the historical development of Christian theology. Objective and reliable" (Barber).

*Brown, Colin. *Philosophy and the Christian Faith*. Downers Grove: IVP Academic, 1969.

> "Brown surveys the thought of over 400 philosophers during the last thousand years, from the Middle Ages to the present day until the book's publication in 1969. The book shows how various thinkers and ideas have affected Christian belief and brings together the lessons Christians can learn from philosophy. Recommended" (**Olsen**)! "The material is succinct and admirably serves the purpose for which the book was written" (Barber).

*+Cunningham, William. *Historical Theology: A Review of the Principal Doctrinal Discussions in the Christian Church Since the Apostolic Age*. 2 vols. Reprint, Carlisle, PA: Banner of Truth, 1960.

> First published in 1860, this classic traces the main doctrinal controversies in the Christian church since the apostolic age.

*Gonzalez, Justo L. *A History of Christian Thought*. Rev. ed. 3 vols. Nashville: Abingdon, 1987.

> "Well documented and clearly written work by an internationally respected scholar of the evangelical wing of the mainline Methodist tradition. Recommended" (**Olsen**).

*Hanson, R. P. C. *Tradition in the Early Church*. London: SCM Press, 1962.

> "A discussion of the relationship between the various sorts of theological and ecclesiastical traditions and canonical Scripture. As an Anglican in the evangelical tradition, Hanson has written in a sound, learned, yet accessible fashion a work that is adequately clear enough to beckon his readers to higher ground, where ecclesiastical bashing might desist" (**Olsen**).

*+?Harnack, Karl Gustav Adolf von. *History of Dogma*. Translated by Neil Buchanan. 5 vols. Philadelphia: Fortress, 1961.

> "In spite of its obvious liberalism, this work is of immense value. Contains perceptive thoughts on the movements within Christendom, and treats the events and circumstances in a generally objective manner" (Barber, 192).

*McGrath, Allister E. *Historical Theology*. See Systematic Theology.

*+Orr, James. *Progress of Dogma*. Evangelical Masterworks. London: Hodder and Stoughton, 1901; Old Tappan, NJ: Revell, n.d.

> The contents of this marvelous volume originated as the Elliot Lectures at Western Theological Seminary in 1897. James Orr discusses the relationship between the development of doctrine and the spread of Christianity and how

doctrinal ideas have risen to the fore in reaction to controversies of different periods of church history.

*+Prestige, G. L. *God in Patristic Thought*. London: SPCK, 1952.

"Classic study of apostolic Christianity as it matured. Not to be overlooked" (**Olsen**)! "A profound mind-stretching treatment" (Barber, 350).

*+Seeberg, Reinhold. *Text-Book of the History of Doctrines*. Translated by Charles E. Hay. 2 vols. Grand Rapids: Baker, 1961.

This seminal work was originally published in German in 1895–98 and has stood the test of time. Seeberg was a professor of church history and systematic theology at the universities at Dorpat, Erlangen, and Berlin. This work covers up through the time of the Reformation. "A monumental work which combines theological acumen with a readable style, and remains an indispensable aid in the study of historical theology" (Barber, 192).

*+Shedd, William G. T. *A History of Christian Doctrine*. 2 vols. 9th ed. New York: Scribner, 1889. Reprint, Minneapolis: Klock & Klock, 1978.

Like Orr's later work, Shedd's fine treatment concentrates on the controversies in church history that shape Christian doctrine. There is an emphasis on the philosophical presuppositions underlying the controversies. It includes a section on different confessions of faith. "To those who wish to learn the lessons of history and who desire to follow the teachings of recognized authority in the field, I heartily commend this fine work" (Barber).

*+Turner, H. E. W. *The Pattern of Christian Truth*. London: Mowbray, 1954.

This book contains the Brampton Lectures of 1954 given by Turner.

Providence

*Berkouwer, G. C. *The Providence of God*. Studies in Dogmatics. Grand Rapids: Eerdmans, 1952.

This volume is a brilliant treatment of the subject. Berkouwer begins with a discussion of the issues surrounding the doctrine up until the middle of the twentieth century. He then discusses his topic in relation to knowledge, sustenance, government, concurrence, history, and miracles. He concludes with a discussion of the problem of theodicy.

*+Flavel, John. *The Mystery of Providence*. Reprint, London: Banner of Truth, 1963.

> First published in 1678, this classic Puritan work is the standard treatment of the subject. Like most Puritan writings, reading this book can be tedious, but mining its riches is worth the effort. A real jewel!

Revelation and Inspiration

*Blomberg, Craig L. *Can We Still Believe the Bible? An Evangelical Engagement with Contemporary Questions*. Grand Rapids: Brazos, 2014.

> This book is a robust defense of the authority of Scripture. Blomberg competently answers the attacks of critics such as Bart Ehrman. He deals with such issues as copies of the text, criteria for selection into the canon, the reliability of Bible translations, inerrancy, the historicity of biblical narratives, and miracles. Readable and compelling!

Custer, Stewart. *Does Inspiration Demand Inerrancy? A Study of the Biblical Doctrine of Inspiration in the Light of Inerrancy*. Nutley, NJ: Craig, 1968.

> This book is a brief study of the doctrine of inspiration in light of the claims of biblical inerrancy. Particularly helpful for laypersons.

?Dulles, Avery. *Revelation Theology: A History*. New York: Herder and Herder, 1969.

> "This book, while not evangelical, is an excellent introduction to the models of revelation throughout history. He effortlessly traces the history of revelation since Greek philosophy. While his discussions are dated, his keen insights keep this book useful" (**Brandt**).

*Harris, R. Laird. *Inspiration and Canonicity of the Bible: An Historical and Exegetical Study*. Contemporary Evangelical Perspectives. Grand Rapids: Zondervan, 1969.

> Although written decades prior to the current surge of interest in canonicity, this outstanding treatment is a must for anyone seeking an overview of the subject. "A masterly approach to the subject of bibliology" (Barber, 56).

*+Henry, Carl F. H. See section on General Studies: Protestant

*Nicole, Roger R., and J. Ramsey Michaels, eds. *Inerrancy and Common Sense*. Grand Rapids: Baker, 1980.

> This book and its contributors are committed to the inerrancy of Scripture as both a biblical doctrine and as the historic view of the Christian church. In addition to the editors, each of whom contributes an article, contributors

include John Jefferson Davis, Gordon Fee, Richard Lovelace, James I. Packer, R. C. Sproul, and Douglas Stuart. In this book, the issues are clarified, the battle lines drawn, and the doctrine robustly defended.

*+Warfield, Benjamin Breckinridge. *The Inspiration and Authority of the Bible*. Edited by Samuel G. Craig. Phillipsburg, NJ: Presbyterian and Reformed, 1948.

This important work was originally published in 1927 under the title *Revelation and Inspiration*. This volume is an edited and expanded version of the original work.

Sacraments

*Armstrong, John H., ed. *Understanding Four Views on Baptism*. Counterpoints: Church Life. Edited by Paul E. Engle. Grand Rapids: Zondervan, 2007.

This helpful volume presents the four major views on Baptism in counterpoint fashion. The four contributors are Thomas J. Nettles presenting the Baptist view, "Baptism as a Symbol of Christ's Saving Work"; Richard L. Pratt Jr. the Reformed view, "Baptism as a Sacrament of the Covenant"; Robert Kolb the Lutheran view, "God's Baptismal Act as Regenerative"; and John D. Castelein the Christian Churches / Churches of Christ view, "Believers' Baptism as the Biblical Occasion of Salvation." John Armstrong provides helpful introductory and concluding articles.

*―――――, ed. *Understanding Four Views on the Lord's Supper*. Counterpoints: Church Life. Edited by Paul E. Engle. Grand Rapids: Zondervan, 2007.

This helpful volume presents the four predominant views of the Lord's Supper in counterpoint fashion. The four contributors are Russell D. Moore presenting the "Baptist View: God's Presence as Memorial"; John Hesselink the "Reformed View: The Real Presence of Christ"; David P. Scaer the "Lutheran View: Finding the Right Word"; and Thomas A. Baima the "Roman Catholic View: Christ's True, Real, and Substantial Presence." Each essay is followed by a response by each of the three other essayists. The editor, John Armstrong introduces the discussions and then gives a concluding word. Excellent treatment and most helpful!

*Berkouwer, G. C. *The Sacraments*. Studies in Dogmatics. Translated by Hugo Bekker. Grand Rapids: Eerdmans, 1969.

A brilliant overview of the Sacraments, Baptism and the Lord's Supper, from a Reformed perspective. The author also offers a critique of the RCC and Lutheran views.

!*Beasley-Murray, G. R. *Baptism in the New Testament*. Grand Rapids: Eerdmans, 1962.

> This comprehensive and scholarly treatment of the subject arose out of the Dr. W. T. Whitley Lectureship during the academic year 1959–60. These lectures were delivered in November 1959 in Regent's Park College at Oxford University and in February 1960 at the Bangor Baptist College at the University College, Bangor, North Wales. There is much scholarly interaction, which makes this a most helpful volume for scholars, students, and pastors. "A learned treatment of the antecedents of Christian baptism" (Barber, 294).

*Bromiley, Geoffrey W. *Children of Promise: The Case for Baptizing Infants*. Grand Rapids: Eerdmans, 1979.

> This helpful volume presents the biblical understanding for infant baptism. A strong apologetic for the practice of infant baptism!

*+Chaney, James M. *William the Baptist*. Reprint, Grand Rapids: Baker, 1982.

> First published in 1877 as an official Southern Presbyterian publication, this helpful volume makes a compelling case in dialogue form for the practice of infant baptism. Excellent for laypersons! Reformed.

!*+Conant, Thomas Jefferson. *The Meaning and Use of BAPTIZEIN*. New York: American Bible Union, 1864. Reprint, Grand Rapids: Kregel, 1977.

> This book was originally published in 1864 under the title *The Meaning and Use of Baptizein*. It is a scholarly investigation of the word *baptizein* in classical and Koine Greek literature including both secular and sacred sources. The book includes its use in the OT Greek versions, as used by the church fathers, and an application of its findings to the NT. It makes a case for immersion as the proper mode of baptism.

Jewett, Paul K. *Infant Baptism and the Covenant of Grace*. Grand Rapids: Eerdmans, 1978.

> This volume attempts to demonstrate the logical inconsistency of equating circumcision in the OT with baptism in the NT. Jewett rejects the traditional Reformed argument for baptizing infants.

*+Murray, John. *Christian Baptism*. Phillipsburg, NJ: Presbyterian and Reformed, 1980.

> In this brief volume (90 pages), Murray presents a brilliant scholarly apologetic for infant baptism and a refutation of immersion as the mode of baptism. Reformed.

*Sartelle, John P. *What Christian Parents Should Know about Infant Baptism*. Phillipsburg, NJ: Presbyterian and Reformed, 1985.

> This brief pamphlet is an excellent handout for Reformed pastors to give their congregants. It informs parents in a readable, easy-to-understand format why they should have their infants baptized. Reformed.

*Schreiner, Thomas R., and Shawn D. Wright, eds. *Believer's Baptism: Sign of the New Covenant in Christ*. NAC Studies in Bible and Theology. Edited by E. Ray Clendenen. Nashville: B & H Academic, 2007.

> The author, a Southern Baptist professor of NT at Southern Baptist Theological Seminary in Louisville, makes a good case for believer's baptism. Schreiner lays a solid biblical and theological foundation for this doctrine. Baptist.

*Smith, Gordon T., ed. *The Lord's Supper: Five Views*. Downers Grove: IVP Academic, 2008.

> This volume has much in common with Armstrong's Counterpoints: Church Life book on the same subject. However, this book adds one more view, "The Pentecostal View." Unfortunately, this is much briefer at only 148 pages, and its essays and responses are not as weighty and substantial as the Armstrong offering. Purchase this book only for the Pentecostal addition.

*Strawbridge, Gregg, ed. *The Case for Covenantal Infant Baptism*. Phillipsburg, NJ: Presbyterian & Reformed, 2003.

> In this volume, sixteen contributors make a compelling case for infant baptism.

*Wright, David F., ed. *Baptism: Three Views*. Downers Grove: IVP Academic, 2009.

> This volume and the Smith book on the Lord's Supper are InterVarsity's attempt to copy Zondervan's successful Counterpoints series. This book reflects a stronger effort than the Smith one. It offers discussion of three views and its contributors are first rate. Bruce A. Ware presents "Believer's Baptism View," Sinclair B. Ferguson the "Infant Baptism View," and Anthony N. S. Lane the "Dual-Practice Baptism View."

Soteriology

Baxter, J. Sidlow. *Christian Holiness: Restudied and Restated*. Grand Rapids: Zondervan, 1977.

> This volume is a compilation of the author's three earlier books, *A New Call to Holiness*, *His Deeper Work in Us*, and *Our High Calling*, all published in 1967. It is a careful study of the doctrine of sanctification for the nonspecialist. In an engaging and warm style, the author traces and refutes different theories of holiness, and then goes on to offer his own view of sanctification.

*Berkouwer, G. C. *Faith and Justification*. Studies in Dogmatics. Translated by Lewis B. Smedes. Grand Rapids: Eerdmans, 1954.

> This excellent treatment of faith and justification consists of seven sections: (1) "Relevance," (2) "The Way of Salvation," (3) "Confessional Reconnaissance," (4) "The Reformation and the Holy Scriptures," (5) "Some Objections Considered," (6) "Justification from Eternity," and (7) "The Value of Faith." "A much-needed discussion of justification and the historical development of the doctrine" (Barber, 220). Reformed.

*———. *Faith and Perseverance*. Studies in Dogmatics. Translated by Robert D. Knudsen. Grand Rapids: Eerdmans, 1958.

> This book is the third study related to justification following Berkouwer's works on justification and then sanctification. "Provides a penetrating study of the Biblical teaching on perseverance from the perspective of the historical Reformed tradition. Does not confine itself to statements about the doctrine drawn from the early era of the Christian church but ably evaluates the teachings of Ritschl, Schleiermacher, Schlink, and Barth. Gives helpful assurance to believers in the midst of a world caught up in the tides of change and transition" (Barber, 221).

*———. *Faith and Sanctification*. Studies in Dogmatics. Translated by John Vriend. Grand Rapids: Eerdmans, 1952.

> This study is an excellent treatment of the doctrine of sanctification and its relationship to theology and Christian living. Of particular interest is the final chapter, "Sanctification and Law." Reformed.

*Demarest, Bruce. *The Cross and Salvation: The Doctrine of Salvation*. Foundations of Evangelical Theology. Edited by John S. Feinberg. Wheaton: Crossway, 1997.

> This book is one of the best and most comprehensive introductions to the doctrine of salvation. Each section contains a helpful historical survey of the

interpretation of the doctrine being discussed. This was the first volume in the Foundations of Evangelical Theology series.

*Dieter, Melvin, et al. *Five Views on Sanctification.* Counterpoints: Bible and Theology. Rev. ed. Grand Rapids: Zondervan, 1996.

This helpful volume presents in the popular Counterpoints format five views on this important doctrine. The five contributors and their respective views are: Melvin E. Dieter, "The Wesleyan View"; Anthony A. Hoekema, "The Reformed View"; Stanley M. Horton, "The Pentecostal View"; J. Robertson McQuilkin, "The Keswick View"; and John F. Walvoord, "The Augustinian-Dispensational View."

!*Morris, Leon. *The Apostolic Preaching of the Cross.* 3rd ed. Grand Rapids: Eerdmans, 1965.

This seminal work is a technical examination of important NT words and what the apostles meant when they wrote them. Not to be missed! "Brilliant word studies on redemption, covenant, propitiation, reconciliation, and justi-fication. Deserves a place in every preacher's library" (Barber, 131).

*+Smeaton, George. *The Doctrine of the Atonement as Taught by Christ Himself.* 2nd ed. Edinburgh: T. & T. Clark, 1871. Reprint, Winona Lake, IN: Alpha, 1979.

This volume is the first in a trilogy. It is a classic and scholarly examination of the doctrine of the atonement as it is presented in the Gospels. Not to be missed! "One of the greatest works on the subject" (Barber, 207). Reformed.

*+————. *The Apostles' Doctrine of the Atonement.* Edinburgh: T. & T. Clark, 1870. Reprint, Winona Lake, IN: Alpha, 1979.

The second volume in the trilogy that was completed with the author's *Doctrine of the Holy Spirit*, this book was formerly published as *The Doctrine of the Atonement as Taught by the Apostle* or *The Sayings of the Apostle Exegetically Expounded.* It is a most thorough exposition of this doctrine from the epistles.

*Sproul, R. C. *Pleasing God.* Wheaton: Tyndale, 1988.

This study is a penetrating look at the doctrine of sanctification written for the layperson. As always, Sproul's prose is engaging and straightforward. Reformed.

*————. *Willing to Believe: The Controversy over Free Will.* Grand Rapids: Baker, 1997.

This book is a popular examination of the Protestant doctrines of man's total depravity and God's effectual grace from a biblical perspective. Sproul traces the controversy over the doctrine of free will from the Augustine-Pelagius debate to the end of the twentieth century. The author is always engaging and easy to read.

*Stanley, Alan P. *The Role of Works at the Final Judgment.* Counterpoints: Bible and Theology. Edited by Stanley N. Gundry. Grand Rapids: Zondervan, 2013.

This informative book attempts to wade through the different views and disinformation regarding the role of works at the final judgment. The four contributors and their perspectives are as follows. Robert N. Wilkin writes, "Christians will be judged according to their works at the *rewards* judgment, but *not* at the *final* judgment." Thomas R. Schreiner's article is titled "Justification Apart From and By Works: At the final judgment works will *confirm* justification." James D. G. Dunn examines the question, "If Paul could believe both in justification by faith and judgment according to works, why should that be a problem for us?" Michael P. Barber provides a Roman Catholic view, "A Catholic Perspective: Our works are meritorious at the final judgment because of our union with Christ by grace." The editor, Alan P. Stanley, attempts to put the discussions into perspective with his concluding essay, "The Puzzle of Salvation by Grace and Judgment by Works."

*+Warfield, Benjamin Breckinridge. *Perfectionism.* Edited by Samuel G. Craig. Phillipsburg, NJ: Presbyterian and Reformed, 1974.

This volume contains the essence of the more than one thousand–page study by Warfield. These articles were written early in the twentieth century, but have lost little of their power and relevance. This book is a brilliant rebuttal against the doctrine of perfectionism. Reformed.

*+Westcott, Frederick Brooke. *The Biblical Doctrine of Justification.* London: Macmillan, 1913. Reprint, Minneapolis: Klock & Klock, 1983.

This book is an important classic study on the doctrine of justification. "The best of evangelical traditions. His treatment of relevant passages underscoring the true nature of justification is objective, his discussion of the finer points of grammar and syntax is done with rare ability, and he expounds the New Testament teaching with consummate skill. The result is a work that handsomely repays serious investigation" (Barber).

Theism

!Helm, Paul. *The Eternal God: A Study of God Without Time*. Oxford: Clarendon, 1988.

> "Rather technical work in Philosophical Theology by an excellent conservative scholar" (**Olsen**).

———. *The Providence of God*. Downers Grove: InterVarsity, 1993.

> "Very fine study by an outstanding evangelical scholar" (**Olsen**).

*Hick, John. *Arguments for the Existence of God*. New York: Herder and Herder, 1971.

> "In this book, Hick concerns himself with evaluating the various iterations of the historical philosophical arguments used in supporting the belief in the existence of God. Hick began his career in teaching as an evangelical and over time moved further and further to the left. Both this work and *The Existence of God* were written relatively early in his academic career" (**Olsen**).

———. *The Existence of God*. London: Macmillan, 1964.

> "This book contains basic philosophical readings selected, edited, and is furnished with an introductory article by Hick. He includes both affirmative and negative points of view, both classical and modern, dealing with the existence of God" (**Olsen**).

!*Kenny, Anthony. *The God of the Philosophers*. Oxford: Clarendon, 1979.

> "Oxford professor Kenny is a true master of the history of philosophy. His prowess jumps to life as he examines some of the divine attributes, such as omniscience, foreknowledge, omnipotence, and eternality. Semi-technical and rewarding" (**Olsen**).

*+Mascall, E. L. *He Who Is: A Study in Traditional Theism*. London: Longmans, Green, 1943.

> "A true classic! Mascall was a leading theologian and priest of the Church of England. He was professor of historical theology at King's College London (University of London). Learned, devout, orthodox" (**Olsen**).

*Owen, H. P. *The Christian Knowledge of God*. London: Athlone, 1969.

*———. *Concepts of Deity*. London: Macmillan, 1971.

———. Christian Theism: A Study in Its Basic Principles. Edinburgh: T. & T. Clark, 1984.

> "These three volumes are from the pen of a true prince of theologians. They are densely packed with a lifetime of study and mature reflection. These are extremely worthwhile studies" (**Olsen**).

*Piper, John, Justin Taylor, and Paul Kjoss Helseth, eds. *Beyond the Bounds: Open Theism and the Undermining of Biblical Christianity.* Wheaton: Crossway, 2003.

> This timely book is a compilation of articles on the doctrine of open theism. The interdisciplinary and interdenominational team of contributors includes Russell Fuller, Chad Owen Brand, Mark R. Talbot, William C. Davis, A. B. Caneday, Michael S. Horton, Stephen J. Wellum, Paul Kjoss Helseth, Bruce A. Ware, Wayne Grudem, John Piper, and Justin Taylor. The book has five parts: "Historical Influences"; "Philosophical Presuppositions and Cultural Context"; "Anthropomorphisms, Revelation, and Interpretation"; What Is at Stake in the Openness Debate?"; and "Drawing Boundaries and Conclusions." Not to be missed!

*Swinburne, Richard. *The Coherence of Theism.* Rev. ed. Oxford: Clarendon, 1993.

*———. *Is There a God?* Oxford: Oxford University Press, 1996.

*———. *The Existence of God.* 2nd ed. Oxford: Clarendon, 2004.

*———. *Providence and the Problem of Evil.* Oxford: Clarendon, 1998.

*———. *The Christian God.* Oxford: Clarendon, 1994.

> "Evangelical. Longtime Oxford professor of the Philosophy of Christian Religion. Each of these five books is important and not to be neglected" (**Olsen**).

Ware, Bruce A. *God's Greater Glory: The Exalted God of Scripture and the Christian Faith.* Wheaton: Crossway, 2004.

> In an engaging and readable manner, Ware attempts to answer how human freedom fits into the doctrine of Divine sovereignty.

———. *God's Lesser Glory: The Diminished God of Open Theism.* Wheaton: Crossway, 2000.

> This book is a brief and readable examination and critique of the doctrine of open theism. Ware explores the implications of this doctrine and how it undermines trust in God.

*Wright, R. K. McGregor. *No Place for Sovereignty: What's Wrong with Freewill Theism.* Downers Grove: InterVarsity, 1996.

> This controversial work is a brilliant defense against freewill theism (open theism). Not to be missed! Reformed.

Theodicy and the Problem of Evil and Suffering

*Berkouwer, G. C. *The Providence of God.* See section on Providence.

*+Hick, John. *Evil and the God of Love.* 2nd ed. London: Macmillan, 1985.

> "This is the book that made John Hick famous. In it, he develops what he coined as the *Irenean Theodicy* that contrasted the Augustinian/Thomist tradition of Theodicy, focusing on the idea of *soul making.* The book was written at Cambridge during a one year sabbatical from Princeton. It is a classic in the study of theodicy and scores of books and dissertations have been written in response to it. Hick does a formidable job of presenting the history of the theodicy discussion among philosophers and theologians, which has been dubbed the most difficult theological and philosophical issue to confront all of humanity. Every pastor *must* think deliberately and deeply about theodicy, in order to address the horrors of life brought to the church in hopes of answers amidst their pain. Tragically, most pastors never do—and it shows" (**Olsen**)!

Chapter 5

Practical Theology

CHRISTIAN LIFE AND SPIRITUAL DIRECTION/FORMATION

*+Augustine, Aurelius. *Confessions*. Translated by Henry Chadwick. Oxford: Oxford University Press, 2009.

> Written in Latin between AD 397 and 400, this autobiographical spiritual classic consists of thirteen books which outline St. Augustine's spiritual pilgrimage from childhood, through his profligate youth, to his conversion. It is widely regarded to be the first Western autobiography written. Hugely influential!

*Benner, David G. *Sacred Companions: The Gift of Spiritual Friendship and Direction*. Downers Grove: InterVarsity, 2002.

> "Spiritual direction is an ancient practice in the church, dating all the way back to the Apostles. But today it has been eclipsed by counseling and discipling. However, spiritual direction is the heart of what pastors do. Benner defines spiritual direction as distinct from teaching, discipling, or counseling, and gives practical advice as to how it ought to be done. A valuable book for any pastor or spiritual director" (**Fleming**).

*+Bernard of Clairvaux. *The Love of God and Spiritual Friendship*. Abridged and edited by James M. Houston. Portland: Multnomah, 1983.

> Bernard (1090–1153) was the towering figure in Christendom in the twelfth century and perhaps even the entire Middle Ages. His basic teaching was that the knowledge of God comes only through devotion to God, in poverty, in simplicity, and in solitude. This volume outlines four major topics: the dignity of the soul before God, the nature and greatness of God's love, devotion to Christ, and spiritual friendship. One cannot overstate the importance of this book in church history.

*+Bunyan, John. *The Pilgrim's Progress*. Reprint, Mount Vernon, NY: Peter Pauper, n.d.

First published in 1678, this classic of the Christian life describes in allegorical fashion the experiences of a believer from conversion to glorification. It is probably safe to say that except for the Bible, this is the most beloved Christian book available in the English language. Spurgeon claimed in his autobiography that he had read this book at least one hundred times. Quite an endorsement!

*+Chambers, Oswald. *Christian Disciplines*. Reprint, Grand Rapids: Chosen, 1985.

This Christian classic concentrates on six major disciplines (or areas of concern) for the growing Christian: divine guidance, suffering, peril, prayer, loneliness, and patience. Chambers is always helpful in his observations and often profound.

*+————. *My Utmost for His Highest*. Edited by James Reimann. Grand Rapids: Discovery House, 1992.

Originally published posthumously in 1935, this book was compiled by the author's wife from his preaching to students and soldiers. It has since become perhaps the best-selling devotional book of all time. It includes brief daily devotional readings for every day of the year. Heartwarming and insightful! This edition is an updated version into modern English. I have read some version of this book cover-to-cover every year for about the past fifteen years, always with great profit. Not to be missed!

*Demarest, Bruce A. *Four Views on Christian Spirituality*. Counterpoints: Bible and Theology. Edited by Stanley N. Gundry. Grand Rapids: Zondervan, 2012.

This volume wades through the confusion of Christian spirituality in counterpoint format. Bradley Nassif wrote the essay on Eastern Orthodoxy, Scott Hahn the one on Roman Catholicism, Joseph Driskill the one on Progressive Mainline Protestantism, and Evan Howard the one on Evangelicalism.

*Ford, Paul F., ed. *Yours, Jack: Spiritual Direction from C. S. Lewis*. New York: HarperOne, 2008.

C. S. Lewis was one of the towering intellectual figures of the twentieth century and perhaps the most influential Christian writer and apologist of his day. This book is an edited collection of his personal correspondence to friends and acquaintances spanning the years 1916 until his death in 1963. His original letters were always handwritten and signed, "Yours, Jack." These letters give the reader a compelling look at the writer's view of the Christian life and deserve to be read and reread.

*Foster, Richard J. *Celebration of Discipline: The Path to Spiritual Growth*. San Francisco: Harper & Row, 1978.

> In this modern classic of the Christian life, Foster demonstrates how the practice of the three disciplines, inward, outward, and corporate, can lead the believer to a deeper inner life. He argues compellingly that there must be a renewal of the classic spiritual disciplines: meditation, prayer, fasting, study, simplicity, solitude, submission, service, confession, worship, guidance, and celebration. "This book is one of the most influential books in the Spiritual Formation movement. It is a very human, non-legalistic approach to the development of spirituality through the development of godly habits. Foster's book has been much debated, discussed, and criticized over the years, but it has held up well, and retained its popularity today" (**Fleming**).

+Fowler, James. *Stages of Faith*. New York: HarperCollins, 1981.

> "This book is pretty much unknown within evangelical Christian circles, but is probably the most influential and insightful book on the subject of faith written in the last century. Fowler was a professor of religion at Emory University in Atlanta, and not an evangelical Christian. His writings about faith are not simply about the Christian faith, but about faith as a condition of human existence. It is a copiously researched book dealing with the development of faith in human condition from infancy to old age. He draws upon developmental psychologists such as Erickson and Piaget, as well as on his own research to develop a six stage model for the development of faith in human life. The six stages are undifferentiated faith of infancy, intuitive faith of childhood, mythic-literal faith of older childhood, synthetic-conditional faith, individuative-literal faith, conjunctive faith, and universalized faith. If all this sounds very academic, it is. Fowler's book can be hard reading, leaning heavily on developmental and psychological theory. The evangelical reader will likely be disappointed that Fowler ignores biblical considerations in developing his ideas. Nevertheless, Fowler's work is of great value for those who have the patience to work through it. What he gives us is a description of the way humans change in their relationship to faith—especially our faith in God—throughout our life. What makes it even more valuable than most books in the same category is his inclusion of the faith development in later life. Evangelical Christian readers can easily see their own faith development, and pastors will recognize these stages in the people they serve. It can be of great help in developing programs of spiritual formation in the local church. If the reader is able to recognize that this is not from a necessarily biblical perspective, and is willing to overlook this, then Fowler's stages of faith can be of invaluable assistance in developing a sustainable, workable, and lasting faith" (**Fleming**).

*Howard, Evan B. *The Brazos Introduction to Christian Spirituality*. Grand Rapids: Brazos, 2008.

> This volume provides an ecumenical and comprehensive overview of the field of spiritual formation in the Protestant, Roman Catholic, and Eastern Orthodox traditions from an evangelical perspective. Extremely readable and user friendly.

*Issler, Klaus. *Living into the Life of Jesus*. Downers Grove: InterVarsity, 2012.

> This book is much more than just one more "how-to" guide to the Christian life. There are many such books that teach how to model Christian behavior. Issler, professor of Christian education and theology at Talbot School of Theology, Biola University, sounds a clarion call to believers that the core problem in their Christian profession and walk is the huge gap between "willing" and "doing" and that the core problem is not so much behavior as it is the transformation of the heart. Issler in an engaging and entertaining manner offers sound biblical strategies to help bridge that gap. This is a must-read for anyone who wants to form Christian character. I suggest that you read it twice: The first time to allow the concepts to digest and marinate in the mind and heart, as well as for conviction. I confess that I was terribly convicted at times. The second reading should be for implementation. Highly recommended!

*Lord, Peter. *Soul Care*. Grand Rapids: Baker, 1990.

> "After over 40 years as a pastor, the author's premise is that 'We do not *have* a soul; we *are* a soul.' 'The church has majored in bringing people to Christ, but minored in . . . nurturing them as believers.' With the goal of growing believers in the image of Christ, Lord includes sections on Understanding Your Soul, Recognizing a Healthy Soul, Achieving a Prosperous Soul, and Healing an Aching Pain" (**Singletary**).

*Lovelace, Richard F. *Dynamics of Spiritual Life: An Evangelical Theology of Renewal*. Downers Grove: InterVarsity, 1979.

> This important study, by a noted professor of church history at Gordon-Conwell Theological Seminary, traces the dynamics of spiritual renewal from Jonathan Edwards to the Jesus Movement. In part 1 the author analyzes the biblical models of both cyclical and continuous renewal and then the preconditions and elements of renewal. In part 2 he turns his attention to renewal in the local congregation, how revivals go wrong, and the like. Though the book is now more than thirty-five years old, its message is still timely. Thought-provoking.

*MacDonald, Gordon. *Ordering Your Private World*. Expanded ed. Nashville: Nelson, 1985.

> This study by former president of InterVarsity Christian Fellowship helps the believer move from a state of physical and spiritual disorganization to a life that is more organized. The author deals with such topics as Use of Time, Wisdom and Knowledge, Spiritual Strength, and Restoration. MacDonald writes with clarity and insight.

————. *Restoring Your Spiritual Passion*. Nashville: Nelson, 1986.

> This book, by someone who lost his spiritual passion and had an extramarital affair, explores how unhappiness and disillusionment manifest themselves in different ways, such as burn-out and depression. It gives a prescription for the unrest and disquiet, which is so much a part of modern life.

*Mulholland, M. Robert. *Invitation to a Journey: A Road Map for Spiritual Formation*. Downers Grove: InterVarsity, 1993.

> "Another modern classic on the subject of spiritual formation, Mulholland writes of the need to conform to the image of Christ through a holistic understanding of our own unique personality, and the application of spiritual disciplines. A good source book for lifelong spiritual development" (**Fleming**).

*Nouwen, Henri. *The Way of the Heart*. New York: Ballentine, 1981.

> "This simple, beautifully written book began as a series of lectures on spirituality for the Yale Divinity School. In it Nouwen discusses the value of the spiritual disciplines of prayer, silence, and solitude. It is a must for anyone seeking to understand the spiritual formation movement and the spirituality of the desert fathers of the church" (**Fleming**).

*————. *Spiritual Direction: Wisdom for the Long Walk of Faith*. With Michael Christensen and Rebecca J. Laird. New York: HarperOne, 2006.

> This book is a composite of Nouwen's spiritual direction course and his unpublished writings to create what is believed to be the definitive work on Nouwen's beliefs on the Christian life. Each chapter concludes with questions under the heading "Reflect and Journal." Christensen and Laird both studied under Nouwen at Yale Divinity School and the former serves on the board of directors of the Henri Nouwen Society.

*+Packer, J. I. *Knowing God*. Downers Grove: InterVarsity, 1973.

> Not yet fifty years old, this book is an acknowledged classic of the Christian life. In 2006, *Christianity Today* designated it as one of the top fifty books

that have shaped evangelicals. In 1993, InterVarsity published a twentieth-anniversary edition with a new preface by Packer as well as Americanized language and spelling. Personally, I prefer the original edition. But however you encounter this book, it is not to be missed!

*Pink, Arthur W. *Spiritual Growth*. 3rd ed. Grand Rapids: Baker, 1996.

"The well-known Bible expositor, A. W. Pink, gives a spiritual analysis of 1 Peter 3:18: 'Grow in grace.' As a call to greater Christian commitment, he expounds the principles of earnest prayer and heartfelt meditation on the Bible. The purpose of growth is to glorify God and to be remade in Christ's image" (**Singletary**). "As with all of Pink's works, this one needs to be studied" (Barber).

*Pratt, Richard L., Jr. *Pray with Your Eyes Open: Looking at God, Ourselves and Our Prayers*. Phillipsburg, NJ: Presbyterian & Reformed, 1987.

"Presents practical, biblical suggestions to improve an individual's prayer life. Principles are conveyed through insights from the Psalms, visual graphics, study questions, and exercises" (**Singletary**).

*Scazzero, Peter. *Emotionally Healthy Spirituality*. Nashville: Nelson, 2006.

"This book, along with its companion volume, *Emotionally Healthy Church*, is a popularly written, non-scholarly work on the need for developing emotional health in a pastor, emphasizing the needs for openness, vulnerability, and transparency and the need for spiritual disciplines. Scazzero is a pastor of a church in Queens, New York, but has studied widely in a variety of spiritual traditions including Roman Catholic and Eastern Orthodox. His work is a valuable corrective to a professional and clinical approach to leadership, following an incarnational model, rather than a transformational model" (**Fleming**).

*Schaeffer, Francis A. *True Spirituality*. Wheaton: Tyndale, 1971.

This book began as a series of messages first preached in Huemoz, Switzerland, and led to the creation of L'Abri. Although more than sixty years old, these messages still retain their intellectual vibrancy and relevancy. Schaeffer was one of the true spiritual giants of the twentieth century and still deserves to be heard and read. "Comes to grips with the problem of reality and the all-sufficiency of Christ, and presents the gospel as the only message to meet the needs of men and women today" (Barber, 221).

Swindoll, Charles R. *Growing Deep in the Christian Life*. Portland: Multnomah, 1986.

> This book by a popular preacher is a basic down-to-earth approach to spiritual growth in the Christian life. Swindoll has the rare gift of taking complex doctrines and making them easy to understand to the layperson.

*+Thomas à Kempis. *On the Imitation of Christ*. Reprint, London: Chapman and Hall, 1878.

> This venerated book is, next to the Bible, perhaps the most widely read devotional work read and is regarded as a true classic. Composed in Latin in the fifteenth century (ca. 1418–1427), it is a handbook for spiritual life. It is comprised of four books, which provide detailed spiritual instructions: Admonitions, Useful for a Spiritual Life, Admonitions Concerning Inward Things, Of Internal Consolation, and Concerning the Communion. This book arose from the *Devotio Moderna* movement of which Kempis was a member. The book's emphasis is on the interior life and withdrawal from the world. It is widely available in inexpensive paperback from numerous publishers. It should not be missed!

*Warner, Larry. *Journey with Jesus: Rediscovering the Spiritual Exercises of Saint Ignatius*. Downers Grove: InterVarsity, 2010.

> The spiritual exercises of Ignatius have rightly been held as models of spiritual direction for almost five hundred years. However, they have been considered to be dense and impenetrable for many people seeking to unlock their riches. Warner, who teaches at Talbot Seminary's Institute for Spiritual Formation, unlocks the door to these exercises guiding the reader through Ignatius's traditional thirty-day retreat approach as well as the nine-month journey. He does not "dumb down" these exercises; rather, he makes them accessible to the average believer.

*Whitney, Donald S. *Spiritual Disciplines for the Christian Life*. Colorado Springs: NavPress, 1991.

> "Whitney's book is an excellent practical argument and development for the importance of spiritual disciplines in spiritual growth. His approach is less mystical and more down-to-earth than Willard or Foster, and can at times seem more legalistic. Nevertheless, it is more accessible to the average layperson. An excellent practical guide for spiritual formation for the practical church. His follow-up volume, *Spiritual Disciplines for the Christian Church*, carries his concepts into the corporate life of the church" (**Fleming**).

*+Willard, Dallas. *The Divine Conspiracy: Rediscovering Our Hidden Life in God*. New York: HarperOne, 1997.

> This book is a modern classic of Christian discipleship. Willard, one of this generation's most compelling Christian thinkers and philosophers, argues for the relevance of God in every area of the believer's life. This book is groundbreaking, insightful, accessible, and warm in spirit. This study was the magazine *Christianity Today's* 1999 Book of the Year.

*———. *Renovation of the Heart: Putting on the Character of Christ*. Colorado Springs: NavPress, 2002.

> This book is another modern classic of Christian discipleship. Willard compellingly outlines how believers can transform the mind, will, body, soul, and social dimension and move to the next level of Christlikeness.

*———. *The Spirit of the Disciplines: Understanding How God Changes Lives*. New York: HarperOne, 1991.

> Since the publication of Foster's *Celebration of Discipline*, there has been a renaissance of interest in spiritual disciplines. Willard stands at the forefront of the spiritual formation movement and is always a delight to read. "Willard is a unique blend of preacher, mystic, and philosopher, who approaches the subject of spiritual formation in a way that is both biblically sound and philosophically deep. Along with his book, *The Divine Conspiracy*, Willard's work has had a profound impact on church life today" (**Fleming**).

CHURCH GROWTH AND EVANGELISM

Conn, Harvie M., ed. *Planting and Growing Urban Churches: From Dream to Reality*. 3rd ed. Grand Rapids: Baker Academic, 1997.

> The message of this book is that the twenty-first-century church must adapt and change form if it is to survive and thrive.

*Cook, Harold R. *Historic Patterns of Church Growth: A Study of Five Churches*. Chicago: Moody, 1971.

> "This book is a short, readable analysis of the patterns of missionary growth among five different missionary groups—the Armenian church, the Celtic church, the Hawaiian church, the Karen church of Burma, and the Batak church of Sumatra. By comparing these groups, Cook develops some common principles for penetrating cultural barriers which are still valid today" (**Fleming**).

*Engel, James F., and H. Wilbert Norton. *What's Gone Wrong with the Harvest? A Communication Strategy for the Church and World Evangelism*. Grand Rapids: Zondervan, 1977.

> "James Engel is well known for developing the 'Engel Scale' for measuring resistance to the Gospel, and progress in receiving it. Engel and Norton are two of the leading proponents of the idea that evangelism is a process, not an event. His insights into the process of evangelism are universally applicable" (**Fleming**).

Ford, Leighton. *The Christian Persuader: A New Look at Evangelism Today*. New York: Harper & Row, 1966.

> "Leighton Ford is well known as Billy Graham's friend, brother-in-law, and second-in-command in the Billy Graham Evangelistic Association. For that reason, if for no other, his words on evangelism are worth reading. While emphasizing the need for personal evangelism, Ford also builds a case for mass crusade-type evangelistic methods. Ford believes that any and every form of sharing the Gospel is vital, and that methods should change with the times" (**Fleming**).

Hunter, George, III. *The Celtic Way of Evangelism: How Christians Can Reach the West . . . Again*. Nashville: Abingdon, 2000.

> "This book draws from the history of growth of the Celtic church of Sts. Patrick, Bridget, and Columba as a model for growth in a post Christian society. A challenging and fascinating read for anyone interested in evangelizing a pre-or post-Christian culture" (**Fleming**).

*Hybels, Bill, and Mark Mittelberg. *Becoming a Contagious Christian*. Grand Rapids: Zondervan, 1994.

> "Bill Hybels is the senior pastor of Willow Creek Church in Chicago, one of the largest churches in America. His simple, down to earth approach to evangelism, emphasizing the building of personal relationships is a must for any pastor interested in encouraging his people to witness" (**Fleming**).

Jenson, Ron, and Jim Stevens. *Dynamics of Church Growth*. Grand Rapids: Baker, 1981.

> This handy little book is a manual of methodologies for church growth. Each of the fifteen chapters is brief and deals with an integral component of church growth: prayer, worship, purpose, diagnosis, priorities, planning, programming, climate, leadership, laity, absorption, small groups, discipleship, training, and evangelism. Much of the material is, at thirty-five years of age, dated, but much is still relevant today.

*Johnson, Ben. *An Evangelism Primer: Practical Principles for Congregations*. Atlanta: John Knox, 1983.

> "Ben Johnson was the head of Presbyterian Evangelistic Fellowship and the professor of evangelism at Columbia Theological Seminary. Johnson's book is a good overall discussion of evangelism in the local church" (**Fleming**).

————. *Evangelism: A Theological Approach*. Philadelphia: Westminster, 1987.

> Pondering the precipitous decline in membership in churches in mainline Protestant denominations, the author concludes that churches must reexamine their approach to evangelism and its underlying theology. This book explores what the author considers to be the central teachings of the Christian faith—humanity, God, Christ, Holy Spirit, the church, salvation, faith, and the kingdom of God—and concludes that these are the basis for evangelism.

*+Kennedy, D. James. *Evangelism Explosion*. 4th ed. Wheaton: Tyndale, 1996.

> This seminal work explains the methodology that became the building blocks for the Coral Ridge Presbyterian Church in Ft. Lauderdale, Florida, helping it to grow from under one hundred members to well over six thousand. The methodology combines a conversational gospel presentation with a lay-mentoring program that has worked miracles in countless churches. "No one has had more influence on the training of Christians for personal evangelism than the late D. James Kennedy of Coral Ridge Presbyterian church. His book and training course *Evangelism Explosion* has been used in tens of thousands of churches in countries across the world. The beauty of his approach is the simple, straightforward style he uses in training people to share their faith, which has been tested countless times in many kinds of churches. Kennedy's approach is not without drawbacks, however. His emphasis on sticking by rules does not leave much room for questioning and debate, and his focus on the next life does not work as well on younger people who seem to assume they will live forever. Nevertheless, for a single, step-by-step approach to sharing Christ, Kennedy's book has never been surpassed" (**Fleming**).

*+Little, Paul. *How to Give Away Your Faith*. Rev. ed. Downers Grove: InterVarsity, 2008.

> This little book is a classic in teaching the art of personal evangelism. Originally published in 1966, it has helped thousands of Christians to be ambassadors for their faith. With humor and insight, Little walks the reader through the nuts and bolts of the gospel presentation.

*+McGavran, Donald. *Understanding Church Growth*. Grand Rapids: Eerdmans, 1970.

> McGavran is the father of the modern church growth movement and this book is his blueprint for churches. "This book is considered foundational to

church growth theory and practice in the late twentieth century. It is essential to understanding the sociological and theological underpinnings of the Church Growth movement" (**Fleming**).

*Moore, Waylon B. *New Testament Follow-Up for Pastors and Laymen: How to Conserve, Mature, and Multiply the Converts*. Rev. ed. Grand Rapids: Eerdmans, 1963.

> The author sees the number one problem the church faces is the problem of spiritual reproduction. People become saved and join a local church, but they never become disciples. They never grow up in the faith and they never reproduce themselves spiritually. This needed book examines NT principles of follow-up and then practical applications of follow-up. Although this book is over a half century old, its message has never been needed as much as it is today.

*+Packer, J. I. *Evangelism and the Sovereignty of God*. Americanized ed. Downers Grove: InterVarsity, 2012.

> "Why is it that Calvinists teach that salvation is a matter of God's grace and not our choice, yet so many of the great evangelists in the West have been Calvinists? Packer does a brilliant job of laying out how the Reformed faith and passionate evangelism are not incompatible. Whether or not the reader believes in predestination or free will, Packer's book will stimulate your thinking about the necessity of evangelism" (**Fleming**). Reformed.

Petersen, Jim. *Evangelism for Our Generation: The Practical Way to Make Evangelism Your Lifestyle*. Colorado Springs: NavPress, 1985.

> This book, by a well-known missionary with the Navigators, is an apologetic for "lifestyle evangelism," an evangelistic tool that enables believers to model the Christian message which eventually leads to sharing the gospel.

*Pippert, Rebecca Manley. *Out of the Saltshaker and Into the World: Evangelism as a Way of Life*. Rev. ed. Downers Grove: InterVarsity, 1999.

> This revised and enlarged edition is an updated version of the original 1979 book. "In 2006, *Christianity Today* voted this book as one of the top 50 books that have shaped evangelicals. It is a practical, common-sense approach to lifestyle evangelism. Pippert uses real-life stories and applies biblical principles to faith sharing as a natural part of everyday life. It includes a study guide for individuals and groups" (**Singletary**).

Ranier, Thom. *The Book of Church Growth: History, Theology, and Principles*. Nashville: Broadman and Holman, 1993.

> "Ranier is the president of Lifeway Christian Resources, the publishing arm of the Southern Baptist Church. He has written several books of interest to

those seeking practical church growth advice, including *Unchristian* and *Simple Church*, which have been bestsellers. In this book, Ranier looks at the history and development of the Church Growth movement of the eighties and nineties, and draws out practical advice for pastors today. His book is one of the most valuable descriptions of this movement, its strengths, and also some of its weaknesses" (**Fleming**).

Stone, Bryan P. *Evangelism after Christendom: The Theology and Practice of Christian Witness*. Grand Rapids: Brazos, 2007.

The author of this book believes that the single most evangelistic practice that the church does is to be the church. He recognizes that Christendom today is in ruins and that the current way of doing "church" with its emphasis on power, status, and statistical success must be jettisoned in favor of a radical, biblical approach grounded in the historical narratives of Israel, Jesus, and the Apostles.

*Sweazey, George. *The Church as Evangelist*. New York: Harper & Row, 1978.

"This book is a practical guide for helping churches think of themselves as evangelistic institutions. The author puts the emphasis on outreach and as-similation of visitors and new members. His approach to visitation and public advertising are pre-Internet, of course, so some of this material is outdated. But his emphasis on evangelism as a whole church phenomena, as well as his practical approach to follow-up and assimilation, are still valid" (**Fleming**).

*Tucker, Ruth. *From Jerusalem to Irian Jaya: A Biographical History of Christian Missions*. Grand Rapids: Zondervan, 1983.

"This book is the best book ever on the history of the world missions move-ment, and is used as a text book in many schools teaching world missions. It tells the story of missions through the biography of the missionaries and evangelists who have led the way. It is a thick book, but well worth the time it takes to plow through it" (**Fleming**).

Wagner, C. Peter. *Leading your Church to Growth*. Ventura, CA: Regal, 1978.

———. *Your Church Can Grow*. Ventura, CA: Regal, 1976.

"Wagner is considered the dean of the 'church growth' movement after his father-in-law, McGavren. His thoughts and writings have been immensely influential in the church, growth, laying down the principles of growth. In *Leading Your Church to Growth*, he deals mainly with the kind of leadership necessary for growing churches. In *Your Church Can Grow*, he deals with the overall principles of church growth" (**Fleming**).

*Warren, Rick. *The Purpose Driven Church: Growth Without Compromising Your Message & Mission*. Grand Rapids: Zondervan, 1995.

> This huge Christian best-seller was written by the pastor of Saddleback Church, the fastest-growing Baptist church in American history. This book shares pastor Rick Warren's five-part strategy for church growth: warmer through fellowship, deeper through discipleship, stronger through worship, broader through ministry, and larger through evangelism.

CHURCH MANAGEMENT

Anderson, Stephen. *Preparing to Build: Practical Tips & Experienced Advice to Prepare Your Church for a Building Program*. Clayton, NC: Anderson, 2011.

> "Every pastor needs at least one source to help them understand the house of worship, when to build or renovate, and how to raise the funds to renovate, modernize, or build. Anderson has written the most comprehensive and practical reference on the subject. This book is essential for growing congregations with facility needs" (**Grigg**).

Berkley, James D. *The Dynamics of Church Finance*. Ministry Dynamics for a New Century. Edited by Warren Wiersbe. Grand Rapids: Baker, 2000.

> "A thoroughly practical guide for developing sound financial practices in church. Recommended for any young pastor, church treasurer, or deacon responsible for setting up a solid financial system for a church" (**Fleming**).

*Friedman, Edwin. *Generation to Generation: Family Process in Church and Synagogue*. New York: Guilford, 1985.

> "Friedman draws on Bowen's systems theory principles, originally developed for family counseling, and applies them brilliantly to the life of religious institutions. His analyses are must reading for anyone who wants to understand why churches behave the way they do" (**Fleming**).

Henry, Jack A. *Basic Budgeting for Churches: A Complete Guide*. Nashville: Broadman and Holman, 1995.

> "A useful guide for writing and promoting a church budget" (**Fleming**).

*Powers, Bruce P., ed. *Church Administration Handbook*. 3rd ed. Nashville: Broadman & Holman, 2008.

> "This book contains practical principles for different types of churches: large and small, urban and rural, traditional and contemporary. It includes sections

on administration, motivating and training volunteers, assessing skills and ministries, planning and budgeting, publications and communications, and employee relations" (**Singletary**).

*Zigarelli, Michael A. *Management by Proverbs: Applying Timeless Wisdom in the Workplace*. 2nd ed. Ostego, MI: PageFree, 2004.

Although the primary purpose of this interesting book is the secular workplace, the twenty-four lessons from the book of Proverbs apply just as much in the local church. The wise pastor will avail himself of the principles outlined here. A real treat to read!

CHURCH POLITY AND OFFICES

*Berghoef, Gerard, and Lester De Koster. *The Elders Handbook: A Practical Guide for Church Leaders*. Grand Rapids: Christian's Library, 1979.

Although this volume is almost forty years old, its principles are both biblical and timeless. It is intended to be, as its title suggests, a complete and comprehensive handbook for elders within Reformed/Presbyterian congregations. It is full of helpful suggestions and good plain common sense. Highly recommended! See also the authors' *The Deacons Handbook: A Manual for Stewardship*. Both are essential resources and should be given to officers upon ordination to sacred office. Reformed.

*Brand, Chad Owen, and R. Stanton Norman, eds. *Perspectives on Church Government: Five Views of Church Polity*. Nashville: B & H, 2004.

In counterpoint format, this book examines the five basic models of church polity that have developed over the course of church history. Daniel Akin writes about the single elder-led Congregational model, James Leo Garrett Jr. about the democratic Congregational model, Robert L. Reymond about the Presbyterian model, James R. White about the plural elder-led Congregational model, and Paul F. M. Zahl about the Episcopal model.

Briggs, J. R., and Bob Hyatt. *Eldership and the Mission of God: Equipping Teams for Faithful Church Leadership*. Downers Grove: InterVarsity, 2015.

Not reviewed for this edition.

*Cowan, Steven B. *Who Runs the Church? 4 Views on Church Government.* Counterpoints: Church Life. Grand Rapids: Zondervan, 2004.

> This informative book follows the counterpoint format in examining the four major approaches to church polity. The four views and respective proponents are: Episcopalianism by Peter Toon, Presbyterianism by L. Roy Taylor, Single-Elder Congregationalism by Paige Patterson, and Plural-Led Congregationalism by Samuel E. Waldron.

*Getz, Gene A. *Elders and Leaders: God's Plan for Leading the Church: A Biblical, Historical and Cultural Perspective.* Chicago: Moody, 2003.

> This book was written by a pastor who is also a scholar and seminary professor. It is biblically based, historically and culturally sensitive, and written with a shepherd's heart.

*Merkle, Benjamin L. *40 Questions about Elders and Deacons.* Grand Rapids: Kregel Academic & Professional, 2008.

> This important resource, by a professor of NT at the Southeastern Baptist Theological Seminary, answers questions relating to church offices in general, the office of elder, qualifications of elders, plurality of elders, and how they are selected, ordained, and removed. There is also a section pertaining to questions about the office of deacon. Extremely informative and essential for church leaders!

Newton, Phil A. *Elders in Congregational Life: Rediscovering the Biblical Model for Church Leadership.* Grand Rapids: Kregel Academic & Professional, 2005.

> This brief treatment of the eldership argues that churches, not just Baptist churches, need to have an elder-based leadership. This book has three parts. Part 1 asks the question: Why elders? Part 2 examines three key biblical texts: Acts 20:17–31; Heb 13:17–19; and 1 Pet 5:1–5. Interestingly, the texts from the Pastoral Epistles did not receive consideration. Part 3 describes how churches can make the transition from theory to practice, how to make the transition to elder leadership. Baptist.

*Strauch, Alexander. *Biblical Eldership: An Urgent Call to Restore Biblical Church Leadership.* Rev. ed. Colorado Springs: Lewis and Roth, 1995.

> This excellent volume explores the office of the elder from the perspective of Scripture. Strauch outlines just what biblical eldership entails and its qualifications. It is pastoral, shared, male, qualified servant leadership. The author sounds a clarion call to return to a biblically based eldership in the church.

*———. *The New Testament Deacon: The Church's Minister of Mercy*. Colorado Springs: Lewis and Roth, 1992.

> This book calls for deacons to free themselves from the shackles of building-maintenance mentality and to involve themselves in compassionate service.

Webb, Henry. *Deacons: Servant Models in the Church*. Nashville: B & H, 2001.

> This comprehensive work focuses on the many aspects and roles of the office of deacon. Baptist.

Wright, Paul S. *The Duties of the Ruling Elder*. Rev. ed. Philadelphia: Westminster, 1972.

> This extremely brief book (88 pages) is primarily a handbook for pastors and elders in Presbyterian congregations. Two chapters deal exclusively with the Session and the pastor.

COUNSELING

Adams, Jay E. *The Christian Counselor's Casebook*. Phillipsburg, NJ: Presbyterian and Reformed Publishing Company, 1974.

> This volume is a workbook designed to be used in conjunction with the author's two previous works, *The Christian Counselor's Manual* and *Competent to Counsel*.

———. *The Christian Counselor's Manual*. Grand Rapids: Baker, 1973.

> This book is the sequel and companion volume to the author's *Competent to Counsel*. They go together and can be used with great profit in confronting people with the biblical answers to life's problems.

*+———. *Competent to Counsel*. Grand Rapids: Baker, 1970.

> "Jay Adams, for better or worse, is a towering figure in the field of Evangelical Christian counseling. His book has had a profound impact on Christian counseling in the last third of the twentieth century on into the twenty-first. The main contribution that Adams has made is his restoration of the Bible as the primary source for Christian counselor. Adams sees nearly all psychological problems as sin-related, and modern psychology as ineffective. He encourages loving confrontation of sin and repentance as the cure for most human ills. The problem with Adams' approach, though, is his distrust and at times antipathy for psychology. This creates a 'one size fits all' approach to counseling that often ignores physical causes of psychiatric disorders, the effect of abuse and neglect, and many other reasons why a person may not

be living in emotional or spiritual health. That being said, Adams if often spot-on in his recommendations not to be ashamed to confront sin when we find it. If the reader is discerning enough to realize that no one approach will answer all problems, then Adams' works and thoughts may be a helpful addition to their counseling library" (**Fleming**).

————. *More than Redemption: A Theology of Christian Counseling*. Phillipsburg, NJ: Presbyterian and Reformed, 1979.

————. *Ready to Restore: The Layman's Guide to Christian Counseling*. Phillipsburg, NJ: Presbyterian and Reformed, 1981.

This volume is a distillation of the author's other works such as *The Christian Counselor's Manual: The Practice of Nouthetic Counseling, More than Redemption: A Theology of Christian Counseling*, and *Competent to Counsel* intended for a lay audience. The author sees the ultimate end of Christian counseling as being restoration.

————. *What about Nouthetic Counseling?* Phillipsburg, NJ: Presbyterian and Reformed, 1976.

Nouthetic counseling has been somewhat controversial in recent decades. This little volume is a question and answer book compiled by the "father" of Nouthetic counseling to allow the uninitiated to gain perspective into the history and biblical foundations of this counseling movement.

*Benner, David G. *Strategic Pastoral Counseling: A Short-Term Structured Model*. 2nd ed. Grand Rapids: Baker Academic, 2003.

"David Benner's book is a good companion and in some ways an antidote to Clinebell's work. Like Clinebell, he gives a short, concise statement of the practice of pastoral counseling, with special care to differentiate it from other forms of counseling. Then he proceeds to discuss practically the stages of pastoral counseling" (**Fleming**).

*Clinebell, Howard. *Basic Types of Pastoral Counseling*. Nashville: Abingdon, 1996.

"Clinebell has been for a generation one of the most helpful resources for pastoral counseling. What makes his book such a stand-out is his inclusion of step by step procedures for counseling a wide variety of pastoral situations. His books break down the pastoral counseling process in simple, understandable steps. The reader should be aware, however, that Clinebell's book does not address many biblical issues. He is not an evangelical in his view of Scripture, and so does not include Scripture much in his counseling methodology. Neither does he deal much with sin (though his section on confrontational counseling is a helpful model for confrontation). If you can get past this, and combine his methodologies with scriptural content, it can be a helpful tool for anyone" (**Fleming**).

*Clinton, Tim, Archibald Hart, and George Chischlager, eds. *Caring for People God's Way: Personal and Emotional Issues, Addictions, Grief, and Trauma*. Nashville: Nelson, 2009.

"A simple introduction to Christian counseling, it provides a practical, step-by-step outline on the basic principles. Designed both for professionals and laypersons, it addresses the basic spiritual issues behind many human problems while encouraging love and listening, and applying biblical truths with psychological insights. It details a wide range of problems that a counselor will encounter, including trauma, grief, loss, and suicide" (**Singletary**).

*Collins, Gary, ed. *Resources for Christian Counseling*. 30 vols. Grand Rapids: Zondervan, 1986–88.

This helpful resource is now out of print, but should be purchased if found secondhand. It can be found on Amazon, Abe, and other online sources. "This multivolume set is perhaps the best and most helpful resource for the Christian counselor in existence today. It was developed by Dr. Gary Collins and spans a host of Christian counseling issues from premarital counseling and guidance counseling to abuse and the occult. Each writer is an unquestioned expert in his or her field, and approach their subject from a decidedly Christian perspective. I would highly recommend this series, if it can be found. These volumes are a continually informative source for Christian counseling theory and material" (**Fleming**).

*Crabb, Lawrence J., Jr. *Effective Biblical Counseling*. Grand Rapids: Zondervan, 1977.

"This is still the classic in understanding psychological issues in layman's terminology. It is in such a wonderful, readable format that the student can enjoy it while learning basic 'effective Biblical counseling' principles. I have used this text in the classroom as well as the counseling room. Dr. Crabb is an advocate of 'counseling by encouragement' through the local church. His 'integrative' approach to theoretical counseling provides a clear pathway to application" (**Baldwin**). "Crabb's book is a good primer for counseling from an Evangelical Christian perspective. Crabb combines the biblical perspective of Jay Adams with a respect for the work of psychologists and psychiatrists. His work is one of the leading writings in the cognitive behavior school of Christian counseling. It is simply written and biblically sound. His book, *Effective Principles of Biblical Counseling*, is a shorter version of what he presents in this book" (**Fleming**).

Cutrer, William R. *The Church Leader's Handbook: A Guide to Counseling Families and Individuals in Crisis*. Grand Rapids: Kregel, 2009.

"Cutrer is the Gheens Professor of Christian Ministry at the Southern Baptist Theological Seminary in Louisville. The book is academic in nature, yet an easy read for most seminarians. Cutrer provides practical advice for specific crises from unexpected pregnancies to end-of-life issues. This handbook is ideal for the inexperienced pastor, as well as the experienced. Cutrer covers preparing for crisis care, preventive measures to help congregations avoid crisis, and how to minister in specific crises" (**Grigg**).

*Kirwan, William T. *Biblical Concepts for Christian Counseling: A Case for Integrating Psychology and Theology*. Grand Rapids: Baker, 1984.

This insightful volume is very helpful for any counselor who wants to be able to integrate biblical counseling with modern psychology.

*+Kubler-Ross, Elizabeth. *On Death and Dying*. New York: Simon and Schuster, 1969.

"This is *the* classic work on the discussion of end-of-life issues. Kubler-Ross developed structure for understanding grief and loss that is used today across the disciplines of medicine, psychology, counseling, and theology. Though it is not a Christian book, it is an essential book for dealing with end-of-life issues" (**Fleming**).

Montgomery, Dan, and Kate Montgomery. *Compass Psychotheology: Where Psychology & Theology Really Meet*. Montecito, CA: Compass Works, 2010.

"I agree with the publisher that 'Compass Psychotheology offers a fascinating and creative perspective on how psychology and theology are partners in understanding human nature, its vulnerabilities and possibilities for transformation.' Having taken the model test and applied it to my own life, I found a clear description of my personality dynamics and was shown how this could allow me to move within the wave of complementary patterns in order to explore some complex personal issues. The Montgomerys also follow the DSM descriptions of personality patterns that allow even clinical psychologists to access and use the material clearly. Written for Pastoral Counselors to apply within their care ministries, the text provides wonderful helps as a resource for assessments and pastoral care" (**Baldwin**).

White, John. *The Masks of Melancholy: A Christian Physician Looks at Depression & Suicide*. Downers Grove: InterVarsity, 1982.

This book is an important study of two problems that plague the Christian church and society. Although written in 1982, its message is quite timely today.

*Worthington, Everett L., Jr. *When Someone Asks for Help: A Practical Guide for Counseling*. Downers Grove: InterVarsity, 1982.

> "I am a big fan of Dr. Worthington's writings and ministry. He has always declared that psychology and our faith as Christian believers can be integrated effectively in Pastoral Counseling in order to train lay counselors and pastoral counselors. The goal of counseling is to be a 'people helper.' The book begins with a good introduction to pastoral counseling and provides great illustrative examples. I really like the simplicity and yet depth of Dr. Worthington's 5-stage problem management model that seems to be applicable to most of the situational difficulties that are common among most people that have needs" (**Baldwin**).

*+Wright, H. Norman. *The Complete Guide to Crisis & Trauma Counseling: What to Do and Say When It Matters Most*. Grand Rapids: Bethany, 2011.

> "This is one of the best resources for trauma and crisis counseling available. Thoroughly biblical and psychologically sound, it deals with all aspects of crisis counseling for professional therapists and pastors. Along with this book should be mentioned the author's *Recovering from Losses in Life* (Grand Rapids: Revell, 2006). This volume covers the subject of grief and loss from a layperson's perspective. It is a worthy companion to the larger *Complete Guide* mentioned above" (**Fleming**).

*———. *Premarital Counseling*. Rev. ed. Chicago: Moody, 1981.

> "Written as a companion to his *Before You Say I Do* classic, Norman Wright provides additional helps to continue the necessity of providing 'Premarital Counseling' for couples seeking to start off their marriages the right way. This book is a classic and I have used it both in the classroom and in my Pastoral Counseling ministry. It is essential to provide help for those wanting to prepare for marriage. Dr. Wright provides the basics to mold into a counseling plan. Churches must realize their responsibility in preparing couples and must provide materials that are practical as well as Biblical. This book allows that direction" (**Baldwin**).

DISCIPLESHIP

Breen, Mike, and Steven Cochram. *Building a Discipling Culture*. Pawley's Island, SC: 3 Dimension, 2009.

> "Breen shares a new approach to discipleship using what he calls 'lifeshapes' to teach the basics of the spiritual life. This, like many other approaches, focuses on the initial disciplines necessary to grow in the Christian faith. His central

concept is a sound one, that we do not build churches to make disciples, but build disciples to make churches" (**Fleming**).

*+A. B. Bruce. *The Training of the Twelve.* Cosimo Classics, 1877; Grand Rapids: Kregel, 2000.

"Bruce's book is a detailed analysis of Jesus' process of making disciples. It is the basis for much that has been written on discipleship today. A classic and a must-read" (**Fleming**). "Unequalled in its field. Shows how Christ disciplined and trained his disciples for the position of apostleship. A most rewarding study" (Barber, 212).

*Coleman, Robert. *The Master Plan of Evangelism.* Old Tappan, NJ: Revell, 1963.

"Coleman's book does a wonderful job of laying out the connections between discipleship and evangelism. To Coleman, they are all the same work of God. Coleman argues that God's plan for conquering the world is to build disciples who can build disciples, multiplying Christ's ministry in others. It is an approach that has proven effective over the years, especially in places most resistant to the Gospel" (**Fleming**).

*Demarest, Bruce. *Seasons of the Soul: Stages of Spiritual Development.* Downers Grove: InterVarsity, 20009

"This book is an absolute gem in the area of discipleship and spiritual development. What makes this book so interesting and useful is that it recognizes the need for a whole-life approach to spiritual development. Growing in Christ is not just growing in knowledge, habits, and feelings, but growth in all and more besides. Demarest recognizes the many different paths described throughout the years to spiritual wholeness devised by Christians, and acknowledges them all to be true. We do not all progress in the same way along the same path, but are discovering a truth greater than all of us put together. It is a helpful volume for discovering our own spiritual path" (**Fleming**).

*+Eims, LeRoy. *The Lost Art of Disciple Making.* Grand Rapids: Zondervan, 1978.

"This book is another classic manual for disciplemaking. Eim's book is mainly aimed at making Christians into useful and productive church members and workers. While this is a worthy goal, it is should not be seen as the end of Spiritual Formation, but only a stop along the way" (**Fleming**).

*Henrichsen, Walter, and Howard Hendricks. *Disciples Are Made Not Born*. New ed. Colorado Springs: Cook, 2002.

> "This book by Hendrichsen and Hendricks is considered one of the best in the field and has proven particularly useful for discipling high school and college students" (**Fleming**).

*Hull, Bill. *Jesus Christ, Disciplemaker*. Grand Rapids: Baker, 2004.

> "This book follows Bruce's approach to disciple making, sketching out Christ's methods for evangelism. It is easier to read than Bruce, and more geared to a contemporary audience. Bill Hull is a recognized expert on small group discipleship" (**Fleming**).

FAMILY AND HOME

Balswick, Jack O., and Judith K. Balswick. *A Model for Marriage: Covenant, Grace, Empowerment and Intimacy*. Downers Grove: IVP Academic, 2006.

> "The Balswicks have blessed readers with another wonderful textbook on marriage. With over thirty years of experience within the context of marital counseling, the book reflects that depth of understanding. With wonderful insights and theological sound writing, this "model" provides great examples and directions. It is unashamedly Christian in its context and approach reminding the reader of God's original intentions for marriage. The book covers many practical issues also including communication and conflict resolution. This is an excellent resource for study and application" (**Baldwin**).

*———. *The Family: A Christian Perspective on the Contemporary Home*. 4th ed. Grand Rapids: Baker Academic, 2014.

> "Now in its fourth edition this classic perspective on the family remains the best text on the subject of the Christian family. I have used this text in most of my classes as a Pastoral Care Professor in the 3rd edition. I am welcoming an updated contemporary version to my list of required texts" (**Baldwin**).

*+Bavinck, Herman. *The Christian Family*. Edited by Stephen J. Grabill. Translated by Nelson D. Kloosterman. Grand Rapids: Christian's Library, 2012.

> First published in 1908 when the institution of marriage was beginning to face enormous challenges that in the succeeding century have grown unabated, this book is both biblical and amazingly contemporary. It is not a "how-to" guide offering ten principles for a healthy marriage, nor does it offer easy

prescriptions. Rather, Bavinck, a brilliant theologian who wrote his *magnum opus, Gereformeerde Dogmatiek (Reformed Dogmatics)*, offers a Christian theology of marriage and the family based on Scripture.

Brandt, Henry R., and Kerry L. Skinner. *Marriage, God's Way*. Nashville: Broadman & Holman, 1999.

"This is a dated, yet detailed reference work on Marriage. The Biblical references are worth the price of the book. The authors seek to present God's plan for marriage and show how any couple can enjoy a satisfying and richly rewarding marriage by approaching the relationship with a Christian standard of love. It is written in a research style and can be used for research very effectively" (**Baldwin**).

*Bridges, Jerry. *The Fruitful Life: The Overflow of God's Love through You*. Colorado Springs: NavPress, 2006.

"The author of the classic work, *The Pursuit of Holiness*, has written another great book. Jerry Bridges takes adequate time in this book to explore the nine aspects of the 'fruit of the Spirit' described in Galatians 5:22–23; 'love, joy, peace, patience, kindness, goodness, faithfulness, gentleness, and self-control.' He then takes the time and effort to clarify the cultivation process by showing us how to practice the fruit in real life. I used this text in several studies of the 'fruit' and was able to use many of the illustrations and explanations. Bridges says: 'these qualities of character can truly mark our lives if we devote ourselves to a twofold pursuit: God-centeredness and God-likeness.' This book can be used in the classroom or personal study on the fruit of the Spirit" (**Baldwin**).

*Chapman, Gary D. *The Five Love Languages: How to Express Heartfelt Commitment to Your Mate*. Chicago: Northfield, 2015.

"Gary Chapman, with over thirty years of applying his concept of 'five love languages' has a new approach to understanding these truths in a contemporary form. In the book he provides quizzes to help you discover your primary and secondary love languages. The five love languages are:

- Words of Affirmation: If this is your love language, you feel most cared for when your partner is open and expressive in telling you how wonderful they think you are, how much they appreciate you, etc.

- Acts of Service: This love language desires doing things that help you.

- Physical Touch: This love language is just as it sounds. A warm hug, a kiss, touch, and sexual intimacy make you feel most loved when this is your love language.

- Quality Time: This love language is about being together, fully present and engaged in the activity at hand, no matter how trivial.

- Giving and Receiving Gifts: Your partner taking the time to give you a gift can make you feel appreciated.

I use these concepts of Love Languages with every pre-marital and marital counseling couple. It always is a great help and always well received" (**Baldwin**).

————. *The Marriage You've Always Wanted*. Chicago: Moody, 2009.

This brief, easy-to-read book examines many of the problem areas that couples face in a marriage. The range of topics is as diverse as why a spouse will not change to the division of household tasks to in-law problems.

*Dobson, James. *Dare to Discipline*. Wheaton: Tyndale, 1970.

This seminar work has undergone numerous reprintings and revisions since its initial 1970 publication. It has been a hugely popular work in the evangelical world in the United States in the past four decades. Discipline as Dobson defines it is not limited to punishment, but rather incorporates self-discipline and responsible living. In an age when the discipline of children has seemingly gone out of style, the author's message is sorely needed today.

Duty, Guy. *Divorce & Remarriage*. Minneapolis: Bethany Fellowship, 1967.

This book takes a biblical look at the issues of divorce and remarriage. Duty sees the crucial questions as twofold: Is dissolution of marriage apart from death possible? Is remarriage ever valid in God's sight?

*Kessler, Jay. *Family Forum*. Wheaton: Victor, 1984.

A very helpful book on how to live life in a family, with your spouse, with others, with yourself, without a spouse, in a broken world, in a permissive world, in a spiritual world, in a real world, and in a changing world. Based on his popular radio program of the same title, Jay Kessler, former president of Youth for Christ/USA and chancellor and president emeritus of Taylor University, utilizes a topical question-and-answer format to deal with just about any kind of question that a believer could face, at least in the world of the 1980s.

LaHaye, Tim, and Beverly LaHaye. *The Act of Marriage: The Beauty of Sexual Love*. Grand Rapids: Zondervan, 1976.

This book is basically a "how-to" handbook on the sexual aspect of marriage.

Laney, J. Carl. *The Divorce Myth*. Bethany, 1981.

> This book is a helpful guide to divorce and remarriage. Of particular value are the study questions at the end of each chapter.

Meier, Paul, and Richard Meier. *Family Foundations: How to Have a Happy Home*. Grand Rapids: Baker, 1981.

> This book examines seven factors essential for a spiritually and emotionally healthy home: a spiritual base, genuine love, gut-level communication, discipline, consistency, setting the example, and proper leadership roles.

*+Murray, John. *Divorce*. Reprint, Philadelphia: Presbyterian and Reformed, 1976.

> This modern classic by the revered professor of systematic theology at Westminster Theological Seminary was first published in 1961. In the compass of just 117 pages, Murray meticulously and brilliantly works his way through the biblical teaching on the subject examining the OT provision, the teaching of Jesus and of Paul, and finally the consideration of practical cases. With divorce continuing to plague the church, this book is needed today as much as it ever was. Highly recommended!

*Petersen, J. Allan. *The Myth of the Greener Grass*. Wheaton: Tyndale, 1983.

> An engaging and shocking look at adultery and marriage. In the thirty-plus years since the book was published, not much has changed except perhaps for the rising incidence of STDs as a result of adultery. This is a "user friendly" read that will help couples to "affair proof" their marriages.

Schaeffer, Edith. *What Is a Family?* Old Tappan, NJ: Revell, 1975.

> This book presents an optimistic view of family life. Drawing from her experiences as a wife, mother, and grandmother at L'Abri, the world-renowned Christian community in Switzerland, the author shares her insights gained as the wife of the brilliant theologian Francis Schaeffer, mother to four children, and counselor and guide to the myriad of people who stopped at L'Abri in their quest for meaning in life. A side note: A few years ago, I sat at a lunch table with my late friend and colleague, the theologian R. K. McGregor Wright, and his wife, Julia Castle, as he shared how his personal search led him to L'Abri as a young college student in the 1960s. My wife and I sat enthralled as he shared his story of his encounter with the Schaeffers.

Smalley, Gary, and John Trent. *The Two Sides of Love.* Lanham, MD: Christian Living, 2005.

> "Originally published in 1990, this book asks the question, 'What strengthens affection, closeness, and lasting commitment?' The authors emphasize communication that is loving and effective. The largest portion of the book is occupied with describing the four basic personality types and explaining how they relate to one another. The authors' premise is that couples must understand one another's individual dispositions before effective communication can take place" (**Singletary**).

*Sproul, R. C. *The Intimate Marriage: A Practical Guide to Building a Great Marriage.* Reprint, Wheaton: Tyndale, 1986.

> In just over 120 pages, Sproul deftly and engagingly deals with six topics: communication in marriage, the roles of the spouses, problems in marriage, divorce, communication and sex, and the institution and sanctity of marriage. The author is sometimes profound and never dull.

*Swindoll, Charles R. *Strike the Original Match.* Portland: Multnomah, 1980.

> Popular preacher and author Swindoll offers fresh, practical advice on rekindling and preserving the fire of marriage. All of his prescriptions are based on Scripture.

White, Jerry, and Mary White. *The Christian in Mid Life: Biblical Guidelines and Inspiration for Men and Women Facing the Challenges of Mid-Life.* Colorado Springs: NavPress, 1980.

> This helpful book enables Christians to navigate the dangers and opportunities of mid-life. Although many books on mid-life crises tend to deal with marriage and its challenges during this period, this volume also investigates how it affects singles as well as the overflow effects on children.

*White, John. *Parents in Pain: A Book of Comfort and Counsel.* Downers Grove: InterVarsity, 1979.

> This book is a how-to manual for parents of children with severe problems. The author is particularly adept at helping parents deal with feelings of guilt, inadequacy, frustration, and anger. Dated, but still helpful because its prescriptions are biblical.

*Wright, H. Norman. *Communication: Key to Your Marriage.* Ventura, CA: Regal, 1974.

> The premise of this book is, as its title suggests, that communication is the key to a happy, vibrant marriage. It offers strategies for dealing with marital

conflict as well as ways that spouses can build the self-esteem of their partners. Bethany House published an updated revised edition in 2012. "An important book" (Barber).

*————. *More Communication Keys for Your Marriage*. Ventura, CA: Regal, 1983.

A sequel to the author's best-selling book, *Communication: Key to Your Marriage*. This book broadens the concept of communication and how it relates
to every facet of human relationships. Very practical!

Yates, John, and Susan Yates. *What Really Matters at Home: Eight Elements for Building
Character in Your Family*. Dallas: Word, 1992.

This books helps parents build character in their families by communicating
eight crucial elements: integrity, faith, a teachable spirit, a servant's heart, self-
discipline, joy, compassion, and courage.

PASTORAL LEADERSHIP

*Bennis, Warren. *Why Leaders Can't Lead: The Unconscious Conspiracy Continues*. San
Francisco: Jossey-Bass, 1989.

Warren Bennis is distinguished professor of business administration at the
University of Southern California and a noted leadership expert. This engaging book exposes the "unconscious conspiracy" that sabotages the plans of
leaders and undermines their vision. Some of these threats are entrenched
bureaucracy, ominous social trends, and mind-numbing routine. The author
identifies the components of the problem and offers solutions. This is a secular book that Christian leaders would do well to read.

*+Bennis, Warren, and Burt Nanus. *Leaders: Strategies for Taking Charge*. 2nd ed. New
York: HarperCollins, 2003.

This excellent book, originally published in 1985, is a modern leadership
classic. Although it is secular in its orientation, its lessons and insights are
essential to Christian leaders. This volume explores the differences between
management and leadership, an important distinction that all executives
must learn. A must-read for anyone trying to lead!

*Biehl, Bobb. *Increasing Your Leadership Confidence*. Reprint, Sisters, OR: Questar, 1989.

"Biehl is a business consultant for several major Christian ministries as well
as large corporations. The manager/executive/leader often has to advise,
identify problems, and offer practical solutions. This book gives 28 sets of

practical, diagnostic questions which can apply equally to individual counseling or to boardroom meetings. It delves past surface situations to find root problems and gives answers" (**Singletary**).

*Blackaby, Henry, and Richard Blackaby. *Spiritual Leadership: Moving People on to God's Agenda*. Nashville: Broadman & Holman, 2001.

The main target audience for this book is the evangelical Christian pastor or para-church leader. The authors attempt to get people to accept the challenge of leadership and then to motivate others to follow them as they work to do the will of God. This book is interesting, informative, and well written. It is amply illustrated with examples from the Bible and the workplace.

Blanchard, Ken, and Phil Hodges. *Lead Like Jesus: Lessons for Everyone from the Greatest Leadership Role Model of All Time*. Nashville: W Publishing Group, 2005.

Ken Blanchard is one of the foremost leadership experts in the United States. In this book, he and coauthor Phil Hodges correlate leadership principles from the life of Jesus along with numerous illustrative anecdotal materials that are both informative and easy to read. The authors focus on four key areas in the life of the leader: heart, head, hands, and habits. They argue that leadership should be transformational and that leaders should adopt a God's-eye view of their lives and leadership patterns.

*DeVille, Jard. *Pastor's Handbook on Interpersonal Relationships: Keys to Successful Leadership*. Grand Rapids: Baker, 1986.

Although published in 1986, the message of this book is timely and still fresh and relevant. It deals with the distinctive challenges of pastoral leadership in that the church functions largely with a volunteer work force. This volume assists pastors to understand the dynamics of pastoral leadership and to embrace the leadership challenge.

*Engstrom, Ted W. *The Making of a Christian Leader*. 9th ed. Grand Rapids: Zondervan, 1978.

The author's premise in writing this book is that "the successful organization has one major attribute that sets it apart from unsuccessful ones: dynamic and effective leadership." Engstrom, the former head of Youth for Christ and World Vision International, explains that good leadership begins with an understanding of tested principles of management and human relations. He provides an outstanding overview of leadership styles, strategies, and personality traits. A must-read for any Christian leader!

*Ford, Leighton. *Transforming Leadership: Jesus' Way of Creating Vision, Shaping Values, & Empowering Change*. Downers Grove: InterVarsity, 1991.

> This engaging volume is an excellent study of leadership using Jesus, the ultimate leader, as the model. Ford calls all to aspire to leadership in the kingdom of God and to emulate the leadership strategies of Jesus. He examines the leadership of Christ under several headings: the leader as Son, Strategist, Seeker, Seer, Strong One, Servant, Shepherd-Maker, Spokesperson, Struggler, and Sustainer. Believers are called to be, as the author argues, transformational leaders as Jesus was. An outstanding book about leadership by a first-rate Christian leader!

*Gangel, Kenneth O. *Team Leadership in Christian Ministry: Using Multiple Gifts to Build a Unified Vision*. Rev. ed. Chicago: Moody, 1997.

> This book is the "Bible" on team leadership in the church and para-church ministries. It is a practical, useful, and easy-to-read manual.

*+Kouzes, James M., and Barry Z. Posner. *The Leadership Challenge: How to Make Extraordinary Things Happen in Organizations*. 5th ed. San Francisco: Wiley, 2012.

> This extraordinary book has, in just over a quarter of a century, become a modern classic among leadership books. Based on extensive research, the authors outline the Five Practices of Exemplary Leadership and focus on organizational challenges. Although this book is from a "secular" perspective, no wise Christian leader dare ignore its insights. A must-read!

*———. *Christian Reflections on the Leadership Challenge*. San Francisco: Wiley, 2004.

> This book shares Christian reflections on Kouzes and Posner's seminal book, *The Leadership Challenge*, and its five practices of exemplary leadership. The list of contributors reads like a Who's Who of Christian leadership in the twenty-first century, including Ken Blanchard, John C. Maxwell, David McAllister Wilson, and Nancy Ortberg.

*Maxwell, John C. *Developing the Leader Within You*. Nashville: Nelson, 1993.

> John C. Maxwell is the guru of Christian leadership studies. This book is not just a Christian book best seller; it has sold over a million copies. There are good reasons for that. This book is an easy and interesting read. It deals with timeless traits and skills that a good leader should possess such as integrity, attitude, vision, self-discipline, influence, and problem solving. Anyone studying the subject of leadership in the late twentieth and early twenty-first centuries needs to be familiar with the writings of John Maxwell. This book is a good place to begin.

*Michael, Larry J. *Spurgeon on Leadership: Key Insights for Christian Leaders from the Prince of Preachers*. Grand Rapids: Kregel Academic & Professional, 2003.

> This book is more than simply a collection of pithy sayings by Charles Spurgeon on the subject of leadership. There is plenty of that, but the real meat of the book is Michael's incisive analysis of Spurgeon's leadership style. Spurgeon was the pastor of the first mega-church and widely regarded as the best and most influential preacher of the nineteenth century. Anyone desiring to learn from his model of leadership should study this book.

Myra, Harold, ed. *Leaders: Learning Leadership from Some of Christianity's Best*. Leadership Library. Carol Stream, IL: Word, 1987.

> This helpful book reads like a panel discussion on leadership with a list of participants who are some of the most well-known Christian leaders of the late twentieth century. Contributors are J. Richard Chase, Richard Foster, Henri Nouwen, Mark Hatfield, Fred Smith, Gene Getz, Everett "Terry" Fullam, Howard Hendricks, Carl F. George, Ted Engstrom, Ed Dayton, Donald Seibert, Truman Dollar, Eugene H. Peterson, and Richard Halverson, answering questions on a range of topics including "Three Traits of a Leader," "Maintaining Integrity Under Pressure," "Setting Priorities," and "Building Spiritual Unity." Easy reading, but informative and challenging!

*Sanders, J. Oswald. *Dynamic Spiritual Leadership: Leading Like Paul*. Reprint, Grand Rapids: Discovery, 1999.

> J. Oswald Sanders, general director of the Overseas Missionary Fellowship (then China Inland Mission) in the 1950s and 1960s, was a well-known twentieth-century Christian leader. This book, like nearly every one of the over forty books that Sanders wrote, is easy to read, insightful, and well worth examining. It was originally published in 1984 with the title *Paul the Leader*. The author takes as his model for leadership the Apostle Paul, who certainly knew a thing or two about the topic of leadership. Sanders highlights the qualities that made Paul such an effective leader and shares them with his readers.

*Schaller, Lyle. *The Change Agent: The Strategy of Innovative Leadership*. Nashville: Abingdon, 1972.

> "In the Seventies and Eighties, Lyle Schaller was one of the most influential writers on church dynamics. Though he is now deceased, his works hold up well. This volume is particularly helpful to pastors and church leaders seeking to overcome *homeostasis*, or resistance to change in a church. Schaller's book gives step-by-step instructions on how to overcome inertia" (**Fleming**).

*Smith, Fred. *Learning to Lead: Bringing Out the Best in People*. Leadership Library. Carol Stream, IL: Word, 1986.

> This excellent little book was written by a Christian businessman who has served as a CEO and consultant to such corporations as Genesco, Mobile, and Caterpillar. It is an easy read and full of nuggets of wisdom and insight. Smith defines leadership as a function of service to a group and believes that leaders cannot be leaders unless they have followers. This book, as its title suggests, is about learning to lead, learning how to get followers to do the work that needs to be done. A must for pastors!

Somervill, Charles. *Leadership Strategies for Ministers*. Philadelphia: Westminster, 1987.

> This easy-to-read volume takes a narrative approach utilizing the case study of a fictitious minister as he serves in different pastorates. The author analyzes his behavior under the following headings: An Identification Strategy (Dealing with Alienation), A Community Change Strategy (Stages of Diffusion), and A Compliance Strategy (Conflict Management). Very helpful for pastors!

Stanley, Andy. *The Next Generation Leader: 5 Essentials for Those Who Will Shape the Future*. Sisters, OR: Multnomah, 2003.

> Andy Stanley is the pastor of North Point Community Church (median age of 30) in Atlanta and the son of noted pastor and writer Charles Stanley. This is a book that has proved to be highly successful in mentoring and shaping Millennials. The author's five essentials are competence, courage, clarity, coaching, and character. This is a brief book that is extremely easy to read and digest.

*Stott, John. *Basic Christian Leadership: Biblical Models of Church, Gospel and Ministry*. Downers Grove: InterVarsity, 2002.

> This study is a compelling exposition of 1 Corinthians 1–4 in which Stott presents an alternative vision of servant leadership. Here he demonstrates convincingly that God is at work even through human weakness. Stott presents a biblical model of leadership based on the Apostle Paul that is out of step with the model of leadership so often portrayed in modern culture.

*Woolfe, Lorin. *Leadership Secrets from the Bible: From Moses to Matthew—Management Lessons for Contemporary Leaders*. New York: MJF, 2002.

> This compelling book contains ten chapters, each of which focuses on a different leadership trait or skill: honesty and integrity, purpose, kindness and compassion, humility, communication, performance management, team development, courage, justice and fairness, and leadership development. Each chapter also contains brief vignettes featuring the leadership skills of Bible characters that are illustrative of each trait or skill. For example, Nehemiah

is regarded as an exemplar of team development as is Peter of humility. Then modern business leaders such as Steve Jobs and Jack Welch are marshaled forth as illustrations of those traits or skills in a modern business setting. A very helpful feature of the book is the section at the end of each chapter titled "Biblical Lessons On" different subjects. These one-sentence lessons are worth the price of the book alone.

*Yost, Robert A. *Leadership Secrets from the Proverbs*. Eugene, OR: Wipf & Stock, 2013.

It would be difficult to evaluate my own book objectively, so I am using one of the many brief reviews that it generated. "Dr. Yost enjoys a depth of ministry experience, both during several pastorates and in academia as a professor and Vice President of Academic Affairs. Given the general impermeability that exists between the two career paths of practitioner and academician, it is a real treat to read a book written by one who intimately knows the heights and depths of both 'houses' of the church. Yost's book is full of insights, lessons, and gems suitable for all audience. It is far more than a treatise on leadership, than a commentary on the Proverbs, or than a drool of popular 'Bible Study' material. While not being overly technical, this book is eminently biblical, full of historical data, wonderful word studies, and is indeed, culturally contemporary. Beyond this, it has a fine bibliography, very helpful appendices, and the refreshing presence of footnotes rather than endnotes. This is a book that provides profoundly helpful material for Adult Bible Studies offered in the context of the local church, as well as rich background for the difficult task of expository preaching through the Proverbs. But beyond the obvious, I recommend this study to the academician who would strive to do what does not come naturally, to go beyond simply informing the students' minds, to warming their hearts with some human pathos, to uplifting their consciousness concerning the needs around them and to inspiring them to do great things in the name of God. Do not miss the promise of this book!" (**Olsen**).

PASTORAL MINISTRY

Adams, Jay E. *Shepherding God's Flock: A Preacher's Handbook of Pastoral Ministry, Counseling, and Leadership*. Grand Rapids: Baker, 1979.

This compilation was originally three books published separately in 1974 and 1975. It combines *The Pastoral Life*, *Pastoral Counseling*, and *Pastoral Leadership* into one handy volume.

*Allen, Charles. *God's Psychiatry*. Reprint, Aida, MI: Revell, 1997.

"Beloved pastor, Charles Allen, first published this book in 1953. It has remained a simple and soul-satisfying comfort for troubled people. It contains plain, encouraging devotional studies from four will-known Scripture passages: the Twenty-Third Psalm, the Ten Commandments, the Lord's Prayer, and the Beatitudes. It gives an empowering spiritual message for hurting, wounded, and discouraged people" (**Singletary**).

*Anderson, Robert C. *The Effective Pastor*. 2nd ed. Chicago: Moody, 1998.

This book, first published in 1985 by the chairman of the Department of Pastoral Ministry at Western Conservative Baptist Seminary in Portland, Oregon, who also has served as a pastor, is a helpful handbook on how to do effective pastoral ministry. It is divided into four parts: "The Pastoral Role," "The Pastor's Relationships," "The Pastoral Tasks," and "The Pastor's Administrative Tasks." Under "The Pastoral Role," Anderson deals with such diverse topics as character and calling, personal life and study habits, and the pastor's wife. Under "The Pastor's Relationships," he deals not only with the pastor's family, congregants, and officers, but also with pastoral visitation and counseling. "The Pastoral Tasks" deals with how to conduct the weekly services and activities as well as the Lord's Supper and baptism, evangelism, weddings, and funerals. "The Pastor's Administrative Tasks" deals with the many "hats" that an effective pastor must wear in the course of his duties: planning and managing, public relations, correspondence, business meetings, support for ministries such as Christian education, music and youth ministries, stewardship, and building programs. A helpful book!

Aten, Jamie D., and David M. Boan. *Disaster Ministry Handbook*. Downers Grove: InterVarsity, 2015.

Not reviewed for this edition.

*+Baxter, Richard. *The Reformed Pastor*. Edited by William Brown. Reprint, Carlisle, PA: Banner of Truth, 1974.

This book, which was first published in 1656 and abridged in 1829, is a true classic of the Christian faith. Reading this book will show the reader just how far afield pastoral ministry in the twenty-first century has drifted from a biblical view of the ministry. "A classic treatment which has been a blessing to pastors since its first appearance. . . . Deserves to be studied in depth" (Barber, 263). "The Puritan tradition held a high view of the person and work of a pastor. No one represents that tradition better than Richard Baxter. Modern readers may find Baxter a tedious read in places, but if one has the patience to keep reading, they may find him a soul who is deeply in love with Christ and his congregation. His emphasis on the Puritan virtues of humility and long-term faithfulness are particularly refreshing in our modern success-driven church" (**Fleming**). Reformed.

Biddle, Perry H. *A Hospital Visitation Manual*. Rev. ed. Grand Rapids: Eerdmans, 1994.

"Biddle is a graduate of Davidson College, Union Theological Seminary in Richmond, VA, and Vanderbilt University. He has also studied at New College, University of Edinburgh in Scotland. Biddle serves the PCUSA denomination and is a prolific writer in the area of pastoral care. This work is excellent for training pastors or laity in the art of visitation. Biddle divides the book into three parts. In part one, Biddle explains what a new minister needs to do upon arriving in his parish to get into the hospital community, an area often neglected by writers. In part two, he deals with sixteen specific types of patients one will visit in the hospital. In part three, the last five chapters of the book deal with such topics as anointing the sick, baptism, and the Lord's Supper, services often forgotten in pastoral care and visitation outside the church building" (**Grigg**).

*+Bridges, Charles. *The Christian Ministry: With an Inquiry into the Causes of Its Inefficiency*. London: Billing , 1830. Reprint, Edinburgh: Banner of Truth, 1967.

This book is, in a nutshell, a masterpiece of the Christian faith. In its almost four hundred pages, it deals with not just preaching but with the entire realm of Christian ministry. For a book that is almost two hundred years old, it is tremendously current and relevant. Its five parts are as follows: part 1, "General View of the Christian Ministry"; part 2, "General Causes of the Want of Success in the Christian Ministry"; part 3, "Causes of Ministerial Inefficiency Connected with Our Personal Character"; part 4, "The Public Work of the Christian Ministry"; and part 5, "The Pastoral Work of the Christian Ministry." Bridges boldly confronts such pastoral sins as laziness in the ministry and spiritual pride. He challenges pastors to actually do pastoral work. In an age when many pastors feel that their work ends with the pulpit, Bridges urges pastors to do the work of visitation and to embark upon a ministry of evangelism, discipleship, and pastoral care. These are aspects of the ministry that are often ignored today. Well worth reading! Reformed.

Callahan, Kennon L. *Visiting in an Age of Mission: A Handbook for Person-to-Person Ministry*. San Francisco: Jossey-Bass, 1994.

"Although somewhat dated, anything written by Callahan is worth reading. The concepts laid out in this book are still valid and should be considered prior to starting a lay visitation program. While he emphasizes training, Callahan pushes the trainees out of the classroom into the laboratory of experience, followed by assessment of the objectives of each visit" (**Grigg**).

Croft, Brian. *The Pastor's Ministry: Biblical Priorities for Faithful Shepherds*. Grand Rapids: Zondervan Academic, 2014.

> Using the Bible as his sourcebook, the author examines what he determines to be the top ten priorities for faithful pastoral ministry.

———. *Visit the Sick: Ministering God's Grace in Times of Illness*. Grand Rapids: Zondervan, 2015.

> "This book is part of the Practical Shepherding series. It lays out a solid biblical theology for providing care for congregants and for providing skilled care for the sick through an organized community of equipped saints" (**Grigg**).

*Croft, Brian, and Bryce Butler. *Oversee God's People: Shepherding the Flock through Administration and Delegation*. Grand Rapids: Zondervan, 2015.

> "This book is part of the Practical Shepherding series. It speaks to the need for delegation to care for the congregation" (**Grigg**).

*Croft, Brian, and Ryan Fullerton. *Pray for the Flock: Ministering God's Grace through Intercession*. Grand Rapids: Zondervan, 2015.

> "This book starts with solid biblical teaching on intercessory prayer, and moves on to the deliberate and intentional practice of prayer. Croft and Fullerton stress the need for pastoral prayer and fasting with both a local and global focus, as well as the need for pastors to gather together for distinct periods of clergy prayer" (**Grigg**).

*Eswine, Zack. *The Imperfect Pastor: Discovering Joy in Our Limitations through a Daily Apprenticeship with Jesus*. Wheaton: Crossway, 2015.

> Winner of *Christianity Today's* 2016 Book Award in the category The Church / Pastoral Leadership, this revealing volume is unlike almost every other book on the pastoral ministry. It reveals with blatant honesty the failures and disasters of a pastor involved in pastoral ministry. It is a timely reminder that God uses imperfect pastors to do imperfect ministry.

*Hiestand, Gerald, and Todd Wilson. *The Pastor Theologian: Resurrecting an Ancient Vision*. Grand Rapids: Zondervan, 2015.

> See review of *The Pastor as Public Theologian* by Vanhoozer and Strachan below. Winner of *Christianity Today's* 2016 Award of Merit in the category The Church / Pastoral Leadership.

Hopkins, Denise Dombkowski, and Michael S. Koppel. *Grounded in the Living Word: The Old Testament and Pastoral Care Practices*. Grand Rapids: Eerdmans, 2010.

> "This is a scholarly work for the more experienced pastor and an easy read for seminary graduates. Hopkins is a professor of biblical theology and Koppel is professor of pastoral theology and congregational care at Wesley Theological Seminary in Washington, DC. The two teamed up to collaborate in developing the pastoral care connection with the Hebrew Bible. The authors insert questions throughout the book for reflection designed to make the reader wrestle with his or her methodology of pastoral care and visitation. While an easy read, this book is designed to make you a better caregiver, and to be used for ongoing training for laity who assist in the caregiving of congregants" (**Grigg**).

*Justice, William G., Jr. *When Death Comes*. Nashville: Broadman, 1982.

> "This small, practical handbook can be used by church staff and laypersons to be more effective in ministering to the grieving. A longtime hospital chaplain, Justice explains the grief stages and describes pitfalls that can create additional pain and frustration for the grieving. Case studies illustrate many of the points" (**Singletary**).

*Justice, William G., Jr., and Richard L. Dayringer. *Training Guide for Visiting the Sick: More than a Social Call*. New York: Routledge, 2005.

> "This is a practical handbook from a Christian perspective for visiting the sick. It provides practical, common sense, and clinical advice. Basic do's and don'ts are explained for ministering to the sick (even the comatose), the dying, and the bereaved. Examples are given from the authors' extensive experiences in hospital chaplaincy. It will profit the professional as well as the layperson and can be used for group training" (**Singletary**).

*Kirkwood, Neville A. *The Lay Pastoral Worker's Hospital Handbook: Tending the Spiritual Needs of Patients*. New York: Morehouse, 2005.

> "Kirkwood has an excellent chapter in which he deals with the dangers of always praying with a patient in which he deals with the ritualization, generalization, superficiality, piety, self-righteousness, and authoritarianism of the one praying. Further, he discusses the benefits of asking permission to pray and he discusses how to use the asking to connect the spiritual needs of the patient" (**Grigg**).

*———. *Pastoral Care to the Aged: A Handbook for Visitors*. New York: Morehouse, 2005.

> "This book serves as a reference for both the pastor and the lay visitor. It does an excellent job of helping the visitor of aged congregants to understand the

seriousness of this ministry and the importance of the aged and their needs" (**Grigg**).

MacArthur, John. *Pastoral Ministry: How to Shepherd Biblically*. MacArthur's Pastor's Library. Nashville: Nelson, 2005.

> John MacArthur is a well-known radio preacher who is the pastor of Grace Community Church in Sun Valley, California, and president of Master's College and Seminary. This book is a collaborative effort with the faculty at the Master's Seminary. It provides a comprehensive picture of pastoral ministry and how to do it. MacArthur is an acknowledged master teacher as evidenced by his preaching ministry at Grace Church and as the featured teacher on "Grace to You," but one wonders how much of the "nuts and bolts" aspects of ministry are actually performed by the author himself and how much is delegated to others.

*+Nouwen, Henri. *The Wounded Healer: Ministry in Contemporary Society*. New York: Doubleday, 1972.

> "Henri Nouwen is a well-known devotional and pastoral writer within the Roman Catholic perspective. This particular book is often as much used and cited in Evangelical as in mainline schools for its description of the life and work of the pastor. While Nouwen's observations largely still hold true, it does have a disadvantage at places of speaking to a 'contemporary' society that is now over forty years old. Nevertheless, many of the themes of technological alienation and disassociation are truer now than they were then. It is considered a 'classic' in its field" (**Fleming**). Roman Catholic.

*Patton, John. *Pastoral Care—An Essential Guide*. Nashville: Abingdon, 2005.

> "There are few books that are written specially about the person and work of the pastor. Patton's work is one of them. Patton argues that the first role of the pastor is to be wise, and defines pastoral wisdom as learning how to apply truth in love. He applies this to basic pastoral work—care for the sick and dying, counseling, visitation, and simply being a caring presence in the community. An excellent book for a new pastor, or a ministry student" (**Fleming**).

*Peterson, Eugene H. *The Contemplative Pastor: Returning to the Art of Spiritual Direction*. Grand Rapids: Eerdmans, 1989.

> "No one has written more or better on the life of a pastor than Eugene Peterson. Several of his books, including *Five Smooth Stones for Pastoral Work*, *Under the Unpredictable Plant*, and *Working the Angles* have spoken to the needs of pastors in many different traditions worldwide. Peterson does not just write about being a pastor—he is a pastor, serving the same congregation

for decades. His books combine the need for pastoral integrity with spiritual disciplines. In this book, he uses three words to define the work of the pastor—*unbusy*, *subversive*, and *apocalyptic*. It is a good corrective for any pastor who finds himself too busy to pray or seek God's true voice" (**Fleming**).

Peterson, Sharyl B. *The Indispensable Guide to Pastoral Care*. Cleveland: Pilgrim, 2008.

"Peterson is a gifted and thorough writer. Her work is scholarly, well written, and suited for research. Her work is unique in several ways, none more noticeable than Peterson's discussion of the key ethical principles of the caregiver. Peterson deals with confidentiality, required reporting, safety, knowing your limits, and making referrals. She also deals with the ethics related to sexual conduct and how it is both immoral and unethical to engage in any sexual conduct with those for whom we provide care. She moves on to discuss communication skills and concludes the book with a discussion of the myriad of types of visits normally required in pastoral care" (**Grigg**).

*Quayle, William. *The Pastor-Preacher*. New York: Eaton and Mains, 1919.

Although this book is now almost a century old, there is much to commend it because Quayle's prescriptions are biblical and thus timeless. Some of his chapters, such as "The Sin of Being Uninteresting" and "The Fine Art of Loving Folks," should be must reading for today's pastor. The original book is folksy and homespun, but still interesting reading. In 2009 Beams of Grace Press in Syracuse, New York, published a reprint edition revised and edited by Steven A. Hite.

Roberts, Stephen B., ed. *Professional, Spiritual & Pastoral Care: A Practical Clergy and Chaplain's Handbook*. Woodstock, VT: Skylight, 2012.

"Roberts' book is just as the title suggests—a resource book for professional ministers, rabbis, and chaplains. The key word here is 'professional.' The model of ministry here is that of an academic specialty along the lines of a psychiatrist or counselor. It addresses the creation of a pastoral theological foundation, but does not specify that foundation. It is assumed each pastor will have his/her own core beliefs going into the study. It addresses the core competencies necessary to provide pastoral and spiritual care, and deals with practical guidelines for hospital visitation, counseling, and end-of-life care, as well as quality assurance and outcome based pastoral work and ministerial ethics. Any evangelical looking for this book to support a biblically based view of pastoral ministry will surely be disappointed. But for those who are already assured of their theological foundations, and are looking for a practical framework for developing their skills of pastoral ministry in either a parish or institutional setting, this book can be of great assistance" (**Fleming**).

Schroeder, Ray. *Growing Your Church and Your Faith through Personal Visitation.* Lincoln, NE: iUniverse.com, 2001.

> "Schroeder, a Presbyterian minister, makes a strong argument that visitation is a sacrament. He outlines the biblical basis for the sacraments being effective symbols of the Lord's love being extended to humanity. He points out that Christ gave his life visiting and meeting the needs of others. He argues that by thinking of visitation as a sacrament, all self-seeking love is rooted out and only Christ-like selfless love prevails. He further argues that personal visitation is to transcend age, and that personal visitation is deeply meaningful to all ages when rooted in Christ-like selflessness" (**Grigg**).

*Shelley, Marshall. *Well-Intentioned Dragons: Ministering to Problem People in the Church.* Minneapolis: Bethany, 1985.

> "Pastors go to new churches looking to minister to sheep. Before long, they discover that some of the sheep are actually dragons. Shelley's book is full of compassionate, sage, and timely advice on how to deal with difficult Christians who oppose us in ministry and in life" (**Fleming**).

*Short, David, and David Searle. *Pastoral Visitation: A Pocket Resource.* Fearn, Scotland: Christian Focus, 2008.

> "This is a practical book especially for young ministers. In this book, Short and Searle deal with difficult questions that inexperienced ministers often struggle with, and seek to avoid. Collaboratively they outline approaches to deal with fear, anxiety, guilt, et cetera. He gives suggestions on dealing with such difficult questions as 'Why has God allowed this to happen?' and does 'Does God still care?' They end the book with a chapter of hymns that can be read or sung. Visitors must remember that hymns, like Scripture, speak to the troubled heart" (**Grigg**).

*+Spurgeon, C. H. *An All Round Ministry: Addresses to Ministers and Students.* London: Watson & Viney, 1900. Reprint, Edinburgh: Banner of Truth, 1960.

> In 1865 Spurgeon inaugurated an Annual Conference of his Pastor's College. He delivered twenty-seven Presidential Addresses prior to his death in 1892. This book consists of twelve of them published posthumously in 1900. These helpful addresses are timeless and run the gamut from "Faith" to "Stewardship" to "The Preacher's Power." Spurgeon's writings never seem to go out of style. "Cannot fail to revive the weary, encourage the dispirited, and rekindle hope in the downcast. An inspiration" (Barber).

*+————. *Lectures to My Students*. London: Marshall, Morgan, and Scott, n.d. Reprint, Grand Rapids: Zondervan, 1972.

> The lectures in this book were initially delivered to Spurgeon's students at his Pastor's College and first published between 1874–94. These addresses, by an undisputed pulpit master, cover such diverse topics as "The Call to the Ministry," "The Preacher's Private Prayer," "On Spiritualizing," "The Minister's Fainting Fits," "The Holy Spirit in Connection with Our Ministry," "The Blind Eye and the Deaf Ear," and "Anecdotes from the Pulpit." A delight to read! "This indispensable work covers every facet of the pastor's life. . . . Deserves careful reading once a year" (Barber).

*Stone, Howard W. *The Caring Church: A Guide for Lay Pastoral Care*. Minneapolis: Fortress, 1991.

> "Stone is a professor of Pastoral Psychology at Brite Divinity School, Texas Christian University. Although a little dated, the book is still one of the best guides for developing a practical lay-oriented pastoral care ministry in the local church" (**Grigg**).

*Stubblefield, Jerry M., and Paul E. Engle, ed. *Serving in Church Visitation*. Grand Rapids: Zondervan, 2002.

> "I find a kinship with Stubblefield in that he links visitation back to the heart of God. From there, he builds a strong biblical basis for churches having an organized visitation ministry. Stubblefield clearly defines the kind of layperson that makes a good visitor. He limits the types of visits to Inreach and Outreach, which I find simplistic. However, overall this is one of the best books on the market for development of a pastoral led lay visitation ministry" (**Grigg**).

Tautges, Paul. *Comfort the Grieving*. Grand Rapids: Zondervan, 2015.

> "This book is part of the Practical Shepherding series and is an easy, but rewarding, read. In it Tautges provides pastors and ministers advice and practical help in shepherding others through painful and difficult losses" (**Grigg**).

*+Thielicke, Helmut. *A Little Exercise for Young Theologians*. Grand Rapids: Eerdmans, 1962.

> "Helmut Thielicke was a pastor and theologian who came from neo-orthodoxy. Whatever his roots, though, this work is a gem which should be read by any student of ministry. Thielicke takes on the mindset of young seminarians with gusto, eviscerating them for failing to recognize that pastoring is about life, not theology. He compares the young theologian to a geologist examining the rocks from the Alps who does not recognize the beauty of the mountains. He appeals to them to recognize that ministry is a mutual learning process, in which

the congregation teaches us, as well as teaching the congregation" (**Fleming**). "A sane, sensible appeal for fruitful communication between the theologically trained pastor and the common people of his church" (Barber, 197).

*+Turnbull, Ralph G. *A Minister's Obstacles*. Grand Rapids: Baker, 1954.

> This little book is like a compilation of "fireside chats" about practical problems and temptations that parish pastors encounter in the ministry. A quick survey of some of his chapter titles are enough to tempt the pastor to read: "The Vice of Sloth," "The Dry Rot of Covetousness," "The Paralysis of Pride," "The Crux of Criticism," "The Vanity of Cleverness," "The Chill of Loneliness," "The Dragnet of Discouragement," "The Waste at Noonday," and "The Rust of Ochronosis." Their lilt sounds like sermon titles. This is a very helpful and practical book. "A valuable, informative, and sympathetic study dealing with the inner struggles and external problems pastors face in discharging their duties. A must" (Barber, 263)!

*———. *A Minister's Opportunities*. Grand Rapids: Baker, 1979.

> This book, written a quarter century later, is the sequel and complement to the author's *Minister's Obstacles*. Each brief chapter is like a "fireside chat" in which the author shares his heart with pastors in the ministry. In this book, Turnbull looks at the other side of the coin, opportunities: "The Stewardship of Time," "The Satisfaction of Study," "The Tools of Learning," "The Worth of a Library," "The Vision of the Ministry," and "The Passion to Preach" to name just a few of the chapter titles. A sheer delight to read!

*Vanhoozer, Kevin J., and Owen Strachan. *The Pastor as Public Theologian: Reclaiming a Lost Vision*. Grand Rapids: Baker Academic, 2015.

> This timely book sounds a clarion call for pastors in this age of anti-intellectualism to reclaim their role as theologians mediating God to the people of their congregations and communities. The call is for pastors to be intellectual as well as spiritual shepherds to their flocks.

*Westberg, Granger E. *Good Grief*. Reprint, Minneapolis: Fortress, 2010.

> "First published in 1960, this book has been an often-used ministry aid for anyone going through the grieving process. Westberg was a professor of medicine and religion at the University of Chicago. The book takes a simple, reasonable approach to the complex problems of death, grief, and life after loss" (**Singletary**).

*Witmer, Timothy Z. *The Shepherd Leader: Achieving Effective Shepherding in Your Church.* Nashville: Nelson, 2006.

> "This book comes from a distinctively Presbyterian/Reformed church context. Nevertheless, Witmer's wisdom and development of scriptural principles make it useful for any branch of Christianity. It is well written, biblical, and practical. It is particularly useful in training lay leaders and under-shepherds in the church" (**Fleming**).

PREACHING

*Abendroth, Mike. *Jesus Christ: The Prince of Preachers; Learning from the Teaching Ministry of Jesus.* Leominster, UK: DayOne, 2008.

> This short book is a delightful examination of the preaching methodology of the Prince of Preachers, Jesus Christ. The author's premise is that preachers need to preach as Jesus did if they want their churches to flourish spiritually. He makes a case that Jesus was an expository preacher who was not afraid to preach doctrine. A joy to read!

*Adams, Jay E. *Preaching with Purpose: A Comprehensive Textbook on Biblical Preaching.* Phillipsburg, NJ: Presbyterian and Reformed, 1982.

> Anybody who has spent much time at all sitting in a church pew has been subjected to a sermon that seemed to meander without rhyme or reason. For some preachers, this is their *modus operandi* and they subject their hearers to their drivel week after week. This book, as does every book by this author, comes right to the point and further sounds a clarion call for preaching with biblical purpose. Brief, to the point, and eminently practical!

*+Alexander, James W. *Thoughts on Preaching.* Reprint, Carlisle, PA: Banner of Truth, 1975.

> This homiletical classic by the first professor to be called to Princeton Theological Seminary in 1812 was first published in 1864. This posthumously published work addresses numerous contemporary issues over 150 years since its publication and deserves to be read and reread. Reformed.

*+Broadus, John A. *A Treatise on the Preparation and Delivery of Sermons.* Rev. ed. Edited by Edwin Charles Dargan. New York: Armstrong, 1903.

> First published in 1870, this book for over a century was considered the gold standard on the fundamentals of homiletics. It still is well worth consulting. The book has been through numerous revisions and is still in print and available in hardback, paperback, and Kindle. "Broadus' book was the standard text

for preaching in the late nineteenth and early twentieth century, and provided the standard outline for the preparation and delivery of sermons for preachers, particularly in evangelical and Reformed churches. His textual, deductive approach was considered the mark of good preaching for several generations. In some circles, it still is. Broadus' approach has sometimes been caricatured as 'three points and a poem,' but still bears up as a dependable approach to the exposition and application of God's Word. Anyone seriously interested in preaching as exposition may still benefit from reading Broadus" (**Fleming**).

*+Brooks, Phillips. *Lectures on Preaching*. New York: Dutton, 1907. Reprint, Grand Rapids: Baker, 1969.

This book is a compilation of the author's messages during the Lyman Beecher Lectures on Preaching delivered at Yale University in 1877. These eight messages by the man known throughout the English-speaking world as the "prince of preachers" consider such varying topics as the Two Elements in Preaching, the Preacher Himself, the Preacher in His Work, the Idea of the Sermon, the Making of the Sermon, the Congregation, the Ministry for Our Age, and the Value of the Human Soul. In these lectures, Brook, best described as a Christian humanist, gives his famous definition of preaching as "the communication of truth by man to men" with two essential elements, truth and personality. Highly recommended!

*Chapell, Bryan. *Christ-Centered Preaching: Redeeming the Expository Sermon*. Grand Rapids: Baker, 1994.

This seminal work by the president and professor at Covenant Theological Seminary is quite possibly the best book on preaching available today. It is a handbook for preparing and preaching Christ-centered expository messages. The author argues convincingly that biblical messages should always be redemptive in approach. Highly recommended. "Chappell's book is a modern classic for the training of preachers. Of particular interest is his insistence that the Gospel be a part of all scriptural preaching. He gives practical guidelines for the development and application of the Gospel when preaching all texts of the Bible" (**Fleming**). Reformed.

*Craddock, Fred. *As One Without Authority*. 4th ed. St. Louis: Chalice, 2001.

"Craddock is the recognized master of the inductive sermon. This book is recognized almost universally as foundational in his approach to preaching to contemporary culture. As the title suggests, Craddock makes the case that preachers in a post-Christian age can no longer rely upon a recognition of their authority in the audience, but must build interest in the subject matter of the sermon. The preacher may see Scripture as the ultimate authority, but he/she can no longer make the assumption that the listener does, even in an evangelical congregation. Preaching is not just an exercise in exegesis; it must also engage the audience in a way that makes them want to hear. Craddock does this with wit and style. His book should be required reading for any preacher seeking to engage the listener today" (**Fleming**).

*+Dargan, Edwin Charles, and Ralph G. Turnbull. *A History of Preaching*. 3 vols. Reprint, Grand Rapids: Baker, 1974.

The first two volumes of this massive work were first published in 1905 as a tribute to Dargan's homiletics professor at the Southern Baptist Theological Seminary, John Broadus. The inspiration for the project came from Broadus's annual lectures on the history of preaching at the seminary. Dargan wrote the first two volumes, leaving Turnbull to complete the project some seventy years later, bringing it up to date by adding preaching in the twentieth century. A sheer delight to read!

*Fasol, Al. *A Guide to Self Improvement in Sermon Delivery*. Grand Rapids: Baker, 1983.

"This volume focuses on the delivery, not the construction, of sermons. It is a good primer for developing oratory skill" (**Fleming**).

Forsyth, P. T. *Positive Preaching and the Modern Mind*. Reprint, Grand Rapids: Baker, 1980.

This book is a compilation of the author's messages during the Lyman Beecher Lectures on Preaching delivered at Yale University in 1907. "Emphasizes the need for including the element of judgment and the element of love in preaching coupled with an ethical reform in doctrine, a practical holiness of life, and a conviction that faith has a basis in history" (Barber).

*Goldsworthy, Graeme. *Preaching the Whole Bible as Christian Scripture: The Application of Biblical Theology to Expository Preaching*. Grand Rapids: Eerdmans, 2000.

This outstanding book was named *Preaching* magazine's Book of the Year for 2000. The author's aim is to provide a handbook that will assist preachers in applying a consistently Christ-centered approach to their sermons. The book has two parts. Part 1 focuses on biblical theology and explains what the author calls his biblical-theological method. Part 2 is essentially a handbook on applying the author's method to the different biblical genres. Highly recommended!

*Greidanus, Sidney. *The Modern Preacher and the Ancient Text: Interpreting and Preaching Biblical Literature*. Grand Rapids: Eerdmans, 1988.

This outstanding book on preaching is a comprehensive, scholarly attempt to fuse the two disciplines of homiletics and biblical hermeneutics. It is an exhaustive examination of how to translate the biblical text into the preached word, a process many preachers have apparently not mastered. The book begins with an examination of biblical preaching, its historical foundations, and then segues into three types of interpretation, literary, historical, and theological. From there, it moves to textual-thematic preaching, the form of the sermon, and then its relevance. The final four chapters, comprising roughly half of the book, is essentially a handbook on how to approach and preach from the various biblical genres. Highly recommended!

*Johnson, Graham. *Preaching to a Postmodern World: A Guide to Reaching Twenty-First Century Listeners*. Grand Rapids: Baker, 2001.

"While not a classic in the sense of Robinson and Broadus, this book is nevertheless profoundly useful in adapting sermon preparation and delivery to today's audiences. It is a much needed study of the profound changes in thought in today's society, and how preaching must adapt in methodology without compromising the eternal Word" (**Fleming**).

Johnson, Patrick W. T. *The Mission of Preaching: Equipping the Community for Faithful Witness*. Downers Grove: IVP Academic, 2015.

Not reviewed for this edition.

Lewis, Ralph L., and Gregg Lewis. *Inductive Preaching: Helping People Listen*. Westchester, IL: Crossway, 1983.

Upon its publication in 1983, this book presented a fresh approach to preaching. The inductive approach is in contrast to the more common deductive one in which the proposition is stated at the beginning of the sermon, with the rest of the sermon logically proving it. The author argues that in today's media-saturated world, the deductive approach to preaching is not reaching people and that a new method is needed.

*Liefeld, Walter L. *New Testament Exposition: From Text to Sermon*. Grand Rapids: Zondervan, 1984.

This excellent book on preaching attempts to bridge the gap between preaching and exegesis. The author defines and describes what expository preaching is and what it is not. He sees the characteristics of a good expository message as being threefold. First, there is a hermeneutical emphasis in that the sermon faithfully conveys the message of the passage of Scripture. Second, there is a homiletical emphasis in that the sermon utilizes a structure and features that fit the biblical passage and help to achieve the goals of the sermon. Third, there is a human need emphasis in that the sermon needs to meet the needs of modern hears. Thus, he bridges the hermeneutical gap between ancient text and modern application.

Lischer, Richard. *A Theology of Preaching: The Dynamics of the Gospel*. Rev. ed. Eugene, OR: Wipf and Stock, 2001.

> This edition is a revision of the author's original 1992 work. The author is the James T. and Alice Mead Cleland Professor of Preaching at Duke Divinity School. He believes that theology and preaching need to be integrated and that the result should be both an oral and an aural experience.

*+Lloyd-Jones, D. Martyn. *Preaching and Preachers*. Grand Rapids: Zondervan, 1971.

> Based on a series of lectures given in 1969 at Westminster Theological Seminary, this thought-provoking collection of essays is a true modern classic on the art of preaching. Lloyd-Jones is always interesting and practical, and often profound. This is a must-read for all pastors who desire to preach biblical messages. "An invaluable textbook on the basic dynamics of Biblical preaching" (Barber). "A sourcebook of inspiration and practical knowledge by one of the last great 'princes of the pulpit'" (**Fleming**).

*Long, Thomas. *Preaching the Literary Forms of the Bible*. Philadelphia: Fortress, 1985.

> "Long's book is a lively and interesting application of preaching across literary genres that challenges us to take into consideration the differences between literary styles within God's revealed Word" (**Fleming**).

*Lowry, Eugene. *The Homiletical Plot: The Sermon as Narrative Art Form*. Louisville: Westminster John Knox, 1980.

> "What Craddock did for inductive preaching, Lowry has done for narrative preaching. He has developed the narrative approach to preaching into a legitimate field of study, while making it accessible to the average preaching practitioner. His narrative outline, often referred to as the 'Lowry loop,' gives structure to storytelling sermons. Also worth mentioning is his book *How to Preach a Parable: Designs for Narrative Sermons* (Abingdon, Nashville, 1989) in which Lowry lays out structural variations for including storytelling in a contemporary sermon. In the postmodern age where narrative forms the structure of almost all communication, Lowry's work is invaluable" (**Fleming**).

*Meyer, Jason C. *Preaching: A Biblical Theology*. Wheaton: Crossway, 2013.

> This important book is essentially a blending of biblical theology with preaching. At least half of the book is an entertaining and informative survey of biblical theology and how it relates to the ministry of the Word. The author, John Piper's successor as senior pastor at Bethlehem Baptist Church in Minneapolis, also reflects on the state of expository preaching today and how systematic theology fits into a preaching program. Highly recommended!

*Mitchell, Henry H. *Black Preaching: The Recovery of a Powerful Art*. Nashville: Abingdon, 1990.

> "African-Americans have always had their unique take on the subject of preaching. But the study of what makes African-American preaching distinct has always been neglected. Mitchell's book addresses this head-on and builds a strong case for the cultural distinctions of Black preaching. Anyone who ministers within the African-American context, or wants to, should avail themselves of Mitchell's learning and wisdom" (**Fleming**).

Perry, Lloyd M. *Biblical Preaching for Today's World*. Chicago: Moody, 1973.

> This book is a brief, accessible, user-friendly guide to the art of biblical preaching. The material here is a reworking of Lyman Stewart Memorial Lectures for 1971–72 which the author delivered at Talbot Theological Seminary in La Mirada, California. This interesting book is regrettably OP. Particularly helpful for undergraduate students!

*Piper, John. *The Supremacy of God in Preaching*. Grand Rapids: Baker, 1990.

> John Piper has obviously drunk deeply from the well that is Jonathan Edwards's life and preaching. This outstanding book on God-centered preaching is an outgrowth of that love affair that the author has had with Edwards. He reminds preachers that their first duty in preaching is to glorify God. This book was honored by *Preaching* magazine as its Book of the Year in 1990.

*+Robertson, A. T. *The Glory of the Ministry: Paul's Exaltation in Preaching*. Reprint, Eugene, OR: Wipf & Stock, 1998.

> This masterful exposition is a wonderful treatment of 2 Cor 2:12—6:10 by perhaps the foremost Greek scholar of his generation. Robertson was the son-in-law of John Broadus. "Includes a wealth of practical, edifying, and usable material" (Barber, 248).

*+Robinson, Haddon W. *Biblical Preaching: The Development and Delivery of Expository Messages*. 3rd ed. Grand Rapids: Baker Academic, 2014.

> This revised edition of Robinson's best-selling book about preaching updates the material that was originally published in 1980 and then revised in 2001. For over thirty years this influential book has been the "Bible" on expository preaching in many colleges and seminaries. The author laments the absence of true expository preaching in this age and then goes on to define and describe what constitutes biblical preaching. The author argues that authentic expository preaching focuses on the "big idea" of a particular passage of Scripture. He then goes on to describe his ten-step method for developing an expository sermon. Finally, he deals with the mechanics of sermon delivery.

This book and Chappel's are the two best modern general books on preaching available today. "Robinson is the true successor to John Broadus when it comes to preaching. His book has become the most widely used textbook on preaching today. Robinson's style is concise and easy to read. His approach to preaching is logical, and his grasp of the subject is absolute. There are many worthy books written on preaching every year, but one would do well to start with Robinson's book before picking up another. What he has done is to lay out a definitive methodology for presenting the complexities of modern sermon preparation" (**Fleming**).

Stevenson, Dwight E., and Charles F. Diehl. *Reaching People from the Pulpit: A Guide to Effective Sermon Delivery*. Grand Rapids: Baker, 1958.

Most homiletics books today focus on the art of sermon construction. This helpful little book, though over a half century old, focuses on the actual delivery of the sermon itself. The authors devote chapters to such often overlooked subjects such as listening, effective voice, ministerial tune, and the use of the body in preaching.

*Stott, John R. W. *Between Two Worlds: The Art of Preaching in the Twentieth Century*. Grand Rapids: Eerdmans, 1982.

"In recent years, there has been a growing questioning of the power of preaching. Stott answers this skeptical tone with a resounding call for the centrality and effectiveness of preaching. Beginning with the apostles and reformers, Stott shows how preaching bridges the gap between ancient wisdom and modern culture. It is an inspirational and practical read for preaching students" (**Fleming**).

*————. *The Preacher's Portrait: Some New Testament Word Studies*. Grand Rapids: Eerdmans, 1988.

This helpful study is an examination, by a master preacher and scholar, of five NT word pictures of the preacher: the steward, the herald, the witness, the father, and the servant. Exceptional!

*Stout, Stephen Oliver. *Preach the Word: A Pauline Theology of Preaching Based on 2 Timothy 4:15*. Eugene, OR: Wipf & Stock, 2014.

A careful and methodical study of the vocabulary, concepts, and examples of preaching in Paul's letters and the book of Acts. The author's purpose is to encourage preachers to consider developing their own preaching according to this biblical model.

*Wiersbe, Warren. *Walking with the Giants: A Minister's Guide to Good Reading and Great Preaching*. Grand Rapids: Baker, 1976.

This delightful book is a sheer pleasure to read and reread. The contents of the book originally appeared in the author's column "Insights for Pastors" in the Moody Bible Institute's magazine, *Moody Monthly*, from 1971–75. The book consists of two parts: "Great Preacher-Authors" and "Classic Books on the Ministry." The eighteen chapters of part 1 offer brief biographical sketches of such preaching luminaries as Samuel Rutherford, F. W. Robertson, Alexander Maclaren, Joseph Parker, Charles Spurgeon, Alexander Whyte, G. Campbell Morgan, A. W. Tozer, and W. E. Sangster to mention just a few. Included in these chapters is a bibliography at the end of each containing biographies about these great men of faith as well as books that they penned. Part 2 consists of thirteen chapters on such diverse subjects as "The Primacy of Preaching," "Humor in the Pulpit," "The Yale Lectures," "Histories of Preaching," "Christian Classics," "Books about the Ministry," and "Bible Concordances." The chapters are brief and easily read in a ten-minute sitting. Early in my pastoral ministry, a chapter was read every day during daily devotions and the book was read cover to cover every year for a span of about ten years. In an age where the printed book seems to be fast disappearing and where reading seems to be almost a lost art, this book challenges the minister to be a reader for the nourishment that great Christian books bring to his soul. Highly recommended!

*———. *Listening to the Giants: A Guide to Good Reading and Great Preaching*. Grand Rapids: Baker, 1980.

This book is the follow-up to the author's *Listening to the Giants*. This volume consists of three parts. Part 1 is the real meat of the book, consisting of thirteen brief biographies of such preaching luminaries as John Henry Newman, J. B. Lightfoot, George Matheson, F. B. Meyer, John Henry Jowett, H. A. Ironside, and William Culbertson. Each biographical sketch is followed by one of the preacher's sermons. Part 2 consists of classic books for pastors. There are chapters on preaching on the miracles, preaching on the parables, sermon series, anthologies, and the like. Part 3 is titled "Miscellanea" and consists of six brief chapters on different topics. This follow-up is not nearly as entertaining as the original, but it is still a lot of fun to read and the sermons are priceless.

Wright, J. H. Christopher. *How to Preach and Teach the Old Testament for All Its Worth*. Grand Rapids: Zondervan, 2016.

Not reviewed for this edition. However, in light of the fact that many preachers ignore preaching from the OT, this volume will be welcomed by many.

URBAN MULTICULTURAL MINISTRIES

Anderson, David A. *Multicultural Ministry: Finding Your Church's Unique Rhythm.* Grand Rapids: Zondervan, 2004.

> "David Anderson has done groundbreaking work in reconciliation and multicultural ministry. He is founder and senior pastor of Bridgeway Community Church in Columbia, MD, lecturer and instructor of cultural diversity, and hosts an award-winning radio talk show on race relations in Washington D.C. He was the first African-American to serve as student body president at Moody Bible Institute. This unique work helps to equip pastors in moving their churches toward greater diversity" (**Grigg**).

————. *Gracism: The Art of Inclusion.* Downers Grove: InterVarsity, 2010.

> "David Anderson encourages churches to take a positive approach in looking at color, class, and culture. Anderson encourages believers to respond to those marginalized and excluded by prejudice and injustice with radical inclusion as reflected by God's heart" (**Grigg**).

*Anderson, David A., and Margarita R. Cabellon. *Multicultural Ministry Handbook: Connecting Creatively to a Diverse World; The Art of Inclusion.* Downers Grove: InterVarsity, 2010.

> "The authors seek to provide a comprehensive manual for pastors and multi-ethnic leaders of faith tackling difficult issues. This is a great book to engage various discipleship groups into candid discussions about race and diversity. A must for urban pastors" (**Grigg**).

*Black, Kathy. *Worship across Cultures: A Handbook.* Nashville: Abingdon, 1998.

> "Kathy Black holds the Bishop Gerald Kennedy Associate Professor of Homiletics chair at the Claremont School of Theology. Although written at the end of the last century, I have not found a better handbook to deal with Christian worship practices across ethnic lines. She deals specifically with weddings, funerals, and worship practices. Every clergy library needs this book for reference purposes, as well as to guide and inspire him in cross-cultural sensitivity" (**Grigg**).

*————. *Culturally-Conscious Worship.* St. Louis: Chalice, 2000.

> "Black deals specifically with the models of bilingual and multilingual worship, as well as the growing complexity of culturally conscious worship in urban areas throughout the world. It also teaches the reader how to blend our differences into unity of worship of our Creator" (**Grigg**).

*Keller, Timothy. *Center Church: Doing Balanced, Gospel-Centered Ministry in Your City*. Grand Rapids: Zondervan Academic, 2012.

> This book, by the pastor of Redeemer Presbyterian Church (PCA) in New York City, provides a theological vision for ministry. He maintains that such ministry should be gospel centered, city centered, and movement centered. Among its many accolades, this book was the recipient of *Christianity Today's* Book of the Year in the Church / Pastoral Leadership category for 2013 and *Outreach Magazine's* Book of the Year in the Leadership category for 2012.

Kirkwood, Neville A. *A Hospital Handbook of Multiculturalism and Religion: Practical Guidelines for Health Care Workers*. Rev. ed. New York: Morehouse, 2005.

> "Neville Kirkwood is more than a pastor, lecturer, and author. He has served in cross-cultural ministry in both India and Australia and holds a Doctor of Ministry degree from San Francisco Theological Seminary. He has written a number of books to help those in pastoral care and visitation. This work serves as a quick reference guide to assist them in multi-faith families, enabling them to promote international harmony, goodwill, and acceptable care to the larger community" (**Grigg**).

WORSHIP

Carson, Herbert M. *Hallelujah!* Hertfordshire, UK: Evangelical Press, 1980.

> This book defines exactly what worship is drawing from the OT and NT as well as the Trinitarian structure. The author discusses such elements of worship as the sermon, the collection, the Lord's Supper and baptism, and the response of the congregation. Interesting and provocative!

*Chapell, Bryan. *Christ-Centered Worship: Letting the Gospel Shape Our Practice*. Grand Rapids: Baker Academic, 2009.

> This book attempts to go beyond the debate over traditional or contemporary worship to explore the historical flow of worship liturgy and how it relates to the gospel. It emphasizes that what is important in worship is substance, not style. Reformed.

Cherry, Constance M. *The Worship Architect: A Blueprint for Designing Culturally Relevant and Biblically Faithful Services*. Grand Rapids: Baker Academic, 2010.

> This book attempts to bridge the gap between worship theory and worship practice. It provides worship leaders with credible blueprint plans for designing worship services that are relevant to all age groups in a twenty-first-century context, but are also faithful to Scripture and Christ-centered.

*———. *The Special Service Worship Architect: Blueprints for Weddings, Funeral, Baptisms, Holy Communion, and Other Occasions.* Grand Rapids: Baker Academic, 2013.

> What the author did for regular worship services in her 2010 book (see above), she does for special services. Indispensable for pastors who need help for those services that are not usually held on Sunday.

*Frame, John. *Worship in Spirit and Truth.* Phillipsburg, NJ: Presbyterian & Reformed, 1996.

> "The author has done an excellent job of laying out for the reader the essential elements of worship, and building a biblical case for variety of musical styles and approaches. It is one of the few textbooks I have found on worship for group discussion that includes both Biblical principles for worship and practical, how-to instructions about how to choose hymns. His follow-up *Contemporary Worship Music: A Biblical Defense* takes on the 'worship wars,' and declares that God's people are still producing good music. But he also is careful to define what makes music 'good' for worship" (**Fleming**). Reformed.

*———. *Contemporary Worship Music: A Biblical Defense.* Phillipsburg, N J: Presbyterian & Reformed, 1997.

> The author, a former professor of apologetics and systematic theology at Westminster Theological Seminary in Escondido, California, is also a classically trained musician who was at first resistant to the use of praise songs in worship services. This book is a vigorous defense for the use of praise songs in worship. Frame interacts in great detail with critics of his position. Reformed.

*Gore, R. J. *Covenantal Worship.* Phillipsburg, NJ: Presbyterian & Reformed, 2002.

> "This book deals with the problems with the regulative principle of worship, which states that only that which is commanded by scripture to be included in worship can be included. Gore argues that this distinction is too broad and vague to give much direction in worship. Instead, he recommends Biblical principles that ought to govern our choice of worship music and styles" (**Fleming**). Reformed.

Jeremiah, David. *My Heart's Desire: Living Every Moment in the Wonder of Worship.* Nashville: Integrity, 2002.

> This book is a plea by a popular radio preacher to experience worship and passion for God every moment of life. Jeremiah is always interesting and biblical.

Kidd, Reggie. *With One Voice: Discovering Christ's Song in Our Worship*. Grand Rapids: Baker, 2005.

"This book focuses on the role music has in worship, focusing on the Psalms of David. What makes this book stand out is that the author is a musician with a broad appreciation of musical styles and a vibrant heart for worship. It is a good study for those who are interested in deepening their appreciation for music in worship" (**Fleming**).

MacArthur, John, Jr. *The Ultimate Priority: John MacArthur, Jr. on Worship*. Chicago: Moody, 1983.

This is another popular book by another popular radio preacher on the importance of worship. Much more detailed than that of David Jeremiah, the emphasis of this work is the biblical teaching about worship. The author argues for a fresh understanding of what worship is.

*Rayburn, Robert G. *O Come, Let Us Worship: Corporate Worship in the Evangelical Church*. Grand Rapids: Baker, 1980.

This helpful book is an instructional manual intended for seminary students on how to conduct worship. In the more than thirty-five years since the book's publication, much has changed in worship styles in many churches in the United States, but this book is still essential in that Rayburn grounds worship in Scripture and not the changing culture. Reformed.

*Tozer, A. W. *Whatever Happened to Worship?* Edited by Gerald B. Smith. Camp Hill, PA: Christian Publications, 1985.

This is the next book that Tozer intended to write prior to his death in 1963. His oft-expressed belief that "worship acceptable to God is the missing crown jewel in evangelical Christianity" led to his desire to write a book on worship. This book is the result of a series of sermons that Tozer preached from his pulpit at the Avenue Road Church in Toronto in 1962. Tozer has been called a twentieth-century prophet as well as mystic. He condemned much of modern worship as simply entertainment and called for a return to true, biblical worship. Tozer needs to be read and heeded today. His voice is sorely missed!

*Wainwright, Geoffrey, and Karen B. Westerfield Tucker, eds. *The Oxford History of Christian Worship*. New York: Oxford University Press, 2006.

An international roster of experts in the field contributed to this compendium of the history of Christian worship from its beginnings through the present. The liturgical traditions of Orthodox, Roman Catholic, Protestant, and Pentecostal churches are explored in this massive (865 pages) and informative volume. An indispensable resource!

*Webber, Robert. *Worship Is a Verb: Celebrating God's Mighty Deeds of Salvation.* 2nd ed. Peabody: Hendrickson, 2004.

> "There are literally hundreds of books written about worship in the church. Most of them may be safely ignored. They are written from every conceivable slant from free worship to liturgy. However, Webber's works, not only in this volume but in his following *Ancient-Future* series of books, ought not be ignored. Webber applies a rigorously biblical approach to worship without falling into the trap of grumpiness either toward traditional or contemporary worship. His books have sparked a renewed interest in liturgical worship in many Protestant and evangelical churches, as he makes a case for the use of ritual and liturgy. Whether or not a person agrees with Webber's conclusions about the value of liturgy, he challenges us to examine the theological foundations of what we do in worship, and to think of fresh ways of presenting deep theological and psychological truths" (**Fleming**).

Bibliography

Barber, Cyril J. *The Minister's Library*. Grand Rapids: Baker, 1974.

———. *The Minister's Library: Periodic Supplement #1*. Grand Rapids: Baker, 1976.

———. *The Minister's Library: Periodic Supplement #2*. Grand Rapids: Baker, 1978.

———. *The Minister's Library: Periodic Supplement #3*. Grand Rapids: Baker, 1980.

Bauer, David R. *Essential Bible Study Tools for Ministry*. Nashville: Abingdon, 2014.

Branson, Mark Lau. *The Reader's Guide to the Best Evangelical Books*. San Francisco: Harper & Row, 1982.

Carson, D. A. *New Testament Commentary Survey*. 7th ed. Grand Rapids: Baker Academic, 2013.

Danker, Frederick W. *Multipurpose Tools for Bible Study*. 3rd ed. St. Louis: Concordia, 1970.

Evans, John F. *A Guide to Biblical Commentaries and Reference Works*. 10th ed. Grand Rapids: Zondervan, 2016.

Glynn, John. *Commentary & Reference Survey: A Comprehensive Guide to Biblical and Theological Resources*. 10th ed. Grand Rapids: Kregel Academic & Professional, 2007.

Lindsell, Harold. *The Battle for the Bible*. Grand Rapids: Zondervan, 1976.

Longman, Tremper, III. *Old Testament Commentary Survey*. 5th ed. Grand Rapids: Baker Academic, 2013.

Rosscup, James. *Commentaries for Biblical Expositors*. Sun Valley, CA: Grace, 2004.

Scholer, David M. *A Basic Bibliographic Guide for New Testament Exegesis*. 2nd ed. Grand Rapids: Eerdmans, 1973.

Spurgeon, C. H. *Commenting & Commentaries*. London: Banner of Truth, 1876; reprint, London: Banner of Truth, 1969.

Author Index